GW00771282

EDYTHE HABER is Professor Emerita at the University of Massachusetts Boston and a Center Associate at the Davis Center for Russian and Eurasian Studies at Harvard University. She is the author of an acclaimed book on Mikhail Bulgakov's early years and of many publications on Bulgakov, Teffi, and Nabokov. She wrote the introduction to Teffi's *Memories: From Moscow to the Black Sea* (2016), which in 2017 was awarded Pushkin House's "Special Award for Best Book in Translation," and has been researching and enjoying Teffi's work for more than 40 years.

"Teffi was the favorite writer of both Tsar Nicholas II and his nemesis, Lenin. Her extraordinary life has been superbly narrated in this fascinating and compelling biography. A tremendous discovery."

William Boyd

"Edythe Haber's book is a labor of love; she has left no stone unturned in her quest to reconstruct Teffi's story. The book combines sharp insights into Teffi's many varied writings with a warm appreciation of the toughness of her life after she left Russia forever in 1919. It is a fascinating account and it will appeal to Teffi's growing band of admirers, but it also speaks directly to a world where millions once again face the challenges and sorrows of lifelong exile from their homelands. Above all, it's a very good read!"

Catherine Merridale, author of *Lenin on the Train* and *Red Fortress*

"Teffi was a Russian literary genius on par with her more famous compatriots: she could be as penetrating as Chekhov, as darkly funny as Nabokov. She was also considered the most 'English' of Russian writers – and her wit can remind one of Saki and Waugh. She was by far the most amusing chronicler of the Russian revolution and the emigration to Paris. Indeed her insights into what it means to be a refugee, what is identity, couldn't be more relevant today. It's high time she joined the ranks of Russian greats, and Haber has brought her out wonderfully."

Peter Pomerantsev, author of *Nothing Is True and Everything Is Possible: The Surreal Heart of the New Russia*

"The fruit of decades of careful scholarship – all the more valuable in view of Teffi's extreme reticence about many aspects of her own life."

Robert Chandler, co-translator of Teffi's
Memories: From Moscow to the Black Sea
and *Rasputin and Other Ironies*

"Teffi claimed to have 'two faces, one laughing and one weeping.' In her penetrating and utterly captivating biography, Edythe Haber reconciles the twinned aspects of this Russian master, who is now, after decades of neglect, gaining recognition not only as a humorist but also as an astute chronicler of her era. What's more, by painstakingly reconstructing the life that gave rise to Teffi's exquisite writings, Haber provides us with invaluable insight into the eternal struggles of exiles and émigrés."

Boris Dralyuk, Executive Editor,
Los Angeles Review of Books

"While most of the major Russian women writers of the first half of the twentieth century have been the subject of important critical biographies in English, this honor has until now eluded Nadezhda Lokhvitskaia, who published under the penname Teffi. Drawing on archival materials, letters, memoirs, and literary texts, Edythe Haber masterfully reconstructs the life of this remarkable woman writer who, on the one hand, contributed significantly to the rich, comic and satirical tradition in Russian associated with figures like Chekhov, Gogol, and Zoshchenko but who, on the other hand, remained acutely aware of how the comedic mode was inherently fraught for a woman. In the process of doing so, Haber succeeds in shedding light on the mechanisms of Russian literary life both at home and in emigration, as well as in foregrounding the special role that humor played in Russian émigré circles. Written with clarity and verve and handsomely illustrated, Haber's *Teffi: A Life of Letters and of Laughter* will appeal to scholars and general readers alike with interests in women writers, exile, and modernism. This is a fascinating and timely biography – one that has particular relevancy in our current age of emigration."

Jenifer Presto, Associate Professor of Comparative Literature
and Russian and Director of Russian, East European,
and Eurasian Studies, University of Oregon

Teffi

A Life of Letters and of Laughter

EDYTHE HABER

I.B. TAURIS

LONDON · NEW YORK

Published in 2019 by
I.B. Tauris & Co. Ltd
London • New York
www.ibtauris.com

ISBN: 978 1 78831 258 5
eISBN: 978 1 78672 439 7
ePDF: 978 1 78673 439 6

A full CIP record for this book is available from the British Library
A full CIP record is available from the Library of Congress
Library of Congress Catalog Card Number: available

Text design and typesetting by Tetragon, London
Printed and bound by CPI Group (UK) Ltd, Croydon, CR0 4YY

*In memory of Professor Vsevolod Mikhailovich Setchkarev
(1914–98), a pioneer in the field of Russian émigré literature,
who introduced me to the pleasures Teffi has to offer.*

"If one would assign the life of an exiled writer a genre, it would have to be tragicomedy."
JOSEPH BRODSKY, "THE CONDITION WE CALL EXILE"

"Life inside a joke is more tragic than funny."
TEFFI, *MEMORIES*

Contents

List of Plates

Teffi's marriage to her second husband, Dmitry(?) Shcherbakov. Photographer G. Mitreutere (Moscow). Courtesy of the Institute of Russian Literature, Russian Academy of Sciences (IRLI RAN), St. Petersburg, Russia.

PLATE 11   Teffi photographed shortly after returning from the front during World War I, where she worked as a nurse and sent dispatches back to the newspaper, *Russkoe slovo. Teatr i iskusstvo*, 3 May 1915, p. 307.

PLATE 12   Cover of Teffi, *Nothing of the Kind* (Petrograd, 1915). Courtesy of Houghton Library, Harvard University.

PLATE 13   Teffi shortly after her arrival in Paris in 1919. Teffi Papers; Courtesy of the Bakhmeteff Archive, Columbia University.

PLATE 14   Natasha Zaitseva in a dress sewn by Teffi (1926). Teffi moved in with the writer Boris Zaitsev and his family in late 1925 and lived with them for about 4 months. Natasha – by then the elderly Natalya Borisovna Sollogub – recalled that Teffi "was so talented that whatever she undertook always turned out well. Until I was 12 years old I always wore someone else's clothes – there was no money [...] And Teffi sewed a dress for me, a real one, a marvelous one!" Courtesy of Pierre Sollogoub.

PLATE 15   Portrait of Teffi, 1920s. Teffi Papers; Courtesy of the Bakhmeteff Archive, Columbia University.

PLATE 16   Teffi at Vichy in manly outfit, 1926 or 1930. Teffi Papers; Courtesy of the Bakhmeteff Archive, Columbia University.

PLATE 17   Teffi and the artist Konstantin Korovin viewing one of his latest works at the Exhibit of Russian Art, Paris, July 1932. Zeeler Papers; Courtesy of the Bakhmeteff Archive, Columbia University.

PLATE 18   Teffi in a group photo at *Illustrated Russia* after Bunin received the Nobel Prize, 1933. Bunin fourth from right, Mark Aldanov to his left. Zeeler Papers; Courtesy of the Bakhmeteff Archive, Columbia University.

PLATE 19   Teffi and Pavel Theakston, the 1930s. Theakston, Teffi's intimate friend, suffered a stroke in 1930, after which she was his principal caregiver until his death in 1935. Teffi Papers; Courtesy of the Bakhmeteff Archive, Columbia University.

PLATE 20   Teffi, bare-backed, on the bank of the Marne River, Marly-le-Roi, France. Summer, 1934. She must have been very pleased with the photo since she sent it to various friends and periodicals, including the Riga newspaper, *Segodnya* (1 Oct. 1934). Teffi Papers; Courtesy of the Bakhmeteff Archive, Columbia University.

PLATE 21   Teffi's daughters, Warsaw, 1935. Helena Buczyńska (left) was a well-known stage and screen actress, while Waleria Grabowska was a translator of her mother's works and member of the Polish Foreign Ministry. Teffi Papers; Courtesy of the Bakhmeteff Archive, Columbia University.

PLATE 22   Teffi's room at 18-bis Avenue de Versailles, 1939. On her bed is her beloved guitar. On the book shelves above are portraits of her literary friends, the most discernible of Boris Zaitsev (center) and, second from the right, Mark Aldanov. The Yakovlev portrait can be seen on the left. Teffi Papers; Courtesy of the Bakhmeteff Archive, Columbia University.

PLATE 23   A mollusk discovered by Professor Konstantin Davydov, named in honor of Teffi. On 1 Jan. 1951, Teffi wrote her daughter Valeria that Davydov had dedicated a recent lecture to her, "since at one time I had mentioned his lecture in print and supposedly made his career." Teffi Papers; Courtesy of the Bakhmeteff Archive, Columbia University.

PLATE 24   Before Teffi's departure from the rest home at Morsang-sur-Orge in early September 1952, two young relatives of the proprietor asked to have their picture taken with her so that "when we're big, we'll show this portrait to our children." Marked by Teffi's daughter, Valeria, in Polish: "Ostatnia fotogr. Mamy" (Last photo of Mama). Teffi Papers; Courtesy of the Bakhmeteff Archive, Columbia University.

Notes on the Text

SPELLING

Russian names are transliterated according to the Library of Congress system, with the following modifications in the interest of readability:

1. Standard English forms of well-known people are used (*Meyerhold*).
2. Names with close English equivalents are anglicized (*Alexander, Maria*).
3. The soft sign is omitted at the end of a word or before a consonant (*Igor, Gorky*); before a vowel it appears as *y* (*Zinovyev*).
4. *–ii* and *–yi* are replaced by *–y* (*Dostoyevsky, Bely*).
5. *y* is used instead of *i* to represent a *y*-glide or soft consonant before an *a* or *u* (*Yakov, Tyutchev*).
6. Initial Cyrillic *e* and after a vowel is given as *ye* (*Yevgeny, Dostoyevsky*).
7. *ë* is given as *yo / o*.
8. Russian words and titles in the notes and text are spelled according to the unmodified Library of Congress system, with the exception of words with a standard English form (*glasnost*).
9. In the text the spelling of Teffi's children's and first husband's names are based on their transliteration from the Russian (Buchinsky, Yelena, Valeria). In the notes I generally use the Polish forms (Buczyński, Helena, Waleria) that they themselves adopted after emigrating to Poland.

MORE ON NAMES

Russian names can be a challenge.

1. Patronymics: Aside from given and surnames, Russians have middle names based upon their fathers' first names. The patronymic

for a son of Ivan, for example, is Ivanovich, for his daughter – Ivanovna. I for the most part omit patronymics except for compelling reasons.

2. Diminutives are variants of Russian first names used for children and young people and otherwise to convey informal, friendly relations (rather like English nicknames). Nadezhda Teffi, for example, is Nadya as a little girl and also to those very close to her as an adult.

DATES

Pre-revolutionary Russia used the Julian calendar, which is 13 days behind the Gregorian calendar, adopted by the Soviet Union in February 1918. For dates I refer to the calendar used at the time.

Teffi rarely dates her letters. Therefore, the dating and chronology are often approximate, based upon the larger context of Teffi's life and times.

TRANSLATIONS

All translations, unless otherwise noted, are my own.

Acknowledgements

My involvement with Teffi goes back many years, and I have many people to thank. I would like to express my gratitude, first of all, to Professor Vsevolod Mikhailovich Setchkarev, advisor for my doctoral dissertation (Harvard, 1971), for introducing me to Teffi and to the then neglected field of Russian émigré literature. I am also indebted to my second reader, Professor Donald Fanger, whose high standards greatly improved the style and readability of my dissertation and have offered a model to me ever since.

I am grateful to the University of Massachusetts Boston for offering a travel grant when I returned to Teffi after a very long hiatus. I cannot thank enough the Davis Center for Russian and Eurasian Studies, Harvard University, for providing me over the years with vital scholarly resources and the opportunity to interact with their stimulating interdisciplinary community. I especially benefited from participation in the Literary Study Group and the Gender, Socialism, and Post-Socialism Working Group, headed by Sonia Ketchian and Rochelle Ruthchild, respectively. I also thank Hugh Truslow, librarian of the Davis Center, Fung Library, for helping me resolve bibliographical conundrums time and again.

Also very valuable was my participation in the Illinois Summer Research Laboratory on Russia and Eastern Europe, University of Illinois, Urbana–Champaign. For all their help, I thank Robert Burger, Julia Gauchman, and Helen Sullivan.

Perhaps the greatest benefit that my return to Teffi has brought is contact with an international community of scholars working on related fields. I am especially indebted to Richard Davies (Leeds Russian Archive, Brotherton Library, University of Leeds), whose scrupulousness, rigor, and intellectual honesty during our collaboration serve as a model that I can only hope to emulate. He has continued to help me in many ways, large and small. One large way was to introduce me to Natalya Borisovna Sollogub (1912–2008), daughter of Boris and Vera Zaitsev, who kindly shared with me her childhood recollections of Teffi.

Also deserving special thanks is the Moscow researcher Tamara Aleksandrova, who generously provided me with her extensive research on Teffi's family and her early years. Other scholars whose collaboration and other contacts have been vital to my project include: Elda Garetto (University of Milan); Lydia A. Spiridonova, Dmitry D. Nikolayev, Yelena Trubilova, and Oleg Korostelyov (Gorky Institute of World Literature, Moscow); and Olga Fetisenko (Institute of Russian Literature, St. Petersburg).

My research benefited greatly from the help of scholars and staff associated with the archives I have visited, who generously shared their time and expertise. Special thanks to Tanya Chebotarev, Bakhmeteff Archive of Russian and East European History and Culture, Rare Book and Manuscript Library, Columbia University (New York); Richard Davies; Margarita Pavlova, Institute of Russian Literature (St. Petersburg); Stanley J. Rabinowitz, Amherst Center for Russian Culture, Amherst College (Amherst, MA); Irina Reshetnikova, Russian State Archive of Literature and Art (Moscow). I am also very grateful to Dmitry Belyayev, Archive of Russia Abroad, Marina Tsvetaeva Museum (Moscow); Yelena Obatnina, Institute of Russian Literature (St. Petersburg); Saundra Taylor, Lilly Library, Indiana University (Bloomington, IN). I thank Ronald Bulatov, Hoover Institution Archives (Stanford, CA), and John Monahan, the Beinecke Rare Book and Manuscript Library, Yale University (New Haven, CT), for sending me important archival material, as well as the anonymous (or forgotten) staff of: Literary Archive of the Museum of Czech Literature (Prague); Houghton Library, Harvard University; Manuscript Division, University of Illinois Library, Urbana–Champaign; Manuscript Division, Russian National Library (St. Petersburg); Manuscript and Rare Book Division, St. Petersburg Theater Library.

I am also most indebted to Robert Chandler, whose excellent translations have earned Teffi a following among English-language readers, and whose enthusiasm for my work has led to many good things. I appreciate the thoughtful reading of my manuscript by Richard Davies and by Professor Katherine O'Connor (Boston University). I would also like to thank Tom Stottor, my highly capable and enthusiastic editor at I.B. Tauris, for his many useful suggestions; project manager, Alex Billington, at Tetragon Publishing, and my excellent, meticulous copy editor, Alex Middleton. Any errors that escaped his eagle eye are wholly my responsibility.

I thank, finally, my late husband, Timur Djordjaze, and my sisters, Zelda and Clara Haber, for their unfailing support and encouragement.

Introduction

Our refugees arrive, emaciated, blackened from hunger and fear, eat their fill, calm down, look around, as if to get their new lives on track, and suddenly fade. Their eyes grow dim, their listless arms droop, and their soul withers – their soul, turned toward the east… We have died. We feared a Bolshevik death – and have met our death here.[1]

So wrote Teffi (Nadezhda Lokhvitskaya, 1872–1952) soon after her arrival in Paris in 1920. The foremost Russian woman humorist of her (and arguably of all) time, she had joined approximately 1 million of her compatriots who fled Russia in the wake of the 1917 Bolshevik revolution and formed what has been called Russia Abroad, with its capitals initially in Paris and Berlin, but with outposts as far-flung as Shanghai and Buenos Aires.[2] Teffi's stories and weekly newspaper columns, which appeared in Russian émigré periodicals throughout the world, gave voice to these dispossessed people, and depicted – with her characteristic blend of sharp wit and affecting pathos – the plights of her fellow refugees: their undying longing for a lost homeland; their acute financial hardships and hapless attempts to adapt to an alien culture; the antagonism and suspicion they encountered in their host countries, especially during the worsening economic and political conditions of the 1930s.

Teffi herself shared the miseries of her émigré readers and demonstrated their resilience in the worst of times. Her life story, together with her literary portrayals of her compatriots, have not lost their timeliness in the light of the repeated displacements during the twentieth and early 21st centuries of mass populations and individuals due to war, revolution, political persecution, natural disasters – and the hostility later refugees have often had to face because of international conflicts that led to their exile in the first place. The story of Russia Abroad remains all too relevant.

And yet, for all that, Teffi is so funny. It has been said that a trait of exilic literature is the "double consciousness" of the writer, focusing simultaneously on "here" and "there," the present and a lost past.[3] Teffi's works capture well the absurdities inherent in such "double" existence, in which former generals work as taxi drivers; royal ladies-in-waiting eke out a living by embroidering; slovenly Olgas strive to reinvent themselves as stylish *Mesdames* d'Ivanoffs. It was this ability to find amusement in adversity – and thereby lighten the burden of her readers – that made her one of the most beloved writers in the Russian diaspora.

Drawing on Teffi's correspondence and other archival material, as well as on her literary and journalistic writing, this book will tell her story in full for the first time and place it within the context of the tumultuous times she lived through. She was already an immensely popular writer in Russia. She had achieved such acclaim that candy and perfume were named after her, and her infectious humor and virtuosic style gained her admirers as diverse as the last tsar and Vladimir Lenin. Although her fame sprang primarily from her humor, Teffi practiced in a wide range of genres, from serious poetry and prose to plays and even popular songs. In my treatment of her literary works, written throughout her very long career, I suggest that they are joined by a single vision: that underlying the absurdity of everyday life, depicted in her comic works, is the same longing (although it sometimes takes ludicrous form) for a more beautiful and meaningful version of self and of the world that marks her poetry.

The variety of Teffi's pre-revolutionary writing brought her into contact with a broad swath of St. Petersburg's literary and theatrical world, and her life therefore offers a panoramic view of the artistic milieu at a time of brilliant flowering of Russian culture, commonly called the Silver Age. Although she was for the most part apolitical, she was also caught up in the many upheavals that shook late imperial Russia: the revolutions of 1905 and 1917; the world war; the civil war following the Bolshevik coup. Her witty and incisive journalistic pieces, moreover, provide both vivid accounts of such major cataclysms and a running commentary on social problems, such as anti-Semitism and crime, which plagued imperial Russia during its final decade.

Within the smaller world of Russia Abroad, Teffi was a yet more vital figure. Her biography casts an especially bright light on the large émigré community in Paris, which established an impressive network of cultural institutions: Russian-language newspapers and magazines, for which she wrote; theaters, which performed her plays; publishing houses, which put out her books. There was also an endless round of literary and philosophical colloquia, lectures, concerts, charitable evenings in which she took part. Teffi became close friends with a number of prominent writers in Paris, and her life vividly recreates both the lively literary atmosphere of the early days of emigration, and the particular difficulties faced by writers in exile, whose medium of expression is their native language and whose material was so often inextricably bound to their native land. With time, some of the vitality was drained from the cultural life of Russia Abroad, and there were growing doubts about the very survival of émigré literature. With the economic and political crises of the 1930s, the situation grew yet more grave, but Teffi, despite acute personal problems, demonstrated her resilience by continuing to divert her readers with her humorous and tragicomic tales (the tragic becoming ever more dominant). In addition, her newspaper pieces offered vivid eyewitness accounts of the deteriorating domestic and world situation that led finally to the outbreak of World War II.

War led to the decimation of Russia Abroad as it had existed in Europe for the previous two decades. Many perished, while others fled elsewhere, primarily to America, but Teffi and some of her aged and ailing contemporaries stayed in France. Despite debilitating illness, which limited her ability to write, she created some of her most ambitious works in her last years, but her remaining years – and those of others of her generation – were few. By the time Teffi died in 1952 an era had ended. Her name for a time faded into obscurity, but during the last couple of decades, after the rediscovery of exiled and repressed writers in post-Soviet Russia, she has achieved renewed popularity in her homeland. More recently, very good translations have brought Teffi burgeoning recognition in the English-speaking world and elsewhere, where her writing has proven fresh and compelling to the present day.[4]

I

"AN INTERESTING BUNCH"
Family Background and Early Years

THE LOKHVITSKYS

In 1911, in a brief autobiography, Teffi traced her literary gift to her great-grandfather, Kondraty Lokhvitsky (1774–1849), "a Mason in the time of Alexander the Blessed" (Tsar Alexander I, r.1801–25), who "wrote mystical poems."[1] Her father, Professor Alexander Lokhvitsky, she went on, "was a famous orator and was celebrated for his wit," while of her mother she noted only that she "always loved poetry and was well acquainted with Russian and especially with European literature."

Thirty-six years later – by then 75 years old and living out the final years of her long exile in France – Teffi turned once again to her forebears. "I'm the last of the Lokhvitsky clan," she wrote the literary critic and historian, Pyotr Bitsilli (1879–1953).[2] They were an "interesting bunch," she added, and she wanted "to write everything I know" about them, since "once I die nobody will take it up." Teffi noted her particular interest in her great-grandfather, who she claimed "corresponded with Alexander I and, on the basis of a dream, foretold the 1812 War, and on the basis of his dream the Golden Gate in Kiev was discovered." Teffi also mentioned a more distant ancestor, a "great-great-grandmother who gave Peter the Great a slap in the face."

Teffi broached the subject with Bitsilli because she was looking for a family chronicle by the nineteenth-century writer Nadezhda Kokhanovskaya (pseudonym of Nadezhda Sokhanskaya, 1823–84), with whom she believed she shared common ancestry. She hoped the book was in the collection of Bitsilli's university library in Sofia, Bulgaria, and, although he did find the work she named, it turned out that she had the wrong title and she therefore gave up the project – which is a shame, since among Teffi's ancestors were some remarkable people who exemplified major currents in Russian society and culture of their times.

The actual title of the book Teffi was seeking is *Old Times: A Family Remembrance*, which – since its reliability is uncertain – might best be regarded as a mythical (or semi-mythical) foundation story of the Lokhvitskys.[3] Kokhanovskaya traces her roots to the middle of the sixteenth century – to Prince Konstantin Ostrozhsky, whose seat, Ostrog, was a major cultural center in Western Ukraine, then part of Poland. The prince had a favorite, a ward whom he called *kokhanets* (from *kokhany*, beloved), from which people created the surname Kokhanovsky – his actual family name forgotten. The prince's sister (or perhaps it was his daughter, says the author) married the poor orphan over her family's objections, and he was soon killed in battle, leaving her with a two-year-old son. The narration then traces the peregrinations of the Kokhanovskys over the following tumultuous century in Ukraine. By the mid-1600s Maria Kokhanovskaya, a widow who was living with her son Kliment in the town of Lokhvitsa, decided to flee their "unhappy homeland" for a Cossack town on the Russian side of the border. When asked where they were from, they responded: "From Lokhvitsa," and so they became the Lokhvitskys.[4] Many years later, in 1709, Kliment, "old and distinguished [*vazhen*], greatly respected," played host to Peter the Great after his great victory over the Swedes at Poltava.[5] It was then that his daughter, Agripina,

> almost raised her hand against Peter the Great. "How dare you? I am the tsar!" "Well, if you're the tsar, *to i robi po tsar'sku* [Ukrainian: then behave like a tsar]," said the Ukrainian girl Agripina… "You have a wonderful daughter!" Peter told Kliment upon his departure. "Seek out a good bridegroom for her."[6]

Kokhanovskaya traces her lineage as far as Kliment's grandson, Yefim Lazarevich, who would have been roughly a contemporary of Teffi's great-grandfather, Kondraty Andreyevich (henceforth K.A.), but, judging by the latter's patronymic, he came from another branch of the family of which nothing concrete is known. His diary reveals that he was a poor boy who earned his keep as a chorister in a Moscow church.[7] (The only reference to a family is passing mention of a visit to his mother, Yevdokia, in 1809.[8]) The virtually uneducated boy's fortunes changed in 1787, when he was hired by Khariton Chebotaryov (1746–1815), a professor at Moscow University and prominent Freemason (at whose wedding K.A. had performed), to teach singing at the boarding school he ran.[9] K.A. was allowed to attend classes in the school, which must have imbued him with the ideals of Freemasonry.

K.A. apparently did not join a lodge and remained a "solitary mystic," but Masonic ideals such as universal brotherhood, love, and equality (shared by later Lokhvitskys) filled his thoughts, poetry, and dreams.[10] His touching words about an old beggar woman attest to his belief in equality: her fervent prayers "moved me so much that I began to cry and thanked the Lord for teaching me through this poor, simple beggar woman how to pray to Him and how to place one's hope in Him."[11] The spirit of brotherly love did not always manifest itself, to be sure, during his service in the tsarist bureaucracy, when, in the face of the malfeasance he observed, he was twice dismissed from posts for making "an unsubstantiated denunciation."[12] Nevertheless by 1808 he reached the rank of collegiate counsellor – the sixth in the civil service – which would have made him a member of the hereditary nobility.

Tsar Alexander I, who in the early 1800s had himself fallen sway to mystical currents, in 1822, alarmed by growing unrest, ordered all Masonic lodges closed, and in the following years his successor, the arch-conservative Nicholas I (r.1825–55), replaced all such universalist ideas with a nationalistic belief in the uniqueness of the Russian people.[13] Whether or not by coincidence, it was precisely in 1822 that K.A. left his government post and, after settling in Kiev, began exploring Russia's national heritage through his new avocation, archaeology.[14] His claim in April 1832 that he had found the very place where the legendary Christianizer of ancient Rus, St. Andrew, had raised his cross was discounted by more learned men, but his discovery later that year of one of the most significant monuments from Kievan Rus' – the remains of the Golden Gate, erected by the Grand Prince Yaroslav in 1037, followed by his unearthing in 1833 of the ruins of the St. Irina Church, built during the same period – earned him ultimately the high esteem of his contemporaries.[15] In 1837 he became the first director of the Archaeology Museum at Kiev University.[16] Of all of her ancestors, K.A. held special appeal to Teffi, and the recent discovery that he may not have been her great-grandfather after all was therefore a shocking one.[17] What is most important for our purpose, however, is Teffi's own understanding of her family background and the significance she assigned it: whatever the truth of the matter, K.A. undoubtedly had an important influence on her sense of her place in the social order and of her literary heritage.

Of her grandfather, Vladimir Lokhvitsky, little is known, except that he was from the merchant estate and had two sons, Alexander (Teffi's father, henceforth A.V.), born in 1830, and Iosif, who became a merchant in the town of Tikhvin, about 120 miles from St. Petersburg.[18] The family was apparently not well off, since it is said that A.V.'s studies caused "great material deprivation," but the boy exhibited a great thirst for learning and managed to enroll in the Law Faculty at Moscow University, from which he graduated in 1852 with a candidate's degree.[19]

Studying law during the repressive regime of Nicholas I might seem a futile endeavor, since the emperor's goal was to stamp out the enlightenment ideal of universal law and concentrate on the particulars of Russian law as it had developed through the ages. Students, as Robert S. Wortman felicitously phrases it, "were to study 'laws' (*zakony*) rather than the general subject of 'law' (*pravo*)"; they were to become "obedient technicians" through "rote memorization."[20] The remarkable professors at Moscow University, however, who included the prominent Westernizers Timofei Granovsky (1813–55) and Konstantin Kavelin (1818–85), managed to circumvent this mandate, looking to a judicial system that would unite the nation through a harmonious edifice of laws and liberate people from the dead weight of tradition.[21] Thus, if in K.A.'s time mysticism offered an escape from the meaningless maze of state service into a world of transcendent values, during the more materialist and rationalist 1840s, the law fulfilled an analogous role.

The law students at Moscow University, as one distinguished graduate recalled, did not "dream of a service career, to take their places next to Gogol's heroes," but aspired to become professors, who, they imagined, inhabited a world of uncorrupted principles.[22] A.V. achieved this ideal early, in 1853 becoming an adjunct at the Richelieu Lycée in Odessa. After the reforming tsar, Alexander II (r. 1855–81), replaced his reactionary father in 1855, A.V. also took advantage of the liberalized atmosphere and began a second career as journalist, at a time when the press was enjoying new rights and influence, when, as A.V. himself wrote, "everyone heeds the voice of our journalism […] it is the only organ of public opinion."[23] Thus, like his grandfather he evinced literary ambition, but in a more prosaic and pragmatic realm, appropriate to the age.

A.V. eloquently pleaded for laying the "great foundations" of an independent legal system, which until then had permitted no open trials, no separate estate of lawyers, and his lofty vision of trial by jury suggests that he shared K.A.'s sympathy for the common people:

These twelve people can […] be from the most humble social classes, and the accused, belonging to the very peak of society, submissively bows his head before them [...] Such an institution will naturally elevate the people's feeling of dignity and conscience greatly.[24]

In 1861 A.V. moved from Odessa to St. Petersburg, where he took up the chair of State Law and the History of Russian Law at the Imperial Alexander Lycée, the premier *lycée* of Russia. After the move his most important books appeared, all of them relevant to the reforms underway, and he made steady advancement in his career, in 1871 (the year before Teffi's birth) becoming a member of the hereditary nobility.[25] At the same time, A.V. shared the liberals' belief in individual achievement, fostered by the reforms: "With the establishment of the legal profession there opens a great and independent sphere of action for talent and action."[26] In 1869 he decided to test his own abilities in the private sphere, leaving his government teaching post to become a defense attorney and joining the many noblemen who began new careers in liberal professions. He was admitted to the bar in 1874 and became a defense lawyer (*prisiazhnyi poverennyi*) attached to the Moscow Circuit Court.[27] At the same time he grew yet more involved in journalism, publishing countless articles in journals intended for the general public and serving as editor of the popular legal newspaper *Sudebnyi vestnik* (Judicial herald).[28]

A.V. envisioned that public trials would serve an educational and even an artistic purpose, and would be

on the one hand, an uninterrupted series of public and free lectures on criminal and civil law; on the other [...] theater in its highest sense, where the dramas are played out not by actors, but by real participants [*deistvovateliami*].[29]

He proved quite right about their theatrical appeal, especially since newspapers covered trials widely and "allowed readers to participate vicariously as members of a jury."[30] Lawyers became celebrities, and among them A.V. a judicial star (his fame was such that in 1877 Dostoyevsky turned to him to represent him in court, but he was too busy to accept[31]). Teffi noted his famous wit, confirmed by the writer Alexander Amfiteatrov: "His jokes were repeated through all of Russia, became proverbs, and many are still remembered to this day."[32]

A.V.'s vision of the educational value of public trials, however, proved unfounded, for in Russia as elsewhere, it was not lofty principles that attracted people, but the sensational and shocking. It was precisely this failure of the educational mission – to inculcate the principle that all defendants, no matter how suspect, had the right to legal representation – that made of A.V. a highly controversial figure. His courtroom activities resulted in vicious "personal attacks, which often rained down upon him" and which reached a peak in 1878 in connection with a trial that caused a furor at the time and was debated for many years to come.[33] It concerned a student, N. Elkin, who, having become affianced to an elderly widow, a Mrs. Popova, managed to wheedle her into giving him 15,000 rubles and the deed to her house, after which he not only broke off the engagement, but evicted her from her own property.[34] A.V. succeeded in getting Elkin acquitted both in criminal and civil court, after which Popova's lawyer filed a complaint, accusing him of defending an immoral person. The criminal complaint was dismissed, but A.V. was convicted at the civil trial and barred from trying cases for three months. Later the Moscow Judicial Chamber disbarred him entirely – a decision that created a storm in the press – but the following year the Cassation Department of the Senate exonerated A.V. on the grounds that the "criterion of individual morality is too elusive."[35] Nevertheless the attacks apparently took their toll, one obituary calling A.V. a martyr, who "bore on his shoulders the independence and freedom of the Russian legal profession."[36]

The attempt on Alexander II's life in 1866 led to a reaction against the reforming impulse, and, after his assassination in 1881, his successor, Alexander III (r.1881–94), reversed many of the reforms. Thus Alexander Lokhvitsky's dream of a new society based on universal legal principles remained unfulfilled – much like the universalist mysticism of K.A. – in the real-world struggle between autocracy and rebellion. In any case, after the disbarment he never fully regained his former renown, and the satirist V. O. Mikhnevich (1841–99) dubbed him shortly before his death in 1884 an "extinguished luminary in the heaven of our national [otechestvennoi] jurisprudence."[37] Perhaps because of this eclipse A.V. had not amassed much material wealth. When he died he "left [...] his large family an insignificant amount of property and a small sum for the funeral."[38]

THE VON GOYERS

The little that is known of Teffi's mother, Varvara von Goyer, indicates that her family was much better off than her husband's. Despite the German surname, descriptions of the family in Teffi's autobiographical fiction suggest deep roots in the Russian Empire. In "The Gold Thimble," the narrator writes that her grandmother gave her a gold thimble when she was seven years old, inscribed *"À ma petite Nadine"* (the French equivalent of Nadezhda).[39] The thimble had been given to her grandmother (also a Nadine) when she too was seven by *"tante Julie,"* who was so pretty that during the Napoleonic war she had to be hidden from approaching French soldiers.[40] The grandmother goes on to tell of her married years, conjuring up the mores of an old-fashioned gentry family:

> The family spent the winter at their estate in the Vitebsk province, the summer at their Mogilyov estate.
>
> An entire procession made the move.
>
> In the lead, in a carriage [*kareta*], were grandmother and grandfather.
>
> Then, in an immense *dormeuse*, were grandmother's mother [...] and her four granddaughters.
>
> "Among them was your mama, Varetta."
>
> Then came a carriage [*koliaska*] with the tutors and the boys.
>
> Then a carriage with the governesses and their children.
>
> Then the cooks and the other servants [*cheliad'*].[41]

The most distinguished member of the family was Varvara's sister, Sofya Aleksandrovna Davydova (née von Goyer, 1842–1915), who exemplified a generation of gentry women who took as their duty the education of the common people and the development of native Russian culture.[42] A prominent specialist and author of many publications in the field of Russian lacemaking (one of which was awarded the Metropolitan Makary Prize in 1885), Davydova's contact with indigent and illiterate craftswomen made her sorely aware of the bleakness of their lives.[43] In 1883 she founded in St. Petersburg the first school for lacemakers, and between 1882 and 1892 organized schools of spinning, weaving, and embroidery in various regions. In addition, Davydova held posts in the Ministry of Agriculture and Ministry of National Enlightenment, and was on many committees devoted to bettering the education of the poor.

Davydova's biography reveals that the von Goyers moved from their estate in the Mogilyov province to Odessa in 1850, where the children (including, presumably, Teffi's mother) received an excellent home education, taught by "the best professors of the Richelieu Lycée."[44] Since Alexander Lokhvitsky began teaching at the Richelieu Lycée in 1853, he must have met Varvara in Odessa, where the couple likely married before departing in 1861 for St. Petersburg.

CHILDHOOD AND ADOLESCENCE

Nadezhda (i.e., Teffi) was born in St. Petersburg 26 April 1872, preceded by three sisters – Varvara (b.1861), Lydia (b.1864), and Maria (1869–1905) – and two brothers, Vadim (b.1862) and Nikolai (1867–1933).[45] A couple of years after Nadezhda's birth, the Lokhvitskys had their seventh and last child, Yelena, and the two youngest sisters – usually identified by their diminutives, Nadya and Lena – figure in Teffi's stories as constant companions during childhood adventures and misadventures.

Teffi wrote of her early years: "My childhood passed in a large, carefree family. We were raised in the old-fashioned way – all together in the same manner." She added: "I had no early experiences of life. Whether this is good or bad is hard to judge now."[46] Although Teffi's traditional, uneventful childhood might seem unlikely given her father's tumultuous public life, it may be that the very busy A.V. entrusted his children's upbringing largely to his wife. Their father's intellect and wit, however, left their mark on his quite remarkable children. And his well-educated wife was unlikely to have had a hidebound approach to child-rearing.

There is little concrete information about Teffi's childhood and adolescence, since she was quite reticent about her private life and no letters from the early period and very little other documentary material have been found. To form some impression of her early years one must turn to her literary and journalistic works with an autobiographical component, attempting to skirt the clearly fictional while adding a few details from other sources. The image that emerges is indeed of a traditional Russian gentry childhood.

The Lokhvitskys, typical of their class, spent the fall and winter in the city, spring and summer at their country estate. Although Nadezhda Lokhvitskaya was born in St. Petersburg and is mostly associated with that city, her earliest urban memories are of Moscow, where her father's position at the Moscow Circuit Court took the family just two years after her birth. Her most evocative description of her early years in Moscow fuses her real life and the fictionalized world she encountered in her favorite reading, Leo Tolstoy's *Childhood*, *Boyhood*, and *Adolescence*, which she "read and reread tens of times":[47]

> Volodya, Nikolenka, Lyubochka [Tolstoy's characters] all lived together with me, they all were so like me, my sisters and brothers. And their grandmother's house in Moscow was our Moscow house [...] Natalya

Savishna – I also knew her well – she was our old Avdotya Matveyevna, grandmother's former serf. She also had a trunk with pictures glued on the lid […] And even grandmother, her stern eyes looking questioningly from under the ruffle of her bonnet, with a flacon of eau de cologne on the little table by her armchair – it was all the same, all kindred […] *Childhood and Adolescence* entered my own childhood and adolescence and fused with it organically, as if I hadn't read it, but simply lived it.[48]

Nadya "read a great deal" as a child, and Pushkin, another favorite writer, also figures in her Moscow memories.[49] When she was six years old and sick with measles, she was given a book adorned with Pushkin's name printed in gold letters. It turned out to be a box of chocolates with a few of Pushkin's poems affixed to the binding. Once Nadya had devoured the candy, she read one of the poems, "The Little Bird" ("Ptichka"), and, although she didn't understand it, she was enchanted by the words and repeated and repeated them until she learned the poem by heart. Later, when she was out playing by the Pushkin Monument, she looked the statue directly in the eye and whispered: "'The Little Bird!' A poem by the poet Pushkin. Your poem." She then proceeded to recite it.[50]

Parents are very little in evidence in Teffi's writings, and the adults with whom the children mostly interacted were the servants. In their youngest years the primary caregiver was their old nanny, who, in the Russian tradition, imparted to her charges the wisdom (or superstition) of the simple people and the riches of the folk language. A little later, "when they were about five," the nanny was followed by the *bonne* (nursery governess), Elvira Karlovna, who "taught the alphabet and rudiments of scripture," and when older still, the children graduated to a full-fledged governess, usually French.[51]

Once spring came, Varvara Lokhvitskaya took her children, with the full panoply of servants, governesses, and tutors, from Moscow to her estate in Volynia. The stories portray the idyllic country life so familiar from classic Russian literature. The older children, already adolescents, gave themselves over to the leisurely, upper-class pursuits of "picnics, horseback riding, games, dances" and regarded little Nadya and Lena as nuisances to be sent away "at the most interesting places."[52]

The little girls found refuge among the servants and other local people of Volynia. The province, now part of Western Ukraine, was even for Russians quite an exotic place. Neighboring eastern Poland (then part of the Russian

Empire) and Galicia (belonging to the Austro-Hungarian Empire), it had a mixed population of Ukrainians, Russians, Poles, Germans, and Jews.[53] The neighboring landowners, all Poles, generally "kept aloof," but the children had considerable contact with more humble segments of local society and absorbed their folk beliefs.[54] An important conduit for local lore was a little girl named Liza in the stories, the daughter of the local priest, who came to study and play with Nadya and Lena.[55] An inspired liar, Liza told the credulous Lokhvitsky girls about her encounters with the Devil and various marvelous creatures. Such folk beliefs made a deep impression on Teffi, and she would choose them as the subjects of some of her best stories.

In 1884, after A.V.'s death, the family returned to St. Petersburg from Moscow. By then *War and Peace* had superseded *Childhood* as Nadya's favorite Tolstoy work, and when she was 13, devastated by the death of the hero, Prince Andrei, she even visited Tolstoy in order to urge him to change the ending. She lost courage, however, and only managed to ask for the great writer's autograph.[56] This occurred soon after Nadya enrolled at the Liteinaya Gymnasium, a girls' classical high school in St. Petersburg, from which she graduated in 1890.[57] One brief impression of her during her school years survives in a letter Teffi received in 1929 from an unidentified man who "recalled the pupil Nadya Lokhvitskaya [...] so vividly, that [...] I could draw your portrait from memory [...] with your flowing hair, with your hat cocked to one side, and perhaps I could even convey your merry wit."[58] In contrast to the institutes for girls that Teffi's older sisters attended, the gymnasiums were academically rigorous, instructing their pupils not only in social graces and domestic skills (as the institutes primarily did), but also in such demanding academic subjects as mathematics and the natural and social sciences.[59] Such a curriculum scandalized an elderly female relative in one of Teffi's feuilletons:

> "They are very careless about young ladies' upbringing nowadays. Now all the attention is given to education. They want to make women scholars out of them. Although they themselves cannot help but understand that for a girl of good society grace is much more important than algebra."[60]

To placate the old lady, the narrator assures her that she doesn't like algebra at all, but her words are doubtless not far from the truth, for the gifts of the Lokhvitsky sisters were literary, not scientific or scholarly. Surprisingly, perhaps, for the daughters of a progressive father and nieces of the socially engaged Sofya Davydova, they were not among the idealistic young women who in the second half of the nineteenth century in Russia studied science and devoted themselves to such useful fields as medicine or teaching. One reason might be that their formative years coincided with the repressive reign of Alexander III, at which time a social and cultural quietism descended on the country. During this "period of deaf-and-dumb reaction," as a contemporary recalled, "the best sort of girls […] in one way or other threw themselves into art […] for a woman who thirsted for freedom and independence had one remaining path: Art."[61] The Lokhvitsky sisters were among such girls.

This period was also marked by a reaction against the utilitarian and tendentious that had so dominated the arts in Russia during the preceding decades.[62] Poets were turning away from civic themes and reviving the notion of "pure art," while in prose – in reaction to the weighty, idea-filled novels that dominated the previous decades (which gave birth to the masterpieces of Tolstoy and Dostoyevsky, among others) – young writers were turning to the more modest genre of the short story.[63] Foremost among them was Anton Chekhov (1860–1904), whose early comic stories, with their conciseness and lack of tendentiousness, their infectious humor and frequent note of melancholy, were a vital influence on Teffi.

The Lokhvitsky sisters kept up with the latest currents in the arts. The artist Alexander Benois (1870–1960), still a teenager, recalls that it was from the "delightful young ladies" Mirra (Maria) and the 16-year-old Nadya (who were summering at a dacha close to his brother's) that he first heard of Dmitry Merezhkovsky (1865–1941), then a budding poet, but soon to become one of the first champions of new modernist trends in literature and later a celebrated historical novelist and religious thinker.[64] By the time he met Mirra and Nadya, Benois himself had organized an informal club devoted to the study of art, which, guided by the conviction that beauty had the power to work spiritual transformation, explored ways of elevating aesthetic culture in Russia.[65] The goal reached fruition about a decade later, in 1898, when Benois and his friends founded the highly influential journal *Mir iskusstva* (World of art), its contributing artists – whose dominant aesthetic was somewhat akin to art nouveau – taking the journal's name. *Mir iskusstva* also published some of the leading young modernist writers, and its editor, Serge Diaghilev (1871–1929), later gained international renown as impresario of the Ballets Russes, for which World of Art members, most notably Benois and Léon Bakst (1866–1924), created brilliant sets and costumes.

JUVENILE WRITINGS

Nadya began to write when she was very young. Indeed, all the Lokhvitsky children wrote poetry, although they "considered this occupation very shameful, and as soon as someone caught a brother or sister with a pencil, notebook, and inspired face, they would promptly begin to shout: 'She's [or he's] writing! Writing!'"[66] This family activity had its consequences, since at least four of the sisters became writers. Aside from Teffi, one other, Maria (under her pen name, Mirra) gained great renown, but Varvara and Yelena also had works published and performed in the theater.[67] The brothers followed very different paths. Of Vadim little is known, but Nikolai had a glittering military career, and in 1917, during the world war, headed the Russian Expeditionary Corps in France.[68]

Nadya at first dreamed of being an artist, not a writer, but revealed from a young age her predilection for the satirical in both her poems and drawings.[69] By the age of 13 she was also writing in a more serious, "official" mode, producing at school two poems in the "magnificent odic style" – one in honor of the tsarina, the other (her first poem in print, apparently in a school publication) to mark the anniversary of the gymnasium.[70] The first of these poems figured in what was apparently Nadya's first contact with a professional literary personage, the editor and writer Ieronim Yasinsky (1850–1931). The two provide rather different recollections of the encounter. Teffi remembered that she first saw him at the home of a school friend when she was about 14. She recited for him a gymnasium ode, which he praised condescendingly, but when she read "something very poetic about a dream and a star," he waxed enthusiastic, even offering to get it published. She refused, however, explaining that her "sister is a poetess, and it would be very ridiculous if the whole family published."[71] Yasinsky recalled that he was at home when two *gimnazistki* visited. "'We are the Lokhvitskys,' began the older one. 'And poetesses,' the younger explained." He was impressed by both their poems, but the 13-year-old Yelena explained that their older sister, Mirra, wrote much better verse than theirs, and that they had decided that "only when she's already become famous and, finally, has died, will we have the right to begin publishing our works."[72]

Shortly afterward Mirra also paid a visit to Yasinsky. By then she had brought some of her poems to the editorial office of the magazine *Sever* (The north), accompanied by Nadya and their nanny.[73] Mirra complained to Yasinsky that the editors had rejected her poems and asked him to judge between her verses and her sisters'. He had to admit her superiority, recalling that her "verses glittered, were polished like precious stones and reverberant like little golden bells." He warned that their erotic content would prevent their publication, but Mirra's poetry did begin to appear in *Sever* in 1889 and soon created a sensation.

In the meantime, Nadya did not entirely keep her promise to subordinate her literary ambitions to her sister's. When she was 16 or 17, that is, in 1888 or 1889, she brought a comic poem, "Margarita's Song" – a parody of the "King of Thule" song from Goethe's *Faust* – to the most popular humor magazine of the time, *Oskolki* (Splinters). The editor, the famous humorist Nikolai Leikin (1841–1906), cut a menacing figure, with his thickset build, crooked shoulders, and crossed eyes staring at her gloomily. Her fright proved justified, for she received his negative verdict a month later: "'Margarita's Song' is totally unsuitable." She writes that "for a secret triumph over the angry editor" she later published the poem no less than four times.[74]

For now, however, her literary career was suspended, as she embarked in 1892 on a new life as wife and mother.

MARRIAGE AND MOTHERHOOD

Nadezhda most likely met her future husband, Vladislav Buchinsky, a lawyer of Polish ethnicity, in Tikhvin, where he served as forensic investigator (*sudebnyi issledovatel'*) and she often spent summers at her uncle's estate. Buchinsky, the scion of an "ancient noble gentry family" from the Mogilyov province, had studied at the elite Imperial School of Jurisprudence in St. Petersburg before taking his post in Tikhvin in 1886.[75] The couple married on 12 January 1892, in Tikhvin, where their first daughter, Valeria, was born and baptized the following November.[76]

Judging from Teffi's fiction, the young couple soon moved on, since descriptions of the dreary and remote town where the husband served do not fit Tikhvin, with its childhood associations and close family ties:

> We lived [...] in a small town in the steppes where my husband served as justice of the peace. What a boring place that wretched little town was! In the summer dust; in the winter the snow would drift higher than the street lamps; in the spring and fall there was so much mud that a troika almost drowned on the cathedral square; they had to pull the horses out with ropes.[77]

The town in question might have been Shchigry in the Kursk province, where the couple's second daughter, Yelena, was born in 1894.[78] In any case, by 1895 the family was settled at Buchinsky's estate, Ryki, in the Mogilyov province, where, judging once more by Teffi's fiction, life became yet more miserable. In three autobiographical stories published in the 1930s – joined by the identical names of the husband and wife, Stanya and Ilka – the husband, who seemed "sophisticated, elegant" during courtship, is now "bored, somnolent, didn't answer questions, just smoked and tossed out hands of solitaire [*shlepaet pas'iansy*]."[79] The adjectives "bored," "nasty [*zloi*]," and "angry" are constantly repeated in descriptions of Stanya, whose narrow moralism seems to Ilka so far from the truly moral that it verges on the demonic: "One should sprinkle them [Stanya and his father] with holy water, read prayers over them. They would crash down on the floor, black smoke would issue from their mouths."[80] The marital conflicts become so fraught that the exasperated Stanya says to Ilka: "I beg of you, go to your clever mama who managed to make such a hysterical creature of you."[81]

In actuality Nadezhda did just that, leaving her husband and children around 1898 and returning to St. Petersburg, where she began a new life as a writer. Her abandonment of her little daughters, while troubling, is perhaps more understandable in the light of family law at the time, which gave fathers exclusive guardianship of minor children.[82] The existence of a third child, however, a son, Janek, who was a mere infant, adds greater moral complexity to her decision. Teffi never mentioned a son, and there was much skepticism when Jan Fryling, a close friend of her daughter Valeria, first spoke of him to the late Teffi scholar Elizabeth Neatrour.[83] Several autobiographical stories by Yelena Buchinskaya, however, published in Polish newspapers in the 1930s, corroborate Fryling's recollection.[84]

The most revealing work, "A Sentimental Story," begins with two little girls, Zu and Buba, sitting in a dark and empty house during a snowstorm, awaiting the arrival of their mother, whom they barely remember. The atmosphere is consistent with Teffi's depiction of the gloomy Buchinsky household:

> The house is empty. It's true that their father, aunt, Zu, Buba, and their little brother live here; there are also a lot of servants. But in spite of that the house is empty, the house is dead, as if the soul had flown from it.

The narrator's dark image of her father – and also his penchant for solitaire – also conform to Teffi's fictionalized portrayals:

> The children are afraid of their father [...] He comes down for dinner,
> then he lays out a game of solitaire on the table, which for the most part
> he doesn't finish; he suddenly sweeps the cards together, gets up from
> the table with a heavy, weary motion, and goes upstairs.

The children know they mustn't talk about their mother, but Aunt Zosya tells
them that she was present when Mama arrived, and "when their little brother
was a couple of months old, Mama left [...] She left for the big city and wrote
fairy tales for grown-ups, and they gave her lots and lots of money for them."[85]
After evening tea, there follows the fullest description of the brother:

> Suddenly their little brother gets up, stretches out his arms, and begins
> to twirl (that's his favorite amusement). He has fair ringlets that fly away
> around his cheeks, and he rocks from foot to foot in such a funny way.
> Zu and Buba get up after him. They twirl and twirl, like wound-up tops.

The children go to bed, and in the middle of the night are awakened by the
arrival of their mother. Buba "grabs something dear, soft, fragrant," and when
she feels tears on her mother's forehead, she says to her: "Don't cry, Mama, I'll
buy you some money."[86] The story concludes in the present day. The grown-up
Zu and Buba have changed little, but

> their little brother is no more – they buried him under the linden tree
> [...] The house is no more either. People came, they burned down the
> house, dug up the garden, destroyed the tree-lined paths, plowed them,
> and sowed them with golden wheat.

Another story, "Jahor," states explicitly that the brother "is no more" because
he went off "to war – from which he was destined not to return."

Teffi translated "A Sentimental Story" and published it – now entitled "The
Old House" – under her own name, with a dedication to Yelena.[87] In her version,
however, all mention of the little brother – and the revealing fact that the
mother wrote popular stories – has been excised, perhaps a testament to the
guilt Teffi felt after leaving her infant son. The question of her relationship with
Janek is further complicated by the Moscow researcher Tamara Aleksandrova's
discovery that Janek lived in the same city as Teffi from 1911 to 1916, when
he was a student in St. Petersburg at the famous Karl May School, noted
for its many prominent graduates and for its two curricula: of the classical

gymnasiums and of schools devoted to applied fields (*real'nye uchilishcha*). Janek, who at first studied in the gymnasium, later transferred to the other division, where he took medical (*sanitarnye*) courses, apparently after the world war began. In 1916 he dropped out without graduating, evidently to join the military. It is not known what Teffi's relations were with her son during his time in St. Petersburg (she never mentions him), but this later contact must have made the pain of his death – and perhaps her own sense of inadequacy as a mother – all the more acute.

That Teffi's feeling of guilt toward her children never fully disappeared is apparent in a letter she wrote to Valeria almost 50 years later, long after she had established very close relations with her daughters. She admitted there that she was a "bad mother," but added in partial self-justification: "In essence I was good, but circumstances drove me from home, where, had I remained, I would have perished."[88]

2

LITERARY BEGINNINGS
1898–1908

Nothing concrete is known about the immediate circumstances leading to Nadezhda's abandonment of her husband and children. A fictionalized version, however, does exist in the immensely popular novel *Keys to Happiness* by Anastasya Verbitskaya (1861–1928), which may contain some kernel of truth.[1] The character in question, Dora, who writes popular feuilletons under the pseudonym "Dezi," tells a visitor that she lost all illusions after her "unhappy marriage… unhappy love… a breakup with [her] husband… a shameful divorce." She "left her husband," she reveals, "for another… […] but he turned out to be contemptible… even baser than my husband." She "lived with him openly, like a wife… For him I abandoned my children." Another man, a Jewish doctor who was worthy of her love, made her realize the shamefulness of her situation and urged her to leave, to work "even as a maid, but to stand on her own feet!" She tried to commit suicide, but the doctor took care of her and she recovered. But then "a month later… he died," after which she separated from her lover and came to St. Petersburg.[2]

Although Verbitskaya's account is clearly sensationalized, the possibility that another man was involved in Nadezhda's flight cannot be discounted. Several of her works depict women trapped in the provinces with tyrannical husbands, in a couple of which the possibility of escape is tied to men who prove unworthy.[3] The fact that adultery was the only grounds for divorcing a wife in late nineteenth-century Russia adds further credibility to Verbitskaya's version.[4] The description of the reaction of Dezi's family once she returned to St. Petersburg, moreover, may be relevant to Nadezhda's situation. Her "whole family," she recounts, "met me like an enemy. They couldn't forgive me for my divorce…"[5] Dezi's family refuses to take her in and, while it is unknown whether Teffi faced the same hostility, a contemporary recalled her squalid living conditions early in her career:

> She lived somewhere on Ligovka, in more than modest furnished
> rooms [rented from] a Finnish woman. There was a sofa in her little
> room from which horsehair and bast were crawling out; on the table
> a poorly cleaned samovar was hissing and there lay cheese, butter, and
> sausage wrapped in paper, student-style. The hostess herself, dressed in
> a red flannelette housecoat with short sleeves, which revealed her very
> beautiful arms, was half lying on the sofa, and by her feet, in the pose
> of Hamlet, lay an enamored young critic.[6]

Getting started as a writer also proved a struggle – especially as an independent
woman writer, whose numbers had grown greatly at the end of the nineteenth
century and some of whom lived in great need.[7]

Moreover, the St. Petersburg literary world had undergone a dramatic
change since Nadezhda left almost a decade earlier. The pallid aestheticism
of the 1880s had given way to a creative outburst in the arts that marked the
beginning of what was later called the Silver Age, which lasted approximately
a quarter-century.[8] The young poets of the 1890s, who, under the influence of
European (especially French) modernism, called themselves symbolists, rejected
materialist, bourgeois society and the realist art it predicated, and turned instead
to a search for transcendent spiritual values, which could not be apprehended,
they thought, through rational discourse, but intuitively – through the use
of symbols and through the sheer power of sound and rhythm – often at the
expense of sense. Decadence – a symptom of *fin de siècle* angst, also derived
from the French – was a feature of Russian symbolism in the 1890s (indeed,
the terms were used interchangeably). The decadents concentrated on the
dark and lurid side of existence – from the banality and ugliness of modern
society to the horrors lurking in the natural world and the satanic forces ruling
the universe. To counter these horrors, they devoted themselves to cultivation
of the self, to making their lives into works of art. This led in some cases to
a celebration in their art (and lives) of unbridled hedonism, the search for
pleasure, wherever it may lead.

The poetry of the symbolists / decadents aroused enthusiasm in some, but
its frequent impenetrability, as well as its sometimes shocking subject matter,
made it the butt of ridicule by others. Most evident in Teffi's early satire is the
mockery, although her own use of symbols and of elaborate sound instrumentation in her serious poetry attests to their influence. Most importantly,
the symbolist dualism – the longing for a transcendent reality beyond absurd
everyday life – had a profound and lasting effect.

*

The changes that had occurred in Russian literature during Teffi's absence from St. Petersburg also had a familial dimension, for Mirra Lokhvitskaya had become a famous poet, closely associated with the symbolists and decadents. Already at the end of the 1880s her verse startled readers with its ecstatic paeans to female sensuality, its bright coloration, its conjuring of exotic and fantastic worlds. Barely out of school, the well-brought-up young St. Petersburg lady was at once identified with the Sappho of her early poem:

> Dark-eyed, marvelous, delightfully slender,
> Filled with inspiration and immortal songs.[9]

Although Mirra's "ecstatic outpourings" have not worn well, in her own time she enjoyed not only great popularity, but achieved official recognition: her first collection, published in 1896, was awarded the Academy of Sciences' Pushkin Prize.[10]

Contemporaries observed that in actual life Mirra bore little resemblance to her poetic persona – that she "wrote bold, erotic poems [...] and was the most chaste married lady in St. Petersburg."[11] It seems, however, that her chastity was compromised in the late 1890s when she had a passionate love affair with the immensely popular symbolist poet Konstantin Balmont (1867–1942).[12] Nadezhda first met Balmont at Mirra's, when "Russia was just in love with [him] [...] People read him, recited, sang him on the stage."[13] The poet, she wrote, was flirtatious: *"Si blonde, si gaie, si femme,"* he said to her, to which Mirra responded: *"*And you are *si monsieur."*[14]

Nadezhda herself soon took steps to improve her literary fortunes, re-establishing her old tie with Ieronim Yasinsky. He recalled:

> Soon Nadezhda Lokhvitskaya somehow quickly grew up, became a fashion plate, got married, and began using another surname [...] she came to me, reminded me of her childhood visits, and announced that she was finally preparing to publish her verse and humorous sketches.[15]

Leonid Galich remembers her

> first debut, long before the beginning of her professional writing career, in the large and crowded living room of I. I. Yasinsky in Chornaya

Rechka [...] Teffi sang her first *chansonettes*, accompanying herself on the guitar, about three engineers and cement-concrete, about red shoes, etc.[16]

Yasinsky was reluctant to publish Nadezhda because of Mirra's objection to the appearance in print of another Lokhvitskaya. "I could not accept a work signed with a famous surname," he wrote Mirra in July 1901. "Nadezhda Aleksandrovna was at my place and read her work, but I did not offer to print it."[17] Only in 1902, when Nadezhda began signing her poems with her married name, did he publish "Four Engineers" (Galich misremembered the number), with two more of her poems appearing the following year.[18]

Another writer, Zoya Yakovleva, now forgotten but then quite popular, might have been more helpful initially. The "dear old writer," as Teffi called her, "always had someone under her wing [*pokrovitstvovala*], was introducing someone to a necessary person, helping with advice and support [*protektsiei*]."[19] It was at Yakovleva's that she made the acquaintance of some prominent literary and theatrical figures, among them the brilliant playwright, director, and dramatic theorist Nikolai Yevreinov (1879–1953), with whom she established lasting relations. She also first encountered Count Aleksei Tolstoy (1882–1945) at Yakovleva's in December 1903. Then a "strapping, stocky student" with a "good-natured face" who wrote symbolist poems, he later became a very popular prose writer.[20] Teffi and Tolstoy developed a close friendship in the early days of emigration before his return to the Soviet Union.

Yakovleva might have played a role in getting Nadezhda's first poem published in August 1901 in the journal *Sever*, to which she herself contributed (and in which Mirra made her debut).[21] Signed "N. Lokhvitskaya," it was sent, Teffi later wrote, by acquaintances without her knowledge. She added that it was "awful" and she "hoped no one would read it."[22]

FIRST WRITINGS

Teffi once remarked:

> I was born in St. Petersburg in the springtime and, as everyone knows, our St. Petersburg spring is extremely changeable: now the sun is shining, now it's raining. Therefore, like the pediment of a Greek theater, I also have two faces, one laughing and one weeping.[23]

These "two faces" peered out at the reader from the very beginning of Nadezhda's literary career. It was her weeping face that appeared in her first poem in *Sever* and in the two other serious poems published in the fall of 1901 in the St. Petersburg journal *Zvezda* (The star). It was also in *Zvezda*, at the very end of the year, that the author unveiled her "laughing face" – and with it the pseudonym "Teffi."[24] In 1902 her satirical works almost entirely replaced her lyrical poems in *Zvezda*, but in 1903 her serious poetry predominated, perhaps because by then her satire was coming out in the popular St. Petersburg newspaper *Birzhevye vedomosti* (Stockmarket news).

During this very early period, Teffi used her real name for her serious writings (after 1901, perhaps due to Mirra's objection, her married name, Buchinskaya) and the pseudonym for her comic–satirical works. The origin of her pen name is uncertain, and Teffi's later explanation only muddied the waters. She recalled that she adopted it in connection with her first play, *The Woman Question*. Since fools are always lucky, she explained, she decided on the name of a fool she knew, Stepan, called "Steffi" by his family (throwing out the first letter to avoid detection by the fool). The name had the added advantage of being sexually ambiguous, since she considered it cowardly to "hide behind a male pseudonym" – a common practice at the time among those who did not wish to be judged as stereotypical woman writers.[25] When the play was a hit, she was too embarrassed to reveal the pseudonym's origin and readily agreed to a reporter's suggestion that the name came from Kipling. The only problem with this version is that *The Woman Question* was produced in 1907, almost six years after Teffi first used her pseudonym. The most plausible source would be two of Kipling's *Just So Stories*, which relate how a lively, mischievous little cave girl named Taffy invented the alphabet and wrote the first letter.[26] There is a problem here too, however, because the *Just So Stories* were published only in 1902 – the year after Teffi took her pseudonym.[27] And so the source may have been the fool Steffi after all.

THE WEEPING FACE

Teffi's first serious poems are quite unremarkable, both formally and thematically. They are hardly touched by the poetic experiments of the modernists and more reminiscent of the doleful but stylistically conventional poetry of the 1880s. The fact that some of the poems were written as lyrics to songs (which were early picked up by famous singers[28]) adds a layer of theatricality that distances the poetic persona from the author. Nevertheless they provide a glimpse of Teffi's mood at this painful period of transition from a conventional if unhappy life as wife and mother to the more treacherous path of a single woman pursuing a literary career.

Her very first published poem, "I had a dream, mad and wonderful…" tells of a dream in which "life called […] to labor, to freedom, and to struggle" – reflecting the poet's longing to escape from the confines of her marriage to a free if difficult life.[29] In the second (and final) stanza, however, she awakens on a dreary autumn day and – using the conventional association of autumn with decline and decay – expresses the fear "that life has passed and dreaming is a joke [*smeshno*]!" (In 1901 Teffi was, after all, already 29!) The very last word of the poem (*smeshno* = funny, ridiculous), is an early indication of the often-painful underpinning of Teffi's humor.

"The Vampire," published a couple of months later, partakes of the demonism and rather lurid style of the decadents, but beneath this stylization lies an allusion to the poet's tormented relationship with her husband. The pale and suffering narrator relates how at night a "bloodthirsty vampire" comes to her. He is "dear," his eyes promise "bliss without measure, without limit, without end," but he drinks her blood. She concludes that the vampire will destroy her, "will bear away my strength and my life."[30]

In the poems published in *Zvezda* in 1903, Teffi reprises the same doleful tone and conventional motifs – the contrasts of dream and reality, spring and autumn, love and death. Now past 30, she continues to bemoan her entrance into the "autumn of life."[31] Still filled with the pain of her unhappy marriage, she declares: "I do not want love. I am wholly filled with anguish."[32] By the end of 1903, however, this dejection disappears, perhaps marking a change in the poet's own life. In "Autumn Confession" – the first serious poem signed "Teffi" – the usual lugubrious mood associated with that season is transferred from the poetess to her male addressee. It is he who regrets their fading love, while she declares: "I kiss you and laugh!" The dominant role of the woman becomes clear at the poem's conclusion:

I believe summer will return,
[. . . . . .]
Again warmed by the ray of love,
I will be happy… with another![33]

Teffi's sudden assertiveness is perhaps connected to her romantic liaison with Leonid Galich (pseudonym of Gabrilovich, 1878 or 1879–1953), which began at about this time and lasted until 1914.[34] Galich was a man of unusually broad interests and achievements. A graduate of the Mathematics and Science faculties at St. Petersburg University, he was at various times a professor at Tomsk and St. Petersburg universities and authored scholarly works in philosophy (both in Russian and German). He also worked in the fields of applied mathematics and physics and was a successful inventor.[35] His journalistic career began when, as a 17-year-old student in need of money, he submitted a satirical poem to a popular St. Petersburg newspaper.[36] Thereafter he wrote on a broad range of political, literary, theatrical, and philosophical issues for a number of prominent newspapers and magazines. He was, it is claimed, "one of the creators in pre-revolutionary Russia of the political feuilleton, a genre that enjoyed great success among readers."[37]

THE LAUGHING FACE

If Teffi's early poetry was derivative and quite pedestrian, from the very beginning she displayed a mastery of satire and humor that was soon to bring her great popularity and to eclipse her "weeping" face. As she wrote ruefully: "'Laugh!' readers said to me. 'Laugh! It brings us money,' said my publishers… and I laughed."[38] Teffi's gift for laughter was considered very unusual for a woman at the time, when major thinkers such as Henri Bergson and Arthur Schopenhauer had gone as far as to assert that women did not have a sense of humor.[39] Humor implies the superiority of the jokester to the butt of his or her laughter – an instrument of power and authority – and indeed in Teffi's earliest satire laughter allowed her to achieve what she struggled toward in her serious poetry and, apparently, in her personal life: ascendancy over men, in particular, over the largely male literary and cultural establishment.

This is striking in Teffi's first satirical poem in *Zvezda*, "New Year's among the Writers," in which she parodies the style and pretensions of various writers at a New Year's party as they introduce themselves to the new-born 1902. She paints a witty group portrait of contemporary literati, among them several with whom she had – or would have – close personal and professional relations. When mimicking Balmont, for example, she mocks his self-aggrandizement ("I am the new god of my native land"), his repeated use of the prefix *pere-* ("trans-," "ultra-") to create such words as *pereplesk* ("transsplash"), *perebal'mont* ("ultrabalmont"), *perepoet* ("ultrapoet"), and excessive sound instrumentation ("*Pushistyi, chistyi, serebristyi*" = "Fluffy, pure, silvery").[40]

In the course of 1902 Teffi published several more witty group satires of writers in *Zvezda*. In June she parodied literary and theatrical figures departing by train on summer vacation. Among them are Merezhkovsky and his wife, the brilliant poet and critic Zinaida Gippius (1869–1945), whose explanation of their late arrival reveals their self-regarding religiosity. Merezhkovsky declares:

> At home I have just held a service
> For the Resurrected Gods…
> […] my hymn of praise –
> I dedicated to myself.

Gippius's egoism takes a more practical form:

> No! I, who love myself like God,
> Am taking a separate compartment![41]

Women writers do not escape Teffi's mockery. A decadent poetess (sounding suspiciously like Mirra – and Nadezhda – Lokhvitskaya, but, of course, not only them) exclaims to the conductor:

> I searched for you! I desired you!
> You fell asleep amidst the fragrant lilies!
> [. . . . . .]
> I am yours, I am yours…

This causes the terrified conductor to call for help.[42] In another poem depicting the writers' return, Teffi parodies a different, more didactic group of "lady writers":

> Let our ardent words
> Force women to go on strike,
> Shaking off their age-old lethargy,
> To establish women's rights,
> And – the main cause of all evils –
> To completely eradicate men.[43]

Teffi published some narrowly topical pieces in *Zvezda* whose significance is lost on the modern reader, but others have preserved their bite. "Lament of the Doctors," for example (inspired by Vikenty Veresayev's *Notes of a Doctor*, which had created a sensation the year before), ironically blames the writer for undermining people's faith in doctors. In the past

> a doctor performed the operation skillfully,
> But by mistake, together with his instrument,
> Sewed up in [the patient] his pince-nez,
> His top hat, watch, handkerchief, newspaper
> And his pocket comb.

The patient didn't survive and

> the doctor, of course, was upset
> When he found out that the capricious patient
> Had carried off his property with him.

Like a "true gentleman" the doctor did not demand restitution, but nevertheless the public was rebuking him. And it is all Veresayev's fault.[44]

In 1903 Teffi became a regular contributor to the popular liberal St. Petersburg newspaper, *Birzhevye vedomosti*, and her witty verse satires began attracting a much broader audience. She recalled many years later that *Birzhevka*, as it was popularly called, "primarily castigated 'city fathers who fed off the public pie,'" and added: "I helped to castigate."[45] She remembered one occasion when she wrote a satirical poem, "Lelyanov and the Canal," directed against the mayor, who had plans to fill in the Ekaterininsky Canal. Tsar Nicholas, it turned out, was against the project and praised the piece, after which the newspaper's publisher raised Teffi's salary by two kopecks.

Actually, Teffi rarely sallied into the political world in *Birzhevka*.[46] Most of her early contributions, as in *Zvezda*, consisted of satirical verse (less often prose) devoted to culture – primarily to the theater. These included amusing observations on visiting artists, such as the renowned American "barefoot" dancer Isadora Duncan (1877–1927), who elicited a rebuke:

> Miss Duncan!
> Why go barefoot
> When tights have been invented?

It is easy to stun our public
With a bare heel!"[47]

Among the relatively few articles on literature, of special interest is Teffi's essay on laughter. Most revealing is her prescription for Russian laughter:

Laughter should be subtle and not banal, and deep; laughter should be sharp and should wound someone, so that in its peals and vibrations drops of blood be felt. Only under these conditions will the Russian diaphragm begin to heave.[48]

Teffi thus characterizes laughter as a weapon, and, indeed, in her own satire, she has transformed herself from the melancholy victim of her early poetry into a gleeful attacker.

Teffi's unique role as a female satirist in the mostly male literary world required considerable fortitude. The provocative literary critic and translator (and later famous children's writer) Kornei Chukovsky (1882–1965) tells of an incident that occurred soon after his arrival in St. Petersburg from his native Odessa. One day he found his Odessa acquaintance, the handsome poet Alexander Fyodorov (1868–1949), writing flowery dedications in copies of his recently published book to various women writers, including Teffi. He told Chukovsky, who had never heard of her, that Teffi was "a popular feuilletonist for *Birzhevye vedomosti*"; that she was "young... witty... making a splash in Petersburg."[49] He added that he was planning "to spend the evening" with her, but when Teffi, a "voluptuous [*pyshnotelaia*], beautiful woman with an open, laughing, rosy face," arrived, she summarily spurned his advances. This embarrassing episode was a mere prelude, for Teffi soon published what Chukovsky characterizes as a "terribly nasty" feuilleton in *Birzhevka*, in which she accused Fyodorov or another writer, Anatoly Kamensky (1876–1941), of plagiarism. She enumerated the many similarities between their two works (both called *The Queen*) and concluded: "Who, finally, is the real queen and who is the vile usurper?"[50]

The accusation aroused a great outcry from both writers, who arranged a trial against Teffi, with the critic and philosopher Akim Volynsky (1861–1926) acting as judge. Chukovsky recalls Teffi's theatrical bravado – which did not quite conceal her trepidation – on the day she faced condemnation:

On her shoulders was a bright gypsy shawl embroidered with crimson flowers. After looking around mockingly at the entire gathering without greeting anyone, she sat down in the passage right in the middle between the two camps. She was cheerful, as if she weren't seated on the defendant's bench, but in a box at the theater, where some amusing spectacle awaited her. But if you looked closely, her calm was affected: her beautiful cheeks were trembling. She kept pulling the crimson shawl more and more tightly around her splendid shoulders, as if she wanted to tear it in half.[51]

Volynsky's verdict was that neither Fyodorov nor Kamensky had copied from the other, but that both had borrowed from Maupassant. The parties were dissatisfied and turned to the Literary Fund for arbitration, but received no satisfaction. Teffi, on her part, did not give up the attack:

> When you compare and read,
> You see clearly – it's plagiarism!
> But you listen and you discover
> That nobody is guilty.
> [. . . . . .]
> "What do we have here – is it simply imitation[?]"
> [. . . . . .]
> "The influence of mysterious forces?
> Telepathy? Hypnosis?"[52]

TEFFI'S TRUE FACE?

Teffi's boldness did not necessarily imply that she had entirely overcome her sense of vulnerability. A couple of prose pieces of 1904 intimate that the dangers were not only from without, that she was experiencing considerable inner turmoil. The sketch "Wingless Souls" begins as a quite light-hearted satire, deriding a hackneyed literary type, the "seeking woman."[53] Her very appearance, Teffi writes, has become codified: "Invariably a pale face [...] Invariably enormous eyes with a melancholy or suffering expression." In the second half of the piece, however, the tone abruptly changes, the writer now treating the literary type as a real human being who is "tormented" because she will never possess "the mighty and commanding spirit – the spirit of creativity."

Alluding to Nietzsche (in great vogue at the time) she divides mankind into two unequal categories: the chosen, "who give the world something new," and "small, imperceptible drones [who] raise the wave of life on their shoulders." She quotes Nietzsche directly: "I love those who do not seek reasons beyond the stars in order to perish, but who devote themselves to the earth, so that at some time the superman might reign."[54] The emotional urgency suggests its relevance to the author herself, who is, perhaps, obliquely expressing her uncertainty as to whether she is one of those "wingless souls" who should dedicate themselves to the earth or a rare creative being who can soar above it.

"Mist," a quite uncharacteristic piece published in *Birzhevka* a couple of months later, betrays the influence of both Nietzsche and the symbolists, and reveals how averse Teffi was to devoting herself to the "dreary" earth and its lowly inhabitants.[55] The narrator first remembers a bright sunny day that filled her with joy until she came upon "a long gray house," in front of which sat an old peddler woman "with malicious, bulging eyes." From both the house and the woman there exuded "the same silent malice," creating a "soft, dully gray fog" that blotted out the sun. In the second, nocturnal, episode the narrator and a man walk arm in arm through the "sticky, dreary mist," which their conversation pierces both upward to the heavenly heights and downward to the subterranean depths. Their ecstatic exchange, however, is halted by another repellant sight, this one suffused with Dostoyevskian pathos: "a strange woman in a big formless hat with a long, wet feather," accompanied by an emaciated dog. At the sight of her "deformed, frightening, dejected" feather, "the turbid mist flowed into [their] souls" and they "silently parted," never to meet again.

In the final episode, the narrator relates how, on a bright autumn day, she saw a magnificent bouquet in the window of a florist shop, a floral microcosm of the transcendent world: "Cold, fragile lilies [...] the six-winged, pure seraphs of the earth!" surrounding a single golden chrysanthemum, "all alive, trembling, like a small sun, like torrid, radiant joy!" But then

> among the lilies something stirred. I saw a dim face, frighteningly familiar, repellently familiar... I saw a wide pale mouth with its corners turned down, a lock of hair, pitiful, flat, that had come undone – and the eyes – tormented, melancholy. A foggy, sticky, cold mist looked out from [the eyes].

Horrified, she realizes it is her face reflected in the mirror behind the bouquet. She concludes: "The mist was – me... I was – the mist." Striking here are the almost identical features of the narrator in "Mist" and the "seeking women" of "Wingless Souls" – their pallor, their eyes (here "tormented, melancholy," there "melancholy or suffering"). She *is*, to her horror, one of those "seeking women," doomed to devote themselves to the dim and ugly earth. The story is also, perhaps, an early reflection of the depression (or neurasthenia, as she calls it) from which Teffi suffered throughout her life.

While it is unclear whether Teffi's acceptance of her earthbound mission was a factor, in her comic–satirical works of 1904 and early 1905 she increasingly turned from the cultural life of the capital to more humble subjects. How she succeeded in creating humorous – even sympathetic – portrayals of the lower classes, given the conflicting feelings of intense pity and equally intense antipathy evident in "Mist," is a question that an unpublished essay on Teffi by the great Soviet satirist Mikhail Zoshchenko (1894–1958) helps to address. He notes her affection for her characters, despite their "banality [*poshlost'*] and stupidity," and finds that what creates a positive impression is their "laughing words" (which he adopted in his own works), making each of them an "aston-ishing fool," a "conversing fool."[56]

Such "laughing words" are central to one of Teffi's earliest fictional works, "The Merry Party," written a few months before "Mist."[57] It centers upon the not very edifying misadventures of a coachman, Vanyushka, who, after arriving late at a party given by a neighboring maid he is courting, is soundly thrashed by the master of the house, who mistakes him for a burglar. The main characters in the story certainly live in a "mist" of ignorance and malice, but, by reproducing their absurd distortions of language, their amusing folk beliefs, and the laughable results of their misunderstandings, Teffi lends them a liveliness and distinctiveness that color the gray with bright hues.

The gray persisted, however, in several serious stories that Teffi published in the magazine *Niva* in 1905. Longer than most of her works and more unobtrusive stylistically, they were clearly written under the influence of Chekhov's serious prose. Although not autobiographical in the narrow sense, they extrapolate from Teffi's own experiences: her past as unhappy wife and her present as a single working woman. Two years before she had published a related story, "The Forgotten Track," in *Zvezda* – Teffi's earliest piece of prose fiction so far discovered.[58] The story begins with an encounter between the heroine, Sofya Ivanovna, wife of the head of the local railroad station, and a "decadent" poet, a visitor to the town. Fearing the jealousy of her irascible husband, she hustles the poet away from the gaping workers and into an empty railroad car. The train suddenly starts to move, and when it comes to a halt at the next station, they are confronted by Sofya's husband. He gloomily helps his wife out and, spying the decadent, shuts him in the car and writes on the door: "To Kharkov via Moscow and Zhitomir."[59]

The underlying triangular plot places Sofya between two very different men: her ill-tempered husband and a "man of art." Although the flight could be interpreted as an escape, analogous to the author's own (albeit in this case aborted), from her miserable provincial life to the world of art, the parodic portrait of the poet speaks against such a simple equation. The "little, skinny gentleman" is hardly a match for the powerful husband, with his "strong hand."[60] Moreover, his outlandish mode of dress – his checked suit, "strange green tie," "pink hose with blue polka dots" – is ridiculed, as is his "modernist" poetry.[61] When Sofya remarks that his poem "is missing a rhyme," he exclaims: "So you need rhyme? Oh! How banal that is! [...] I hate them! I enfold a free thought in free forms, without bounds, without measures, without..."[62]

The earliest of the *Niva* stories, "The Day Has Passed," portrays another woman living with a tyrannical husband in the provinces, whereas the other two works published in the magazine in 1905 offer rare and revealing glimpses of poor, solitary office workers – among the many women from impoverished gentry families compelled at that time to earn their own keep.[63] The title of the first and more complex story, "Princess's Ruby," at once introduces a dualistic strain, counterposing the past of the heroine, Aglaya – when her wealthy father, later ruined, called her Princess – and the present pitiful state of the poor and sickly office worker. All that remains of her "royal" past is a pale pink ruby, which reassures her that even in the midst of deprivation she is a higher being: "Only a real princess can go around so ragged and shabby because she loves a little colored stone!"[64]

The story begins when the male protagonist, Rudanov, who knew her father years before, encounters Aglaya in her office while visiting St. Petersburg and begins to visit her at home. Aglaya arouses in Rudanov the conflicting emotions of intense pity and equally intense revulsion experienced toward the underprivileged in Teffi's earlier works – the feelings growing to the point that he paradoxically contemplates marrying her precisely because "she's a cripple and ugly and stupid."[65] Aglaya herself harbors some hope when her ruby disappears, for she assumes that Rudanov took it to make a stickpin for himself – a sign of his feelings for her. This infuriates him, and when "her trembling, cold hand, wet from tears," touches him, a "shiver of revulsion" overpowers his "gnawing pity" and he flees to his native Odessa.[66] Only when passing through

St. Petersburg the following spring does he discover that Princess has died, as if without her ruby life was impossible. On his return home, Rudanov learns that his tailor found the stone in his jacket lining, and this arouses his half-forgotten feelings for Aglaya, for which he can find no resolution:

> He thought about the little dead Princess, and the old gnawing pity quietly crawled in and latched onto his heart [...] And all those thoughts, endless, oppressive, wound and unwound [...] and he succumbed to them [...] not knowing how he was to blame, but finding no justification for himself.[67]

Katerina, the poor office worker in "Platypus," evokes no such conflicting emotions of pity and repulsion, but, even though she is neither sickly nor ugly, her life is miserable. She works long hours at a monotonous job, made all the worse because a clerk, whom everyone calls Platypus, is slandering her in order to further his own position. In the course of the story he succeeds in getting Katerina dismissed. When she passes Platypus's apartment on the way home that evening she is about to turn away, but changes her mind: "Let him look at her, she's not the one who'll lower her eyes in any case."[68] What she sees has an unexpected effect:

> Platypus lay jacketless on a sofa by the wall, his back to the window. He hid his face right in the corner and was breathing heavily like a horse who had been driven too hard [...]
> And right by the window, in front of a table covered with torn brown oilcloth, stood a little old woman with a swollen yellow face and a strange flat head, as if she had been beaten on the crown all her life.
> Katerina Nikolayevna quickly walked away from the window.
> A kind of quiet, sharply resonating note began gnawing deep under her heart, began growing, strengthening, and, drowning out the previous spitefully buzzing one, merged with it and both died out.

In "Platypus," Teffi transfers the physical and psychological impairments from the poor working girl to her victimizer, who himself emerges as victim in the larger scheme of things. Pity dissolves the feelings of revulsion and outrage – a compassion for all unfortunates that infuses the best of Teffi's mature writing. And during the revolutionary year of 1905 she had the opportunity to manifest her sympathy not only in literary works but through direct action.

THE 1905 REVOLUTION

The many ills besetting the Russian Empire in 1905 – growing worker unrest, the calamitous war with Japan, mounting discontent with the tsarist government's autocratic ways, to mention a few of the most critical – created a combustible situation. The spark that set off what is known as the first Russian revolution was a mass workers' march held in St. Petersburg on Sunday, 9 January. When the unarmed crowd arrived at the Winter Palace, the military killed over a hundred people and injured many more.[69] As news spread of what came to be called Bloody Sunday, strikes and peasant revolts broke out throughout the Russian Empire.

Educated public opinion, except for the most reactionary, was united against the government, and a broad spectrum of political factions sprang into action, from the moderately liberal Constitutional Democrats (Kadets); to the Socialist Revolutionaries (SRs), the heirs to the Russian nineteenth-century revolutionary movement; to the Marxist Social Democrats (SDs), themselves split into the Mensheviks and the more extreme Bolsheviks. As Teffi remembered 45 years later: "Russia suddenly moved to the left. Students were agitated, workers were striking, even old generals grumbled about the wretched system [*skvernye poriadki*], and sharply commented on the person of the tsar."[70] Teffi herself was among those infected by the spirit of revolt. A friend of hers, Konstantin Platonov – the son of a senator, who, "to the bafflement of his father, had close ties with the Social Democrats"[71] – introduced her to a number of prominent Bolsheviks, including Lev Kamenev, Alexander Bogdanov, and Alexandra Kollontai.

Platonov urged Teffi to go and study with Lenin in Geneva, which, not surprisingly, she did not do, but in March 1905 she published a poem, "The Banner of Freedom," in the Geneva Bolshevik newspaper *Vpered* (Forward).[72] The poem (dedicated to Platonov) is narrated by poor "worker-bees" – seamstresses who labor day and night sewing fancy clothes for the rich. On a holiday they witness others dancing in the dresses that caused them (the bees) so much misery, and that night, back at their sweatshop, the bees declare:

> We sewed together strips of red silk
> [. . . . . .]
> We sewed the bloody banner of freedom.[73]

Throughout most of 1905 the tsar's attempts to quell the forces of revolution were belated and insufficient. After the proposal to create a constituent assembly, or *duma*, was issued in early August, Teffi reacted with a column in which the narrator, recovering from a prolonged illness and unaware of recent events, is visited by a lady who is the very personification of radical chic. The visitor informs her of the latest reforms, but when the narrator asks if there is freedom of speech, she replies: "Well, yes, well, of course... *Enfin, je ne sais pas* [...] Well, to be sure, freedom of speech, but it's forbidden to talk about it."[74]

Teffi managed to write this amusing feuilleton at a very painful time for the Lokhvitsky family: on 27 August Mirra died at the age of 35. The cause remains unclear. It was said that she died of tuberculosis, but there is apparently greater evidence that she had heart problems.[75] Teffi's comment to a correspondent many years later suggests underlying psychological and spiritual causes:

Mirra (Masha) was sure she was under a spell [*porchennaia*] and asked very seriously for a witch doctor [*znakharka*] to be found. The doctors didn't understand her illness. They found that her heart was healthy, but she died of heart seizures.[76]

Meanwhile revolutionary events were moving apace, and in response the tsar issued a manifesto on 17 October that introduced universal suffrage (for men) and various civil liberties. One result was the immediate appearance of an opposition press, including the first legal Bolshevik newspaper in Russia, *Novaia zhizn'* (New life). It began publication on 27 October, its editor in chief the poet Nikolai Minsky (1855–1937), who was not a Bolshevik but like many writers and artists that year was infected by revolutionary fever.[77] Teffi and Galich joined him on the editorial board as non-Party members (although, according to one of the Bolshevik participants, they "made out at the time to be Marxists or Marxist-leaning [*marksistvuiushchikh*]"[78]). The literary contributors to *Novaia zhizn'* included a diverse collection of contemporary writers, ranging from the symbolist Balmont to the realist Ivan Bunin and the revolutionary Maxim Gorky. The newspaper created a sensation – which the Bolsheviks ascribed to the immense enthusiasm of the working class, but Teffi attributed to interest among the intelligentsia: "The novelty of a union between the Social Democrats and the decadents [...] and Gorky to boot, intrigued everyone greatly."[79]

In the very first issue of *Novaia zhizn'*, Teffi's sketch "18 October" depicts the streets of St. Petersburg the day after the tsar issued his manifesto. She begins with a vivid description, using the visual iconography common in revolutionary art: the masses united in a "mighty and triumphant procession";

the red banners outlined against the gray sky, which "meander like gigantic dark streams of resurrected triumphant blood."[80] Interspersed among the patches of revolutionary rhetoric are little vignettes suggesting that the chasm between the classes, portrayed with such pained intensity in some of Teffi's early works, has been bridged: "A soldier, a lady in white gloves, a student, a worker, an officer, a bureaucrat with a cockade, a woman in a kerchief, a sailor. All are together."[81] In conclusion Teffi returns to the revolutionary imagery of the beginning, as the banners "lead their people, their great host, forward, through the black night, to a new dawn, to a new life."[82]

In the following issue, Teffi republished her poem "Banner of Freedom," now entitled "The Bees."[83] She was then asked to return to her usual satirical métier and chose a formidable target for the 1 November issue: Dmitry Trepov (1850–1906), the former governor general of St. Petersburg, who had been removed from office after the October Manifesto. In response to his plaint that

> I was for all of Russia
> The protector and patron!

the narrator – playing on the second meaning of *patron* in Russian (bullet) – retorts that Trepov himself had commanded the troops: "Do not spare the bullets [patrons]" ("*Ne zhalei patronov*").[84] That evening, Teffi writes, "everywhere – in the streets, in trams, in clubs, in living rooms, at student gatherings – they repeated the joke."[85]

Teffi's involvement with *Novaia zhizn'* proved short-lived; indeed, from the start the relations between the Bolsheviks and the literary staff were strained. She recalled that from her first encounters with the Marxists she found their conversations "about some kind of congresses, resolutions, and 'co-optations,'" incomprehensible.[86] In general they "were uninteresting and did not arouse respect":

> They never talked about Russia's destiny; they were never disturbed by the things that tormented the old revolutionaries, for which they went to their death. Life passed them by. And often some important event – a strike at a large plant, some major revolt – caught them unawares and stunned them by its unexpectedness [...]
>
> But life interested them very little. They were buried up to their ears in congresses, co-optations, and resolutions.[87]

Lenin arrived from exile in November, and Teffi developed an antipathy to him too. His appearance she found unassuming: "Nothing about him promised a dictator. Nothing expressed spiritual fervor. He spoke, gave orders, as if he were doing a job, and it seemed as if he himself was bored – but nothing could be done about it." He "behaved simply, without any pose," but saw people as no more than material:

> Each person was good insofar as he was necessary for the cause. And if he wasn't – to hell with him. And if someone was harmful or simply inconvenient, one could strangle him. And he did all this calmly, without malice, and reasonably. One might even say good-naturedly. It seems he also looked at himself not as a person, but as a servant of his idea. These obsessed maniacs are terrifying.[88]

Once Lenin took control, *Novaia zhizn'* was filled more and more with Party matters, and soon an incendiary article of Lenin's forced Minsky to flee abroad. Shortly thereafter the entire literary section resigned and *Novaia zhizn'* became a Party organ. The newspaper was shut down by the police on 3 December 1905, after having published 28 issues.

By the end of 1905 the tsarist government was regaining control, although unrest continued for another year and a half.[89] Opposition in the press also went on, and after her association with *Novaia zhizn'* ended, Teffi's works appeared in various satirical journals. One poem, published in 1906, indicates that, although she was by then disillusioned with the Bolsheviks, her faith in bloody revolution had not died. She describes an old lioness mauled by hyenas, who anticipate devouring her cubs as well. They wait in vain, however, for the cubs will not come until "they grow, become strong, turn into powerful, strong, invincible lions […] They will come…"[90]

Anti-government satire continued until 1908, but grew milder, due in part to greater government restrictions, but also, no doubt, to fading revolutionary fervor. The poems and prose sketches Teffi contributed to periodicals in 1907 and 1908 are more reformist than revolutionary, and more and more she returned to literary and social themes.[91] Thus, in "Jews and Russian Literature,"[92] Teffi responded to a controversial article of the same name by Chukovsky, in which he asserted that Jews cannot really understand Russian literature because of their non-Russian origins.[93] Teffi directs Chukovsky's argument against him, asking: "Where are Kornei's roots?" (in Russian a

play on words: *"Gde zhe korni u Korneia?"*). She then poses a long series of
rhetorical questions, which, following his logic, casts doubt on his ability to
understand not only Russian, but world literature: did he battle Attila? Did
he eat manna with Moses? Did he crawl into the bathtub with Marat? She
concludes that everyone is capable of understanding the literature of other
races with one exception:

> But what is Kornei's race
> That no one has understood him?

TEFFI AMONG THE MODERNISTS

By 1905 Teffi was apparently earning well enough to move into her own apartment at 10 Saperny Lane, the same house where several important cultural
and intellectual figures lived. Almost 40 years later, Galich remembered the
"enormous house with three inner courtyards," whose inhabitants included
the religious philosophers Nikolai Berdyaev (1874–1948) and Anton Kartashev
(1875–1960), the writer and founder of "mystical anarchism" Georgy Chulkov
(1879–1939), Teffi, and Galich himself.[94] Two of Teffi's neighbors, Berdyaev
and Chulkov, were putting out a new literary–philosophical journal, *Voprosy
zhizni* (Questions of life), and invited her to contribute. She never did, but it
was at the editorial office that she first met the modernist prose writer Aleksei
Remizov (1877–1957), who was serving as business manager.[95] He recalled 45
years later: "I made your acquaintance 11 October 1905 [...] And you were
Teffi with an addition: Lokhvitskaya's sister."[96]

According to Galich, the St. Petersburg artistic and philosophical avant-
garde met almost daily in Chulkov's flat, and Teffi, who in her memoirs
refers to Chulkov as a "friend," was no doubt often present.[97] E. Anichkov
also remembers seeing the "merry and unfemininely clever Teffi" at the celebrated salons held in the apartment of symbolist poet and learned Hellenist
Vyacheslav Ivanov (1866–1945), and his wife, the writer Lydia Zinovieva-
Annibal (1866–1907), atop a six-story house next to the Tauride Garden, and
hence called the Tower.[98] The poet Sergei Gorodetsky (1884–1967) left a vivid
account of a typical evening there:

> A large garret with a narrow window looking right out at the stars.
> Candles in candelabra… We gathered late… We argued long and stormily

[…] After the debate, toward morning, the poetry reading began […] Many excellent things that became a part of our literature were heard here for the first time…[99]

It is startling that the Tower's visitors were breathing this rarefied air during the revolutionary year of 1905. Berdyaev remarked that he was "struck by the contrast. In the 'tower' refined conversations of the most gifted of the cultural elite were taking place, while below revolution was raging. These were two separate worlds."[100] Teffi and Galich were among those who managed to exist in both – which in some respects were not so very separate, for Ivanov envisioned an analogous "cultural historical revolution."[101] This would be a kind of spiritual–aesthetic parallel to the uprising on the streets, its source the theater, which he believed should return to its ancient roots in ritual, should reject modern conventions that separated the audience and players so that all could be joined in "collective action."[102] Ivanov's theories provided the foundation for the literary–theatrical circle Torches (Fakely), which, as Galich wrote rhapsodically in early 1906, would provide "the seed of a future theatrical–mystical chorus, a future 'commune' [obshchina] of artists."[103] The circle included major modernist poets and critics, while on its periphery, Galich added, was the "colorfully mystical Teffi (N.A. Buchinskaya) with her deep and transparent symbols."[104] The great experimental director Vsevolod Meyerhold (1874–1940), still near the beginning of his career, headed the Torches Theater project (the theater itself never materialized), with Teffi a member of the organizing (initsiativnaia) group.[105] She later recalled:

Several years ago, when the extremely talented V. E. Meyerhold was not yet a director on the imperial stage but only burned and dreamed, he often spoke within a circle of sympathizers about the theater of the future. About the "real" theater.

He had his own theory […] I remember it was founded somehow mathematically, geometrically […]

We all burned and dreamed together with Meyerhold and believed in him […]

"Down with the footlights!" squealed some.

"Down with the stage!" another recommended.

"Collective action!" someone in the corner hooted.

We burned![106]

The appeal of such mystical unity to Teffi, disturbed as she was by class divisions, is obvious. Nevertheless, she could not wholly accept Meyerhold's abstract schemes, and she wrote that he and Chulkov decided that an "apparent wall" separated them. She concluded: "They were right."[107]

FYODOR SOLOGUB

Teffi, by all accounts, never moved beyond the periphery of Ivanov's circle, but she did develop a quite close and lasting relationship with another famous symbolist, Fyodor Sologub (1863–1927).[108] In her memoir of the poet, Teffi writes that she first met him in connection with "The Bees." After she read the poem at the university in August or September 1905, she was told that "Sologub has written your 'Bees'" – that he revised it "in his own manner" and was about to publish it.[109] When the two were introduced, Teffi confronted him, declaring that "it's not good to take somebody else's thing like that." He retorted: "It's not good for the one it's taken from, but for the one who does the taking it's not bad." She laughed and said that she was very flattered that he liked her poem, to which he replied: "Well, so you see. It means we're both satisfied."[110] A few days later Sologub invited her to one of his Sunday literary gatherings, which she thereafter attended regularly.[111]

Sologub, the son of servants, came from an entirely different world than most other modernist writers.[112] After spending ten harsh and tedious years as a village teacher, he took up a post in St. Petersburg in 1892 and began publishing his poems and stories, which combined a stylistic purity and clarity (rare among the symbolists) with a decadent obsession with death, cruelty, and evil forces ruling the universe.[113] His "precision and frequent attention to the minutiae of life," in line with Teffi's own stylistic practice, helps to explain the affinity between the two.[114] When Teffi met Sologub in 1905, he was a school inspector, living with his consumptive sister in housing provided by the school. She remembers that he was "about forty, but […] he seemed old to me. Not even old, but somehow ancient […] An always tired, always bored face."[115] Teffi recalls his modest apartment, with its icon lamps, its "small dark study" strewn with manuscripts, where he "treated his guests to peppermint cakes, ruddy rolls, pastilles, and honey cakes, for which his sister went somewhere across the river on a horse-drawn trolley."[116] At these "very interesting" meetings of "close literary friends" – among them the poets Alexander Blok, Nikolai Gumilyov, and Andrei

Bely – Sologub read from his novel *The Petty Demon* and the first part of *A Legend in Creation.*[117]

Teffi also befriended Sologub's sister, Olga Teternikova, and, shortly before her premature death in June 1907, sent her flowers, which, she claimed in the accompanying note, were "enchanted": "As soon as they bloom you will immediately get better."[118] Teffi recalls that after she died, Sologub wrote her a "very nice and tender letter," to which she responded: "I am deeply touched that at such a painful time you remembered me […] Olga Kuzminichna was so dear, radiant [*iasnaia*], affectionate. I am comforted that I knew her at least for a short while."[119]

Later that year two events occurred that radically changed Sologub's life. The first – the publication of *The Petty Demon* in book form – at once transformed the obscure writer into a celebrity. Teffi sent him a newspaper clipping that paired Chekhov's "Man in a Case" and Peredonov of *The Petty Demon* as "typical examples of the bureaucratic flora growing within school walls," and commented: "Look, dear Fyodor Kuzmich! They are already referring to you in editorials. Soon they'll begin to refer to you in government decrees." It was also in 1907 that Sologub met the writer and translator Anastasya Chebotarevskaya (1877–1921), whom he married the following year and at once abandoned his quiet life. They moved into a large apartment and bought gilt chairs, and "the quiet chats were replaced by noisy crowds, with dances, with masks."[120] Among the frivolous activities was a game involving the substitution of part of a word with another, semantically related but contrasting. In a letter to Sologub of 2 May 1908, Teffi engaged in the game, asking such questions as "Why do they say Ge-orgy [*gai*-orgies] and not *triste*-drinking bouts?" A few days later she sent Alexander Izmailov (1873–1921), literary editor of *Birzhevka*, one of her funniest early stories, "In Place of Politics," in which a family becomes addicted to the same game.[121] The piece was, Teffi wrote in her cover letter, "for the most refined taste! The activity I describe has gripped the entire circle of modernists."[122]

Teffi observed that Sologub's sudden fame and his constant social whirl had a negative effect on his creative life. Only "in his verse was he his former self, solitary, tired; he feared life and loved the one whose name he wrote with a capital letter – Death […] 'The Knight of Death,' I called him."[123] At times Teffi herself seemed to be playing with Sologub's fascination with death. Due to her illness and high fever, she wrote in November 1908, "at night death came and said to me: 'kiss me, bunny [*zain'ka*]!' But she [death is feminine in Russian] didn't seduce me."[124]

Aside from Sologub's salon, the two came into contact at other literary gatherings and frequently went together to the poetic circle founded by Konstantin Sluchevsky: "Perhaps we can go and return on the last train, i.e., at 1:00," Teffi wrote him in May 1908. "If you don't go, I can't go either. Such is the law of nature."[125] They also did good literary turns for one another: Teffi wrote a favorable review of Sologub's *Drops of Blood*; he tried, albeit unsuccessfully, to get her play, *Queen Shammuramat*, produced by the Komissarzhevskaya Theater.[126] In August 1908, after the play failed to appear in the symbolist journal *Zolotoe runo* (The golden fleece), Teffi asked him to "tell them they are swine. They won't believe me!" She later included the play, renamed *The Noon of Dzokhara*, in her poetry collection *Seven Fires*, with a dedication to Sologub. For all that, Sologub remained something of a mystery to Teffi: "It was difficult to understand what kind of person Sologub was," she wrote. "Neither did I understand his attitude toward me. It would appear he was totally indifferent."[127]

MODERNIST ANTIPATHIES

Despite Teffi's frequent interactions with the symbolists and their influence on her poetry, there were limits to her sympathy – and no one seemed to arouse her antagonism more than the Moscow poet Andrei Bely (1880–1934). This is expressed with particular fervor in her review of Bely's poetry collection *Ash*, published in *Rech'* (Speech) at the end of 1908.[128] Teffi criticized *Ash* not for the poet's usual verbal acrobatics, but for his unexpected adoption of the themes and style of the nineteenth-century civic poets, especially of Nikolai Nekrasov (1821–78). The result, she concluded, was "tiresome and boring […] Poor words in poor combinations."[129] Within a few days, as Teffi later recalled, the editor of *Rech'*, the leading Kadet Pavel Milyukov (1859–1943), offered to send her a copy of a letter in defence of Bely from Zinaida Gippius (written under her pseudonym, Anton Krainy) so that Teffi could reply in the same issue.[130] Gippius wrote – her piece as much a rebuke of the reviewer as a defense of Bely – that anyone who does not feel the genius of Bely's lines "Over my native land / Arose Death" "does not know what either 'native land' or 'death' or 'arose' is."[131] She concluded:

Neither I nor Andrei Bely, nor any of us living people have any business with you. I have a native land, I have my human heart, my present hour, my life, my death, our life, our death… And of course it has never entered your mind that there is life, there is death.[132]

Teffi wrote that she was so "stunned" by this ad hominem attack that she reacted with uncharacteristic malice.[133] She denied the genius of Bely's lines, pointing out that since 1906 "there was literally not a single editorial in progressive newspapers without the words 'the specter of death is hanging over Russia.' […] And now a 'genius' has arrived and […] said the same thing – and this is a revelation."[134] The accusation that she, who had been actively involved in the revolutionary struggle, did not know the meaning of "native land" and "death" – especially coming from one who had retreated abroad at the time – particularly stung Teffi: "We lived through terrible years. But you were not with us then."[135] Her ire finally overflowed into an unbridled – and unseemly – attack on Bely: "I don't like him, that old slobberer [*sliuntiaia*] and poseur."[136] In his memoir, *Between Two Revolutions*, Bely reacted to Teffi's attack with a kind of ferocious glee: "I am proud: Teffi so disliked these lines that she declared in print: 'I don't like that old slobberer.'"[137]

The reason for this mutual animosity is not entirely clear. Obviously Bely's affectations profoundly annoyed Teffi, but she was tolerant enough of the poses of others, so common in the Silver Age. Possibly the underlying cause of her hostility was the sense of complacent superiority that emanated both from Gippius's article and from Bely's works. Teffi – who, it seems, had by then abandoned hope of ascending to the Nietzschean heights – might have been especially irritated that Gippius excluded her from the category of "living people."

3

ASCENT

1908–15

By 1908, after all the revolutionary solemnity of recent years, Russia longed for laughter – and not, as Teffi recalled later, the usual "Russian 'laughter through tears invisible to the world,'" but the simple, merry variety.[1] She wrote in 1910:

> Laughter is now in style [...] Books of humor go through three editions in three or four months and the demand for them keeps rising. Humor magazines are mentioned even in speeches delivered under the bell of the State Duma. Theatrical entrepreneurs are longing for a good merry comedy and beg tearfully: "Why, write something, the kind of thing that makes your throat begin to tickle with laughter!"[2]

Such laughter crossed cultural lines, infecting both the elite and the unsophisticated. Teffi's earliest works already spanned the spectrum from serious poetry to light newspaper pieces, so it is not surprising that this atmosphere fostered her talent and augmented her fame.

THE THEATER

Teffi already revealed an aptitude for dramatic form in her earliest newspaper pieces, many of which were written in dialogue. Her flirtation with Meyerhold and the Torches circle left her dubious about radical modernist experimentation in the theater, and in a 1909 review of a book by another experimenter whom she admired, Nikolai Yevreinov, she countered his dramatic theories with her own view of the theater as a kind of intricate, absorbing game:

The actors meet, collide, create a drama. A drama not of the hero, not of the heroine, not of the noble father, not of the villain – a drama as something whole, as a chess game is whole, in which neither pawn, king, nor queen is interesting, but what is interesting is what is created with their help – the game itself.[3]

This notion of drama as play, in which psychology is subordinate to a clever plot, explains much about Teffi's path as a dramatist. Her first play, *The Woman Question*, was staged in 1907 at the St. Petersburg Maly Theater, one of the first private theaters in Russia, which, unlike the state-subsidized imperial theaters, had to make a profit and therefore, in the disapproving words of the Soviet *Theater Encyclopedia*, "began to orient itself toward the tastes of Philistine, petty bourgeois circles. Melodrama, pseudo-problem plays, thoughtless entertaining plays, began to form the basis of its repertoire."[4]

The Woman Question was among the theater's light entertainments, but it is hardly "thoughtless." Rather, it applies a light touch to a burning issue of the time: women's rights. The heroine, 18-year-old Katya, propounds not only equal rights for women, but a total reversal of gender roles. She immediately applies the principle to her own situation, insisting that she will not marry her fiancé until she becomes a doctor and he performs the household duties. She then falls asleep and dreams that this hoped-for reversal has taken place. The conceit serves as a kind of double-edged sword. On the one hand, the absurdity of claims of women's inferiority becomes apparent, but on the other the dream shows that when women dominate they behave much the same as men. Aunt Masha, now a general, sings racy songs and tells off-color jokes, while all the visiting "military women" flirt with the male servant, Styopka (clothed in a lace apron, a bonnet, and a ribbon around his neck).[5] Finally Katya's fiancé declares (like Katya in her waking life) that he is breaking the engagement because marriage will mean slavery. She is then awakened by her father and announces that she will marry her fiancé after all, since "we are all the same good-for-nothings [*driani*] […] What joy! We're all alike."[6]

Katya's conclusion does not refute the principle of women's equality, only the more extreme notion of female superiority, but the distinction was lost on a female reviewer, who asserted that the play "wittily, gracefully, amusingly, and bitingly mocked feminism, the vain attempts of women to compare themselves in all ways with men."[7] She also noted the play's "extraordinary success. The public roared with laughter and applauded with abandon."

Other of Teffi's "jokes" appealed not only to a mass audience, but to the elite. By 1908 the theatrical avant-garde, in its tireless search for new forms, turned to the cabaret, which had spread across Europe a decade or so earlier.[8] In place of the conventions of realistic theater, there was a call for short sketches characterized, as one critic wrote in 1908, by "freedom, lightness, originality, improvisation, and refined simplicity."[9] For all the lightness, the critic stresses, this new endeavor was "serious," since it could produce "true innovation in form." Its seriousness, as Meyerhold wrote a couple of years later, would not preclude entertainment, the "healthy and pleasant relaxation" necessary for the modern "cultured man," after the "anxieties and alarms" of his working day.[10]

The first such cabaret, "the Bat" (*Letuchaia mysh'*), was created by Moscow Art Theater actors in February 1908, and St. Petersburg followed suit at the end of the year. The Theatrical Club had rented Prince N. Yusupov's splendid town house for the purpose, and two competitors were vying to become the resident theater: one initiated by Meyerhold, the other by Zinaida Kholmskaya (1866–1936), an actress at the Maly Theater and co-publisher (with her husband, the theater critic Alexander Kugel, 1864–1928) of the journal *Zhizn' iskusstva* (The life of art). Although the former was the favored candidate, the Theatrical Club board made the unusual decision of accepting both theaters, which were, moreover, to occupy the space on the same days: Meyerhold's "the Curved Shore" from eight to 12 and Kholmskaya's "the Crooked Mirror" from midnight to three in the morning.[11] While it was assumed that Meyerhold's production, supported by "almost the entire cream of the St. Petersburg artistic intelligentsia," would be superior, to everyone's astonishment it was a flop, while the Crooked Mirror, which drew upon the talents of lesser known figures, created a sensation.[12] One such figure was Teffi, whose short play in verse *Love through the Ages* was performed on opening night, 5 December 1908.

Meyerhold's endeavor failed, according to Lyubov Gurevich, because "everything is too finished [...] there is not that bold cartoon-like quality [*eskiznost'*], which has its special charm, especially in such 'illegitimate' [*nelegalizovannykh*] forms of art."[13] The Crooked Mirror, in contrast, was "simpler, more primitive," she added. This was in keeping with the dramatic credo of its artistic director, Kugel, who promoted "the living charm of the so-called low forms of art."[14] Kugel's emphasis on the simple foundations of the theater was congenial to Teffi's vision of a play as a kind of plot-driven game. Her *Love through the Ages*, to be sure, is not structured around a unified plot, but a theme (love) whose development over time is traced in a series of scenes.[15] Written in a mixture of verse and prose, with songs and amusing costumes adding to its entertainment value, the piece traces love from the pre-human period until the fortieth century.[16]

The first pair of lovers are monkeys, whose primitive version of love is revealed in the refrain they both sing:

> Ah, our language is so simple,
> Only look at our tail,
> When it begins to wag,
> Everyone understands
> That the apple of love
> Is calling – "Pick me, pick me."[17]

After a comical look at love in the thirteenth and eighteenth centuries, the play arrives at the present time, the male figure a symbolist poet, attired in evening dress with a green tie and sky-blue shoes, his beloved a nanny goat. The final scene takes place in the fortieth century. Appearing prominently on the stage is Mikhail Artsybashev's scandalous novel *Sanin* (published the year before the production), under whose influence evolution has come full circle: the couple has regressed to its simian state and sings the refrain from the play's beginning.

Love through the Ages was a success, praised by one critic as "a very graceful, light, and airy little thing."[18] Soon after, at the very end of December 1908, the theater staged another of Teffi's playlets, *The Men's Congress* – clearly a response to the First All-Russian Women's Congress, which had convened earlier that month.[19] Much simpler than *Love through the Ages*, it consists of a single scene in which the men react to women's demands for equal rights with the usual clichés about male superiority, but then undercut their position by revealing their own inferior attainments. Finally, the congress reaches a compromise: if women "want to be given rights and duties equal to men [...] we'll agree to half. Let them take our duties, and as far as rights are concerned, they can wait a little longer."

Such fast-moving and witty playlets soon spread from elite to popular theaters, a phenomenon that had occurred somewhat earlier in Western Europe.[20] In January 1909, Veniamin Kazansky, a former actor, founded the Liteiny Theater, which (albeit under different names and directors) existed until the advent of Communism and was to be the main producer of Teffi's plays.[21] The genre was so popular that in the fall of 1912 alone no fewer than 12 new miniature theaters opened in St. Petersburg.[22] Teffi (whose case for the virtues of brevity applies to her prose as well as her plays) explained the appeal, contrasting how an ordinary drama and a miniature convey the same plot: a woman has killed her husband and suspects that her grandmother knows. The former is filled with repetitions, pauses: "Maria: 'Grandmother!' (Silence.) Maria: 'Grandmother! Are you here?' (Silence.) Maria: 'Grandmother, why are you silent? After all, I know you're here.' The old woman: 'What?'"[23] Teffi remarks that the dialogue will go on like this for half an hour, especially if the grandmother is a little deaf. In comparison, the miniature compresses the scene into one speech: "Grandmother! Come here! And don't pretend. I know very well that you hear everything and understand everything. Well, yes. I killed him. I! I! Do you hear? Well, now you can go and drink your tea." Teffi comments: "And the old woman leaves in a flash, because she has exactly two minutes to write her will, burn down the house, and hang herself."[24]

In a 1911 feuilleton, Teffi illustrated how the miniature suited the tempo of modern life, portraying a typical bourgeois – a stockbroker – who falls asleep at the opera but is stimulated by the speed of the miniature theater:

First they'll scare him with a d-r-r-rama.
Someone will quickly slaughter someone, in a flash [*likho*] […]
Before the stockbroker has time to blow his nose out of sympathy for the corpse, he is being tickled behind his ear, as if with a peacock feather, with a hilarious farce.
Before his heaving diaphragm has time to calm down, they are already serving up on the stage mimo-eurythmics with feeling [*s nastroeniem*], in order to ennoble his soul […]
Then a pint-sized opera, then a pint-sized comedy and a movie – *Nut Gathering in Northern Guinea* – to the music of *Lohengrin*.
The stockbroker is pleased.[25]

Teffi's miniature plays continued to appear throughout the 1910s and were regularly greeted enthusiastically by the critics and the public.[26] Yevreinov attests to her skill as a dramatic miniaturist: "no one like N. A. Teffi could with a single phrase pass sentence on her hero, literally nail him down with a precise, capacious, and funny testimonial."[27] Although her dramatic pieces are considered a minor part of her output, she wrote: "I personally have felt satisfaction only in my theater pieces […] It is only in the theater that an author can observe the direct effect of her work, and her success there is real success."[28] Her daughter Valeria recalled: "She personally worked on the staging of her plays, giving the actors very valuable directions and often sketching the designs for the costumes with her own hands."[29]

SATIRIKON

For all her theatrical success, Teffi's greatest renown came from her humorous feuilletons and stories. Two associations, formed in 1908 and 1909, respectively – with the magazine *Satirikon* (Satyricon) and the Moscow newspaper *Russkoe slovo* (Russian word) – transformed her from a popular St. Petersburg literary figure to a celebrity on a national scale.

The genius behind *Satirikon* was the humorist Arkady Averchenko (1884–1925), who, soon after arriving in St. Petersburg from Kharkov in early 1908, wandered into the office of the humor magazine *Strekoza* (Dragonfly).[30] By then the venerable publication and its equally ancient rival, *Oskolki*, were, as Teffi recalled, "barely breathing. Their crude [...] humor amused very few."[31] *Strekoza*, therefore, was not only happy to publish Averchenko's very funny stories, but in a month's time made him secretary of the editorial board.[32] He soon persuaded the publisher, M. G. Kornfeld (1884–1978), to close the expiring magazine and to replace it with a satirical journal. Aleksei Radakov (1877–1942), one of the talented staff artists, thought up the name *Satirikon*, taken from the novel by Petronius, whose depiction of the decadent life of Nero's Rome may have seemed suitable to late imperial Russia.[33]

Teffi remembers (no doubt with comic exaggeration) how her own association with *Satirikon* began. One day her maid announced: "*Strekoza* has arrived."[34] A short brunet entered and informed her that he wanted to transform the magazine into a literary journal, but she declined to collaborate. Then a couple of weeks later the maid again announced the arrival of *Strekoza*, but this time in the form of a "tall blond."[35] Since she had a bad memory for faces, she decided it was the same person and told him, much to his amazement, that they had already spoken. It turned out that the first *Strekoza* was the publisher, Kornfeld, and the second Averchenko, who convinced her to join the new publication. *Satirikon*, with its very talented writers and artists, was a resounding success, and Teffi and Averchenko became its most popular writers. By 1913 conflicts arose between Kornfeld and his staff – principally over money, apparently – and the best contributors (including Teffi) resigned.[36] They founded a new magazine – suitably called *Novyi Satirikon* (New Satyricon) – leaving the old *Satirikon* an empty shell, which ended its existence the following year.

Although political and social satire figured prominently in *Satirikon*, especially in its early years, contemporaries especially welcomed its simple, merry laughter. "During the years of revolution," wrote one, "they laughed bloody tears. There was satire, but no laughter. The appearance of *Satirikon* signified the birth of laughter. Alongside political satire there were delightful works created by the genius of inoffensive laughter."[37] Teffi's were among such "delightful works," her best pieces achieving a new level of mastery of the prose miniature. She did not, however, publish frequently in the magazine and later recalled that she was "more a guest artist [*gastrolersha*] than a permanent staff member."[38] Nevertheless, in the public's mind she was firmly ensconced as one of its main writers, perhaps because most of her books were put out under its imprint.

Satirikon, although intended for a mass audience, also attracted members of the artistic and literary elite. The cover of its first issue (1 April 1908) was adorned with a drawing by Léon Bakst and works of other World of Art members appeared from time to time. Symbolist and post-symbolist poets and prose writers also made their appearance. Chukovsky noticed this paradoxical intermingling, observing with feigned astonishment that in a single issue of the magazine "you will find vicious mockery of the poet Kuzmin [...] but you don't even have to turn the page to see the following line: 'So-and-so, so-and-so, and – M. Kuzmin – are regular contributors to the journal'!"[39] On *Satirikon*'s pages, he added, you will find poems by Blok and other modernists, but you need only randomly open the journal and "will read there with astonishment [...] about 'pimply decadent dandies.'" Chukovsky concluded that contemporary readers were pleased with this because, tired of the lofty abstractions of symbolism and disillusioned by the results of the 1905 revolution, they have lost faith in all high-sounding ideals.

An affinity between the *Satirikon* writers and the modernists has been observed and attributed to the so-called "crisis of symbolism," dating back to Alexander Blok's 1906 play *The Puppet Booth*, which replaced the poet's "unattainable Beautiful Lady" with the "earthly Columbine, a cardboard fiancée."[40] A rapprochement has also been noted between the literary and art journal *Apollon* (Apollo), founded in 1909, and *Satirikon* – their very names suggesting a connection with the Nietzschean concepts of the Appollonian and Dionysian (satyrs being companions of Dionysus).[41] *Apollon* published a broad range of modernist writers, but a group of younger poets, who later called themselves acmeists – and who included such major figures as Nikolai Gumilyov (1886–1921), Anna Akhmatova (1889–1966), and Osip Mandelstam

(1891–1938) – came to predominate. The acmeists reacted against the other-worldliness and insubstantiality of the symbolists, and espoused instead clarity, a celebration of the concrete, material world for its own sake. Some of the young *Apollon* poets published in *Satirikon* – Gumilyov and Sergei Gorodetsky with particular frequency – and the exhortation of Mikhail Kuzmin (1872–1936) in his famous essay "About Beautiful Clarity" (1910) applies not only to them, but to the Satyriconians as well – and to none more than Teffi:

> write logically, observing the purity of your native speech […] be eco-nomical in your means and stingy in your words, precise and genuine – and you will find the secret of a marvelous thing – *beautiful clarity* – which I would call *clarism*.[42]

RUSSKOE SLOVO

Becoming a staff writer for *Russkoe slovo* – the most widely read and highly regarded newspaper in Russia – was an important event for Teffi, both pro-fessionally and financially. Founded in 1895, it was modeled on Western European and American dailies, and with its first-rate columnists, network of correspondents all over Russia, and bureaus around the world, by 1917 reached a circulation of over a million.[43] *Russkoe slovo*'s large circulation and generous honoraria attracted many famous writers. Tolstoy's essay on Shakespeare appeared there for the first time in 1906. The symbolist poet Alexander Blok, who published some poetry in *Russkoe slovo*, wrote in his diary: "Considering ten people for each copy (that's a minimum), that's about 2,500,000 people."[44]

Teffi's output during her first year was enormous, her columns at times appearing two or three times a week. She recalled that her early pieces were expected to focus on minor urban ills, such as "the unsanitary state of cab yards and […] 'the difficult position of the modern laundress,'"[45] but the description is misleading, for from the beginning her pieces focussed more on the cultural scene. Some do have political content, but the satire is relatively mild and sometimes buried in a primarily apolitical work. Only at the end of "Exhibition of the Newest Inventions," for example, does she turn to a menacing – not to say prophetic – device:

> This thing is called an "automatic informer [*shpik*]." It's a small appa-ratus that landlords will be required to place in every apartment. The

apparatus contains a camera and a phonograph. In this way the "auto-matic informer" will record and print everything that happens in your apartment. Once a month the appropriate person will come, will take the apparatus to the appropriate place, will look over the recordings, and if necessary will call the appropriate person to account.[46]

At first fiction was not part of Teffi's assignment, but was slipped in as small vignettes to illustrate the main themes of the articles. Soon that changed, however, at her own request:

I would like on a certain day – let's say on Sunday – to send you a small humorous story and not a feuilleton. It's much more interesting, more amusing, and more enjoyable [*veselee*] for the reader. Thus I would send you two pieces a week: one a humorous feuilleton, the other a little story [...] I've already published stories with you, but I've always had to spoil them a little in order to fit in with the topical. I'd like to pay greater attention to the artistic finish of my pieces, since then they would remain for collections.[47]

The de facto editor, Vlas Doroshevich (1864–1922) – known as "king of the feuilletonists," whose pithy style had greatly influenced Teffi and other minia-turists – interceded for Teffi.[48] She later recalled his words: "Let her write what she wants and how she wants [...] You can't haul water on an Arabian steed."[49]

Beginning around April 1910, Teffi's stories started to appear in *Russkoe slovo* alongside her topical feuilletons, and many of them, together with her *Satirikon* pieces, were collected in her books of humor, the first of which came out in 1910. Thereafter a major new collection was published almost yearly – invar-iably in multiple printings – and supplemented by many cheap editions. Her humor brought her such fame during the 1910s that perfume and candy bore her name.[50] As the émigré writer Mark Aldanov remarked: "Hardly any other writer in Russia has ever had such an enormous circle of readers as Teffi."[51]

All told Teffi's output during the decade or so preceding the October 1917 revolution was prodigious. Her reply to a questionnaire in 1915 gives an idea of the creative process that fostered such productivity:

When I sit down at my desk my story is completely ready, from the first letter to the last. If even one thought, one phrase is not clear to me, I can't take up my pen.

In a word, the most vivid and intense process of creation takes place before I sit down at my desk.

That is play. That is joy [...]

I always write at once – almost all my things are written in one sitting. I don't like to reread and polish. I only correct a thing that has pleased me for some reason. That happens very rarely.[52]

POETRY AND PROSE COLLECTIONS: 1910–15

Seven Fires, Teffi's only book of poetry published in Russia, came out in 1910, the same year as her first collection of humorous stories. It is hardly surprising that the verse was overshadowed by the prose, but *Seven Fires* was also generally well received, especially in the popular press – the *Russkoe slovo* reviewer even declaring that he "would take Teffi's little book in preference to all the Vyacheslav Ivanovs."[53] Among the elite critics the reception was more mixed. Gumilyov praised the poems' "literariness in the best sense of the word," whereas the influential Moscow symbolist Valery Bryusov (1873–1924) was dismissive, finding only "modernist commonplaces" and concluding that "Mme. Teffi's necklace is made of fake stones."[54]

Bryusov's critique has some validity, for the collection's themes and imagery recall those of many poets of the age.[55] And it is true that Teffi's at times heavily alliterative style and gaudy imagery smacks of excess, leading D. S. Mirsky, in his classic history of Russian literature, to write: "The verbal pageantry of the symbolists is best vulgarized in the poetry of Teffi."[56] Most of the poems in *Seven Fires* date from the second half of the first decade of the twentieth century – a time when symbolism's phenomenal success with the broad reading public led to simplification and popularization among its many imitators – and Teffi was certainly swept along by the fashion.[57] Even Gumilyov acknowledged a certain artificiality in the poems, but took it to be purposeful. The reader does not see the poetess's true face, he writes, but a "mask, which she wears with festive grace and, it seems, even with a barely perceptible smile."[58] The *Russkoe slovo* review also made a virtue of the book's derivative imagery:

> Here there are pure irises and lilies, and luxuriant chrysanthemums, and silver wreathes of lilies-of-the-valley, and the "pale blue midnight hour" and "lunar mists" and trembling icon lamps, and white marble

colonnades, and steps, and a pale and beautiful moon and women in white garb and the "azure trembling" of summer twilights.

[...] All this rather refined, fairy-tale like, operatic beauty is a typical product of our age [...] But it is genuine beauty and genuine poetry.

More recently, *Seven Fires* has been considered to be a parody, and some of the poems do sound suspiciously like Teffi's early spoofs of Balmont and others.[59] Yet it is doubtful that the poems are parodies pure and simple, for it is precisely from behind her masks that Teffi often reveals her true self. And, although *Seven Fires* at first seems an anomaly among Teffi's works, the collection introduces themes and imagery that recur in both her serious and her comic prose.

The poems of *Seven Fires* range greatly in style and theme, from sultry evocations of distant times and climes to the revolutionary "The Bees" and the popular "Song about Three Pages," which entered the repertory of the celebrated singer Alexander Vertinsky (1889–1957). Teffi strove to unite all of these into an aesthetic whole, taking the "seven fires" of the title – seven precious stones – as rubrics for the sections of the collection.[60]

Seven Fires is imbued with the usual symbolist dualism, with a moribund earth contrasted to the transcendent sphere – primarily to the sun, which figured so prominently in symbolist imagery since Balmont's 1903 collection *Let Us Be Like the Sun*.[61] The sun dominates the final "Topaz" section (subtitled "Visions of the Land of Sennaar," another name for Babylonia), and the final work, the play *The Noon of Dzokhara* expresses the symbolist dualism most fully. It portrays Queen Shammuramat, who is suffering from unrequited love for the enemy prince Arei. In the course of the play Arei is taken captive, but has been killed – a fact that the queen at first refuses to admit, making love to the corpse. When she finally acknowledges his death, Arei becomes a symbol for the entire earthly world: "Dead is the earth for me," she declares, "dead are people, and there is nothing save for me!"[62] The queen now longs for a higher love: "The winged sun – my soul – burns with love [...] Will I be with you, dead ones?"[63] She goes to the window and lowers the drapes behind her, and when the slave girls open the drapes they find only an empty window, a blue sky, and white doves flying toward the sun.

In the poems of the "Topaz" section the sun is portrayed as a god of absolute brightness and power, who offers escape from this world through both sensual love and death. The sun is not, however, an unambiguously positive force, for it is also associated with the cruelty and suffering to which Teffi already demonstrated great sensitivity in her earliest works. In "The Sacrifice," for example, the human sacrifice to the "winged sun Ashur" trembles "before the joy of the strong," and even his worshippers are blind and dumb beggars before their god.[64] And it is not only in pagan antiquity that earthly beings are subject to such cruelty from a higher power. In "Gulda" blighted creatures, akin to the pitiful victims of Teffi's early prose – "Starving children on crooked legs! […] an old bird, grown blind in its cage!" – die in torment

> so that Princess Gulda might embroider
> The ruby pattern of happiness for the pedestal of God.[65]

"Marionettes," which has the clearest ties to Teffi's comic writing, conveys the world's deadness and cruelty in an entirely different stylistic register – through the image of a puppet show, so common among the modernists. A marionette couple whirls in an endless dance, and the woman longs to achieve true communion with her partner:

> Oh, if only you could glance at me,
> Kindle in yourself a living soul!
> With my love I would break the spell
> Of our endless, our cursed path![66]

The puppet, whose love is incapable of awakening "a living soul" in her partner, is but a variant of the queen in *The Noon of Dzokhara*, whose love fails to arouse her dead lover. And the cruel gods are replaced by children laughing at the spectacle that so torments the puppet – pointing to the pain that so often underlies Teffi's humor.

The nocturnal celestial bodies also figure in *Seven Fires*, but are more elusive than the burning sun. The distant stars (a repeated image in Teffi's serious stories) do not, like the sun, attest to the cruelty of the higher sphere, but – as "mute gods" who bewitch through their "silence" – to its unresponsiveness.[67] The moon is a more sinister presence, exploiting traditional lunar associations with illusion, madness, the diabolical. Its blandishments sometimes take physical form, but its principal prey is the soul, to which it reveals the "rapture and anguish of the impossible dream."[68] This "impossible dream" – the lure of illusion – is a vital component of Teffi's artistic vision, especially in her comic works. If union with the brilliant sun brings ascent from the everyday world through ecstatic love and (sometimes cruel) death, the inconstant moon opens a tempting escape from everyday life through illusion.

BOOKS OF HUMOR

The prestigious Shipovnik Press published not only *Seven Fires*, but also Teffi's first collection of humorous stories – a testimony to the high regard in which humor was held at the time. The book was uniformly praised by the critics. Kuzmin favorably compared Teffi's natural Russian humor in the Chekhov manner to Averchenko's "American" variety, with its "fantastic lack of verisimilitude," and concluded, rather condescendingly: "We do not know if the author will test her strength on other forms of prose, but even practicing this kind [...] she can make a pleasant contribution, with her powers of observation, merriment, and literary language."[69]

Later volumes all received high praise. Typical are comments on her 1914 collection *Smoke without Fire*; awarding Teffi "first place" among contemporary humorists, the critic praised her style as "refined and simple, the dialogue – her favorite form – lively and unforced; the action unfolds quickly, without superfluous details, and sincere merriment is effortlessly conveyed to the reader."[70] Some, such as Chebotarevskaya, noted the sadness intermingled with her comedy, Teffi's "almost elegiac humor."[71] Her position as a woman writer – and, more unusually, a woman humorist – evinced contradictory responses. Chebotarevskaya found in her works a "feminine softness," whereas another writer asserted that her "caustic sarcasm" set her apart from other women writers.[72] And her fellow Satyriconian Arkady Bukhov stated bluntly: "In general Teffi writes so cleverly and beautifully that even her enemies would not call her a woman writer."[73]

For support of these contrary views of Teffi's humor – "feminine softness" and "caustic sarcasm" – one need look no further than the beginnings of her first two books. The epigraph to the first volume, taken from Spinoza's *Ethics*, presents a sunny view of the comical: "For laughter is a joy and therefore is in itself a blessing."[74] The quote is preceded in Spinoza by the observation: "Between derision (which I name an evil [...]) and laughter I recognize a great distinction."[75] The subtitle of Teffi's second book, "Humanoids" (*Chelovekoobraznye*), however, suggests something very close to derision. In the opening sketch, also entitled "Humanoids," Teffi (clearly under the influence of Nietzsche) distinguishes between genuine humans, who are created by God and pass on to their offspring a "living, burning soul – the breath of God," and humanoids, the product of evolution, who, after many centuries of labor, have succeeded in evolving from the lowly worm to "a humanoid creature."[76] Such humanoids, central to Teffi's comic vision, conform to the view in the poem "Marionettes" of people as puppets living in a dead and meaningless world.

There are two main types among Teffi's "puppet people": the fool and the failure. The former, as defined in the sketch "Fools," is not, as is usually thought, characterized by ignorance or irrational behavior, but, on the contrary, is convinced that he "knows everything" and is invariably guided by certain axioms.[77] His primary quality is his "absolutely unshakable seriousness" and impenetrable self-satisfaction, which no external evidence can break down.[78] The self-satisfied fool, living by some axiom or other, is the most ubiquitous character in Teffi's early comic stories. Some of her fools seem quite sympathetic at first, but soon drive others to distraction. There is, for example, Pavel Pavlych in "An Acute Illness," who constantly "said things that were impressively well founded. 'Well, put on your coat today and you'll be warmer […] yesterday you didn't wear your coat and you were colder.'"[79] At first his companions like him very much, but soon his solemn truisms infuriate them. One exclaims: "How dare he tell me that a toothache is unpleasant! […] The smart aleck! The scoundrel! The beast!"[80]

The second category of humanoids, the failures, are portrayed – like the unfortunates in Teffi's earliest prose – with an admixture of sympathy and distaste. They can be as rigid and stupid as Teffi's pompous fools, but it is within this category that she at times expands the bounds of her characterization, allowing her heroes some depth and genuine humanity. This is particularly true of women. A particularly successful example is the 40-year-old Migulina in "The Rosy Student," who, although a successful doctor and lecturer, is a failure in love. On social occasions her unprepossessing appearance and certain absurd verbal rigidities (such as addressing even a single interlocutor as "ladies and gentlemen" [gospoda]) make her an object of ridicule.[81] The student of the title decides to begin a mocking flirtation with her, explaining to his aesthete friends that "perhaps I am too refined, but I am attracted by this woman's unhatched [neotshelushennyi] Eros."[82]

During the student's "courtship," Migulina's greater attention to her appearance – she thickly powders her face, tries to paint her lips red, "but for some reason they came out lilac" – makes her seem ever more ridiculous, but at the same time the narrator creates sympathy by adopting her point of view, conveying her growing embarrassment, fear, bewilderment.[83] Finally the student ends the flirtation, declaring: "I have awakened the eternal feminine in her. I have hatched her Eros." He judges his prank "a funny business [smeshnaia shtuka]," but Teffi gives Migulina the last word – the emotional effect of the student's words reversed when repeated by her lilac lips: "'Yes… yes… a funny business, ladies and gentlemen…' her lilac lips replied with a trembling smile."[84]

As "The Rosy Student" illustrates, victimization – a recurrent theme in Teffi's early serious works and in *Seven Fires* – is also a feature of her humorous stories. A particularly graphic example is "Easter," which tells of a man whose boss snubs him at an Easter service, after which he goes home and vents his rage upon his wife, who in turn yells at her daughter. The daughter scolds the cook, the cook her helper, and the final victim is the innocent cat. The cat's feelings at the end of the story could be taken as the norm for Teffi's defenseless victims:

> She hid behind the garbage can, sat for a long time, not stirring, understanding that a powerful enemy might be looking for her.
> Then she began to pour out her grief and bewilderment to the garbage pail. The pail preserved an apathetic silence.
> "Meow! Meow!"
> That was all she knew.[85]

In "Marionettes" Teffi stresses the mechanical nature of the puppets (emphasis added):

> Fancy clothes, smiles, and fine manners
> Are such *strong and straight springs*!
> To the right a *cardboard beau* was looking,
> [. . . . . .]
> His little *glass eyes* shone;
> *Two small screws* strongly clasped my waist.[86]

In his essay "Laughter," Henri Bergson defines the comic as "something mechanical encrusted on something living," and indeed in her humorous stories Teffi often superimposes the mechanical or inorganic upon a living being.[87] In "The Seer," for example, she wishes that providence would enliven the appearance of her pale, meek characters by dipping "its brush into any paint at all – even green."[88] Their eyes, she goes on, are "so alike that they seemed like wretched bone buttons – exactly half a dozen – seated in pairs."

An impression of a person as a thing is also imparted by a rigid expression that does not change to fit the situation. Thus, the father, sitting at the dinner table in "In Place of Politics," looks "as if he had just been dragged from the water and hadn't yet come to. However, this was his usual appearance, and no one in the family was upset by it."[89] Speech, as in "The Rosy Student," is also marked by illogical rigidity, and the written word often contains set formulas having little to do with the concrete situation. An extreme example occurs in "The Letter," in which the hall porter includes the following information in a letter he writes for the illiterate wet nurse: "I bow low... [...] the season is in full swing... And in the intoxication of masquerade pleasures we surrender ourselves to the ardor of mad passions..."[90]

Many of Teffi's early comic stories impart a sense of the void beneath the artificial surface of things. Ideals and feelings melt away under her mocking gaze, leaving a comic equivalent of the dead world of the poetry. This is especially true in her many works devoted to love. "Happy Love," to cite a typical example, describes a love tryst from the point of view of both the man and the woman, who, as they effusively declare their love, think how much they dislike one another.[91] "The Brooch" shows not only the counterfeit nature of love, but more broadly the fragility of social relations. In this cleverly constructed anecdote (which Teffi also adapted for the theater), a cheap pin is enough to ruin four relationships: between husband and wife, husband and lover, wife and lover, and maid and steward. The tone of the tale is on the whole light-hearted, but it ends on a dark note, as the wife thinks:

> We lived so well, everything was comfy-cozy [*shito-kryto*] and life was full. And then this damned brooch descended on us from out of the blue and just like a key it opened everything [...] And what's the reason for it all? How can it all be made cozy again? What can be done [*kak byt'*]?[92]

The answer to this urgent question, as some of the stories discussed suggest, lies in deceit, often self-deceit. The sketch "About Diaries" points to the most common types of self-deception among Teffi's humanoids. The narrator remarks that a man keeps a diary for posterity, hoping that after his death someone will read it and appreciate his profundity. A woman does not care about future generations; she writes for some Vladimir Petrovich or Sergei Nikolayevich and therefore concentrates exclusively on her alluring appearance.[93] This male pretense at wisdom and female pretense at beauty account for the many pompous fools and middle-aged coquettes in Teffi's stories. The first category has been discussed, but the coquettish matron is as omnipresent in Teffi's works. In "Resort Types" the conflict between the beautiful façade and the unappealing truth takes the form of a struggle between corset and stomach:

> "You fool! Fool! You old hag!" the stomach worries. "You should drink lots of nice hot coffee with cream and with a lovely rich Danish [*krendel'*] and take a nap on the sofa for half an hour or so. Who are you going to impress with your corset, with your old mug? You're over fifty, after all."
>
> "Cheer up! Cheer up, there's no need!" the corset popped up. "Patti married a baron when she was sixty, Ninon de Lenclos ruined her own grandson. You'll have time to rest up in the grave."
>
> "First of all, what do we need Patti's baron for," the stomach did not give in, "when we have our lawful Ilya Petrovich? And in the grave, mother mine [*matushka*], you won't get coffee for any amount of money."[94]

The gap between pose and actuality takes extreme form in "The Demonic Woman" – this favorite type among the decadents differing "from an ordinary woman primarily by her manner of dress. She wears a black velvet cassock, a chain on her forehead, a bracelet on her leg [...] and a portrait of Oscar Wilde on her left garter."[95] Teffi underlines the pose by juxtaposing the demonic woman's dramatic statements and a simple prose translation of her utterances. This is how she requests herring and onion:

> "Herring? Yes, yes, give me herring. I want to eat herring, I want to, I want to. Is that onion? Yes, yes, give me some onion... I want to eat, I want banality, quickly... more... more, look, everyone... I am eating herring!"
>
> In essence, what happened?
>
> Her appetite was simply acting up and she felt like having a little something salty. But what an effect!
>
> "Did you hear? Did you hear?"
>
> "She mustn't be left alone tonight."
>
> "?"[96]

The transformation of dull, prosaic reality through style sometimes takes a more literary form. In "Life and Works" the journalist Saturnov, who is supposed to be writing of his trip down the Volga, remains in his room and writes of the Volga of his imagination. He notices some stylistic excesses, but thinks "it would be a shame to correct it, because it's beautiful. Devilishly beautiful."[97] He then lavishes his "devilishly beautiful" style onto a hawker selling cucumbers in the courtyard:

> "We are turning toward Samara. Now we already have another sight. Now we have cucumbers."
>   "Green cucumbers!" [cries the hawker.]
>   "Cucumbers, cucumbers everywhere – whole fields of cucumbers. We are drowning in cucumbers and our souls are suffused with their fresh merriment. The cucumber! How much meaning this word has for the heart of a Russian man!"[98]

Another example of style getting the upper hand occurs in "Letters." After dinner Sergei Ivanovich writes a letter to Vera Petrovna from his country estate:

> "My dear, I miss you so much that I literally can't eat a thing…"
>   "But the *botvinya* [cold fish and vegetable soup]," his conscience suddenly pricked him.
>   But after a short struggle style conquered the *botvinya*.[99]

This process of style conquering *botvinya*, which occurs with such regularity in Teffi's early humorous stories, shows the need for her characters to escape from life's emptiness and boredom into a more beautiful or meaningful world. In other words, the underlying theme of *Seven Fires* reappears here, but in the comic mode, where the "beautiful world" is not only far from the transcendent spheres of the poetry, but invariably fraudulent – and therefore funny.

In Teffi's early prose, as in *Seven Fires*, the ideal sometimes proves to be illusory, but is superior to reality. "Nightingale Dreams" points to the necessity of illusion for a meaningful life. The narrator is riding through the country in a post carriage one lovely moonlit night and hears a nightingale for the first time. She ponders on "how much I've been whirling about […] and now this song, so simple, so quiet, gives me the brightest and truest feeling of beauty."[100] Under its influence she decides to reject a well-to-do suitor and marry the poor, idealistic Alyosha. Only later does she find out that what she took for a nightingale song was the coachman's whistling. She concludes: "That is how I dreamed and purified my soul through true beauty, listening to the whistle of a pockmarked coachman. What nightingale, from what fairy tales, would have done more for me?"[101]

So if the symbolists' heavenly spheres play no part in Teffi's humorous stories, her characters still seek escape from the dead world through illusion – her ordinary humanoids through pose and self-deception, her more developed natures through some higher ideal, which, illusory or not, is all that gives life meaning. A duality is established, not between a higher and lower reality, but between dead life and meaningful illusion.

The importance of illusion in Teffi's world makes her especially value those with a rich imagination – an important reason for her fondness for children, who in her stories are typically blessed with a gift for fantasy. In the sketch "Toys and Children," the narrator advises her readers to give children toys that allow the imagination free play:

> If you give children a suitable stick, that is, one they can sit astride, for them it will possess a head and legs and a tail and mane, and even a character. It will be a horse.
>
> If you give them a wooden horse, they will put a hat and warm sweater on it and sit it down to read a book. Because all the attributes of a horse are apparent, one has to think up new ones, since to play means to fantasize.[102]

"An Earthly Treasure" provides a witty summary of Teffi's case for fantasy. She differentiates between the two Russian words for a lie, the coarser *vran'e* and the more neutral *lozh'*. A *lozh'*, she writes, is a perfectly rational phenomenon: people always tell a *lozh'* with a practical goal in mind. *Vran'e*, on the other hand, is done merely for the love of it, from inspiration, with no thought of personal gain. It is, in other words, the same as fantasizing. Teffi ends the sketch: "And who knows, perhaps in another ten or twenty years, having stopped using unnecessary and expensive electricity, we will get our light and heat and transport with the help of simple fibbing energy [*vral'naia energiia*] – that mysterious earthly treasure."[103] Indeed, in Teffi's comic world, inhabited mostly by puppets caught up in a meaningless whirl, this "fibbing energy" is already the principal motive force, bringing light and heat for which there is no other source.

LAUGHTER ON LIFE'S SAD PATH

"The Good Deed of the Elder Vendimian" provides insight into Teffi's vision of the humorist's role in this cruel world. The story takes place in a desert settlement in the distant past. On the New Year, Vendimian, a pious and virtuous old man, notices that people have put sandals outside their houses in the hope that someone will leave them a gift. He is disconsolate because he is poor and can give nothing, but decides to leave his own sandals outside, thereby giving others a chance to do a good deed. When he checks in the morning, however, all he finds is a dead mouse in one sandal and spittle in the other. At first he is in despair, but then he is comforted by the thought that both pranksters "ran home laughing at the thought that [...] I would be grieved."[104] He concludes: "And shouldn't I, a weak and destitute old man, be endlessly happy that I could give my brother at least a minute of bright joy on life's sad path?" Vendimian is happy that, although he couldn't make people good, at least he could make them laugh. Similarly, Teffi, who exhibits little faith in human goodness, pities people on "life's sad path" and makes their burden lighter through laughter.

"Beyond the Wall," one of Teffi's strongest early stories, is a rare instance when genuine feeling illuminates her puppet world. It tells of two elderly women, Mme. Lazenskaya and her landlady, Mme. Shrank, who has invited her to break the Lenten fast. Through most of the story the usual pecking order is at work, with Shrank, the dominant personality, lording it over her poor tenant. The vulnerable Lazenskaya meekly accepts the barrage of insults, but – absurdly – her patriotic pride is wounded when Shrank declares that Russians, unlike Germans, "never have earthquakes." She retorts: "You think I'm poor, so I have no fatherland!... You should be ashamed! Everyone knows that Russians have had an earthquake!"[105] She then rushes off to her little room without eating any *paskha* (an Easter confection), and through the open window vent feels a bit of the outside world of nature and the Easter season – the "strong and moist smell of spring [...] the quiet drone of the Easter church bells."[106] At first Lazenskaya is upset by this "echo of faraway, alien joy" and the sight of the wall outside her window: "endless, flat, gray," but then she hears Mme. Shrank order the cook to "tell Mme. Lazenskaya to come and drink coffee when her foolishness passes [...] There's a piece of *paskha* here." Lazenskaya understands that the cook went to bed long before and that Shrank was saying this for her alone to hear. This moment of unexpected kindness, however slight, coincides with a change in the endless wall, which is no longer gray, but "has just barely turned pink under the crimson rays of the rising sun. The lively breeze of daybreak audaciously knocked against the vent." The comic–pathetic Mme. Lazenskaya sees only a pale reflection of the splendiferous suns of *Seven Fires* on the grim gray wall enclosing her life, but even that – coupled with an instant of uncharacteristic kindness by her land-lady – grants Teffi's comic creation a fleeting glimpse of the heavenly flame.

4

FEASTS AND PLAGUES

1910–16

THE SMOLDERING VOLCANO

There was a dark underside to the humor so prevalent in Russia in the years preceding World War I. As one historian of the period notes: "This carefree, slightly infantile, always talented merriment was called forth in order to muffle the anxiety filling the air, the fear gnawing at the soul, to forget the horrors of life."[1] A drawing by the World of Art member Yevgeny Lanceray (1879–1946), which appeared in *Satirikon* toward the end of 1909, encapsulates the underlying troubles haunting Russian society at the time. The reader's eyes first alight upon the kind of elegant scene so beloved of St. Petersburg artists: a formal park, classical statues, graceful greenery. As one's gaze travels downward, however, one beholds an ugly, violent act. A poem, "Two Worlds," signed A.G. (Alexander Glikberg, the real name of the talented *Satirikon* poet Sasha Chorny, 1880–1932), serves as a caption:

> In the depths of an overgrown park
> [. . . . . .]
> Bunches of roses and white lilies
> Exude a piquant calm.
> Clouds float over the garden;
> A white youth bearing grapes
> Has pressed his torso against a white maiden –
> And by their feet, beneath heaven's caress,
> Brother has grabbed brother by the throat
> For a dirty crust of bread.[2]

"Two Worlds" could serve as an emblem of Russia as a whole at that time. On the one hand the economy was surging and the political situation had stabilized, but on the other there was a deep sense of disquiet, of living on a volcano.[3] Teffi commented on the spiritual malaise in her *Russkoe slovo* feuilletons. She described the steep rise in suicides, a phenomenon that had spread to all strata of Russian society: "High-schoolers, old men, seamstresses, policemen, women students [*kursistki*], old women in almshouses, merchants' sons, workers, people of all ages and stations voluntarily depart from life."[4]

Teffi also wrote quite often about other social problems, especially about crime and anti-Semitism. Of particular interest are her articles on a 1913 case that, according to the famous police detective Arkady Koshko, "caused a sensation not only in St. Petersburg, but in all of Russia."[5] Teffi considered the brutal murder by privileged youths of a certain Mme. Timé, the wife of a railroad ticket collector, symptomatic of the times and typical of St. Petersburg in particular. Whereas a Moscow crime was usually guided by instinct, the accused in the St. Petersburg case were "very cultured people": "In Moscow [...] Carousing, drinking bouts, smoke-filled rooms [*mutnyi chad*], intoxication, nobody understands anything. Here – everything is weighed, calculated, and, the main thing, proper."[6] The crime, moreover, undermined societal norms, since in the past everyone understood that a bandit was "a wild, burly fellow," but now you looked at the manicured hand of the young man sitting next to you at a dinner party and thought: "He's so nice... But hasn't he killed someone and then gone for a manicure?"

Teffi addressed the problem of anti-Semitism numerous times, including in a feuilleton on the sinking of the *Titanic*. She acknowledged the bravery of others, but asserted that the most heroic were third-class passengers: "our fellow countrymen, destitute Jews from the Mogilyov province." For if some "Moishe from Mstislav's last scream was not a curse, then truly, of all those who perished on the *Titanic*, it was precisely he [...] who was the greatest and the most beautiful hero."[7] In 1913 Teffi devoted no fewer than four feuilletons to the Beilis case, involving a Jewish workman in Kiev accused of the ritual murder of a Christian boy. In one she relates how Americans on a tour of the Roman catacombs – reacting to their guide's comment that contemporaries of the early Christians believed they drank children's blood because they "were profoundly ignorant and suffered from various wild superstitions" – pulled out an article on the Beilis case and whispered: "Russians, Russians."[8]

The anxiety engendered by these ills plaguing Russian society, and by a deeper foreboding of looming catastrophe, only increased people's need to have fun. Newspapers juxtaposed accounts of catastrophe and of merriment – in 1910, for example, printing notices "of balls and masquerades alongside a chronicle of the cholera epidemic that had flared up in the capital."[9] *Satirikon* was a major participant in this "feast during the plague" (the Pushkin title often applied by contemporaries to this period), sponsoring annually a mammoth masquerade ball. In 1911 as many as 3,000 people attended, and among the works performed was Teffi's operetta *Popsy*, with music by M. Chernov.[10] The Satyriconians also satisfied the public's demand for light entertainment by staging readings. At one such event, probably in 1912, Teffi brought along the poet Igor Severyanin (1887–1941) in what was apparently his first public appearance.[11] The audience was quite bewildered by his hedonistic poems, but they were soon to bring Severyanin enormous popularity.

This hedonism was manifested about a year later in the rage for the sexually provocative tango, which had spread from the bars and bordellos of Argentina to conquer Europe and America.[12] In April 1914, Teffi wrote that the dance had become so pervasive in Russia that the consumer market was flooded with "tango" fabrics, greeting cards, candy, boots, and soon after she became enmeshed in a controversy that pointed to the tango's "suspect" status.[13] The chronicler in the magazine *Teatr i iskusstvo* (Theatre and art) wrote that she was supposed to chair a debate on the dance, but half the participants – including Teffi – did not show up. When she explained that she "had 'unwillingly' agreed to participate," a reporter responded:

> Of course it is very sad that the talented writer found herself in such an unpleasant position. But it is still more unpleasant that Mme. Teffi, although "unwillingly," agreed to lend her name to a "literary affair" like the debate on the tango.[14]

The frivolous mood was also much in evidence in the unprecedented number of gatherings, "literary, artistic, theatrical, professional, and amateur, creative associations, regular meetings, 'Saturdays,' 'Thursdays,' 'Wednesdays,' in private homes and in public places – in clubs, halls, theaters."[15] Teffi remembers in a late memoir that she too held a salon, dubbed by the poet Vasily Kamensky (1884–1961) "blue Tuesdays" because of her blue wallpaper.[16] She imagines telling a provincial visitor about her guests:

> "And who is that near the door?" he asked.
>> "That's Gumilyov. A poet."

"And who's that he's talking to? Also a poet?"

"No, that's the artist Sasha Yakovlev."

"And who's that tuning the piano?"

"That's the composer Senilov. Only he's not tuning, he's playing his composition."

[...]

"And who is that skinny woman on the sofa?"

"That's Anna Akhmatova, the poetess."

"And which of them is [the husband] Akhmatov?"

"Akhmatov is that same Gumilyov."[17]

Teffi wrote that she was especially fond of Gumilyov, who dedicated his poem "The Fairy Tale" to her. He rarely came to her blue Tuesdays, she recalled, but they liked to meet for quiet chats.

Teffi also visited popular artistic haunts, including the Vienna Restaurant, where she first met the popular writer Alexander Kuprin (1870–1938), often accompanied by drunken, rowdy companions.[18] At one of her visits in 1913, Teffi made such an impression on the Crimean writer Vadim Bayan that he wrote: "I recently visited [the Vienna] and was again enchanted. Most of all I liked Teffi, whom I saw for the first time. And my brother writers concluded: Vadim Bayan / Is drunk on Teffi [*Vadim Bayan / Ot Teffi p'ian*]."[19]

An establishment that played a far more significant role both in Teffi's life and in St. Petersburg artistic culture was the celebrated literary and artistic cabaret the Stray Dog, which opened on New Year's Eve 1911/12 in the cellar of a historic house on the corner of Mikhailovskaya Square and Italian Street.[20] Conceived as a "cabaret exclusively for actors, artists, and writers," it operated, at least in theory, as a private club, with admission limited to those who were opening new paths in the arts.[21] Teffi was a "Friend of the Dog," a category that, according to one of its founders, Boris Pronin (1875–1946), included "people who did substantial things for the Dog. Teffi was a Friend because – she was Teffi."[22] The cabaret was envisioned as an alternate space, an underground, nocturnal refuge (open from midnight to daybreak) from the "heartless" outside world. The murals in the main room, painted by Sergei Sudeikin and featuring brilliant, exotic birds and flowers (inspired by Baudelaire's *Fleurs du mal*), greatly enhanced the illusion of escape to an enchanted world, "transporting the cellar's visitors far beyond the limits of their real place and time," as Yevreinov put it.[23]

The founding principle of exclusivity of the Stray Dog soon was compromised and the cabaret became what has been called a "Noah's Ark," the gathering place of rival camps – symbolists and acmeists coming together with the more radical futurists – a heterogeneous collection of poets united by their categorical rejection of traditional literature, summed up by their call to "throw Pushkin, Dostoyevsky, Tolstoy, etc., etc. off the steamship of modernity."[24] The atmosphere fostered spontaneous creativity, but also provided a fertile breeding ground for what was then deemed "deviant" behavior – sexual practices of all stripes, drug addiction, alcoholism.[25] In her memoir of Mikhail Kuzmin, Teffi writes quite equably about the atmosphere, in particular about the homosexual ambience of the poet's circle: "all beginning poets, young, almost boys, a whole restless herd […] who all worshipped Oscar Wilde." From among their number some "celebrated poets" emerged: "Georgy Adamovich, Georgy Ivanov."[26]

Teffi appears in a number of memoirs about the Stray Dog. Pronin remembered that she "was wholly one of us, was often at meetings, she liked the Dog very much."[27] Others, rather surprisingly, emphasize her shyness. One habitué recalls that she was "very quiet, flatly refusing to read any of her humorous stories aloud. 'I cannot conquer my timidity. My business is to write, not to read.'"[28] A contrary impression is recorded by A. Shaikevich:

> In a red fox boa, in a black velvet dress, a woman with a clever, inspired face comes out on the stage. She reads one of her new "sly songs" – "The princess donned her green dress." "Bravo, Teffi… – Teffi, come here" – the fresh voice of Akhmatova, so familiar to all, resounded from somewhere in the cherished, intimate space of the Dog.[29]

In any case, by early 1914 Teffi was apparently confident enough to perform at a number of events.[30] She usually participated in programs featuring the acmeists, whose poetry, marked by clarity and restraint, she found most congenial. She was much less kind about the futurists' wild verbal experiments and public buffoonery. In 1913, she described how, upon first perusing the notorious miscellany *Sadok sudei* (usually translated as *A Trap for Judges*), she thought it was written in some other Slavic language, but when she managed to decipher it, found "everything was so simple and so boring. Simple stories, simply and badly told."[31] In her late memoir of Kuzmin she claimed that she "didn't go to […] performances where poets went around in blouses [*kofty*] and roundly cursed from the stage, parrying the curses of the audience," but in 1913 she wrote with some sympathy – although with considerable irony – about their readings:

I liked the futurists' performances and am truly sorry they've ended.

Well, where now will we see a gentleman in a blouse coming out on stage and starting to swear?

[...]

"Hey, you fools! I spit on you! Tfoo!"

"It's a fool we're hearing it from!" the audience merrily hoots in response.[32]

The futurists, she asserted, have accomplished what theoreticians of modernist theater a few years before had yearned for: communal action, the destruction of the footlights: "The footlights are destroyed by a pickle flung over them and back." She countered the charge that the futurists are untalented and play the fools: "To play the fool well requires enormous intensity of fantasy, requires creative power."

Such literary matters, however, were soon overshadowed by world events.

THE VOLCANO ERUPTS: WAR

In June 1914, Teffi was in Marienbad (in the modern-day Czech Republic), "peacefully dieting," as she recalled 25 years later (when another world war was looming).[33] A young German officer with "sentimental eyes" informed her compatriots that he was studying Russian, but when they asked him to say something in their native language, he "affectionately uttered: 'Zcroundrel! Dog! Zon of a bitch, I need your horzess!'" This German may well be a darkly comic fiction, but Teffi's description of how she, together with crowds of tourists, was evacuated from Germany the day war on Russia was declared (5 August) is probably close to the truth.[34] She was not to go abroad again until 1919, and then not as a carefree tourist, but as an exile.

When Teffi returned to St. Petersburg, she found a city gripped by patriotic fervor – one outcome the change in August of the city's German-sounding name to Petrograd. An Imperial Manifesto (*Vysochaishii manifest*) had been published, calling on the people to "forget internal discord" – a summons that the populace seemed to heed, at least temporarily.[35] Literary circles were infected by the general mood and produced a flood of patriotic, anti-German works. The Stray Dog made some half-hearted efforts to support the war effort, including some performances of a military bent, but on the whole the atmosphere of unbridled frivolity and tomfoolery continued unabated.[36] It would not go on for long, however. On 11 February 1915, the brash young futurist Vladimir Mayakovsky (1893–1930), interrupted the program to deliver his poem "To You!" – clearly addressed to those sitting before him (who included Teffi[37]). The poem describes the reaction of a mortally wounded officer who "suddenly saw how you, with your lip smeared from meat cutlet, are lewdly humming Severyanin!"[38] The reading, Pronin remembers, "had the effect of thunder, there was even fainting."[39] The incident brought the cabaret to the attention of the police, who found on the premises dozens of bottles of wine (now officially forbidden). The Stray Dog was closed 3 March 1915.[40]

Meanwhile, during the fall of 1914, a scandal involving Teffi dramatically altered her personal life. Dr. Nyurenberg – a celebrated physician favored by writers and other cultural figures – was visiting Teffi when Galich stormed in and fired five shots, hitting Nyurenberg in the neck, hand, and arm. He also shot at Teffi, but missed, and then turned himself over to the local police station, where he stated that he had warned Nyurenberg of the danger facing him if he continued his visits.[41] The doctor was close to death, but survived, and decades later Galich revealed the consequences of his crime to Ivan Bunin:

> I sat in Vyborg Prison, accused of premeditated murder [...] and if it weren't for the war department, which insisted that I be [...] quickly shoved [...] onto the staff of the supreme commander [...] then God knows what I would have been good for.[42]

Nothing more is known about Teffi's relations with Dr. Nyurenberg, but when he died in April 1917 (apparently of unrelated causes), she wrote an obituary describing his total dedication to his calling and his miraculous diagnoses.[43]

Because of her extreme reticence about her personal life, there is virtually no trace of Teffi's other liaisons (reputed to be many) – including with Dmitry Shcherbakov, who was to become her second husband. The most substantial evidence of the marriage is a communiqué written during the civil war stating that a Captain Shcherbakov (no first name given) died in Paris 16 April 1919, and requesting that his widow, *"Madame Stcherbakoff, écrivain connu TEFFY,"* be informed.[44] Other military documents identify Shcherbakov as a courier to White commander Admiral Kolchak, who was traveling to Siberia via Western Europe with Staff Captain of the Cavalry (*Shtab-Rotmistr*) Tolstoy-Miloslavsky.[45]

Another piece of evidence of the marriage is an undated studio photograph of Teffi, in which she is identified in the catalogue as "N. A.

Buchinskaya-Shcherbakova."[46] Who precisely her husband was has not been firmly established, but evidence points to Dmitry Shcherbakov, a landowner and friend of Kuzmin, to whom Teffi dedicated a story, "The Author," from her 1913 book *Carousel*.[47] In her memoir of Kuzmin, she alludes to their "mutual friend," "D. Shch.," who accompanied the poet on his rare visits to her.[48] In his diary, Kuzmin mentions a Shcherbakov quite often, a few times in connection with Teffi, and a Dmitry Shcherbakov wrote rave reviews of a couple of Teffi's plays.[49] In Teffi's memoir of the artist Ilya Repin, finally, she recalls a "Shch.," "a landowner of the Kovno province, a great aesthete, a friend of Kuzmin's." She gave him her portrait, which disappeared during the revolution and was later found hanging among the icons in one of the peasants' huts.[50]

Shcherbakov, who, according to Kuzmin's diary, took part in many of the activities of his circle, was most likely gay. It may be that after the male domination that had so oppressed Teffi during her first marriage and the possessive passion that had driven Galich to attempt murder, she found a companionate marriage with a homosexual an attractive alternative.

By the end of 1914 Teffi was contributing to the war literature in a variety of genres, from patriotic verse and satire to serious stories included in her 1916 book *The Lifeless Beast*. She recited "The White Garment" – apparently her earliest war poem – in late December 1914, at a gathering at Sologub's, which, according to a newspaper report, was attended by "almost all the poets of the new school."[51] Although not on the highest level artistically, it is noted for its Christian theme – rare in earlier Teffi, but to become quite common during the war. It was later anthologized a number of times and set to music by Vladimir Senilov.[52]

In January 1915, Teffi volunteered at a St. Petersburg military infirmary, which provided the setting for several stories included in *The Lifeless Beast* as well as for a satire, "Two Natures." The latter, published in *The Shield* (a miscellany compiled by Leonid Andreyev, Maksim Gorky, and Sologub with the goal of combating anti-Semitism), portrays high-society ladies volunteering at an infirmary. The patroness, Anna Pavlovna, informs the others of two new arrivals, one very pleasant – a recipient of a St. George's medal – and the other very unpleasant – a Jew. She has the decorated soldier put in a prominent place and offered all possible comforts, and the ladies are in ecstasy over the "astonishing grandeur of the Russian soul."[53] When they discover that this soldier and the Jew are one and the same, Anna Pavlovna can only babble: "This soldier, you see, has two natures [...] We gave cigarettes to the St. George recipient and a Jew is smoking them! We placed a bed of honor for the St. George recipient and a Jew is sprawled out on it!"[54]

In March 1915, Teffi traveled to the front in the dual capacity of nurse and journalist. A striking photograph published in *Teatr i iskusstvo* – she is clad in a nurse's headdress, a rifle in one hand and a sword in the other – attests to the publicity value of the trip, but that was not its only purpose, for it resulted in serious and affecting reportage.[55] Teffi's description of a field hospital in "Near the War," for example, conveys both the horror of war and the resiliency of the wounded:

> There is a strange figure pacing along the platform; a human figure, but on its shoulders is an immense white sphere instead of a head. In the sphere a tiny chink has been made for one eye, and a little lower there is another chink, a cigarette dangling from it. But the sphere behaves very cheerfully and independently. It seeks a more comfortable seat for itself in the car and merrily slaps the orderlies on the back.[56]

In August 1915, Teffi put out a small collection of war stories and feuilletons, including "Near the War."[57] The following year she included the best and least topical of them, together with other serious works written between 1909 and 1915, in *The Lifeless Beast* – the best book she published in Russia.

THE LIFELESS BEAST

It might have been Teffi's war experience that led her to include in *The Lifeless Beast* those among her earlier works that penetrate beneath the comical, artificial surface to reveal genuine feelings, both negative and positive. Indeed because of the greater seriousness of many of the stories she found it necessary for the first time to write a preface in order to "warn the reader [that] there is a great deal that is not funny [*neveselogo*] in this book." She added rather grimly: "I issue the warning so that those looking for laughter, when they find tears – the pearls of my soul – won't turn on me and tear me to pieces."[58]

The inclusion in the collection of stories written over a prolonged period offers an opportunity to trace Teffi's development as a writer of serious fiction. While the earliest work, "Shamash" (1909), depicts in the heightened style of

Seven Fires the mass annihilation of worshippers of the sun god, "The Hare," published three years later, conveys an analogous vision of the injustice of the world order in miniaturized form, through an incident involving a single peasant woman and a small animal.[59] The timid, gentle Matryona, on her way home with the money she just received from a landowner, rescues a hare and wraps its wounded paw in the same scarf where she secured her gold rubles. She feels deep sympathy toward the animal, imagines their happy future together, but then he runs away with her money. After she chases him in vain, the story ends with the cawing of a crow, the sound – *tak* (yes) – affirming the complicity of all of nature in the injustice suffered by Matryona: "A crow rose up from a post and began flapping like a black rag through the gray sky and loudly approved of everything: '*Ta-ak! Ta-ak!*' It turned toward the forest, made haste, bore the news. '*Ta-ak! Ta-ak!*'"[60]

Matryona's victimization by an animal is, to be sure, uncommon in Teffi, who in her many stories about "lesser" creatures generally portrays them as morally and emotionally superior to humans. In "Steam," for example, a snoring woman, with her "obtuse" face, is contrasted to her dog, who in its dreams re-enacts animal love, "inhuman, devoted, timid, and selfless."[61] Among people, it is primarily children who exhibit such emotional wholeness, and *The Lifeless Beast* contains some charming pieces about the joys and minor trials of the young. Some of the most interesting stories in the collection, however, depict powerfully the loss of childhood joy in the face of life's ugliness and cruelty.

"Little Devil in a Jar" (1915) – which, like "The Hare," demonstrates Teffi's mastery of the miniature form – begins on Palm Sunday, when the narrator was seven years old. It is a beautiful spring day and life seems "endless," its "joys [...] indubitable, whole, and bright."[62] For the holiday the girl receives a toy devil in a jar, who dances when she presses the film covering the opening. The devil, glittering in the sunlight and laughing, at first only adds to the joy of the day, and the little girl joins in his laughter and spinning, and makes up a song. But then the film breaks, water leaks out, and the devil become menacing: "Thin but pot-bellied [...] And his eyes protruding, evil, white, astonished."[63] The girl tries to placate him, making a bed for him in a matchbox, but he is not assuaged, and the next night she surrenders her bed entirely to him. The following day she exclaims: "I love you, devil!"[64] and when she bursts out crying that evening her parents decide she is ill and put her to bed. The little girl, however – in thrall to the devil – cannot be cured so easily: "I knew that when the grown-ups leave, I would crawl out of bed, find the devil's jar, crawl into

75

it, and would sing my little song […] and spin all my life, spin all my endless life."[65] The ending reverses the joy evoked by the singing and spinning and the words "endless life" at the beginning of the story, while the shift to the future tense broadens the significance of what has been an amusing anecdote – intimating that the child will forever be prey to evil forces, will spin endlessly, like the marionettes of the poem. Especially striking is the image of the narrator crawling into the devil's jar. She, instead of the toy, will amuse others all her life – a fitting emblem for Teffi herself, capturing as it does the anguish aroused by the constant imperative to entertain.

The title piece, "The Lifeless Beast" (1912) – one of Teffi's most widely praised works – depicts with greater psychological and emotional depth the painful transition from childhood to joyless adulthood. The story begins at a Christmas party, where the little girl, Katya, is given a stuffed animal – a woolen ram. It seems alive to her, "with […] human eyes […] and if you pulled his head down, he bleated affectionately and insistently: 'Ba-a!'"[66] But she is at once told that the ram is "lifeless."

The party proves to be the happiest moment of the story, because before long the marriage of Katya's parents falls apart and they disappear from her life. She is left alone with her nanny and some servants – rather menacing peasant women who whisper endlessly about the family scandal. An added horror is the squeaking that fills the house at night; nanny's explanation only makes matters worse: "Rats are running around and just you wait, they'll bite your nose off!"[67] Katya's one comfort is the "lifeless beast," who unfailingly gazes at her with affection and understanding and whose "human eyes" distinguish him from the people surrounding her, portrayed through animal imagery – the nanny, who "bared her teeth like an old cat"; the peasant women with their "fox faces."[68] But of course the ram is not alive, and one of the servants cruelly taunts Katya that the end of the increasingly tattered toy is inevitable: "A living body eats and drinks […] but however much you slobber onto a rag, it'll fall apart all the same."[69] Katya tries in vain to bring the "lifeless beast" to life by having him eat and drink and bleat by himself, and when a teacher arrives and orders all toys, including the ram, banished from the nursery, she is terrified: "It's bad for a lifeless creature! […] He can't talk, can't call."[70] That night, however, the impossible seems to occur. Katya hears the ram cry out by himself, but this longed-for sign of life signals the very opposite: the ram is being torn apart by rats.

In response to this horror the little girl withdraws from the hostile adult world, burrowed in her bed, covered her head [...] She was afraid that nanny would wake up, would bare her teeth like a cat, and she and the fox-like peasant women would get a good laugh over the woolen death of the lifeless beast.[71]

At the conclusion, Teffi gathers together previously discrete details – the scurrying rats and bleating ram; the "fox-like peasant women" and the nanny's bared teeth – transforming what seemed a loose narrative into a tightly knit, tragic anecdote. The story ends with a very brief paragraph: "She grew totally quiet, pressed into a ball. She will live quietly, quietly, so nobody would find out anything." The use of the future tense here, as in "Little Devil in a Jar," expands the significance of the story, intimating Katya's lasting alienation.

The instances of victimization and cruelty in Teffi's "peacetime" stories in *The Lifeless Beast* are inevitably amplified in her depiction of war. At the same time, however, she shows how the conflict – by creating cracks in the old, ossified social order – provided a broader field for genuine feeling and human connection to seep through.

"Yavdokha" (1914), the first of the war stories, is also the most unremittingly bleak. The peasant heroine is so poor and benighted that, like some of the characters from the lower orders in Teffi's earliest works, she seems barely human. Her only companion is a hog to whom she devotes all her waking hours, yet even he will be slaughtered for someone else's Christmas dinner. At the beginning of the story Yavdokha receives a letter from her son, Panas, who, she learns for the first time, is in the army. Since she is illiterate, she has to go to the village to find someone to read it. It turns out that the letter is not from Panas at all, but from a comrade, who writes: "Your son Apanasy has ordered you to live a long life [*prikazal dolgo zhit'*]" – words traditionally uttered on the deathbed.[72] Yavdokha misunderstands and thinks they refer to her son's friend, and that evening she thinks: "Panas sent a letter, he'll send money too [...] I'll buy bread.'"[73] The narrator comments: "And there was nothing else." Thus the tolls of war are made all the more grievous by Yavdokha's benightedness.

Teffi's experience at the Petrograd infirmary shortly after she wrote "Yavdokha" brought about a striking change in her depiction of the peasantry, the mixed feelings of pity and disgust replaced by a strong emotional connection with the peasant soldiers. In "Daisy" the change is all the more striking because at first the title character – very much a creature of her set – is seeking a spot in an infirmary because, as her monocled friend Vovo Bek puts it: "All the ladies from high society [work in infirmaries] [...] And a nurse's uniform will probably be very becoming on you."[74] When Daisy wangles an assignment and arrives at the infirmary, however, her preparatory preening goes unnoticed and she is sent to assist a doctor who is removing a bullet from a soldier's leg. While Daisy holds the leg the direct tactile connection works an emotional transformation:

> She felt his every quiver and to each one she responded with a kind of new, intense tenderness in her soul, and when, finally, the doctor [...] showed her a round black bullet on his bloodied palm, she began to tremble all over with joy and barely held back from crying. "Lord, what happiness! Lord, what happiness!"[75]

After the operation the soldier, Dmitry, smiles "with the simple childlike smile of a grayish, pockmarked, bearded peasant" and says: "Thanks, my dear. It was much easier for me because of you, my white [-clad] sister!"[76] Daisy then receives a call from Vovo, but hangs up without answering and, returning to the patient, says:

> "Thank you, Dmitry, for feeling good. I'm happy today, and never have been before... It's because you feel good that I'm so happy."
> And she suddenly felt embarrassed because he might not understand her.
> But he smiled with the simple, childlike smile of a grayish, pockmarked, bearded peasant.
> He smiled and understood everything.

The physical shortcomings of the soldier ("grayish, pockmarked") are eclipsed by his "simple, childlike smile," and Yavdokha's inner darkness replaced by Dmitry's understanding.

"The Heart" tells of a rare instance of genuine human connection in a peacetime setting. The story concerns an outing to a monastery by a rather frivolous party: a medical student, nicknamed Medicus; a teacher, Polosov; a woman landowner, Lykova; and an actress, Rakhatova. Their conversation as they make their way through the swamp that leads to the monastery at first suggests that this will be one of Teffi's tales of light-hearted flirtation, but a darker note is struck when Polosov jumps on the rickety plank and they feel, "hidden under the green velvety carpet, a sticky, oozy, marshy death."[77] Although nature's gay surface soon dispels the sense of peril, the party has another unnerving experience when they arrive at the monastery: they witness a monk throwing water over an enormous, hacked-up fish, and "suddenly something trembled in one of the middle pieces; trembled, thrust, and the whole fish responded [...] 'It's the heart contracting,' said Medicus."[78] This sight makes no lasting impression on the visitors either, and that evening they find it very funny when a monk asks if they have come for confession. Rakhatova decides as a lark to take up the idea, and the following morning she and Lykova are amused by the timorous, shabbily dressed old monk who conducts the confession. But then they witness a transformation in the monk: after he asks Rakhatova if she has "any special sins" and she answers that she does not, "his whole face trembled and radiated fine little wrinkles and smiled with childish joy" as he cries out "thank God!"[79] Alluding to the earlier description of the hacked-up fish, he is compared to "a large, chopped-off heart on which a drop of living water had fallen, and it trembled, and because of it the dead, chopped-off pieces trembled." Rakhatova – just such a "dead, chopped-off piece" – asks herself: "What is this? [...] Can it be I'll start crying?" She at once attributes her reaction to fatigue, but when the party rides back and the other characters chatter away, she and Lykova remain silent – a hint that a trace remains of the sympathy and love that the monk imparted to them. The topography of the story, finally, adds a symbolic dimension. It is constructed as a series of concentric circles: the swamp surrounding the monastery – the enticing, but treacherous natural world; the monastery itself – a microcosm of human society. And at the very center a monk – the heart – vivifying the otherwise dead world.

THE VANISHING OLD WORLD

"A Quiet Backwater," published in 1915, serves as a kind of requiem for the old life threatened by war and soon to be destroyed by revolution. The story takes place on an abandoned estate where the only human inhabitants are two old servants, Pelageya and Fedorushka – "a retired laundress and retired coachman."[80] In the extended metaphor that begins the story, the "quiet backwater" is contrasted to a turbulent river – an allusion not only to restless human striving in general, but to the agony of war:

> There, in the open space, waves pine and toss. They are rushing about from side to side, as if from madness and pain, and suddenly in a last

desperate effort they leap, fling themselves up to the sky and again crash down into the dark water.[81]

For now the backwater, a "blue-eyed little lake – the joy of ducks – and a bunch of stiff reeds growing in the front garden," remains untouched.

The inhabitants of the estate, separated geographically from the turmoil of the world, are further isolated by old age, their deafness and forgetfulness cutting them off even from one another. They hardly seem more human than the pitiful Yavdokha, but their oneness with nature endears them to the reader. The harmony between man and beast is most apparent when Pelageya expounds upon the name days of various animals and of the earth itself, but is disconsolate when she cannot recall the cow's name day: "Now you won't remember, and by not remembering, you'll offend her, scold her or something, and that's a sin […] And there up above her angel will weep…"[82] At the end this forgetfulness pervades the landscape of the quiet backwater, adding a note of pathos to the tranquil atmosphere: "The night outside the window is blue. It reminds one of something, but it's impossible to remember what […] The river has left. It's forgotten the reeds." The elegiac mood is reinforced by the intimation that all the "quiet backwaters" of old, patriarchal Russia will not long survive the wildly rushing waves of Russian history.

5

A FAREWELL TO RUSSIA, PAST AND FUTURE

1915–19

THE BEGINNING OF THE END

In the course of 1915, the war took a precipitous turn for the worse for Russia, and as the expectation of rapid victory faded, so did popular support for the tsarist regime. The most divisive figure in the Romanov entourage was the "mad monk," Grigory Rasputin (1869–1916), who was in fact not a monk at all, but a peasant religious zealot famed in roughly equal measure for his power as a mystical healer and for his unbridled debauchery. In April 1915, Teffi had a couple of curious encounters with the so-called "elder."

It all began with two enigmatic telephone calls – one from the brilliant, idiosyncratic writer and philosopher Vasily Rozanov (1856–1919), the other from Alexander Izmailov. Neither dared name Rasputin on the phone, and it was only when Izmailov met Teffi face to face that he told her that a certain M—ch had proposed to a certain F. that the latter invite a select company, including some writers, to observe Rasputin. In his book on Rasputin, Edvard Radzinsky reveals that M—ch was Ivan Fyodorovich Manasevich-Manuilov and F. a figure close to Rasputin, Aleksei Frolovich Filippov, who had decided to invite the writers, but only on condition that their identity be concealed.[1] Teffi hesitantly accepted, although she writes that she "felt moral nausea from the whole hysterical atmosphere surrounding the name of Rasputin."[2] She conveys some of this hysteria in her description of two dinner parties she attended right before the encounter. At the first, Ye., an imperial maid-of-honor, described how Rasputin's fixed gaze had caused her "terrible heart palpitations," and, when she did not at once agree to visit him, how "he placed his hand on [her] shoulder and said, 'Come without fail.'" At the second dinner, her hosts repeated the usual rumors swirling around Rasputin – "about bribes, [...]

about German pay-offs, about spying, about court intrigues."[3] Although Teffi discounted much of this as "vulgar, stupid lies," she suspected that "there was, nevertheless, some living, unfabricated source [...] that fed all these legends."[4]

Rozanov entreated Teffi beforehand to broach erotic subjects (with which he was obsessed), but Rasputin was more interested in seduction than conversation. He ordered Teffi to come visit him and touched her shoulder, as he had with Ye., but this time the technique failed. The touch seemed to rebound to Rasputin himself, who "convulsively moved his shoulder and began groaning quietly."[5] A little later he jotted down one of his poems and presented it to Teffi with the inscription: "To Nadezhda. God is love. Love. God will forgive. Grigory."[6] The session suddenly ended when Rasputin was urgently called to the tsar's summer palace. He left orders that Teffi remain, but she again resisted. With her sharp eye for artifice, Teffi assumed at first that Rasputin's behavior was a pose: "Here he is, Rasputin, with his repertoire. That artificially mysterious voice, intense face, imperious words. So all of this is a tried and true technique."[7] Yet she herself was not entirely satisfied with her explanation, for the "physical torture" he experienced when repulsed seemed genuine. As for Rasputin's political power, Teffi had her doubts:

> For a person who pursues a serious political line, Rasputin didn't seem serious enough to me. He twitched too much, his attention was too easily distracted, he himself was so totally muddled. He probably gave in to persuasion and bribes without particularly thinking it over and weighing the consequences. The very force he wished to master was carrying him off somewhere [...] and he was racing in a whirlwind, in a tornado, himself lost.[8]

A few days later a second gathering took place at Filippov's, this time Rasputin looking even more gaunt, tense, his piercing eyes deeply sunken, and now, more than before, everything was cloaked in mystery. Teffi discovered that the elder had been aware of the writers' identity all along, and wondered whether they were pawns of someone from his entourage: "Who among them are from the secret police? Who is a candidate for a hard labor camp? And who is a secret German agent?"[9] This time Rozanov urged Teffi to draw out Rasputin's religious secrets, and she questioned him about the heretical Khlysty (Flagellant) sect, in particular about the rite of "rejoicing" (*radenie*) – frenzied dancing culminating in sexual acts, which purportedly led to the descent of the Holy Spirit.[10] Rasputin did not directly respond, but instead began a mad dance:

He tore from the spot [...] and, running away from the table [...] suddenly began jumping, dancing, thrusting his knee forward, his beard shaking, and all the time spinning, spinning... His face was confused, tense, he was rushing, jumping unrhythmically, as if not obeying his own will, frenzied, unable to stop...[11]

The sight was horrifying yet irresistible, "so weird, so wild, that, looking at him, I wanted to squeal, fling myself into the circle, and also jump and spin as long as my strength held out."

Afterward Rasputin resumed his effort to lure Teffi, but his tone was much darker:

Only come, for God's sake, as soon as possible. We'll pray together [...] Well, they keep wanting to kill me [...] They don't understand who I am, the fools. A sorcerer? [...] They burn sorcerers, so let them burn me. There's one thing they don't understand: if they burn me it's the end of Russia.[12]

As she prepared to leave, he appeared "terrifying [...] and completely mad," entreating her: "Only remember..." On their way home, Teffi commented to Rozanov about how strangely Rasputin had latched on to her and speculated that it was "because of *Russkoe slovo*."[13] Yet this scheming Rasputin did not easily jibe with the "completely mad" figure she had just seen. And so Rasputin remains an enigma to the very end.

The consequences of the writers' encounters with Rasputin did, however provide an answer to Teffi's questions about Rasputin's entourage. Several days later Izmailov informed her about a newspaper article stating that Rasputin often met with writers to whom he told "amusing anecdotes" about extremely highly placed people.[14] This led to a police interrogation of Filippov, and Izmailov warned that they too might be questioned and would certainly be placed under surveillance. What was "most disgusting and astonishing" about the whole business, he added, was that Filippov saw a paper on his interrogator's desk written in M—ch's hand. Teffi asked incredulously whether M—ch could have been working for the police, and Radzinsky's biography confirms her suspicions.[15] In conclusion Teffi writes that she never saw Rasputin again, but after his assassination at the end of 1916 she recalled his words:

"They'll burn me? Let them burn me. There's one thing they don't know: if they kill Rasputin, it's also the end of Russia.

"Remember!... Remember!..."

I remembered.[16]

While Rasputin and his circle were engaged in their nefarious acts, the war-time economy was quickly crumbling. There were, on the one hand, unscru-pulous speculators who amassed immense wealth and, on the other, critical shortages, which created intolerable conditions among ordinary people.[17] In September 1915, Teffi portrayed the actions of speculators in a Petrograd café. A "gentleman" approaches the narrator's table and strikes up a conversation with her escort:

"Do you have tin?"

"No, but I have gauze."

"I also have gauze, but I don't have tin."

[...]

The conversation, so similar to exercises used to teach oneself a foreign language, amazed me.[18]

Because of the severe shortage of consumer goods, in February 1916, Teffi advised her readers how to deal with the scarcity of flour: "close your eyes and, concentrating with all your might, repeat seventeen times distinctly and loudly: 'I do not want flour! I do not want flour! I do not want flour!'" After that you will say: "Flour? [...] Qu'est que c'est such a thing?"[19]

Despite such crises – and perhaps because of the need to escape from harsh reality – theatrical life went on. Among the light works that enjoyed considera-ble success in Moscow at the beginning of 1915 was André Rivoire's comedy *Le bon roi Dagobert* (1908), translated from the French in rhymed couplets by Teffi and her sister Yelena.[20] Of greater significance was the production at Moscow's Maly Theater of *Satan's Hurdy-Gurdy*, Teffi's only full-length play written in Russia. She completed it at the end of 1915 and in mid-December telegraphed the Maly's director, Alexander Sumbatov-Yuzhin (1857–1927), urging him to stage it.[21] He must have quickly agreed, since later that month she signed a contract and the premiere took place in late February or early March 1916.[22]

Satan's Hurdy-Gurdy reveals both Teffi's "laughing" and "weeping" faces, but with mixed success. In general critics praised the comic episodes, but considered the serious segments unoriginal and ineffective, only Teffi's loyal husband, Dmitry Shcherbakov, giving the play an unqualified rave when it opened in Petrograd in November.[23] Critics were quite right about the play's lack of originality, for the banality of provincial life had been a common theme in Russian comedy since the eighteenth century, and the heroine, Ardanova – a young wife trapped in an unhappy marriage – is not only a familiar figure in Russian and world drama, but appeared already in Teffi's early stories. As in "The Forgotten Track," the heroine comes close to running off with an outsider, the lawyer Dolgov, but in the end he fails her. In justifying himself, Dolgov expresses an underlying theme in Teffi's works, the illusory nature of the ideal, calling Ardanova's longing to escape "a dream about a beautiful land called 'Never.'"[24] He also introduces familiar symbolism, describing the townspeople as "corpses, marionettes, wound up by old Satan long ago and forevermore," and even admits that he is "a corpse like all of them, and I also whirl to Satan's hurdy-gurdy."[25] Dolgov advises Ardanova to give up seeking "Never" and to lead the human puppet show: "You'll be [...] a provincial lioness, queen of the marionettes!"[26] In the end they kiss, signaling Ardanova's acceptance of that role – one that well describes Teffi's own position within her comic universe.

Before the war Teffi went abroad annually, sending back her travel impressions to *Russkoe slovo*, but since such jaunts were now impossible, she explored instead various parts of the Russian Empire. In June 1916, she went north to the Solovetsky Monastery and the White Sea port Arkhangelsk, then in July headed south to the Caucasus, where she ran into the comic poet Lolo (pseudonym of Leonid Munshtein, 1866–1947) and his wife, the actress Vera Ilnarskaya (1880–1946), with whom she is pictured on the pages of the journal they edited, *Rampa i zhizn'* (Footlights and life).[27]

Once back in Petrograd in October, Teffi found nothing had changed: "The same queues are milling about, wet, huddled, like a homeless dog."[28] The severe shortages even changed the forms of feminine ostentation in her stories. One particularly extravagant banker's wife, for example, a Mme. Karfunkel, came to the theater with a leg of veal because "you can't get veal nowadays for any amount of money, but she got hold of it somewhere."[29]

If such satire seems rather lightweight given the profound crises facing Russia in late 1916, on 6 December Teffi indicates that a crucial reason was the censorship. She notes how delighted she was that she had gotten hold of a ticket to the Duma, because "I'll be able to write a fiery feuilleton tomorrow evening on... the weather, on... the theater, or even on... the high price of butter and the streetcar crush."[30] In another piece published the same day,

Teffi defines the public mood through a characteristic Russian word, *zliush-chii*, which, she explains, "is by no means only an intensified degree of the word *zloi* [angry]."[31] Anyone "can feel angry at someone," she goes on, but a *zliushchii* person needs no particular object; he is "simply *zliushchii* and that's that." To convey the fetid atmosphere, Teffi returns to one of her favorite images, all-enveloping fog: "On the streets it's murky [...] There is no sun. Well, maybe there is, but it's not visible because, due to human malice, a black mist is surging and concealing the sun." In one of Teffi's most pointed feuilletons, written about a month preceding the February 1917 revolution, she lists new phrases that reveal the ills of Russian society and concludes: "The pig is triumphant."[32]

In early February 1917, Teffi expressed her attitude toward the times in a play, *Evolution of the Devil*, staged by the Crooked Mirror and directed by Yevreinov. In a review (the only remaining trace of the miniature) Shcherbakov describes it as "full of humor, now light, now malicious, interspersed with paradoxes and brilliant witticisms."[33] True to its title, the play traces the evolution of the devil through the centuries, from the once great Satan to a "petty demon," who has joined the speculators to "cheat little people." In the end, however, he himself is cheated and cries out: "Man, God's pride, where are you? Shoo! [*Chur menia!*] Shoo."

REVOLUTIONS, FEBRUARY AND OCTOBER

Teffi wrote of the tumultuous opening of the State Duma on 14 February 1917 – a key event in the gathering political crisis. A pro-Duma demonstration was planned to mark the occasion, but was prevented, Teffi hints, by police action.[34] But soon after, on 23 February, a protest held in Petrograd on International Women's Day grew into a general strike that brought the city to a halt and led finally to the collapse of the tsarist government. Nicholas II (r.1894–1917) abdicated on 2 March and the Duma formed a Provisional Government, which was supposed to rule until the election of a Constituent Assembly.

Teffi depicts the exultation by ordinary people at the overthrow of the monarchy in several stories. "The Average Man" tells of one Gerasim Shchurkin: "If you were to draw a straight line from the most magnificent minister to the sweeper of the horse-railway tracks, right on the fold would be Gerasim Ivanych Shchurkin."[35] He and his wife have been renting a room to a radical student, whom they were planning to evict after two visits from the police. But now soldiers conduct a search and exclaim: "Aha! A comrade lives here," and then the student himself arrives and cries: "Free-edom! Long live the republic!"[36] Shchurkin, his fears allayed, "jumped onto the windowsill and [...] cried out as loud as he could: 'The policeman is a fool!'" He adds: "I felt like it and screamed. That's how I am [...] The free citizen Gerasim Ivanych Shchurkin."

This optimism, however, was short-lived, for the Provisional Government was unable to implement reforms during wartime, and disillusionment soon set in – a process vividly portrayed in Teffi's writings. A couple of lighter satirical pieces, published in *Novyi Satirikon*, mock the conflicting feelings of the upper classes about the revolution. In "Napoleon," Baron Shnup insists that he is on the side of revolution, since he and his aristocratic associates are now "unemployed proletarians. We've all been chucked out of the ministry."[37] In "The Revolutionary Lady" Sophie brags to her friend, Marie, of the many meetings she has attended, but as soon as the topic shifts to a strike among the poor, Marie cries: "Akh, *finissez*! How horrible it all is!"[38]

A number of feuilletons in *Russkoe slovo* treat these mixed feelings more seriously. In May Teffi mocked the increasing anxiety of those who, on the one hand, were terrified by exaggerated rumors of violence, but on the other went to revolutionary meetings and after listening meekly to the speeches of "Marxists, evolutionist–socialists, maximalists and syndicalists," gave money and felt "at the forefront of the revolutionary movement."[39] A few days later, in an article provocatively entitled "Deserters!" Teffi conceded that the lower classes were wreaking destruction, but still fervently defended the revolution.[40] She declared that the intelligentsia was expecting a miracle – that "the same common people [*narod*], who for centuries were stupefied by vodka, oppressed, crushed by a lack of rights, by illiteracy, poverty, superstition, and hunger," would at once reveal "a great and shining soul." Now that the revolution has uncovered these horrors, she continued, "the road is open to a free struggle with evil," and she urged those retreating from the cause, to whom she applied the strong term "deserters," to join in, even if their worst fears were to prove justified: "And if everything collapses [...] may each of us be able to say: 'My forces were weak and small, but I gave of them totally.'"

Teffi's own revolutionary sympathies, however, emphatically did not extend to the Bolsheviks. Her contempt, which dated back to 1905, is expressed in a feuilleton of late June 1917, in which she attributes the setbacks they recently suffered to their lack "of political intuition to a rare and striking degree," their failure to anticipate workers' movements, which at best they have joined "*post facto*."[41] She goes on to give a withering portrait of Lenin: "Average height, gray complexion, completely 'ordinary.' Only his forehead is not good, very prominent, stubborn, heavy, not inspired, not seeking, not creative." This "sincere and honest preacher of the great religion of socialism" (as she rather surprisingly calls him) lacks "the fiery tongue of the Holy Spirit; there is no inspiration in him, no flight, and no fire." Alluding to the party's practice of joining forces with criminals, she is still harsher on Lenin's followers, calling them "Leninists, Bosheviks, anarchist–Communists, thugs, registered house-breakers," a "satanic smorgasbord [*vinegret*]."[42] Yet she makes clear that she has not abandoned the ideal of socialism: "What immense work – to again raise up the great idea of socialism and cleanse [it] of all this garbage!"

Teffi reveals her own stunning lack of foresight when she asks rhetorically: "Is not the word 'Bolshevik' now discredited forever and irrevocably?" But she was not sanguine. The following month she wrote of the ineffectiveness of the Provisional Government, the growing chaos in the army, with "crowds of idlers scurrying around" in the rear, "arm in arm with wenches [*devkami*]," while soldiers at the front spent their time gambling and going to Bolshevik rallies.[43] On 22 October she bemoaned the weakening government, the collapse of industrial production, massive workers' strikes, the steady erosion of freedoms.[44] Only a couple of days later, on the night of 24–25 October, the Bolsheviks carried out their coup in Petrograd, taking over the Winter Palace and arresting the ministers of the Provisional Government.[45]

The Bolsheviks' takeover in Petrograd was essentially bloodless, but the intelligentsia was horrified by the destruction and defacement of precious artifacts in the tsar's former palace and the residences of the wealthy. Teffi was among the members of the Society for the Preservation of Artistic Buildings and Art Objects, which was organized by Sologub after the February revolution but whose task became especially urgent following October.[46] "We demanded protection of the Hermitage and of picture galleries," Teffi recalled in her memoir of Sologub. "We petitioned, went to [Commissar of Enlightenment] Lunacharsky [...] But we got nothing for our troubles."[47]

An action that affected Teffi more directly was the closing of opposition newspapers. *Russkoe slovo* was shut down on 26 October, although it was permitted to reopen on 8 November and for a time continued its criticism of the Bolsheviks.[48] In a November feuilleton, for example, Teffi referred ironically to positive developments under the new government, such as a decrease in crime: "There have been fewer robberies lately [...] This can be explained by the fact that this business [...] has been monopolized by the government."[49]

Such criticism could not be tolerated for long, and in late November *Russkoe slovo* and other unfriendly periodicals were permanently shut down. But then in January 1918, journalists from *Russkoe slovo*, including Teffi, opened another newspaper, called *Novoe slovo* (New word). When it was closed 2 April, the determined staff opened yet another paper, *Nashe slovo* (Our word) on 11 April, which lasted until 6 July.[50]

There were other valiant attempts to maintain an independent press during the first half of 1918. Teffi's *Yesterday*, made up of some of her recent feuilletons and stories, came out at that time, and *Novyi Satirikon* eked out its existence until August, with Teffi's works appearing there until the very end. The magazine's satire, to be sure, became milder, mostly focusing on some of the absurdities attendant upon social upheaval. Thus, in "A Future Day," Teffi imagines the changes in one noble household. The former carter, Terenty, is master and the old owners – a woman doctor and a botany professor – servants. A messenger (himself a former vice admiral) comes and informs Terenty that he is supposed to give a lecture at the university:

> "What kind o' lecture?"
>> "It says it's at the Philology Department."
>> "Whi-ich?"
>> "Philology."
>> "Phalala, phalala – you yourself are phalala."[51]

Despite his bewilderment Terenty goes to the university and addresses his audience:

> Comrade universities. Now, I used to be a carter, and now I'm gabbin' about phalala. Because, you see, you need higher education. And we can't let a *burzhui* [slang for bourgeois] get near you. He'll teach you such things you can't even pronounce.

CIVIL WAR

In a March 1918 feuilleton, Teffi reflected on the disintegration of the Russian Empire as civil war spread throughout its vast expanse. She adapted a favorite image – the Devil twirling his helpless victims, only now the evil spirit was manipulating not just one or a few individuals, but the Russian Empire:

> You look at the map and are astounded [...] for some reason Russia came into being, stuck together [...]
>
> And suddenly some wily devil poked his stick somewhere near Moscow and began spinning Russia like a whirlwind top.
>
> "Whee-ee-ee!"
>
> The pieces are flying in various directions like sparks.
>
> The Crimea! The Caucasus! Poland! Little Russia! Lithuania! Finland! The Baltic region! Siberia! Kazan! Whee-ee-ee! More! More! Cities! Seas! Kingdoms! Principalities! Free lands! More! More! Soon only the stick will remain...[52]

The capital was not doing well either, for ever more severe shortages were making life intolerable. "It's wretched, it's cold," wrote Teffi during the winter of 1917–18. "They provide electricity for only five hours a day. There's no firewood."[53] During that terribly harsh winter the food shortage was especially acute, with flour so scarce that the bread ration was down to four to six ounces a day.[54] Hunger gave rise to a kind of psychosis, Teffi wrote in June: "People eat with horror, with despair. They've stopped stocking up [...] People simply eat right here, on the spot, as much as a person can get down."[55]

After the Bolsheviks moved the capital to Moscow in the spring matters grew even worse – no doubt an important factor in Teffi's decision to leave Petrograd for Moscow.[56] (A May 1918 issue of *Rampa i zhizn'* noted her arrival "from hungry Petersburg" and her delight at "Moscow's bread."[57]) Yet the perilous political climate was surely an even greater factor. An incident that occurred at the very beginning of 1918 signaled Teffi's precarious position: an actress who performed works by her and Averchenko on New Year's Day was warned that "if she dared read stories offending the present government, she would be summoned to Smolny [the Bolshevik headquarters] and the theater would be closed."[58] She was arrested the following day and warned after a lengthy interrogation that "she must not dare 'to earn her bread through slander of the people's government.'" (She was subsequently released.)

In a feuilleton written while still in Petrograd, Teffi summed up the appalling state of the formerly glittering capital: "We live in a dead city [...] On the streets are the corpses of horses, dogs, and quite frequently people [...] At night dark, frightened figures steal up to the horse corpses and carve out pieces of meat."[59] She talks of arrests: "Someone released from a Petrograd prison tells about executions [...] Nobody knows anything for certain, but in the dead city they are always talking about death and always believe in it."[60] Later, when in Kiev in October 1918, Teffi described in greater detail the terror gripping Petrograd. She quotes a typical conversation between two acquaintances who meet on the street:

"He's arrested, arrested. It's not known where…"
   "They've been executed, both of them…"
   "It's said they were tortured… shhh… Somebody's listening in."
And suddenly his face adopts an unnatural, carefree expression and his trembling lips whistle "Pretty Girls of the Cabaret." What does it mean?
   It means that he had to step over a thin stream of blood coming out from below a closed gate.[61]

In contrast to Petrograd, "Moscow is still alive," Teffi wrote in the same Kiev feuilleton, although her description makes it sound as if it was suffering its death agonies:

Mad motor cars race, with a whistle and a whoop. Rifle shots enliven the black silence of nocturnal streets. Moscow is being robbed and stabbed. It's still alive, still protesting, jerking its legs, and pressing a foreign passport to its heart.

Moscow offered Teffi a reunion with her daughter Gulya (Yelena) – the first evidence of contact between the two since Gulya's childhood. *Rampa i zhizn'* reported that mother and daughter appeared together in May at the premiere of the Bat: "During the intermissions the old Moscow journalists tried in vain to amuse [Teffi], while the young ones gave their attention to one of the creations of the talented writer – her young daughter Yelena Buchinskaya."[62] The article is accompanied by a photograph with the caption: "Yelena Buchinskaya (creator of word-eurhythmia)." By this time Gulya had completed her training in Warsaw and had already been on the stage for a few years.[63] During the 1915–16 season she joined the Polish Theater in Moscow, where, it seems, she developed ties with the futurists and studied eurhythmia (an art form based on gesture, defined by its founder, the theosophist Rudolf Steiner, as "visible music, visible speech").[64] In late 1918, Gulya performed at the Domino Café in Moscow, "dancing to […] the languid, oriental declamation" of "the unbalanced, unstrung, but […] handsome Armenian, Alexander Kusikov."[65] At some point thereafter Gulya left Moscow, and Teffi's friend, the writer Sergei Gorny (pseudonym of Alexander Otsup, 1882–1949), recalled many years later that he "often met your Gulka in Kharkov, which was then occupied by the Whites."[66] The Polish theatrical encyclopedia confirms that she did appear in a futurist cabaret in Kharkov. She then moved south to Constantinople, where she played in a Russian cabaret, and by 1922 had joined her sister and father in Poland, where she had a stellar theatrical and film career.

Teffi also contributed to Moscow's theatrical life with an operetta, *Catherine II* – co-authored by Lolo with music borrowed from Offenbach.[67] Produced in August 1918, it was a great success, Teffi later wrote, and even influenced the development of Soviet musical theater, since it revealed operetta's potential as satire to Vladimir Nemirovich-Danchenko (1858–1943), co-director of the Moscow Art Theater and founder of several musical theaters.[68] Teffi's old artistic life, however, could not go on for much longer, given the political situation. In *Memories*, a darkly comic depiction of her final months in Russia and her treacherous path to exile, she writes of a short trip to Petrograd (probably in late August) and an encounter there with her "young friend Lyonya Kannegisser," who insisted they meet on "neutral territory."[69] She considered this a "boyish pose," and only on 30 August, after he assassinated M. S. Uritsky, chief of the Petrograd Cheka (secret police), did she realize the deadly seriousness of his words.

When Teffi returned to Moscow people were still caught up in the social and cultural whirl: "Along the black nocturnal streets, where passers-by were strangled and robbed, we ran to hear the operetta, *Silva*, or listened to young poets reading their own works and one another's, howling with hungry voices, in shabby cafés packed with an audience in torn overcoats that smelled like wet dogs."[70] (Very likely among the cafés was the Domino, where Gulya was performing.) Signs of danger were unmistakable, however. Many people – whether actively critical of the Bolsheviks or simply because of class origin – have mysteriously vanished, "and it was difficult to find out where [someone] was: in Kiev? Or there, from where he will not return?" Others "floated out of the fog, whirled about, and faded into the fog."[71] Among the latter, it seems, was Teffi's husband, Dmitry Shcherbakov, since she tells the same story as in her memoir of Repin about her stolen portrait ending up among the icons in a peasant hut.

Given the alarming situation, Teffi decided it would be best to absent herself from Moscow for a while, and an opportunity arose in the person of an "entrepreneur" from Odessa who went by the pseudonym Guskin, because of his "terribly difficult" (Jewish) surname.[72] Guskin, whose Odessan turns of phrase and malapropisms provide comic relief in the dark civil war narrative, urges Teffi to go with him on a reading tour to Kiev and Odessa. In Moscow bread will soon disappear, he warns, but in Ukraine "the sun is shining, you read a story or two, you take the money, you buy butter, ham, you're all filled up and sit in a café." Any doubts she had about this dubious character are quelled by Averchenko, who is going on tour to Kiev "with some other pseudonym." The two *Satirikon* stars, together with two actresses in Averchenko's entourage, decide to travel together.

Within a few weeks the party sets off through blood-soaked Russia and finally approach the Ukrainian border, where they have their most chilling encounter, with the local "commissar of the arts."[73] The man, whom Teffi dubs Robespierre, is wearing an "enormous, splendid beaver coat" – the blood-encrusted bullet hole in the back confirming that it was pilfered from one of his victims. He is surrounded by an equally sinister suite, its most frightening member an ordinary looking young woman, but with "no eyes, no brows, no mouth."[74] This barely human creature recalls the disturbing depictions of the underclass in Teffi's earliest fiction, but with a crucial difference: revolution has upended the social order, and now it is she whom "everybody obeys. She herself carries out searches, she herself judges, she herself shoots."[75]

Guskin, practicing his usual wiles, succeeds in extricating his charges from Robespierre's grip, and at last they managed to cross into Ukraine. The first sight of Kiev, still occupied by the Germans in accordance with the Brest-Litovsk Treaty, was overwhelming: "The whole world (Kievan) is full, overloaded with edibles [...] Stores are crammed with ham, sausage, turkeys, stuffed suckling pigs. And on the streets, against the background of the stuffed suckling pigs, are *tout Moscou et tout Petersbourg*."[76] A second glance, however, is more disquieting: "The first impression – a holiday. The second – a [railroad] station, a terminal right before the third bell. The hubbub is too anxious, too voracious for a joyous holiday. There is alarm and fear."[77]

The cultural life of Kiev was indeed at fever pitch, as Teffi learned from a former staff member of *Russkoe slovo* whom she ran into: "The city has gone crazy! Just open the newspapers – the best names from the capitals! In the theaters the best artistic forces [...] They're expecting new plays from you. *Kievskaia mysl'* (Kievan thought) wants to invite you to join their staff."[78] After amicably ending her association with Guskin, Teffi did begin writing for the newspaper and for other Kievan periodicals. She also took an active part in the theatrical life, she and Lolo (who soon turned up) reviving *Catherine II* and collaborating on a second play, *If You Don't Apply Grease, You Won't Get Going* (*Ne podmazhesh' – ne poedesh'*).[79]

Because Kiev was so packed with refugees, Teffi had to stay at first with friends of one of the actresses in her Moscow party. She then managed to get a room at the François Hotel, which was ramshackle, her room terribly drafty, and Teffi at once correctly prophesied (or so she writes): "I will get the Spanish flu with complications in my lungs."[80] By the time she recovered, toward the end of November, she found that the mood in Kiev had changed dramatically. Rumors were spreading about the approach of Ukrainian nationalist forces, led by Simon Petlyura, and people "began to talk about Odessa."[81] Refugees kept streaming in, however, among them the actress Tamara Oksinskaya, who was to be Teffi's landlady during her final years.

Petlyura entered Kiev in the middle of December 1918, at which time the Germans, defeated in the world war, beat a hasty retreat. In late January 1919, the Bolsheviks were approaching and the Russian refugees began to flee. Teffi wrote in what was apparently her last Kiev feuilleton: "Petersburg–Moscow mugs have disappeared. Presses are closing. Beauty salons are emptying out. As if swept off by the wind they have flown down the globe. Odessa! Constantinople! Princes' Islands!"[82] In all probability Teffi left Kiev right before the retreat of Petlyura's forces on 2 February. She describes the turmoil at the railroad station at her departure, the "people running and rushing about in panic," and later, as the train was making its halting way to Odessa, the shooting outside the windows.[83]

In Odessa Teffi found the same people as in Kiev, caught up in the same feverish whirl, despite the approaching Bolsheviks and the epidemic of robberies by Odessa's notorious bandits:

Theaters, clubs, restaurants were filled all night [...]

In the morning, stupefied by wine, gambling, and cigar smoke, bankers and owners of sugar refineries came out of their clubs and winced at the sun with enflamed eyelids. And for a long time they were followed by the heavy, hungry eyes of shady types from Moldavanka, who were picking up scraps and leftovers by entranceways, digging into nut shells and sausage skins.[84]

Teffi made the acquaintance of the province's "young, gray-eyed governor, Grishin-Almazov," who kindly offered her a "wonderful room" in the London Hotel.[85] Each day at six o'clock she invited over old friends and new acquaintances, and recalls in particular the "dear faces [...] reflected in the mirror over the fireplace: the dry, pedigreed [face] of Ivan Bunin, his wife's profile, like a pale cameo, and the brigand Alyosha [Alexei] Tolstoy and his lyrical wife, Natasha Krandievskaya, and Sergei Gorny, and Lolo, and Nilus, and Pankratov."[86] Vera Bunina (1881–1961), who was apparently among the new acquaintances, left a description of her hostess:

> She gives the impression of being a very talented woman. She sang [...] her little songs [...] very well [...] She dressed in such a way that one was first struck by her fur, the brightness of her silk jacket [*kofta*], her puffed-up hair, and then, at long last, her face.[87]

Vera and her husband, Ivan Bunin (1870–1953) – one of the best-known of the writers who left Russia after the revolution, whose consummately wrought poetry and prose eschewed modernism in favor of the classic Russian realist tradition – soon became one of Teffi's best friends.

The future Soviet writer Yury Olesha (1899–1960), then an aspiring young poet, offers another view of Teffi in Odessa, which reveals that she and her circle continued their love of pose so prevalent in Russia's artistic circles before the revolution. He writes of his encounter with Alexei Tolstoy in 1918 (in fact, it must have been 1919), accompanied by a mustachioed man whom he addressed as Amari but who turned out to be Teffi, whose "superb [...] stories we know by heart."[88] The poet Maximilian Voloshin (1877–1932), who also appeared in Odessa that spring, seemed at first to be role-playing as well, with his "thick, square beard, tight curls, [...] round beret, flowing cape, short pants, and gaiters."[89] His purpose, however, was deadly serious, for his poetry declamations at government offices were meant to secure freedom for those caught up in the civil war killing machine. In his effort to rescue the poetess Yelizaveta Kuzmina-Karavayeva (1891–1945), later known as Mother Maria, one of the towering figures of the Russian emigration, Voloshin enlisted Teffi, who interceded with the governor and helped win her freedom.

Teffi's most poignant encounter in Odessa was with a man she identifies as her "old friend M.," who had crossed the vast Russian Empire from Vladivostok to Odessa as a courier for the White leader Admiral Kolchak.[90] Since the beginning of the war, she writes, this "profoundly civilian man, a landowner," had "served in the army [...] After the revolution he went to his estate and when his native town was besieged by Bolsheviks, was chosen dictator."[91] M. told her in a self-deprecating tone about his further adventures on the Volga:

You remember about five years ago a fortune-teller said that not long before my death I would serve in the navy. And everyone laughed at me: a big, fat [fellow], and he'll put on a cap with ribbons. Well, it came true. I'm going to Paris now, and then via America to Vladivostok, back to Kolchak.[92]

Teffi writes that he very much wanted to take her with him, but because of the terrible weather and friends' assurances that they would take care of her, she refused. M. departed, and a month later died in Paris.

The details Teffi gives of M.'s life coincide with the White Army documents concerning her husband, Shcherbakov. In *Memories* she writes that when she arrived in Paris, the Russian consul gave her what remained of M.'s belongings: a ring with a black opal. An "adventurer," she was told, had "robbed M. bare," but "didn't dare touch the black opal."[93] She recalls that she and M. had both bought black opals from the artist Alexander Yakovlev, and blames M.'s stone for the many convulsions that rocked his once-peaceful life and had "enveloped [her life] in its black fire."[94] Most striking is Teffi's inclusion among the calamities brought on by war and revolution of his "absurd [*nelepaia*] marriage" – of course, giving no clue that the marriage was to herself.

As spring approached, Teffi writes, Odessa was swept by a surge of optimism, for people were expecting allied reinforcements to join the French division already in the city. Buoyed by the positive mood, writers began to set up some of the institutions that defined their pre-revolutionary life, and a newspaper, *Nashe slovo*, began to appear around the middle of March. Its "mood," Teffi recalls, was "militant and cheerful," but her contribution was in "total dissonance."[95] She expressed her deep misgivings in "On the Cliff of Gergesenes," drawing a parallel between the swine in the Gospel story (Matt. 8:28–32), who, possessed by devils, fling themselves off a cliff, and the "rabid swine" among the refugees in Odessa, "speculators, former secret police, former Black Hundreds, and other former [...] scoundrels."[96] She conjectures that just as there must have been "meek, frightened sheep" at Gergesenes, so there are in Odessa, but the "rabid" and "weak" are running for different reasons: "the rabid herd is running from the Bolshevik truth, from the principles of socialism, from equality and justice, while the meek and frightened [are running] from the falsehood, from the black Bolshevik practice, from terror, injustice, and violence."[97] Even now Teffi believed in a "Bolshevik truth," perverted by their "black practice."

In her final Odessa feuilleton, "The Last Breakfast," published on 20 March 1919, Teffi compares "merrymaking Odessa" to a convict savoring his last meal before execution: "Clubs and restaurants are filled to the hilt. They're devouring chicken at eighty rubles a drumstick. They're blowing their 'last little million' on *chemin-de-fer*. Bloated stomachs, bleary eyes, and a visa all the way to the Krokotokatu Islands […] Cold, dreary days. Eerie nights."[98] The end of Teffi's Odessan life was indeed near. On 23 March she learned that the French were abandoning the city, and that those who had fled all the way "down the map from the north" were now frantically preparing to run still further, across the border to Turkey.[99] Among those who had vanished were "friends" who had assured her that they would look after her, and only at the last minute – to the sound of approaching gunfire – did "engineer V" appear (Sergei Gorny, an engineer by profession), himself abandoned by friends.[100] He had two passes for a ship, the *Shilka*, headed for Vladivostok, and terrified of traveling alone, begged Teffi to accompany him, posing as his wife.

The small overcrowded ship turned out to be a highly unsuitable means of escape, since its command had disassembled the engine and abandoned the vessel. Furthermore, there was no food or coal, and provisions had to be commandeered at gunpoint from another ship. Since the *Shilka* had no work-ers to load the coal, some of the passengers – "elegant young men in foppish suits" – were recruited to perform the menial job.[101] Although they took it at first as a joke, they not only hauled the coal, but "entered into the role," adopting the stevedores' language and singing their songs. Teffi compares the sight to theatrical experiments of the recent past, except in this case it was not a performance: life itself forced the actors to play the role, as it would compel them again and again to reinvent themselves in emigration.

While on the *Shilka*, Teffi observed other young men whose prospects were far darker. There were the young officers who boarded the ship in Sevastopol – "handsome, smartly dressed boys [who] were merrily trading remarks […] singing French songs," and who would soon face death just as "smartly. Bravely and merrily."[102] And there was the stoker, who revealed during a night-time conversation that he was actually a St. Petersburg youth who had visited Teffi's apartment, where they "talked about gems, about the yellow sapphire," but who was now planning to fight the Bolsheviks.[103] The stoker brought back to Teffi the vanished evenings in St. Petersburg: "The sultry, nervous ladies, refined young men. The table adorned with white lilacs." Then she thought of what was awaiting the boy, how he would "press his weary shoulder to the stone wall of a black cellar and close his eyes…"[104]

While the ship was docked in Novorossisk, Teffi traveled to Ekaterinodar (now Krasnodar) to attend a performance of her works. On the train she observed other young men – soldiers from the front, "exhausted, filthy, tormented," who, in contrast to the jolly officers, laid bare the true, horrifying face of war.[105] The cry of one of the soldiers that night is testimony to their emotional deadness: "Since 1914 I've been tormented, tormented, and now I've... died."[106] The contrast between these living corpses and the military elite Teffi encountered in Ekaterinodar – the last bastion of imperial pomp – is striking. That evening at the theater the glitter – "the embroidery on the uniforms, the gold and silver of the galloons" – was on full display.[107] At the end of the performance, the author came out for a bow: "My last bow to the Russian public on Russian soil," Teffi comments. This gathering was also a "last bow" for the tsarist elite, soon to vanish forever from Russia.

Teffi conjures up a final chilling image, emblematic of the vanished bohemian world. As her train approached the resort of Kislovodsk, she spied "a scrap of rope [...] It is a gallows."[108] This is where they hanged the "well-known female anarchist G.," whom Teffi remembered from earlier days: "Beautiful, young, bold, merry, well dressed" – one of those anarchists who seemed like "masquerading braggarts. Nobody took them seriously."[109] But revolution played its tragic trick and killed G. in good earnest: she "stood right here, looked, squinting, at her last sun and smoked her last cigarette. Then she flung away the butt and calmly threw the taut noose around her neck."[110]

Teffi concludes her memoir with a comment on literature and life, remarking that writers are often criticized for their unsatisfactory endings, but in this regard are only imitating life. She had planned to remain on the *Shilka* until Vladivostok, where she would rejoin M., but the high command refused to grant the little ship permission to make the hazardous voyage. Therefore, she had two choices: remain in strife-torn Russia or cross the border. She took the latter path, assured by people: "You'll return to your homeland by spring."[111] She thought: "A marvelous word – spring. A marvelous word – homeland." She did not return to Russia in the spring, of course, but – a bad ending, indeed! – was fated to live out the rest of her life in exile.

6

MIGRATION

1919–24

STAMBOUL

Constantinople was the first foreign stop for Teffi and others who had fled southward until they reached Russia's watery southern border. When she arrived in the late summer or early fall of 1919, conditions were terrible after the Ottoman Empire's loss in World War I, the country lacking the resources to house and feed the hordes of penniless and traumatized Russians who swept onto its shore. Teffi remembered how she arrived in Constantinople "without possessions and without money" and was housed with some of her compatriots in an empty school: "The cold was terrible [...] Rain, dampness. Life was hungry [*Zhili golodnovato*]."[1] She recalls that one day, when "they were drinking tea without sugar and gnawing on stale bagels," they felt that they had reached "rock bottom," but then decided the bottom was not so bad: "Hot tea, easy-going chitchat. Like English five-o'clock tea."

In an early essay Teffi wrote about other hardships she faced in Constantinople. For one thing, although there were money changers on every block, they were unwilling to accept Russian currency: "What state stands behind your bank-note?" they asked. "Russia? Ha-ha!"[2] And the apartment situation was appalling. Teffi recreates a typical conversation with a landlady: "'Do you want to hang your picture on that nail?' she asked. 'I consider it my duty to warn you that it's not a nail, but a bedbug.'" The bug, it turned out, was but one of a multitude: "The small corner sofa – an essential accessory of a Constantinople room – is so densely stuffed with various insects that they successfully replace springs."[3]

Nevertheless Teffi, ever fascinated by the East, was drawn to Constantinople, although the city did take getting used to: "At first it seems too bright, pungent, achingly sharp," she wrote. "Its fruit is too sweet, its *shashlyk*, turning on mechanical spits, is too succulent, its hard candies on peddlers' trays too brightly colored; the peddlers shout too loudly, the smell of its fragrant grasses is too pungent." But once "you get used to it," she added, "the pungency and brightness and loudness, all will convey one joyous whole – Stamboul."[4] The relief Teffi felt after her escape from the dangers and deprivations of civil war is palpable, for here a "soul-rending scream" at six in the morning was simply the "bagel vendor" selling his goods.[5] And once outside, she was immersed in a world of plenty, of "fruit, tomatoes, grapes, pastries, shrimp, rolls, brooms, boot brushes, halva, shoes – everything to gladden a person, inside and out."

It is not known how Teffi survived in Constantinople with apparently little more than the clothes on her back. Many relief organizations sprang up there, and perhaps she received aid from one or more of them.[6] Or it may be that acquaintances helped her and also facilitated her path to France. In any case, by the first days of 1920 Teffi had made her way to Paris.

PARIS: 1920–2

Because of its devastating losses during World War I, France actively recruited Russian refugees to work in its factories and mines.[7] Estimates of the number who settled there vary greatly, but most place the total in the hundreds of thousands, with about 40,000 living in Paris alone by 1930. The émigrés were a diverse group, the stereotypical penniless but feckless White Russian aristocrat but a part of the mix. The largest segment, for obvious reasons, consisted of former military men, but there were also many from the lesser nobility and the urban middle class, as well as skilled workers and those who lived off the land (including Cossacks). The political spectrum was also very broad, ranging from unrepentant monarchists to liberal Kadets, revolutionary SRs, and Mensheviks. And, of course, Russian writers and artists were drawn to Paris, which from the earliest days became one of the main cultural centers of the Russian emigration, its only rival Berlin.[8]

Teffi must have felt relief upon arriving in Paris after the chaos and destruction of civil war. She began at once to take part in the new émigré cultural life, making contact with literary and artistic acquaintances who were already planting the seeds of Russian culture abroad. Two of her poems were published in February 1920, in the second (and last) issue of *Griadushchaia Rossiia* (Russia of the future), the first émigré literary journal.[9] Soon after, in February or early March, she hosted what humorist Don-Aminado (1888–1957) claims was the first émigré salon in Paris in her small room in the Hôtel Vignon, near the Madeleine Church. Among the guests was the writer and artist Alexander Koiransky (1884–1968), who told an anecdote about a retired general who came to the Place de la Concorde, looked around, and said, in an untranslatable play of French and Russian: "This is all good, even very good but… *que faire? Fer-to ke?*" (In Clare Kitson's translation: "But, well… *que faire?* What is to be done? Fair's fair, but *que* bloody *faire* with it all?"[10]) Teffi, enchanted, exclaimed: "My dear, make me a present [of it]!" to which the gallant Koiransky replied: "I would consider it an honor! Take the general and my heart in the bargain!"[11] Teffi used the generous gift in "Ke fer?" published on 27 April 1920, in the first issue of the newspaper *Poslednie novosti* (The latest news). The piece has remained Teffi's most famous work, the general's remark, as Don-Aminado wrote, becoming "a proverb, a constant refrain of émigré life."[12]

Teffi later recalled quite fondly the Paris of 1920 and 1921, when exile was still a novelty and, as many assumed, only temporary: "Although life was penniless, it was turbulent [*burnaia*] and interesting."[13] She formed close ties with a number of well-known writers, among them the Bunins, who arrived in Paris at the end of March 1920, and stayed at first in the spacious apartment of the poet Mikhail Tsetlin (1882–1945) and his wife Maria (1882–1976) – both from wealthy Jewish families and with a radical past, but by then adamantly anti-Bolshevik. They became the "literary center" of Russian Paris, their apartment a place where writers "often met, […] read our new works."[14]

There were also more informal get-togethers in one or another of the writers' modest flats. Teffi was an especially frequent visitor at the house on Rue Raynouard where the Bunins had moved by July 1920, joining the Tolstoys and Balmonts. Bunina's diary entry for 24 April 1921 captures the warm, informal relations that existed among the friends: when she arrived home that day she "found Yan [her pet name for her husband], still in his robe, conversing with Natasha [Tolstoy's wife, the poet Natalya Krandievskaya-Tolstaya, 1888–1963] and Teffi. They had come to get us for dinner at a restaurant, where Landau [the writer Mark Aldanov, 1886–1957] would also be."[15] At times Teffi herself played hostess in her hotel room, as in early 1921, when she invited the Bunins to join her and an eminent guest from Berlin, V. D. Nabokov (1870–1922), father of the writer.[16]

Aside from purely social visits at Rue Raynouard, Teffi attended meetings of the Guild of Poets, founded in mid-July 1920. Chaired by Bunin, with meetings often held in the Tolstoys' apartment, the Guild had as its mission "bringing together the Russian poets in France" and arranging "public lectures, the publication of a journal, etc."[17] One collection, which included Teffi's 1915 poem "Fedosya," did come out later in 1920, but the Guild, like a number of other Russian publications and cultural endeavors of 1920 and 1921, proved ephemeral.[18] Exceptions were two periodicals that became mainstays of the Russian diaspora: the newspaper *Poslednie novosti*, edited by the prominent Kadet Pavel Milyukov, and the journal *Sovremennye zapiski* (Contemporary annals), founded by a group of SRs. Both survived until the German occupation of Paris in 1940.

Two important writers' organizations also trace their origins to these early days: the Union of Russian Writers and Journalists in Paris, among whose goals were the protection of authorial rights and financial aid to needy members, and the Committee to Aid Russian Writers and Scholars in France.[19] To raise money, the groups adopted the old Russian tradition of holding benefit "evenings," at one of the earliest of which (30 May 1920) Teffi, Bunin, and Tolstoy read their works.[20] Humorists were often featured, as at the "Literary Evening Named '*Que faire?*'" (13 May 1921), at which Teffi, Alexander Yablonovsky, and Don-Aminado debated that urgent question, and the "Evening of Terrific [*strashnykh*] Optimists," when, on New Year's Eve 1921, the trio again joined forces.[21]

Publishing houses also began to appear in Paris and other émigré centers. By late 1920 Yevgeny Lyatsky (1868–1942), formerly a St. Petersburg literature professor, founded Severnye ogni (Northern lights) Press in Stockholm, and Teffi promptly contacted him about putting out a book of hers. When he proposed a very small volume, she offered two books instead, explaining that otherwise "materially it turns out to be a very meager enterprise."[22] Lyatsky agreed, and *The Black Iris* and *The Way We Lived* – both composed of works previously published in Russia – appeared the following year.[23] In 1921 several other collections by Teffi came out in various émigré centers – the most significant *A Quiet Backwater*, consisting primarily of stories from *The Lifeless Beast*, published in Paris.[24]

Teffi's many activities during her first couple of years in Paris might leave the impression that she was quickly adjusting to life in exile, but her writings and her correspondence tell a different story. Her feuilletons and stories, which came out with astonishing frequency in *Poslednie novosti* in 1920 – many collected in her 1923 book *The Lynx* – express in acute form the homesickness she shared with her fellow refugees. In "Nostalgia" she writes:

> Our refugees arrive, emaciated, blackened from hunger and fear, eat their fill, calm down, look around, as if to get their new lives on track,

and suddenly fade. Their eyes grow dim, their listless arms droop, and their soul withers – their soul, turned to the east.[25]

When Teffi herself looked east, what she saw was chaos, the total annihilation of the social structure she had earlier mocked but now viewed as essential for survival:

> The everyday [byt] – the flesh of our lives – has died. Only chaos remains, and our spirit soars over the abyss. How can you live that way – over an abyss? It's absolutely impossible, you know. If you don't crash down today you will tomorrow.[26]

If Teffi saw bloody death reigning in revolutionary Russia, she found spiritual death among the exiles. "We don't believe in anything," she writes in "Nostalgia," "don't expect anything, don't want anything. We have died. We feared a Bolshevik death – and have met our death here." In "Raw Material" she observes the deadness among Russian artists and intellectuals:

> People will soon stop talking about Russian art, Russian literature – especially Russian literature [...] Nobody is able to work [...]
> They say, "Remember – I wrote... Remember – I said..." They're remembering their living life in this one here, beyond the grave.[27]

The double image of death in the early feuilletons – the spiritual death of the refugees and the physical death of those they left behind – is hardly surprising, given the circumstances. What is striking is the degree to which the vision of death in life conforms to Teffi's pre-émigré works (both her serious poetry and her comic prose). Exile, moreover, only intensified her earlier perception of life's meaninglessness. In her portrayal of emerging émigré society in "Ke fer?" the narrator, adopting the tone of a dispassionate scientist, describes *Leryussy* (*les russes*) as a tribe whose customs even defy scientific laws: "We, the so-called *Leryussy*, live the strangest lives [...] We do not hold together through mutual attraction, like the planetary system, for instance, but – contrary to the laws of physics – through mutual repulsion."[28] In this world not only are natural laws reversed; so are the meanings of words:

> *Leryussy* [...] are distinctly divided into two categories: those selling Russia and those saving it.

The sellers enjoy themselves [*zhivut veselo*]. They go to the theater, dance the foxtrot, keep Russian cooks, eat Russian borsht, and regale those who are saving Russia [...]

The saviors present a different picture: they scamper about day and night, writhe in the snares of political intrigues, travel somewhere, and unmask one another.

They regard the "sellers" good-naturedly and take money from them for the salvation of Russia. They hate one another with a white-hot hatred.[29]

The pose and deceit earlier practiced by Teffi's comic characters also continue – indeed, prove all the more necessary for exiles, forced to fashion themselves anew. The process can be seen in the 1920 story "Two Meetings." The first meeting takes place at a seedy little seaside house, called, incongruously, the Grand European Hotel, where Andrei Nikolayevich, lately a heart-throb and officer of a "famous drunken regiment", encounters Irina Petrovna, formerly a governor's wife.[30] Out of habit he engages in flirtatious banter, but then "gave a start [...] looked around at the dirty sand, rags, tin cans, and rusty ivy, and said [...]: 'It's finished! Russia has died.'"[31] By the time of the pair's second meeting, on the Rue de la Paix, however, Andrei is transformed: elegantly dressed, he announces his "exalted" mission: "To build young Russia with these hands."[32] He has thus become one of the "saviors," although his absurd task – "the electrification of waterfalls in the Warsaw region" – undercuts his lofty speech.[33]

Like Andrei, albeit in less extreme form, ordinary émigrés need to mask their impoverished lives. Even so simple an activity as inviting friends over for tea requires deception. "If you are a true refugee and live in one room," Teffi advises her readers, "you must without fail give your premises an elegant look: throw out the dried-out cherry pits that are stuck in your ashtray [...] You can conceal the wash basin under a carelessly unfolded Japanese fan."[34] To lend polish to one's conversation, one shouldn't talk about everyday cares, but "about the opera or apparel. Only you definitely mustn't tell the truth: 'I don't go to the opera – I don't have the money.'" Instead you should raise everything to a higher plane and declare: "The French don't even understand Tchaikovsky," or: "Paquin is repeating himself!"[35]

If in emigration the deadly social world of Teffi's early stories has been transferred to Paris, the locus of the longed-for "other" has shifted from some unattainable, transcendant sphere to her lost homeland. In "Nostalgia" the essence of Russianness is embodied in the endearing emotionality of the Russian peasant:

> Every peasant woman among us knows – if there is great sorrow and you need to lament a little – go to the forest, embrace a birch tree, strongly, with both arms, press it to your breast, and rock with it […] with our own, white, Russian birch!
> But just try that here.
> *"Allons au Bois de Boulogne embrasser le bouleau!"*
> Translate the Russian soul into French… What? Did it cheer you up?[36]

The poem "Homesickness" is a rare instance when Teffi indulges in self-revelation. She confesses that she has "also shed tears over our Russian birch tree," longs to see again a wily Russian peasant, the Moscow Kremlin, Lobnoe Mesto (execution place) in Red Square. Her nostalgia has now reached such a peak, she concludes, that to relieve it she needs the birch, the peasant, and Lobnoe Mesto "all together!"[37]

After Teffi's outpouring between April and December 1920, her name almost entirely disappeared from the pages of émigré newspapers during the next two years. The political figure and journalist Grigory Aleksinsky (1879–1967) recalled many years later that she was unable to write due to her extreme homesickness.[38] He suggested that she write poetry, and some of her verse appeared in 1921 in the Prague weekly he was publishing, *Ogni* (Fires).[39] She also published several poems and serious stories in 1921 and 1922 in the Berlin journal *Zhar-ptitsa* (Firebird), later included in *Passiflora* and *Twilit Day*.

Teffi's situation grew yet more critical when she fell seriously ill during the summer of 1921. In July she wrote Bunina from the health resort Contrexéville, in the Vosges Mountains, complaining of her "truly terrible condition," and on 9 August Bunina noted in her diary that "Teffi has been taken to Paris and placed in a city hospital […] If it has come to a hospital it means she has no money. Is it possible that her rich friends can't do anything for her?"[40] The illness, which turned out to be typhus, did indeed leave Teffi penniless, and in July she asked Bunina to arrange for her to receive 700 francs from the Committee to Aid Russian Writers and Scholars (of which Bunina was a member), then in September requested 2,000 francs more, in part to repay the publisher Tikhon Polner (1864–1935), who had helped defray her hospital costs.[41] Teffi apparently remained in need, since on 4 February 1922 the Tsetlins held a benefit concert for her with the participation of French performers, including the famous music hall singer Mistinguette.[42]

GERMANY: 1922–3

During the early years of exile, many artists and intellectuals, tormented by the loss of their homeland, were driven by a deep-seated restlessness to wander from one European country to another, and Teffi was no exception. Germany proved most attractive because of the low cost of living for those with hard currency. While Berlin was the main Russian center, many residents of France flocked to Wiesbaden, in the Rhineland, since it was occupied by the Allied powers until 1929 and they could enter without a visa.[43] Teffi took advantage of this situation, and from approximately March to November 1922 spent the better part of her time in the city.[44] Don-Aminado described her public demeanor to Bunin that July: "Teffi is in Wiesbaden, singing to her guitar, dressed all in white."[45] In a couple of letters to Bunina, Vera Ilnarskaya gossiped about Teffi's "affairs of the heart": Teffi's "Paris love affair [*roman*] – Dr. Goldenstein – arrived recently, and we kept expecting a duel with her Wiesbaden affair, but the doctor preferred to retreat with a broken heart."[46] Another lovelorn Parisian, the dramatist and journalist Vladimir Binshtok (1868–1933), also turned up, and organized a Teffi evening with money from the Committee to Aid Russian Writers and Scholars. When Ilnarskaya asked about help for her husband, Lolo, Teffi told her that the committee gave money "only for an operation, a funeral, or to those with whom Binshtok is enamored." The distraught Ilnarskaya asked Bunina whether this was true or "was Teffinka lying, as usual?" In a second letter, she described Teffi's Wiesbaden romance:

> Teffi has recovered: she jumps around like a she-goat, has gotten herself an admirer – a general, not too young, it's true, but on the other hand he's one of the directors of the Voluntary Fleet [*Dobrovol'nyi flot* – the Soviet shipping agency]: that means he has money – they're selling Russian ships! That gives him the chance to treat her lavishly [*shikarno*] [...] Good for Teffinka, she doesn't miss a beat here, and Binshtok is working [for her] in Paris.[47]

As so often, however, Teffi's surface frivolity concealed her inner distress. Her correspondence reveals her anxiety about her daughters in Poland, and she must have been worried about her brother, Nikolai, who had not yet returned from Siberia, where he went in February 1919 (after the dissolution of the Russian Expeditionary Force in France) to aid Kolchak.[48] (He was to return to France in the fall of 1922.) But it was the fate of Teffi's beloved sister Lena that caused her the deepest anguish. In a letter to her old St. Petersburg acquaintance Akim Volynsky (now chair of the Petrograd Division of the Union of Writers), she made a "fervent plea" for him to help her sister, who was "living very, very badly." If she could be "settled in a dormitory and receive a ration," she added, "she would be saved."[49]

Teffi must have received a devastating response, for soon afterward she wrote Bunina that her "favorite sister, the only thing that bound me to Russia, has died."[50] In *Memories*, she recalls that on Easter, 1919, while she was on board ship, her "sister came [to her] as a little girl, the way I loved her most of all," and "only three years later [i.e., in 1922, when in Wiesbaden] would I find out that on that very night, thousands of versts from me, in Arkhangelsk, my Lena was dying…"[51] Teffi described to Bunina the effect of this loss: "Now I feel completely empty […] And in four days I grew thin and black and silent." Typically, she found it best to hide her grief from those around her: "I am not telling the Lolos anything."

In the fall of 1922 Teffi moved from Wiesbaden to Berlin, commonly called by Germans "Russia's second capital," since it had been inundated by an estimated 100,000 Russians – not only émigrés, but those from Soviet Russia who took advantage of the not yet insuperable barriers to travelling abroad.[52] The Russians settled primarily in the southwest of the city, which had six Russian banks, three daily newspapers, 20 bookshops and 17 major publishing firms.[53] The last were a lure to émigré and Soviet writers alike, and it is said that in 1922 and 1923 more Russian books came out in Berlin than in Moscow and Petrograd.[54] Teffi benefited from this abundance, publishing three books there in 1921: *The Lynx*; *Passiflora*, her best poetry collection; and *Shamram*, a collection of light verse in the Oriental style.

PASSIFLORA

As early as 1921 Teffi broached Lyatsky with the idea of publishing a collection of her verse:

You probably don't know that my first book, which made my name, was a book of poems put out by Shipovnik. Since then I haven't put out a new [volume of] poems, although I've published quite a few of them and they are very popular [...] I often receive letters asking where people can get my poems. That has led to the idea – shouldn't I publish a book? And to a second idea – shouldn't I propose the book to you?[55]

Lyatsky did not act on Teffi's proposal, and therefore she took advantage of the opportunity to publish it in Berlin. The collection includes poems written from as early in 1912 – some in the gorgeous style of *Seven Fires*, others in the light and playful mode of many of Teffi's songs, and still others, inspired by the war, marked by solemn rhetoric. The most characteristic poems, however, adopt a starkly simple, terse style, her subjects no longer the sultry slave girls and pagan priestesses of *Seven Fires*, but small, meek people. The writer, moreover, no longer places herself above her humble subjects, but figures as one of them.

In the diminished world of *Passiflora* the deities of Teffi's earlier works – both pagan (the sun god) and Christian – have been reduced to their floral equivalents. In "The Sunflower" (1914) the poet, abandoned by the "great, cruel luminary," has planted a sunflower in her little garden.[56] She pleads with it to disperse the gloom and nurture in her the "free and proud" soul of a poet. But if darkness should nevertheless prevail, she concludes, she and her like "shall drown out our groans with laughter" – laughter once again figuring here as an emanation of pain. In the title poem, "Passionflower," Christ's Passion is re-enacted in the botanical world, the flower, with its cruciform petals, acting as Christ's emissary:

> You are a white forest apostle,
> An evangelist of the field![57]

In the end the poet places herself in this miniaturized world, accepting the flower's suffering as her own: "And I will take to my heart your bloody stigmata."

In *Passiflora* the longing to escape everyday reality – characteristic of Teffi's first collection – continues, but the object is sometimes a distant Nordic realm reminiscent of Russia. In "My Land" (1922), the setting is bucolic, the style folk-like. The narrator is at first plowing in "a dewy meadow," then undergoes a metamorphosis characteristic of Russian folk epics, turning into a swan who "swam around grayish-blue lakes" and "cast a spell on the devil of the black forest…"⁵⁸ Teffi repeats the images of the white bird and blue lake in other poems – a "swan of the northern blue lakes"; "a white bird" that she imagines "is knocking against the glass with its wing" on sleepless nights – creating a mythical picture of her lost homeland.⁵⁹

Death figures in *Passiflora*, as it did in *Seven Fires*, both in its positive and negative aspects – as escape to a superior realm and as cruel punishment. It plays the former role in "The Silver Ship" (1920), one of Teffi's most highly praised poems.⁶⁰ Symbolist dualism is embodied in its form, with both of its stanzas juxtaposing a higher reality and surface appearance. The poem begins with the arrival from on high of a majestic, black-sailed "silver ship with purple edging," then contrasts this grand image with the perception of ordinary people, who see only "the moon […] playing on the waves."⁶¹ In the second stanza the ship, ascending "above the starry stillness," departs with the poet, but people again do not understand and say: "And so she died today…" Thus the vulgar conception of death is a misunderstanding of its true nature: a flight through interstellar space to a transcendent sphere. In contrast, "My heart was meek" (1912), written in the starkly simple style characteristic of *Passiflora*, emphasizes death's injustice, the narrator questioning why so small and harmless a creature as she has suffered such a fate:

> When your voice resounded,
> I only began trembling all over,
> I only unlocked the door…
> Why did I die?⁶²

The wartime poem "Angelica" (1915), written in the style of oral spiritual verses (*dukhovnye stikhi*), seeks a justification for the most miserable of deaths – that of a blind beggar woman, Fedosya. The poem contrasts her outward appearance, "old, humpbacked, ugly [*khudorozhaia*]," to her beautiful soul, "blue-eyed, golden haired, radiant" [*sineokoi, zlatokudroi, iasnolikoiu*]," which is called Angelica.⁶³ When she dies Angelica is received joyously in heaven, but the harmonious image of earthly suffering rewarded beyond the grave is undercut when the poet returns to Fedosya's ignominious earthly end, "buried, forgotten, under a fence."⁶⁴ The note of doubt is expressed in the final lines, where Fedosya's blindness is shared, figuratively, by all of God's children who

> do not see, Lord,
> Thy radiant Divine joy!"

"The blessing of God's right hand" (1922) questions divine justice in a far harsher, more impassioned tone, perhaps because – judging by the date affixed to the poem, 7 August 1921 – Teffi wrote it when she herself was facing death from typhus:

> The destruction of the meek, the joy of the basely depraved –
> Barabbas is acquitted and Christ crucified
> [. . . . . .]
> And in order to make it come out even and smooth
> We are promised reward beyond the grave...
> [. . . . . .]
> I am dying...
> [. . . . . .]
> And like everyone I'll depart, and like everyone not understand...
> And, weeping, I try with my little candle
> To illuminate the great Divine darkness![65]

In her later, serious prose Teffi will repeatedly struggle to penetrate this "Divine darkness," as her own world grew more and more bleak.

Among the Russians who came to Berlin were those, like Boris Pasternak and Andrei Bely (and Teffi's friends the Tolstoys), who were to return to Soviet Russia, and others, such as the outstanding poet Vladislav Khodasevich (1886–1939) and the major prose writers Ivan Shmelyov (1873–1950) and Boris Zaitsev (1881–1972), who were to become vital forces in émigré literature. Zaitsev and his wife, Vera (1878–1965), who had left Russia the previous June with their small daughter, Natasha, were soon to become Teffi's best friends. Among Boris's oldest acquaintances in Berlin was Pavel Theakston, whose English father had owned the factory near Kaluga where Zaitsev's father was chief engineer.[66] Teffi most likely first met Theakston there, and the attraction must have been immediate, since she dedicated *Shamram* to him.

Despite new and old acquaintances, Teffi was unhappy in Berlin, as she wrote her friend, the celebrated actress Yekaterina Roshchina-Insarova (1883–1970): "Things are very bad in Berlin. I don't fit in [*ne podoshla*] at all and lead a very solitary life."[67] In February, matters got much worse, for again Teffi fell "seriously ill," had to undergo an operation, and "almost died," Zaitseva wrote her good friend Vera Bunina.[68] On 11 March the Blue Bird Theater held a benefit for "ailing Teffi" and even two months later it was reported that she "is recuperating a little," but "is cut off from literary work for a prolonged period."[69] While at a sanatorium outside Berlin, Teffi received an invitation from Milyukov to contribute to a weekly Paris newspaper, *Zveno* (The link), which since early 1923 had been coming out on Mondays (the day off for *Poslednie novosti*, of which Milyukov was editor).[70] Teffi accepted the offer with the stipulation that she receive five dollars per feuilleton because of the "wildly high prices" in Berlin.[71] It seems no agreement was reached, since she later offered the newspaper's co-editor, M. Vinaver, two feuilletons for six dollars each, explaining: "You can't imagine how expensive life is here! Especially medical treatment. A mud bath now costs 150,000 [marks]!"[72] Apparently they came to terms, because two of Teffi's feuilletons appeared in *Zveno* in early September 1923. The first, "The Dollar," describes Germany's galloping inflation, which, she asserts, accounts for the fevered gaiety and frantic spending: "Why be frugal when all the same you can't stash away and save money. Today you've stashed a thousand marks and tomorrow it will turn out that you've stashed one pfennig."[73] Because matters have been getting steadily worse, she adds, foreigners have been leaving in droves. By the time this feuilleton was published, Teffi had joined the hordes: she returned to Paris in August 1923.[74]

BACK IN PARIS

After Teffi's arrival in Paris, she settled once again in a little hotel, this time on Rue Jacob on the Left Bank. The material remnants of the old aristocracy must have struck a sympathetic chord:

> My *quartier* – St. Germain – is well known from ancient novels on aristocratic life. Old, boring, smelling of rats and book mold [...] Old shops of old antique dealers. Chipped gilded furniture with upholstery of faded tapestry is displayed in the windows, sad, like the corpse of an old plundered woman.[75]

In "The Return" Teffi reflected on the changes she found among her compatriots:

> The Russians who stayed in Paris for the past year and a half or two have all been more or less set up. The Russian culinary and tailoring "arts" have thrived most. There is a large demand for Russian cuisine and Russian seamstresses.[76]

Underneath it all, though, little had changed. Those who in Russia enjoyed an exalted status were still engaged in menial work:

> Exactly as before an admiral, well known in his day, is braiding ladies' belts from colored straw; a famous general, who commanded Russian troops on the French front, is writing invoices at a firm; a famous scientist, celebrated for his dangerous expeditions, is expediting deliveries [*sluzhit v ekspeditsii*] at a fashionable store; hundreds of Russian engineers, officers, lawyers, journalists, teachers, are grinding bolts at an automobile plant and unloading cars at freight stations; doctors, students, officers are in the retail herring trade, officers ride around as taxi drivers and serve as waiters; the wives and widows of generals are sewing, embroidering, knitting, working by the day, and singing in gypsy choruses. In a word, it's all the same. Only what formerly tormented, humiliated, disturbed them, what seemed like the mockery of fate, they now accept as necessary – it's a good thing, they say, that we have that at least.[77]

As for Teffi herself, she had no need to abandon her profession, since she apparently overcame her writing block, and in late 1923 her stories and feuilletons began appearing in numerous émigré newspapers, with particular frequency in *Zveno* and in the Riga daily *Segodnya* (Today).[78] She also wrote for the popular magazine *Illiustrirovannaia Rossiia* (Illustrated Russia), beginning with its first issue in January 1924.[79]

In late 1923 and early 1924 Teffi also resumed her involvement in social, cultural, and charitable events, participating in, for example, concerts to aid the Union of Russian Writers and Journalists and the Union of Russian Students.[80] As before, however, the lively surface of her life concealed her inner disquietude, which emerges most vividly in her correspondence with Lyatsky. Since publishing Teffi's books in Stockholm, he had become a professor at the Charles University in Prague and also took advantage of the generosity of the new Czechoslovak state toward the Russian emigration by founding a publishing company, Plamia (Flame), and a weekly newspaper, *Ogni* (Fires).[81] The former published Teffi's *The Twilit Day* in 1924, while her feuilletons and stories appeared in *Ogni*.

Judging from their correspondence, a striking change had taken place in Teffi's relationship with Lyatsky since Stockholm. The earlier letters, though cordial, are impersonal and businesslike, but beginning in 1923 they point to a romantic attachment.[82] (Lyatsky was married, but his wife had not left the Soviet Union and they had perhaps divorced.[83]) Thus, Teffi wrote on 3 October 1923, when Lyatsky was in Paris: "How much I needed you, both yesterday and today." If they could meet, she continued,

> we would go somewhere now, right away, where there is music. You have warm, silken hands. And we would look into one another's eyes so brightly that it would seem to the waiter serving us as if today were a sunny day.[84]

In other letters the abrupt insertion of business matters raises the suspicion of some calculation behind such amorous outpourings. For example:

> You know – I sometimes want so much to see you as soon, as soon as possible. [She draws a picture of a burning candle.] […]
> P.S. Do you remember you said that my stories would be translated into Czech? Yes? Will they? Truly?[85]

To be sure, Teffi had many practical issues to discuss with Lyatsky: aside from a book of her stories, she was prodding him to put out a collection of her verse, a volume of Mirra's poetry, and a book by her brother on "the Russian question in the Far East."[86] In any case, she does seem to have forged a genuine emotional bond with her "brother in neurasthenia," as she called him. With Lyatsky she could remove the mask of laughter and reveal her genuine feelings. She wrote of her lifelong depression:

> I am suffering from an immense, unconquerable sadness. My whole life has been spent in a struggle against it. To a horrible degree [do uzhasa].
> I didn't sleep at all last night and listened and looked, as it [the night], rustling, stirred like a shadow in the corner.
> All day I've been sitting with my eyes closed. I'm terribly weak.
> I have to untangle all this somehow. But I can't. I don't know how.[87]

Elsewhere she described her social life as a refuge from melancholy and loneliness: "I often spend time in society. It's very painful. But not to do so is still more so."[88] In her most detailed comment on the disparity between her mood and her behavior she applied the spinning image, so common in her works:

For several days I've been terribly unhappy. For no definite reason.

I press myself to your heart and cry so much.

How ridiculous [*smeshno*] it is to live in this world! You know, just these days I've been whirling the most, been the brightest and merriest, like the pivot around which all our Paris parties twirl. I'm like a top – I whirl and sing, whirl and sing, and if I stop – I'll crash down.[89]

Teffi did indeed "crash down": on 6 May 1924, she again fell critically ill. About a month later Zaitseva wrote Bunina that Teffi was "slowly fading [...] I'm afraid she'll die soon [...] She can't move at all. She has a fibroma (terrible hemorrhaging, uninterruptedly for six weeks, which weakened her heart, and because of her heart they can't operate)."[90]

Teffi's illness – the third in four years – left her once again critically short of money, and it was Lyatsky who came to the rescue, arranging a grant from the Czech government. When she received official notification, as well an advance from Plamia, she thanked him "for so many things at once that I don't even know where to begin."[91] Teffi was staying in a sanatorium at the historic house La Vallée-aux-Loups – Chateaubriand's retreat in the early nineteenth century and later a summer residence for Madame Récamier – which was located in Châtenay, adjacent to Sceaux, where the Zaitsevs had settled, and their proximity drew them closer.

By July Teffi was feeling well enough to resume writing and at the sanatorium wrote her memoir of Rasputin and a series of pieces on Chateaubriand.[92] Now she had to face the prospect of moving back to Paris, which she dreaded because she would "again have to look for a room, hustle, not find one, and stay at the most wretched [place] because I'm impractical and stupid."[93] When she returned around the middle of September, she did indeed move to another "wretched" hotel room, again on Rue Jacob, and complained to Lyatsky that her "way of life is idiotic: at 9 p.m., when people are making visits, going to the theater and the cinema, I, in the Chateaubriand manner, go to bed [...] I don't see anyone and am very bored."[94] Lyatsky's visit at the end of September must have livened things up a bit, although Teffi's description of him to the Zaitsevs suggests that any romantic feelings had by then vanished (or perhaps she was again concealing her feelings): "Terrifying. In galoshes. Glittering teeth."[95]

It was apparently soon afterward that Lyatsky proposed marriage, but Teffi's response, in October, suggests that she was more offended than flattered: "You are tormented by loneliness and you want to plug up that black hole [...] What a modest role you assign me in your life! I am not the end, but the means."[96]

This was clearly the end of their romance, and when Lyatsky traveled to Paris about a year later, he was accompanied by a new wife, Vidoslava Pavlovna, a writer and translator.[97] As for Teffi, while she was still at La Vallée-aux-Loups, rumors had reached Lyatsky of her liaison with another man and, although she denied it, it is likely that by then she had grown close to Pavel Theakston. Although the romance with Lyatsky thus ended – and despite occasional professional conflicts – the two remained friends through the years. Teffi owed him a great deal, nothing more than for the publication of *The Twilit Day*, which came out in October 1924.[98]

THE TWILIT DAY

The Twilit Day is composed entirely of serious works, some of which return to the Russian past, others reflecting the painful reality of exile. The former emphasize the emotions, continuing the exploration, begun in *The Lifeless Beast*, of those instances when spontaneous feeling breaks through the stultified surface of human relationships. This occurs most powerfully in one of Teffi's best works, "Solovki," which depicts a pilgrimage to the Solovetsky Monastery in the Russian far north (which Teffi had visited in 1916).[99] The opening description of a ship crossing the White Sea to the remote island monastery recalls images associated with Russia in *Passiflora* – the watery expanse, the white birds, in this case gulls. Another feature of the north, the white nights, figures in the initial description of the sun, which appears to be rising and setting at the same time (suggesting one meaning for the collection's title, *The Twilit Day*). The image alludes as well, perhaps, to Christian death and resurrection, supported by the ship's "gold cross" visible "high above" and the statement: "The ship was holy, it was called the Archangel Michael."[100]

The ship's passengers, to be sure, are anything but "holy": they engage in the same banal conversation and reveal the same peccadilloes as most of Teffi's characters. The plot focuses on the peasant Semyon Rubayev and his wife Varvara, whom he is bringing to the monastery to atone for her "downfall" with another man. At first Varvara remains unrepentant; even during evening confession she feels "as if her entire soul has fallen into a sleep of dull, miserable obstinacy."[101] But the next morning the cry of a *klikusha* – a woman whose hysterical shrieks and unbridled behavior are ascribed to diabolical possession – brings about a stunning visceral reaction, having nothing to do with conventional morality:

Varvara clenched her hands tightly [...] she felt her legs and shoulders begin to tremble in rapid and large heaves, her face stretch out as if glued to her cheekbones, her stomach swell, roll up under her throat, and a wild scream fly out from the dark depths of her body, contorting and tearing it apart and striking her temple with red lights: "Aay. Ye-es. Ye-es."

For an instant she thought: "I should stop..."

But something forced her to strain more and more, scream more loudly [...] give herself over more strongly, intensely, to the scream, once more, more, still more... Oh, if only they don't prevent me, let me drag it all out...[102]

The next thing Varvara knows she is lying on the floor, a feeling of release spreading until "her body became entirely empty. As if something heavy, inflated, black, left it with the scream."

Varvara has been liberated from the deadening resentment that had so oppressed her, but only at the cost of her sanity, for she has become a fool in Christ, who loves everyone and longs to wander to holy places. Freed from petty earthly concerns, she (like the poet in *Passiflora* – and the queen in *The Noon of Dzokhara*) looks to the white birds in the sky and says: "Sweet sky, light... Gulls... Gulls..."[103] Varvara's cry – an emanation of Russia's irrational, soulful spirit – can be regarded as an expression of Teffi's own pained love for her homeland. The collection's title, *The Twilit Day*, taken from an 1854 poem by Fyodor Tyutchev, ends with lines that sum up Teffi's feeling for Russia: "You are both bliss and hopelessness."[104]

"Marcelina" also recounts a case of spontaneous emotional release, although on a smaller scale. The narrator recalls that when she (Nadya) was nine years old and learned that the 16-year-old Polish maid Marcelina was caught stealing, she at first was terribly excited, imagining ever worse punishments awaiting the servant girl. But when the housekeeper expresses pity for Marcelina, Nadya undergoes a sudden change:

A warm sweet pain slowly spread under my breast, near my heart, made my arms and legs go numb, clouded my eyes, began ringing quietly in my ears.

"Pi-ity..."

All the excitement of the entire day flickered and went out like an extinguished electric bulb.[105]

That evening Nadya feels the "sweet pain" more and more intensely, and when she hears news of a conflagration nearby, she (like Varvara in "Solovki") reacts viscerally, independent of her conscious will:

> I saw my hands stretch out, my palms struck the table, began to grab convulsively, tug, crumple the tablecloth – someone else's hands, I had no control over them […] and there, deep inside, my anguish [*toska*] beat with excruciating pain and screamed through my throat with someone else's voice, which I had never heard.[106]

Someone splashes her face with water and carries her to her room, where she finally calms down and falls asleep.

In the stories devoted to émigré life in *The Twilit Day* such love and pity are little in evidence. On the contrary, the 16-year-old title character in "Lapushka," who has been living with her family in a shabby hotel room for four years, feels only resentment toward her parents, who in their hope of returning to Russia have neglected her education. They in turn are intimidated by their unattractive, sullen daughter, and her mother, Lizaveta Petrovna, who earns a paltry sum from embroidering (while her father rarely stirs from the couch), hesitates to ask her to go to the Galeries Lafayette to buy beads. Lapushka readily agrees, however, because once outside she puts on powder and lipstick and "walks just like everyone, alongside well-dressed ladies."[107] She is completely seduced by the Parisian world of appearance, which "the whole world knows [about] except for Russians."[108] When Lapushka enters the store, the sensual pleasure she feels at the sight of the fabrics – especially of a ribbon, "orange, patterned in gold, exactly like a piece of the sun" (again the sun!) – suggests an unfulfilled longing for beauty.[109] She at first resists the temptation to steal the ribbon, but after overhearing a Frenchwoman's exclamation – *"Vraiment il n'y a que ça dans la vie!"* – she succumbs.

The story ends that evening, when Lizaveta Petrovna, anxiously waiting for her daughter, receives a call from the police. Lapushka finally arrives and at once locks herself in her room, emerging only in the morning, when she is seized by uncontrollable emotion, but the very opposite of the love and pity of "Solovki" and "Marcelina":

> Frenzied joy flared up in her malicious eyes like a little fire, and it was evident that she could no longer keep quiet. "You… you… are paupers!… You're waiting for that Russia of yours? […] I ha-a-ate you!"[110]

She then walks out, leaving behind her devastated parents.

"The Limit," one of Teffi's longest works, most fully embodies the corrosive, egoistic spirit that Teffi observed in émigré society. It is one of her rare works with a male narrator, who – with his overly developed consciousness, owes much to the protagonist of Dostoyevsky's *Notes from Underground*. Not surprisingly, "The Limit" falls short of Dostoyevsky's masterpiece, for Teffi does not share her great predecessor's ability to create a compelling fusion of the psychological, philosophical, and stylistic levels of her narrative. She hampers herself, moreover, by choosing a modern means of communication – the telephone – since the repeated and lengthy calls from the hero to a stranger strains credulity.[111] For all its shortcomings, however, "The Limit" is a key text, its ideas and imagery recurring in Teffi's later serious works.

The hero of "The Limit" manifests to an extreme degree a trait typical of Teffi's more ordinary characters – the need to conceal his true self behind a protective veneer. He declares: "The main thing is not to lose your outward appearance, life's form. Or else it's kaput."[112] Underlying this need for self-defense is his notion that love – and life in general – entails a constant battle for dominance – a view that has already ruined his marriage (although he and his wife genuinely care for one another). While trapped in this egoistic love, the narrator recognizes another variant – uniquely Russian, based not on domination, but on pity, and which he associates with the *rusalka*, the Russian water nymph. The *rusalka*, he asserts – unlike the sensuous Western mermaid –

> knows one cannot tempt a Russian soul with the body alone. One must capture a Russian soul through pity. Therefore what does a *rusalka* do? She weeps […] If she simply sat or beckoned or something – some might not approach. But if she weeps, how can you help but approach?[113]

He goes on to contrast the word "love" (*liubov*'), used only by the educated, to the common people's term, "pity" (*zhalost*'). Love he considers quite the opposite of pity: "You know, there are people who enjoy eating oysters. It's said of these people that they love oysters. And rightly so. The concept to love always includes the concept to devour."

The torments brought on by unhappy love are so great that they lead the narrator, like the poetic persona in "The Blessing of God's Right Hand," to question divine justice and beneficence. He asserts that even Jesus's Passion could not compare to human suffering: "God's Son screamed on the cross […] And He suffered 'in the name of.' Many can [suffer] in the name of, and with joy. But simple human senseless suffering – who can overcome it without a murmur?"[114] He too scoffs at reward in the afterlife: "To make things even they thought up bliss beyond the grave […] You understand, I don't want it. There is a limit, after all." He also rejects the grandeur of nature, even of its most exquisite creature, the butterfly: "Now, as for nature […] Have you seen the head of a butterfly under a microscope? My dear, you couldn't think up such a sinister mug if you tried. And it is a symbol of beauty. Ha! Ha!"[115]

The only thing that dulls the pain is the passage of time, but the hero rails against that as well:

> What an unparalleled horror! A person flails about [*mechetsia*] day and night, screams from intolerable pain, bites his hands […] And when he grows numb from pain – because there's a limit to everything – […] it means time has taken its toll ["*vremia vzialo svoe*].[116]

This indeed happens at the end of "The Limit." After a break of four months, the narrator calls his interlocutor to tell her that he has visited his now former wife, who is living at a dacha with her present lover. The night after his arrival she came to his bed, but no trace of feeling remained, for they – like so many in Teffi's world – are now spiritually dead: "Maybe she […] wanted to check if I had died," he comments. "She was probably sure about herself."[117]

Although the narrator of "The Limit" cannot, of course, be identified with his creator, he does express her views on some fundamental questions. His comment on laughter suggests another tie: "I laugh and joke. I'm simply a merry person. The sick do not dare to be pessimists […] That's Nietzsche. They don't dare. Because otherwise people will notice that they're ill and will tear them to pieces."[118]

7

RUSSIA ABROAD

1924–31

At the very end of 1924 Teffi's hotel life ended for a time when she moved in with the Zaitsevs, who since August had been living in Balmont's former apartment together with Vera's niece, Lelya Komissarzhevskaya, an actress with the Bat (and future wife of its director, Nikita Baliev). When Lelya went on tour, Teffi took her place, and the months she spent with the Zaitsevs were among the few truly happy episodes of her long émigré existence. Natasha Zaitseva – by then the elderly Natalya Borisovna Sollogub – recalled the time:

> Our whole family loved Nadezhda Aleksandrovna Teffi and she loved all of us – including me. She was so talented that whatever she undertook always turned out well. Until I was twenty I always wore other people's clothes – there wasn't any money […] But Teffi sewed me a real dress, a marvelous one.[1]

Teffi paints an affectionate portrait of Natasha in "The Little White Flower": "serene [iasnaia], pale, with blonde Russian braids like mine when I was eleven years old."[2] In a letter to Boris of September 1925, she wrote movingly about her feeling of kinship with the entire Zaitsev family:

> As for my tenderness toward you, never doubt it, because it's *organic*. Not only spiritual [dushevnaia], but bodily. We are of the same tribe […] Our blood, the smell of our skin, its color, our soft hair, everything is of the same sort – our own! To a rare degree. Never have I met such close relatives. Natasha is my daughter, Verusha my sister, you – no, you're not my brother, but rather a nephew.[3]

Teffi wrote Lyatsky contentedly about her time with the Zaitsevs: "I'm living a cozy family life. I don't go anywhere."[4] In fact, she went out quite often, and Bunina describes one instance – a party at the end of January 1925 – when Teffi, the philosopher Fyodor Stepun, and Bunin were "the main center of serious–jocular conversations."[5] On such occasions Teffi left notes that the Zaitsevs "always read aloud and roared with laughter [*uzhasno khokhotali*]."[6]

If the relations among the inhabitants of 2 Rue Belloni were high-spirited, however, they were hardly carefree. Teffi's finances were strained due to one of her periodic writer's blocks, but she was much more worried about the Zaitsevs, and at the beginning of 1925 she appealed "in secret" to the Bunins: "They're frivolous, they're so terrified they don't sleep nights [...] They have to pay for the apartment on the 23rd and they owe 700 francs. If the committee doesn't give them 1,000 – it's curtains."[7] They did not receive the full amount, but Lyatsky again came to the rescue, arranging a monthly stipend from the Czech government.[8] In September, despite her own shaky finances, Teffi herself responded to Zaitsev's desperate need: "Consider that you have 500 francs," she wrote him. "It's my September [money] from the Czechs. I'll put off [getting] my sumptuous wardrobe until October."

Teffi lived with the Zaitsevs for approximately four months, from December 1924 until the beginning of April 1925, when she left for Nice. "Thank God, she's healthy," Zaitseva wrote Bunina on 10 April. "I've gotten terribly close to her [*uzhasno szhilas'*]. A marvelous woman."[9] That summer the Zaitsevs sublet their apartment while visiting friends in Provence and Teffi took a room at the Hôtel Édouard VI, on the Place de Rennes, across from the Gare Montparnasse. She wrote Lyatsky that she was living "a European life again, i.e., with an elevator, a telephone, servants, etc., etc.," and urged him to come to Paris "as soon as possible, or else I'll go away somewhere – it's really very hot and stifling."[10] She failed to mention that she was planning to leave with another man, Pavel Theakston.

On 14 July, Teffi wrote the Zaitsevs of their coming trip, and her affectionate, almost maternal description of Theakston suggests how close they had grown: "Poor Pavlik is on a diet. He eats only melon and artichokes. He's grown quiet and utterly kind, so you just feel like crying!" She seems to have established a comfortable relationship with a man who, in contrast to her first husband and Galich, did not strive to dominate (perhaps because he was married, although by mutual consent he and his wife led separate lives[11]). In the obituary Teffi wrote after Theakston's death in 1935, she emphasized other traits that must have attracted her: his generosity, which was so boundless that during the civil war he even tipped his would-be executioner; his "festive [*prazdnichnyi*]" nature and "light, joyous soul" (so different from her own).[12] Theakston's mild manners are surprising in one who was very much a self-made man, who had to go to work at a very young age, due to his father's early death. After working in banks for several years, he found employment at the Russo-Belgian Metallurgical Society, where by 1898 he had ascended to the directorship. In 1906 he served as head of the Prodamet syndicate, the largest industrial organization in Russia, and after the October revolution Lenin asked him to become head of the People's Commissariat of Trade and Industry – an offer he declined, allying himself instead with the White movement.[13]

After traveling with Theakston to "various beautiful places" in July and August, Teffi again had to face the problem of where to live in Paris.[14] The housing crisis dashed any hope of rejoining the Zaitsevs, and she found no better option than to stay at the hotel opposite the Gare Montparnasse, although it was "inconvenient, expensive." For her readers, however, Teffi emphasized the positive: "I adore Paris. I find it pleasant to hear it knocking, honking, ringing, breathing all the time, right here alongside me."[15] The many functions of her only table encapsulate the inconvenience of living in such a cramped space, while the objects piled up there support Teffi's dual image as serious writer and frivolous female: "On top […] is an inkwell, paper, face powder, envelopes, a sewing box, a cup of milk, flowers, a Bible, candy, manuscripts, perfume."

In the fall of 1925 Teffi was well enough to become involved in a couple of ambitious artistic endeavors. On 8 October she and her old *Satirikon* colleague, the talented poet Pyotr Potyomkin (1886–1926), became co-artistic directors of a theater, House of the Actor, but, after staging several programs of miniatures, it closed by the end of the year.[16] More successful was the illustrated magazine *Perezvony* (Chimes), published in Riga and backed financially by Nikolai Belotsvetov, Theakston's brother-in-law.[17] With the energetic support of Teffi and Theakston, Zaitsev became head of the literature and art department of the journal, which was published between November 1925 and October 1927. It featured many well-known writers of the older generation, including Bunin, Balmont, and Remizov, as well as Teffi.[18]

Teffi also resumed an active social life. At the end of 1925 she and Theakston went slumming in the Latin Quarter with the Yevreinovs and others. Teffi and Yevreinov "cultivated their fantasy, recounting the biographies – made up on the spot – of the public dancing around them – apaches, pimps, and other suspicious types."[19] She also attended a ball the Yevreinovs gave in January 1926, and reportedly was her old flirtatious self: "She didn't miss a single dance, and her tango with the then handsome artist Verbov evoked unambiguous remarks and smiles [...] All those close to her, after all, knew her 'romantic character.'"[20]

Aside from such purely social activities, Teffi took part in a number of fundraising events in late 1925 and 1926, among them a joint literary evening with Remizov, which took them to Brussels at the end of March 1926. Teffi's notes to the Remizovs before the event show her at her disorganized best. First she announced that she had forgotten the first name and patronymic of their hostess; then she wrote that she had lost the address of their Brussels hotel, adding that she was coming late because: "I'm sick as a dog!"[21]

In general there was a dizzying number of cultural events sponsored by the Paris Russians in the late 1920s, and Teffi was overwhelmed by invitations. Even when she was being treated for a "kidney ailment" in Vichy in May 1926 (from which she soon recovered), the invitations kept coming, "now to a congress of suffragettes, now to various celebrations," she complained to Zaitseva. On a typical day – 31 October 1926 – Teffi's and Don-Aminado's "Evening of Optimists" had to compete with three public lectures, a couple of concerts, and meetings of the Society of Russian Chemists, the Russian Student Christian Movement, the Republican-Democratic Association, and the Society of Artillery Officers.[22] The peak of the 1926 season was a gala held on 12 December marking the 25th anniversary of Zaitsev's literary career, called by *Poslednie novosti* "a genuine holiday of Russian culture abroad."[23] But Teffi's evening the following February crossed the Russian border, featuring as it did the American variety star and toast of Paris, Josephine Baker.[24]

Teffi also partook of some of the intellectual offerings of the emigration. She and Theakston were admirers of the prominent religious philosopher Boris Vysheslavtsev (1877–1954), and from November 1925 to April 1926 attended his lecture series "The Social Philosophy of Christianity."[25] (He later referred to them as "my faithful students [*slushatelei*]."[26]) Judging from a pamphlet with a similar title, in his talks Vysheslavtsev condemned Communist materialism and found the true roots of social justice and equality in Christian love and freely offered sacrifice.[27] Teffi, who was disillusioned with the Soviet "solution" but whose writings expressed her deep anguish at the condition of the poor and oppressed, must have found Vysheslavtsev's explorations of Christian justice and equality compelling.

At the end of 1926 Teffi's financial situation became more stable after she began to write regularly for the Paris newspaper *Vozrozhdenie* (Renaissance), to which she had been making occasional contributions since its founding in June 1925. In November 1926, she reluctantly agreed to the offer by its editor, the respected economist and political figure Pyotr Struve (1870–1944), of 300 francs for a "humorous miniature of about 150 lines" (although she had requested 400).[28] Struve had succeeded in attracting some of emigration's best writers and thinkers to *Vozrozhdenie*, which had gained a large readership, exceeded only by that of *Poslednie novosti*.[29] Struve himself left in 1927, after a falling-out with the publisher, former oil magnate Abram Gukasov (1872–1969), and the newspaper's politics, initially moderately conservative, grew more strident and reactionary. The literary section, however, remained very strong.[30]

Now that her work situation was more secure, Teffi was determined at long last to abandon hotel life, and in the summer of 1927 she moved into her first Paris apartment, at 25 Boulevard de Grenelle, not far from the Soviet embassy. She was now able to entertain a wider circle of friends, but the Zaitsevs still occupied a special place. They were frequently invited to outings in Theakston's car and to meals at local restaurants (the prosperous Theakston paying, naturally). Zaitseva wrote Bunina about one such ride, in the Bois de Boulogne, after which "Pavel Andreyevich treated us at the Rôtisserie Périgourdine." She concluded: "Teffi is like family to me. I see nothing but good things from her."[31]

In Theakston and the Zaitsevs Teffi acquired a kind of surrogate family in exile, but in 1927 she had what was apparently her first direct contact with her actual family after many years. Her daughter, Valeria, suffering from health problems, came to Paris in May, and she and her mother – also in need of a cure – soon left for the spa town of Aix-les-Bains.[32] Teffi clearly enjoyed the company of her daughter, who served in the Polish foreign ministry and was also known for her translations into Polish of her mother's stories.[33] She wrote Zaitseva from Aix – with a combination of amused irony and pride: "Valichka has been busy with my education: she painstakingly (with concealed horror) corrects my mistakes in French [...] We live peacefully."

In late October Teffi went to Warsaw to see her daughters. She intended to visit "incognito," but word of her arrival was soon out and "her apartment was besieged by Polish journalists."[34] Their articles stressed Teffi's popularity in Poland, which the *Segodnya* reporter attributed in large part to her daughters, one of whom "is the famous Polish actress Buchinskaya, the other the no less famous translator." The trip not only united Teffi's family; it placed her in closer proximity to Russia than she had been since her departure. The effect was very powerful:

At one time it [Poland] was our door to Europe. Now it is a door to Russia. A closed one. One feels it very strongly, Russia. You capture the breeze from the east with your breath, you capture the smell of Russia's autumnal fields, doleful but free, with boundless horizons.[35]

Teffi remained in Warsaw for over a month, sufficient time for her to gain some perspective on the Paris emigration. At the beginning of her trip, she wrote of the impoverishment of the Russian language in exile, but after spending a month in Poland, she had greater appreciation of the French émigré community:

The Russian colony in Warsaw is a small provincial town. The Paris colony in comparison is a capital.

In Paris there are public figures, writers, five Russian newspapers, a theater, lectures, discords (ideological and personal), fashion studios, schools, charitable evenings.

In Warsaw a small refugee community is barely breathing.[36]

Teffi left Poland on 28 November and by early December she was back in Paris, looking "refreshed and prettier," according to Zaitseva.[37] All told 1927 was quite a good year. Teffi had begun writing regularly for *Vozrozhdenie*, had at last found a decent apartment, and had re-established ties with her daughters. Another happy event of late 1927 was the publication of *The Small Town*, Teffi's most popular émigré book and the first to appear since 1924.

THE SMALL TOWN

The Small Town contains some of Teffi's best-known comic stories, but its satire was criticized by some for its excessive negativity.[38] Most disturbing for Teffi must have been Zaitsev's review in *Sovremennye zapiski* – especially since she herself had asked him to write it, commenting in her self-deprecating way: "You'll find two or three stories that are not too bad. (The rest are trash, no need to mention them.)" The scrupulously honest Zaitsev, however, did not ignore what he considered the book's deficiencies, and even wondered whether Teffi was still "a humorist at all," since she saw "primarily the bad, the deformed, the worthless." He concluded that the book, while "brilliantly written," was "full of unquenchable melancholy."[39] Teffi found an unlikely defender in Nina Berberova (1901–93), the best-known woman writer of the younger generation, for the two were never on good terms. Responding to those who found the book "very malicious," Berberova, asked: "Is it not simply because *The Small Town* is a truthful book?"[40] She too found Teffi's works "no longer humorous," but considered this positive: "They are at times so penetrating (and at the same time so dynamic) that with all their merry bitterness they stay in your memory for a long time."

The title piece of *The Small Town* – Teffi's most famous work after "Ke fer?" – exemplifies the book's negativity (or truthfulness – the two not mutually exclusive). The town in question, the Russian community in Paris, is first distinguished by the skewed nature of its institutions – and, by implication, of its values: "It [...] had about forty thousand inhabitants, one church, and an inordinate number of taverns."[41] The occupations of the town dwellers are also lopsided: young people mostly "worked as [taxi] drivers," whereas older men "kept taverns or worked in these taverns," and women "sewed dresses for one another and made hats." Aside from these usual human categories, the town's population included "ministers and generals," who mostly produced "debts and memoirs." Another feature of the town – to an even greater extent than in "Ke fer?" – is the mutual animosity of its inhabitants, who "hated one another so much that it was impossible to bring together twenty people of whom ten were not the enemy of the remaining ten."[42]

The selfishness and mutual animosity of Parisian Russians are themes in a number of the stories in *The Small Town*. "The May Bug," one of the few wholly serious stories, shows the dire effect of such hard-heartedness on a wounded veteran, Kostya, a penniless invalid whose entire family perished during the civil war. His only hope is one Zhukonokulo, a former family tutor whom his mother treated kindly. Zhukonokulo, however (who reminds Kostya of a repulsive May bug – *maiskii zhuk* – a play on the first syllable of the tutor's odd name), indignantly denies any obligation, and Kostya runs off, thinking bitterly:

No, bug, you are obliged [...] we shielded you with our breasts, bug, we gave our lives [...] I was crippled, shell-shocked. You fawned on me then, bug, flattered me, and made up poems about me, saying I was a hero. And now you have nothing to do with me.[43]

Kostya then shoots himself.

Most of the stories in *The Small Town* are lighter in tone and focus on the struggles of a rootless people. "The Conversation," a dialogue between Nikolai, who lives in Paris, and Ivan, a resident of Berlin, concentrates on their loss of language. When Nikolai tries to persuade Ivan to move to the French capital, the latter asks, "What *Bezirk* is the cheapest?"[44] They continue:

> "Lord, why, you've completely forgotten how to speak Russian. Why, who in the world says '*Bezirk*'?"
> "Then what is it in Russian?"
> "In Russian it's called *arrondissement*."

They continue to mix in French and German words and to stumble over tricky Russian lexical items until both men end up in tears.

Economic necessity leads some in Teffi's stories to adopt a French identity wholly, with predictably risible results. Thus, the seamstress in "Hedda Gabler" sheds her real name, Olga, and calls herself "Madame Elise d'Ivanoff." The creator of *"fantaisies,"* she promises to "drape [a client] in emerald silk," but Olga's slovenly appearance and the mundane objects she comes up with while looking for this wondrous fabric – a piece of sausage, a dirty spoon, a herring – undercut her attempt to pass for a chic French designer.[45]

One type of character who escapes Teffi's generally negative view of Parisian Russians in *The Small Town* is what the French have dubbed *l'âme slave* – the Slavic soul. In her introduction to the newspaper variant of the story, "L'âme slave," she explains the source of the concept:

> It's been almost five years now since Paris has been jam-packed with Russians, and Parisians are still amazed at our senselessness [*bestoloch'*], our messiness, our senseless kindness, the absurdity of our entire life. They look and can't understand a thing. In the final analysis they have found a word for all this: *"âme slave"* – the Slavic soul.[46]

This "senseless kindness" is exemplified by the poor émigré couple the Yegorovs in the story's first episode. They are finishing their meager dinner in a seedy French restaurant when the stage show begins, and Yegorov, horrified by the awful singing of the older performer – and ignoring the fact that he is "quite stout" – decides that his family must be starving for him to humiliate himself so.[47] As they leave, the Yegorovs give the Frenchman their last franc and 50 centimes, but what transpires after the performance – the singer eats a filling dinner at the restaurant, then goes to a café where an adoring *"petite"* is in ecstasy over his talent – shows how misplaced the sympathy of the "Slavic souls" is.

In "Marquita," one of the best works in *The Small Town*, both protagonists possess Slavic souls (although one of them is a Tatar). The story opens in a typical Russian café, where the performers hide behind artificial identities – an apache dancer is actually a failed seminarist and "the gypsy singer, Raisa Tsvetkova" is Raichka Blum.[48] Only the heroine, Sashenka, behaves naturally when she sings her number, "Marquita," and later, when she kisses her little son, Kotka. When a rich Tatar sends over a box of candy for Kotka, however, Raichka urges Sashenka not to drag the child around, since "a woman should be Carmen. Cruel, fiery."[49] But it is precisely Sashenka's maternal qualities that appeal to the Tatar, Asayev: "She has stolen my heart. She kissed her little boy – she has a soul." Sashenka in turn, revealing her irrational Slavic soul, is attracted to Asayev precisely because of his ugliness: "He needs to be loved tenderly […] His nose is covered with some kind of little holes and he snorts."[50] Such sentiments point to a happy union, and Asayev does come close to proposing, but he backs away after Sashenka, whom he invites to a fancy restaurant, acts the part of fiery Carmen, even talking slightingly of her son, while her "soul quietly wept."[51] Sashenka returns home and tells Kotka: "There's someone who will love you and me, and keep us warm. It won't be long now…" But Asayev glumly concludes: "She is a demon. There was a mistake […] It's over!"[52]

A simpler story, "Wings" (dedicated to Vera Zaitseva), is built on a contrast between two visitors to the narrator, one an ordinary woman, the other a Slavic soul. While the first is complaining about money and her impractical husband, the second arrives: "Golden curls, joy, gray stockings on shapely legs, a shaggy little feather in her hat […] kisses, lipstick – a whirlwind."[53] She is in ecstasy over her husband precisely because he has just given away their last centime: "Well, isn't he enchanting! […] A remarkable man!"[54] She then flies out, leaving behind a glove and a feather from her hat. The narrator blows the feather out the window, its ascent toward the sun reproducing in miniaturized form the recurring bird imagery in Teffi's works (hence the story's title): "It floated forth, caught by the wind, flew, was carried straight to heaven, small, grayish-gold in the sun."

LIFE'S REVERSALS: 1928–31

1928 began on a cheerful note, with the writers' annual New Year's ball featuring a piece by Teffi, *The Monstrous Wet Nurse and the Surprise Steed*.[55] The

1 Caricature of Teffi's father, Alexander Vladimirovich Lokhvitsky, a law professor who after the 1864 judicial reform of Emperor Alexander II became a celebrated and controversial criminal defense lawyer. *Galereia russkikh deiatelei*, no. 2. St. Petersburg, 1870.

2 Teffi's sister, Mirra Lokhvitskaya. For her poetic paeans to feminine sensuality she was famous at the turn of the nineteenth and twentieth centuries as the "Russian Sappho."

3 Teffi's brother, General Nikolai Lokhvitsky, commander of the Russian expeditionary force in France during World War I, later a prominent émigré monarchist. *Novoe vremia* (St. Petersburg), 30 July 1916, p. 8.

4   Photograph of Teffi from the early twentieth century.
Photographer D. Sdobnov.

5 Scene from "Love through the Ages," Crooked Mirror cabaret, 5 Dec. 1908. The scene shows contemporary love: a symbolist poet and a nanny goat.

ДВА МІРА.

Въ глубинѣ глухого парка
Переброшенная арка
Мирно дремлетъ надъ водой...

Листья небо заглушили.
Купы розъ и бѣлыхъ лилій
Дышатъ пряной тишиной.

Облака плывутъ надъ садомъ.
Бѣлый отрокъ съ виноградомъ
Къ бѣлой дѣвѣ станъ прижалъ, —

А у ногъ, подъ лаской неба,
Изъ за грязной корки хлѣба
Брата братъ за горло сжалъ...

А. Г.

6 *"Two Worlds," Satirikon*, 12 Dec. 1909, p. 5. Courtesy of Houghton Library, Harvard University. The illustration by Yevgeny Lanceray and poem by Sasha Chorny contrast the elegant, classical side of the Russian capital and the desperate condition of its poor.

ХУДОЖЕСТВЕННОЕ ОБЩЕСТВО ИНТИМНАГО ТЕАТРА—СПБ.

Воскресенье, 26 Января 1914 г.

„ВЕЧЕРЪ ЛИРИКИ".

Поэты:

Анна Ахматова, М. Кузминъ, Ив. Рукавишниковъ, Вл. Пястъ, Рюрикъ Ивневъ, Моравская, Н. Гумилевъ, Г. Ивановъ, О. Мандельштамъ, Тэффи, Н. Кузнецовъ.

Музыканты:

А. Зейлигеръ, Д. Карпиловскій, Д. Зиссерманъ, В. Гольдфельдъ, Л. Штримеръ, I. Чернявскій, Л. Цейтлинъ, Абрамянъ, Эренбергъ, Е. Кушелевская, Богдановская, Гольда Гутманъ, Соломея Граузанъ.

Ведринская   Актеры:

Валерская, Волоховъ, Блокъ, Глѣбова-Судейкина, Глаголинъ, Крамовъ, Голубевъ, Миклашевская, Лось, Егоровъ, Тиме, Суворина

Начало вечера въ 11½ час

Входъ исключительно по приглашеніямъ Художественнаго Совѣта „Бродячей Собаки" и по предварительной записи г.г. дѣйствительныхъ членовъ О-ва. Плата — 5 руб. Актеры, поэты, художники, музыканты и „друзья Собаки" 1 руб

7 Program of "An Evening of Lyrical Poetry," the Stray Dog, 26 January 1914. Teffi shares the program with Anna Akhmatova, Mikhail Kuzmin, Nikolai Gumilyov, Osip Mandelstam, Georgy Ivanov, and others.

8 Drawing of Teffi by Alexander Yakovlev, 1914.

9 Teffi and her guitar, 1915.

10 Photograph of Teffi, identified as N.A. Buchinskaya-Shcherbakova, née Lokhvitskaya, 1915 or 1916. This is one of the few traces of Teffi's marriage to her second husband, Dmitry(?) Shcherbakov. Photographer G. Mitreutere (Moscow). Courtesy of the Institute of Russian Literature, Russian Academy of Sciences (IRLI RAN), St. Petersburg, Russia.

11 Teffi photographed shortly after returning from the front during World War I, where she worked as a nurse and sent dispatches back to the newspaper, *Russkoe slovo*. *Teatr i iskusstvo*, 3 May 1915, p. 307.

12 Cover of Teffi, *Nothing of the Kind* (Petrograd, 1915).
Courtesy of Houghton Library, Harvard University.

13   Teffi shortly after her arrival in Paris in 1919.
Teffi Papers; Courtesy of the Bakhmeteff Archive, Columbia University.

14 Natasha Zaitseva in a dress sewn by Teffi (1926). Teffi moved in with the writer Boris Zaitsev and his family in late 1925 and lived with them for about 4 months. Natasha – by then the elderly Natalya Borisovna Sollogub – recalled that Teffi "was so talented that whatever she undertook always turned out well. Until I was 12 years old I always wore someone else's clothes – there was no money […] And Teffi sewed a dress for me, a real one, a marvelous one!" Courtesy of Pierre Sollogoub.

15 Portrait of Teffi, 1920s.
Teffi Papers; Courtesy of the Bakhmeteff Archive, Columbia University.

16 Teffi at Vichy in manly outfit, 1926 or 1930.
Teffi Papers; Courtesy of the Bakhmeteff Archive, Columbia University.

17 Teffi and the artist Konstantin Korovin viewing one of his latest works at the Exhibit of Russian Art, Paris, July 1932. Zeeler Papers; Courtesy of the Bakhmeteff Archive, Columbia University.

18 Teffi in a group photo at *Illustrated Russia* after Bunin received the Nobel Prize, 1933. Bunin fourth from right, Mark Aldanov to his left. Zeeler Papers; Courtesy of the Bakhmeteff Archive, Columbia University.

19 Teffi and Pavel Theakston, the 1930s. Theakston, Teffi's intimate friend, suffered a stroke in 1930, after which she was his principal caregiver until his death in 1935. Teffi Papers; Courtesy of the Bakhmeteff Archive, Columbia University.

20 Teffi, bare-backed, on the bank of the Marne River, Marly-le-Roi, France. Summer, 1934. She must have been very pleased with the photo since she sent it to various friends and periodicals, including the Riga newspaper, *Segodnya* (1 Oct. 1934). Teffi Papers; Courtesy of the Bakhmeteff Archive, Columbia University.

21   Teffi's daughters, Warsaw, 1935. Yelena (Helena Buczyńska, left) was a well-known stage and screen actress, while Valeria (Waleria Grabowska) was a translator of her mother's works and member of the Polish Foreign Ministry. Teffi Papers; Courtesy of the Bakhmeteff Archive, Columbia University.

22 Teffi's room at 18-bis Avenue de Versailles, 1939. On her bed is her beloved guitar. On the book shelves above are portraits of her literary friends, the most discernible of Boris Zaitsev (center) and, second from the right, Mark Aldanov. The Yakovlev portrait can be seen on the left. Teffi Papers; Courtesy of the Bakhmeteff Archive, Columbia University.

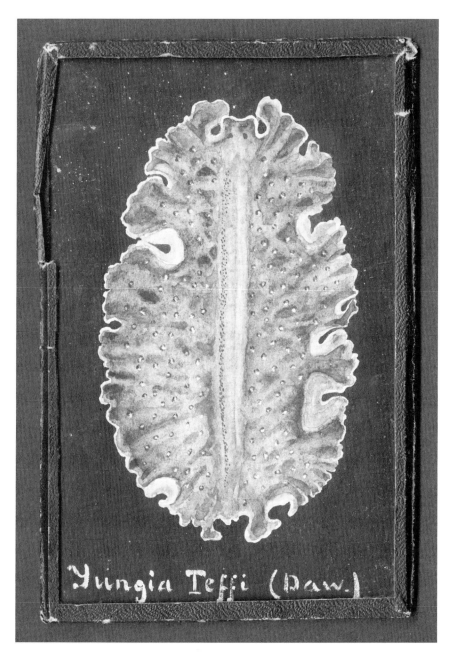

Yungia Teffi (Daw.)

23 A mollusk discovered by Professor Konstantin Davydov, named in honor of Teffi. On 1 Jan. 1951, Teffi wrote her daughter Valeria that Davydov had dedicated a recent lecture to her, "since at one time I had mentioned his lecture in print and supposedly made his career." Teffi Papers; Courtesy of the Bakhmeteff Archive, Columbia University.

24 Before Teffi's departure from the rest home at Morsang-sur-Orge in early September 1952, two young relatives of the proprietor asked to have their picture taken with her so that "when we're big, we'll show this portrait to our children." Marked by Teffi's daughter, Valeria, in Polish: "Ostatnia fotogr. Mamy" (Last photo of Mama). Teffi Papers; Courtesy of the Bakhmeteff Archive, Columbia University.

"pantomime–ballet," staged by Yevreinov and reminiscent of the frivolous and witty playlets the two had put on for the Crooked Mirror, is a parody of chivalric tales, replete with mistaken identities, disguises, the switching of babies. To augment the absurdity, men played not only most of the female roles, but those of such non-human parts as the horse, the moon, and even the moon's reflection.[56] Twenty writers – among them Zaitsev, Georgy Ivanov, and Berberova – took part in the performance.

All in all, the end of the 1920s was a time – all too transient, it turned out – of relative calm and stability for Teffi. By then her social activities were following a well-established pattern. The Zaitsevs still figured centrally, and she also remained close to the Bunins, whom she saw both in Paris and – during summer trips in Theakston's car – in Grasse, where they were living for the better part of the year together with three young writers: Galina Kuznetsova (1900–76), who had a passionate love affair with Bunin; Nikolai Roshchin (1896–1956); and Leonid Zurov (1902–71), with whom Bunina developed an intense and enduring maternal relationship. In Paris Teffi continued to take part in many social and charitable activities – the latter an indication of the continuing severe hardship within the émigré community. Her ability to help impoverished writers increased in 1928, when she joined the governing board of the Union of Russian Writers and Journalists, a position she maintained for many years.[57] Aside from participating in activities to aid literary and theatrical colleagues, Teffi supported causes benefiting other segments of émigré society. Her call to aid a kindergarten suggests that the plight of émigré children especially moved her:

The children behave freely and simply [...] but a kind of strange sorrow flickers sometimes in those tender, transparent eyes [...]

I am told their names. Here is the daughter of an engineer; her mother works as a *femme de ménage*. Here is the daughter of a colonel – her mother embroiders. Here is the son of a famous aviator who died of cancer. Here is a tiny boy with a pale, inspired face [...] who was born a month after his father was executed.[58]

Teffi also participated in appeals for disabled veterans "who sacrificed their lives for Russia, who suffered mutilation, wounds, lost their health, who are now cripples"; for émigré doctors, who "not only treat the indigent free of charge and operate free, but also in difficult cases pay for their hospital stay."[59] Teffi's description of the 1929 Miss Russia competition, for which she served as a judge, indicates the penury of young émigré women, willing to suffer such humiliation for what must have been a meager prize. Describing how a French "specialist" "passes [his hand] along her neck […] pulls her dress tight to reveal the shape of her breasts and waist," checks that she is not wearing a bra, lifts her skirt above the knees, even examines her teeth and ears, she called for an "end [to] this senseless and immoral nonsense!"[60]

Teffi's own life had achieved a level of security, but she still felt vulnerable. "I […] regard my future [as a writer] very gloomily," she wrote Zaitsev in the summer of 1928, and "it is really very worrying to stake my existence on whether P.A. [Theakston] will feed me or not." She was therefore always looking for a chance to earn a little extra, and was dismayed when she didn't receive an invitation to a congress of Russian émigré writers sponsored by the Serbian government in late September 1928 – especially since she expected it to result in a monthly stipend of 1,000 francs. She finally did wangle an invitation, after meeting the congress organizer, Alexander Belich, at the Bunins', but decided not to go after all.[61] Her efforts were not totally in vain, however, since her book *The June Book* was included in a series sponsored by the Serbs.

The failure to obtain 1,000 francs from the Serbs was followed by a more serious blow when, in January 1929, the Czechs ended their stipends to Teffi and other writers. Teffi wrote Lyatsky for help: "We are all wailing and hoping you would and could defend us for at least a year."[62] His influence, not surprisingly, proved insufficient, and even Bunin, whose income must have been considerably higher than Teffi's, was "in a panic," his wife noted, adding later: "Yan is very worried about how and on what we'll live."[63]

Teffi wrote of her precarious finances to Don-Aminado: "I want to change my trade. It's impossible to live on literature any more. It's unprofitable and boring."[64] As the final word suggests, her problem was not only monetary. The boredom she was experiencing reflected the larger crisis émigré writers were facing after a decade in exile. The issue had been heatedly discussed at the Green Lamp – a series of colloquia initiated by Merezhkovsky and Gippius in 1927.[65] At the second meeting, entitled "Russian Literature in Exile," Gippius asserted that the émigrés had so far been unable to create anything new, and even concluded that Russian literature abroad "does not exist," since it "does not reflect *internally* either the Russian political catastrophe or the experience of exile." In the heated discussion that followed, the Menshevik journalist St. Ivanovich was yet more pessimistic, predicting that "it is [only] a matter of time" before émigré literature died out entirely.[66]

Teffi, who attended the meetings, had observed even earlier that Russia was slipping away: "We are forgetting the everyday life of our sunken Atlantis, our dear old life," she wrote in 1925. "At times our memory, just like the sea, unexpectedly tosses up some splinter, scrap, fragment from the drowned world, forever lost, and you begin to examine it with sadness and tenderness."[67] In 1928, she wrote of one such object, a "dear old Russian *ottomanka*" (a large sofa with cushions instead of a back), which "floated up on the waves of memory" but will only "crash down once more into the abyss."[68] It was, perhaps, her acute awareness that the past might soon be irretrievably lost that led Teffi to commit to paper her memories of the revolution and civil war. Her memoir, serialized in *Vozrozhdenie* beginning in late 1928, differed from others, she emphasized in her preface, because her subjects were not "illustrious, heroic figures," but "simple non-historical people who seemed amusing or interesting."[69] The word "amusing" seems at first jarring, given her grim subject matter, but after so much time had passed, Teffi was able to depict the terrible events she had witnessed with sufficient dispassion to uncover the comical – or more accurately, a distinctive blend of the comic grotesque and the tragic. The humor only accentuated the horror, as Tsetlin remarked: "The laughter and bitterness in Teffi's book are so funny, and thereby it achieves a double impression: what nonsense and what sadness and what horror!"[70]

Another reaction to the ineluctable retreat of the Russian past was a turn to French subjects, to people Teffi came across, such as *femmes de ménage*, the husband of a concierge, a manicurist.[71] Some of the stories are quite successful and were included in her *June Book*, but she concluded in a 1930 feuilleton that the French would forever remain alien to her. She looks at a subway conductor and thinks that a French writer could capture him in a few strokes (as she did her Russian subjects): "A gesture, a turn of phrase, a small detail, insignificant to us – and he's done."[72] As for her: "To feel him enough so you could speak, think, and act for him? Never."

If Teffi felt it impossible to penetrate the inner life of the French, she and other émigré writers sought at least to find a niche for themselves in the French literary world. By the end of the 1920s the number of encounters between French and Russian émigré writers was increasing, and a particularly ambitious undertaking was the Studio Franco-Russe, initiated in 1929 by the young Russian writer Vsevolod Fokht (in French Wsevolod de Vogt, 1895–1941).[73] A series of "*rencontres*" was organized, the main goal to foster greater contact between the younger generation of Russian writers and their French counterparts – although it was considered essential that the "masters" of the older generation

(Teffi among them) attend.[74] Fokht succeeded in enlisting the support of several French writers and editors, and arranged for publication of the meetings' transcripts, as well as translations of works by Russian participants.[75] Monthly meetings were held for about a year and a half, between October 1929 and April 1931, and Teffi attended regularly through November 1930, but remained silent.[76] Despite this lack of active participation, two of her stories, "Solovki" and "Marquita," appeared in a supplement to *France et monde* in 1929.[77] The editor stated that her "remarkable stories" would be included "in an Anthology of Modern Russian Writers," which apparently never came out.[78]

The Russo-French meetings came to an end in April 1931, when Fokht suddenly abandoned literature and left for Jerusalem to become a monk. A more fundamental reason for the termination, Livak observes, was the growing fissure within the French literary world between those, like the founders of the studio, who looked to religion for a solution to Europe's problems, and those who turned to the Soviet experiment.[79] As the latter faction gained dominance in the 1930s, interest in émigré writers inevitably waned. The largely negative attitude of the émigrés toward Soviet literature and culture widened the gap. An example is Teffi's comments on Boris Pasternak in a review of a 1929 volume of Bunin's poetry. Contrasting Bunin's clarity with the obscurity of Pasternak's verse, she recalls the condescending advice of Ilya Ehrenburg (1891–1967) – a Soviet writer then living and working in Paris – "to ponder, read deeply, in order to comprehend this talent" – and compares "such hard labor" to that of "a scavenger rummaging [...] through a pile of rags and broken crockery [...] to fish out a silver spoon."[80] The following year Teffi criticized harshly the staging of Gogol's *The Inspector General* by her old acquaintance Vsevolod Meyerhold. She sorrowfully concluded that this "very talented director" had become a mere jester for his "lord and master [*barina-boiarina*]," the Soviet government: "And the laughter of jesters has never been either merry or joyous."[81]

This marginalization of Russian writers in France was symptomatic of an overall shift during the 1930s in the formerly welcoming attitude of the French toward foreigners, due to the deteriorating economic and political situation. To make matters worse for Russians in particular, in January 1930 a sensational kidnapping took place – apparently by Soviet agents – of General Alexander Kutepov (b.1882), head of the largest émigré veterans' organization, the Russian All-Military Union (ROVS).[82] A strike by approximately 6,000 Parisian taxi drivers (mostly Russians) ensued, followed by a mass meeting of about 3,000. Bunina wrote in her diary: "Terrible news since morning: 'Kutepov has disappeared.' Everyone thinks it's the Bolsheviks." A few days later she noted that the Zaitsevs were "in a fighting mood. They want to find Kutepov, no matter what."[83]

This incident occurred a few months after the New York stock market crash in October 1929, but the crisis spread slowly to France, and in the émigré literary world the new decade began much as the old one had ended.[84] There was the usual writers' ball, benefits, meetings of the Green Lamp and the Studio Franco-Russe.[85] Things had changed little by July 1930, when Teffi went to Vichy, bothered once again by a kidney ailment. She witnessed there the onset of the high season – the arrival not only of the elegant international set (the "big fish"), but of the "small fry [meloch'] who feed off [their] leavings."[86] The latter, perhaps, gave her the idea for her *Adventure Novel*, which she began soon after, in August, and which took place in much the same milieu – of "frivolous, enigmatic young things with pet dogs [ruchnye sobaki], sultry boys, [...] representatives of the best fashion houses, fortune-tellers, pimps, money lenders, and hotel thieves."

From Vichy Teffi moved to the less celebrated resort at Saint-Nectaire in the Auvergne. While there she received a letter from a distant acquaintance, Alexander Amfiteatrov (1862–1938). Formerly a very popular writer with revolutionary leanings but now an ardent anti-Bolshevik who had moved far to the right and was living in fascist Italy, Amfiteatrov invited Teffi to contribute to a collection of Russian émigré humor in Italian translation.[87] She agreed only reluctantly because of her low opinion of émigré humor, but did ask him if he could find a publisher for a whole book of hers in Italian. She explained that she was not seeking glory, but needed the money: "I have a sister and niece in Russia who are dying of hunger and I am their only hope and support!" (She was evidently referring to Varvara, her only surviving sister.) Amfiteatrov responded enthusiastically, and thus began their copious, affectionate correspondence, which vividly evokes their increasingly difficult lives.

Teffi's difficulties, indeed, began almost immediately. In the fall of 1930 (probably in October) Theakston suffered a serious stroke while in Copenhagen, and it was decided that she (not Theakston's wife) go with his son Seryozha to bring him back to Paris, after which she took on the daunting role of principal caregiver.[88] At the end of December, Zaitseva wrote Bunina:

You probably know already that Pav[el] Andr[eyevich] Theakston is very ill. He is paralyzed on the right side and hasn't been able to speak [...] Teffi is dead tired. She's been looking after him for two months, although they have a nurse there, but every other day she sleeps over, and she's always there during the day.[89]

By then, moreover, the Great Depression was affecting the Russian emigration, including the Theakstons. "In general things are very bad here," Zaitseva wrote Bunina a couple of days later. "Crashes all around. You know the Theakstons are ruined."[90]

More generally the crisis was weakening the financial underpinnings of the émigré literary world. In early 1931 Teffi wrote Bunin: "We are living on a volcano and everything is flying [...] in the wrong direction."[91] At first glance she seemed to be doing relatively well, what with her weekly feuilletons in *Vozrozhdenie* and (sometimes in slightly altered form) in *Segodnya*. *The June Book* was coming out later that year, and *Memories* and *An Adventure Novel* in 1932, while at the end of February 1931 she received an advance of 1,000 francs for an Italian translation of *An Adventure Novel* by Amfiteatrov's wife, Ilaria.[92] This flurry of publications, however, signified not so much a flowering of the book trade as something close to its death throes. Teffi accepted very low honoraria from *Vozrozhdenie*, she wrote Zaitseva (1,500 francs for the memoirs, 1,000 for the novel), "because right now it's tough with books." Her attempt to get a second book published in Belgrade ended in failure and, despite Amfiteatrov's indefatigable efforts, most plans for Italian editions came to nothing. (*An Adventure Novel* did come out in 1932, but aroused no interest.[93])

Teffi's money problems grew more severe when she quit writing for *Segodnya* at the end of 1931 – the reason *Vozrozhdenie*'s displeasure at her pieces coming out in Riga on Sundays, the same day as in Paris. When *Segodnya* ignored her request to print her on Mondays, Teffi severed the tie, explaining to the editor that conditions had so deteriorated at *Vozrozhdenie* that they were firing and cutting the pay of staff members. She was "the only one whom they haven't touched so far," and she couldn't risk her position, since "no other newspaper can pay 500 francs per feuilleton."[94] In August Teffi wrote Amfiteatrov in more concrete detail: "They've stopped publishing poor sick Lolo. Those whom Gukasov in his time lured from *Poslednie novosti*, like Zaitsev and Khodasevich [...] have had their fees cut in half." By December, the situation had grown yet more dire: "Office employees are falling ill from malnutrition. One has just been buried. Two have consumption. The master [Gukasov] goes from desk to desk like a plantation owner. It's ve-ry bad."[95]

Despite her precarious situation, Teffi refused to take part in another venture of 1931: the revival in Paris of *Satirikon*, published by the same Kornfeld as the St. Petersburg original and edited by Don-Aminado.[96] Teffi warned Amfiteatrov in February not to contribute without an advance because "Kornfeld [...] is a swindler" who had owed her money since 1914. "I was stupid not to listen to you," he admitted the following fall: "Well, did I ever think that the miserable 600 francs *Satirikon* swindled from me could become practically a question of life and death?" Although Teffi herself was badly off, she was moved by his plight and offered him her advance for one of the Italian book projects. He refused, retorting on 27 December: "What a capitalist you've turned out to be!"

THE JUNE BOOK

Teffi's next books of fiction, *The June Book* and *An Adventure Novel*, are devoted in large part to an exploration of the nature of love. While a frequent theme in Teffi's earlier works, especially marked is the influence of her 1929 talk at the Green Lamp, "On the Unity of Love."[97] According to Irina Odoyevtseva's rather mocking account, Teffi had prepared a long, erudite lecture on asceticism, but the audience, anticipating something amusing, drowned out the speaker's learned comments with unbridled laughter.[98] Teffi's talk may well have elicited such a response – this happened all too often when she attempted to be serious – but Odoyevtseva misremembered her topic, which – far from asceticism – was passionate or "burning love [*liubov'-gorenie*]." Such love, to be sure, need not be physical: it "can germinate everywhere. Both in Sodom and Gomorrah and in the meek soul of a contemplative person or ascetic."

Conspicuously excluded from Teffi's account is the egoistic love of "The Limit." She is exploring instead "selfless and sacrificial [love], the very same that, in the word of the apostle, 'does not seek its own.'" Even such love, however, is not sanguine in her view, for she agrees with the view she ascribes to the religious philosopher Vladimir Solovyov (1853–1900) that "especially strong love is for the most part unhappy" – and, she adds, is "lonely." Mutual love is not even essential; the emotion itself is precious "even [if] the object has no significance." She expands on the adage that "love is blind," asserting that "the one who loves never sees the beloved and endows him with qualities he does not have." Teffi concludes with the vision of Abba Dorofei, a North African saint, who saw the world as a circle, with God at its center: "The closer souls are to God, the closer they are to one another, and vice versa: the closer they are to one another the closer they are to God." This is true of all who love – saints and sinners, even animals and plants:

> The ecstatic nun with stigmata on her hands [...] the dark Sodomite sinner [...] the old woman with her poor geranium [...] and St. Francis's brother – the hare who clung to him – and God's servants, the dandelion and the violet.

Both the ecstatic and somber aspects of Teffi's vision of love are reflected in *The June Book*, although the latter predominates. The book received high praise from critics, but the writer and critic Mikhail Osorgin (1878–1952) warned readers not to expect Teffi's usual laughter. On the contrary, he found an "overabundance of tragedy" and concluded that "if it weren't for the great and traditional [Russian] art [...] of transforming dead curses into living sadness, how terrifying would be the 'merry' stories of Teffi, one of the most intelligent and most clear-sighted [*zriachii*] contemporary writers."[99]

The title story, "The June Book," to be sure, is an exception, since it most fully embodies Teffi's ecstatic view of love. It centers on an unlikely triangle: Katya, an adolescent from St. Petersburg spending the summer at her aunt's country estate; her doltish cousin, Grisha; and an unattractive servant girl, Varvara, who is infatuated with Grisha. The denouement occurs one evening when the jealous Varvara bursts into Katya's room and starts tickling her – not playfully, but tormentingly – and Katya calls out desperately for Grisha. When he comes to the rescue, she hugs him hysterically, and in response he kisses her, and the "strange warmth of Grisha's lips" arouses new feelings in Katya.[100] After he leaves, Katya cries out to God and longs to confess, but cannot find the right words. She turns to nature on this splendid white night, when all is in harmony except for the girl: "All of 'them' knew something. This little human creature only thought."[101] Katya recalls words uttered by the Father Superior of the local monastery: "June [...] a book of untold secrets" – and only then finds the right words to address God: "Lord [...] blessed be Thy name... Thy will be done..."

Katya's yielding to God's will and to the mysteries of nature does not imply, however, that she will be happy, for her moment of ecstasy does not negate her previous judgment that Grisha is a fool. A poem she read earlier by the nineteenth-century poet A. K. Tolstoy (1817–75) expresses Teffi's idea that one never really sees the beloved:

You see in him not *his* perfection
[. . . . . .]
For you he is merely the pretext you have found [...]
For [your own] secret thoughts, torments, and bliss.[102]

The blindness of love is a constant in *The June Book*. This is true even of "The Wife," one of Teffi's most nuanced and sympathetic portrayals of conjugal relations. Manya, the wife of a gifted composer, Alexei, is a model of sacrificial love, but the painful irony is that her devotion often makes matters worse, and her well-meaning advice – for example that he should play his nocturne louder and add bells – reveals how poorly she understands his art. Despite the genuine love and sympathy the couple shares, the conflict between Aleksei's creative needs and Manya's practical concerns finally erupts and Manya's accumulated grievances spill out: "Am I really a woman? [...] It's not for myself I'm suffering – for yo-u-u-u! If I leave you you'll croak in a garret! Go aw-a-a-ay!"[103] Alexei leaves, and the "clear and joyous evening" contrasts with the stifling atmosphere of his flat. The "flaming-golden" sunset fills his soul with "inexpressibly blessed harmony" and, remembering Manya's warning that he will "die in a garret," he thinks: "My poor thing, my dear... Is that really so bad?"[104]

Commenting on the pain and frustrations of human love in "On the Unity of Love," Teffi recalls the queen in *Noon of Dzokhara*, who makes love to a corpse: "Are not living objects – insolent, coarse, and stupid, who offend love [...] – worse than a quiet corpse?" In "My Quiet Traveling Companion" Teffi goes further, endowing a particularly lowly object – a piece of sealing wax – with the precious human attributes of devotion and loyalty. The narrator traces the path she and her "little friend" trod together over the past decade and in the process sums up her wanderings over those years – from Petrograd to Moscow, Kiev, Odessa, Novorossisk, and finally into exile.[105] When the narrator is hospitalized in Berlin and her landlady brings her the "little gnarled piece," she sees in it virtues too often lacking in people: "human sadness, care, and affection, and fear for me, and devotion."[106] But in the end it too disappears.

"Moonlight" serves in certain respects as an antipode to the "The June Book," for if the adolescent Katya experiences the first tremors of love, the heroine of "Moonlight," the 78-year-old Anna Aleksandrovna, has outlived all human attachments. Living in a room rented from unsympathetic strangers, she doesn't feel close to her daughter, whom she remembers as a "plump little girl, merry and affectionate," but who now "is struggling against old age, loneliness, and depression."[107] Like Katya, Anna is deeply affected by the nocturnal sky, but if the girl feels the terror and ecstasy aroused by first love, for the old woman only the terror remains. Even when she has a heart seizure and is gasping for air, she dreads going to the window, beyond which "is horror. An immense sky [...] the black branches of winter trees on the dead face of the moon."[108] When she does drag herself there, however, she asks (addressing herself in the third person): "What is she so afraid of? [...] She has nothing."[109] Looking up at the "immense, moon-filled sky," she murmurs: "Here it is – my majestic abode, my rest. Accept me, Lord…"

Both "The June Book" and "Moonlight" end with a view of the nocturnal sky and submission to God's will, but if Katya feels a oneness with the awakening nature of June, for Anna the bare winter branches point to extinction. The old woman, who has lived through all that still awaits Katya and been left with nothing, is prepared to abandon the earth, to escape – like the poetic persona in "The Silver Ship" – to a higher moonlit sphere. In *The June Book*, where love, even in the best of circumstances, proves inadequate, death remains the final escape.

AN ADVENTURE NOVEL

An Adventure Novel represents something of an anomaly among Teffi's works. It is her only novel, its sub-genre unusual both for the writer herself and, as Soviet literary theorists of the 1920s were wont to complain, for Russian literature as a whole.[110] As one reviewer declared, perhaps too categorically: "Among Teffi's works there have been no such books, Russian literature has known no such books, and in the long chain of 'émigré novels' one can find nothing even distantly approaching it."[111]

Teffi's adventure novel does indeed conjure up a world very different from the mass of her short stories, which depict ordinary people caught up in the mishaps of everyday life. Here instead she tells a sordid tale of passion and crime set in the netherworld of Russian Paris and peopled by ageless *cocottes*, boyish *danseurs* "gracefully swaying between gigoloism and criminality," and a variety of other shady types.[112] But if the plot and character types represent a new departure, in other ways the work remains very characteristic of the writer who, known primarily for her very short stories, has also written a novel of small proportions. And just as in her shorter works she favors the "lightweight" genres of the feuilleton and comic tale, popular with the public but rather suspect to the serious literary critic, here again she chooses a popular but not quite respectable form, an adventure story – or, more accurately, a crime novel.[113] As in many of her works, moreover, the novel's unpretentious exterior represents a kind of camouflage. Zaitsev perceptively noted: "Aside from the visible appearance, the dramas, the clashes, there is something behind the scenes, difficult to recount, and usually most cherished by the author. This second plane of art is very strong in *An Adventure Novel*."[114] The existence of a "second plane" is in general characteristic of Teffi's writings, while in its exploration of the varieties of love, it is most closely related to *The June Book*.

The basic plot is quite simple. The heroine, Natasha, a beautiful 35-year-old model for the Parisian fashion house of Manel, meets a mysterious young man at a restaurant, who calls himself Gaston Luqué. He is clearly dishonest. He drops into her life and disappears unexpectedly, with no warning, and Natasha suspects a liaison between him and the beautiful, ageless *demimondaine*, Lyubasha von Wirch. Yet she develops a passionate attachment to Gaston, and he draws her into his shady activities. The dénouement occurs at a German resort, where Gaston receives a letter that greatly upsets him. From a small fragment he drops after tearing the letter up, Natasha manages to piece together: *"elle l'aime," "jeune," "faut renoncer."*[115] Gaston leaves, and several days later acquaintances tell Natasha that their friend Lyubasha has been strangled and Zhorzhik Bublik has been arrested. They show Natasha Zhorzhik's picture in a newspaper, and it turns out to be Gaston. The novel ends with Natasha, crazed with grief, drowning.

The plot movement of *An Adventure Novel*, with Natasha leaving the calm surface of everyday life to descend ever further into Gaston's disturbing, irrational world, confirms the novel's two planes of existence. Before she met him her life was superficially successful, but boring and empty. Even her relations with men (including a former husband) had always been strangely unemotional, "brief and boring, and not one of these men who had approached her by chance had searched for warmth, an intimacy of souls."[116] Throughout the novel Natasha's outward existence "flowed on evenly and as usual"; indeed, the more she becomes entangled with Gaston, the more successful is her professional life, until she finds out at the end that Manel has decided to make her director of the fashion house.[117] This outer success means nothing to her, however, for the only thing that has ever truly touched her is Gaston, who has brought into her life the disturbing excitement of a "crime film, an adventure novel."[118] This "adventure novel," however (or, given the double meaning of the Russian word, "adventure romance" or "affair"), based as it is on cheap fiction and cinema, exists only in Natasha's imagination. Like Teffi's comic characters, but in a different emotional register, she creates an illusory world as an alternative both to her empty everyday life and to the dreadful reality underlying Gaston's deceit. At the beginning deception actually reigns on both sides. Natasha (the name itself a pseudonym for Marusya Dukina) pretends to be a rich Englishwoman, while Gaston's identity is left vague. He soon finds out who she really is, but a web of deceit surrounds Gaston until the very end. Natasha believes that she desperately wants to know the truth – "finally to emerge from the fog of anxiety, conjectures, and suspicions" – but in actuality this desire is itself dubious, since in the course of the novel there are so many hints of Gaston's identity that, when it is revealed, Natasha herself admits: "It was as if someone were telling her over and over again a long familiar story."[119]

Natasha's imagined "adventure romance" has blinded her to the truth, but more important is the nature of her love. One night, when Gaston, distraught and frightened, comes to sleep at her place, she understands she should avoid seeing him, but when he trembles in his sleep and says in a tone of inexpressible anguish, *Ich habe Angst, Mama!* she reacts: "My boy, poor boy! I won't leave you!" Teffi defines such maternal feeling as "the most bitter and heroic image of love." It "will forgive everything, accept everything, bless everything. 'My boy!' said Natasha and doomed herself and began to cry from pain and happiness."[120]

Natasha's love, despite her awareness of Gaston's flaws, transforms him into her little boy, Goss. She thinks:

> "Why have I bound up my life so grotesquely with this punk [*mal'chishka*]? [...] He's stupid, he's dishonest... [...] If I had simply gotten a poodle, I wouldn't be as lonely as I am with him."
>
> Gaston, childishly puffing out his upper lip, was diligently filing his nails. Natasha glanced at him and senseless pity, like warm tears, flooded her soul.
>
> "Poor lost boy. Goss! Why are you so pale today? Can it be you haven't eaten?"[121]

Lyubasha, the other main female character in the novel, in important ways stands as Natasha's negative double. Both women are very beautiful and about the same age, but if Natasha embodies maternal love, the liaison between Lyubasha and Gaston appears to be of the duel-like variety explored in "The Limit."[122]

Lyubasha's relationship with her husband, Baron von Wirch, one of Teffi's hapless failures, introduces yet another variant of love. People assume that the baron knows about his wife's affairs, but an incident related by Lyubasha's friend, the manicurist Fifisa, contradicts that assumption. One day, while Fifisa is waiting for Lyubasha, the baron unexpectedly drops in and she makes him some fried eggs. While he is eating, Lyubasha arrives, followed by a jealous American lover, whom she orders out, but then notices the baron:

> He tilted his face back – all nostrils, and a piece of egg was quivering in his beard [...] He was so very terrifying! For some reason I was especially scared of that egg in his beard [...] And the baroness turned completely pale, but she laughed: "Griva, Griva, what's the matter?" And he kept stammering and suddenly: "Who was at your place just now?" And, would you believe it, she lost her head![123]

The comic sight of the cuckolded husband with egg in his beard does not amuse but terrifies Fifisa, and later Lyubasha herself cries hysterically: "I'm afraid, I'm afraid, I'm afraid!" Her fear is justified, for she, like Natasha, will die for love, although in her case the result of duel-like passion.

There is yet another plane of existence in *An Adventure Novel* – the irrational, associated with dreams and premonitions, and symbolized by watery expanses. Early on, a fortune-teller predicts that Natasha will return home by water and warns her: "Fear water!"[124] Later Natasha's thoughts about Gaston take the figurative form of a watery death:

> he muddied the water of her life like sea sepia, and in this black water a monster was stirring somewhere that would destroy her, and she didn't see it and didn't know its name – but felt it was there and cried in her sleep...[125]

The night before she drowns, Natasha dreams that the fortune-teller's augury has come true – that she has returned to her childhood home, where relatives, all dead, are awaiting her.

The morning after Gaston leaves, Natasha avoids the water; she walks about the town, "but not toward the sea [...] not toward abysses, not toward the angelic-rosy dawn. No, instinct still drew her toward life."[126] The other abyss that figures in the novel is the night-time sky, "the heavenly firmament, without beginning and without end," which arouses – to a greater extent than in "Moonlight" – horror and unadulterated despair. The evening after Gaston's departure, Natasha, still clinging to life, looks out at the abyss, "a black gap, not below, but through all the sky and all the earth and all of immeasurable space," and fully acknowledges her total solitude:

> She is alone in the world, in shameful solitude [...]
> And previously she had also always been alone. Unneeded by anyone, uninteresting. A model for other people's dresses.
> [...]
> Love had come and had given her soul only cold, hunger, and fear. In this love she had also been alone. Lonely.[127]

The following day Natasha – typically in Teffi's world – puts up a final defense through artifice, getting her hair bobbed and dyed red, but this ruse cannot protect her from the truth about Gaston, which she learns that day. Afterward she "feels nothing but deadly fatigue and boredom," although accompanied by "strange laughter" – once more affirming the tragic source of Teffi's laughter.[128] Natasha then looks for the rich Dutchman whom she, at Gaston's bidding, has been luring for dubious purposes, hoping he will give her the money she needs to return to Paris. She thinks she sees him far out in the water, and only when she is very deep does she realize she imagined it. A ship cuts off her path, making her end inevitable.

Natasha faces death calmly:

> And there was nothing in the world. Neither her life with Gaston, nor her love for him [...] nor the horror of her final hours [...] She felt only calm surprise that all this could have been so significant and so terrifying![129]

Surrendering to death, Natasha, like Anna in "Moonlight," invokes God's name and God's will, but even her attempt to cross herself results in "a sharp, burning pain [that] struck her when she breathed, burned her brain" – a final sign of an unjust, cruel universe.[130]

A couple of days later Germans sitting on the beach discuss a newspaper account of Lyubasha's murder: "'They've arrested the baroness's husband, a degenerate, almost an idiot, who lived off his wife's money.' 'Since the day of the murder [...] the baron has been behaving very suspiciously. He has been laughing continuously...'" Teffi does not state explicitly who the murderer is and Lyubasha's hysterical fear of her husband makes the baron a plausible perpetrator, but it is more likely that Gaston committed the crime and that the baron's grief, like Natasha's, accounts for his laughter.

On that same tranquil evening Natasha's body washes up on shore, but even this discovery does not disturb the serene atmosphere, as a fisherman's son, seeing her bobbed head, cries out joyously: "We caught a boy!" The irony of this image of life's cares dissolving into the peace and beauty of nature is underlined by the appearance of a sentimental German pastor, accompanied by a young friend whom he fears will be sullied by talk of the murder, "that sordid Parisian drama of degenerates, high-society cocottes, and pimps." He points instead "to the rosy distance, which promises marvelous happiness" – a scene that includes, ironically, Natasha's body: "The quiet of the sea and the blessedness of the sky and even the peaceful human toil – over there fishermen are carrying something dark, it must be their evening catch – and the silvery, joyous little voice of a child…" The pastor's view of nature excludes the hidden passions and vices that operate in Natasha's circle, and yet the presence of her body in this idyllic scene (not to speak of the entire novel) shows its inadequacy.

Earlier the narrator put forth another view, repeating the butterfly image from "The Limit": "Whoever has seen under a microscope God's most enchanting creation, symbol of earthly beauty – the butterfly – will never forget its nightmarishly sinister mug. For us the world of monsters is transformed by the film of 'seeing small' [*maloviden'ia*]."[131] In *An Adventure Novel* Teffi dissolves the "film" and reveals the world of monsters it conceals. It is doubly ironic that the optimistic character at the end of the novel is a Christian clergyman, for it is in the dark world of sin and suffering that the model of Christ has significance. Natasha, who suffers for the sins of others and dies for love, is following Christ's path, and the priest's vision, by ignoring the hidden planes of human life, proves not only inadequate, but also unchristian. One can, nevertheless, accept his final words (and the final words of the novel), although one is bound to put a darker interpretation on them than he intended: *"In manus Tuas, Domine."*[132]

8

A SLIPPERY SLOPE

1931–6

Theakston's illness brought an immediate halt to Teffi's involvement in émigré social and cultural activities, and, in late February 1931, the couple abandoned Paris altogether for La Colline, a Russian sanatorium in Saint-Antoine, in the hills above Nice.[1] By Easter Theakston's condition was improving, there were "masses of flowers" everywhere, Teffi wrote Zaitseva, but her mood remained very dark: "If I'm not terrified I'm bored, and if I'm not bored, I'm terrified." Later that spring Seryozha Theakston's visit broke up the monotony a bit, but a very unpleasant incident involving his crazed former lover forced his father and Teffi to make a precipitous departure from Nice to Uriage, a resort near Grenoble.[2] On 19 July Theakston described the town to Zaitseva (writing with his left hand): "Picturesque [...] A large, shady park, a nice green lawn."[3] Teffi wrote Bunina that Theakston "is recovering well and my 'mission' is coming to an end," but she was overly optimistic, for in late November it seemed to Zaitseva that he was "melting away."[4]

The deepening economic crisis added to Teffi's woes. In her 1932 New Year's greeting to Amfiteatrov she complained that, although she had spent the holidays working, "not everyone wants to pay me for the work," and a few weeks later described the broader anxiety gripping her circle: "Everyone is worried, angry, and unsociable. So am I." The mood among Russians in France grew still darker when on 6 May a Cossack named Paul Gorgulov assassinated the French president, Paul Doumer.[5] In the uproar that ensued those on the right accused Gorgulov of being a Soviet agent, while the left placed him in extreme anti-Communist émigré circles. It turned out that he was deranged and had acted alone, but his crime aroused already burgeoning anti-foreign – especially anti-Russian – sentiment.[6] The news about Gorgulov, Teffi wrote the Zaitsevs in July, "greatly tormented" her, thus further exacerbating her already bleak mood. He was sent to the guillotine on 14 September.

During the summer of 1932 Teffi and Theakston found some respite at the "enchanting Château des Ombrages" in Marly-le-Roi,[7] but as their vacation was ending, Teffi wrote Amfiteatrov of her dread at seeing her panic-stricken colleagues:

If you could see Merezhkovsky's bewildered eyes, bulging with horror! If you could hear a kind of nervous quacking [? *khrebtovoe kriakan'e*] from Gippius! B. Zaitsev's timid little laugh! That alone could make you sink into neurasthenia. And so I have.

Teffi's life that fall proved even worse than she feared, for in November she fell violently ill, pressure from work aggravating the situation: "I'm as weak as a fly now," she wrote Amfiteatrov, "and I've broken a record: they pumped me full of camphor and strychnine, sat me down, and I wrote a feuilleton because we're forbidden to skip any – the plantation owner [Gukasov] would whip us."

The crises of the 1930s raised further doubts about the very survival of Russian literature abroad – a topic upon which Teffi spoke at the celebration of the publication of the fiftieth issue of *Sovremennye zapiski* on 30 November 1932:

Russian literature is barely alive, barely breathing; there are no publishing companies and only thanks to *Sovremennye zapiski* can we get to know new works by our writers. Young people are gradually leaving Russian literature for European [literature], young Russian writers are no longer inspired by Tolstoy and Dostoyevsky, but by André Gide and Marcel Proust...[8]

Because of the growing numbers of indigent writers, Teffi warned Amfiteatrov before the writers' ball in January 1933 not to expect anything from the take, but she promised to set aside some money for him from her own evening, to be held later that month. The benefit, which featured performances by "tiny ballerinas from the studio of M[atilda] Kshesinskaya" and the famous Japanese modern dancer Yeichi Nimura, "went brilliantly," according to *Vozrozhdenie*, but one successful evening, of course, could change nothing.[9] An event of far greater moment occurred the following November and immensely lifted the spirits of the entire Russian emigration: the awarding of the Nobel Prize in Literature to Ivan Bunin. Zaitsev's article on the first page of *Vozrozhdenie* expressed the joy that many must have felt:

> The Russian writer Ivan Bunin has been crowned […] and in his person our literature and Russia have been crowned […] Still more astounding, and for our émigré hearts especially intoxicating, a Russian **émigré** has been crowned […] This is, of course, a holiday. A true Russian one, the **first** after so many years of humiliation and misfortune […] Russia is not forgotten.[10]

About a week later Teffi wrote Vera Bunina expressing "how happy we all are that the long-awaited triumph of Ivan Bunin has at last arrived!" She added that Theakston "even cried a little from joy. It was he who composed the splendid telegram congratulating Iv. Al."[11] By then Bunin had arrived in Paris and, although Teffi could not leave Theakston alone to attend the 16 November reception at *Vozrozhdenie*, she called to let him know "that she 'joined them with all her heart.'"[12] And she did attend the celebration at the Champs-Élysées Theater on 26 November, of which *Vozrozhdenie* wrote ecstatically that "you couldn't count all the émigré 'celebrities'" in attendance.[13] Teffi, however, remarked sourly to Amfiteatrov: "Neither the Merezhkovskys nor Shmelyov nor Balmont nor Remizov were at the celebration […] It's bad. Spiteful and petty. It was very painful for [Bunin]." In general Bunin was "very sad and bewildered," she added, since "he, poor thing, now receives only abusive anonymous letters. That's how our fellow countrymen express their national pride." Teffi had anticipated this reaction in a feuilleton, "Triumph," which she characterized as a "friendly 'defense'" of Bunin. It tells of an indigent Russian scientist who has been awarded a large prize, after which his countrymen, although at first overjoyed, decide that he should give away virtually all the money. When someone asks "how he is going to live," another responds: "He's lived up until now, after all, so he'll go on living."[14]

There were indeed expectations that Bunin would share his award, and he did set aside 10 percent for Russian writers and organizations, but the gifts only created widespread discord – especially since Bunin decided to leave the distribution of the money to a committee.[15] Teffi wrote Bunin of her certainty that he himself had decided on her "royal [*tsarstvennyi*] gift" (reportedly of 2,000 francs).[16] She also received a pair of gloves from Vera and responded that she was "very touched" that, "despite how tired and busy you were […] you found the time and inclination to make me such a sweet gift."[17]

Teffi's joy at Bunin's award was tempered by the death on 5 November of her brother, General Lokhvitsky.[18] His funeral was attended by a large contingent of military dignitaries and former Russian aristocrats, with Grand Prince

Kirill (1876–1938), cousin of the last emperor, sending a wreath.[19] Judging from Teffi's remarks to Amfiteatrov, Nikolai's death did not touch her very deeply – and she certainly felt no sympathy for her brother's political views: "I feel sorry for my brother, but was not close to him and saw him rarely […] He was a decent chap [*dobryi malyi*], but a snob and… a *Kirillovets* [supporter of Kirill's claim to the Russian throne]!" Nevertheless, the death, on top of other cares, probably contributed to another period of ill health: "I'm insanely tired," she wrote Amfiteatrov. "Exhaustion brings insomnia, migraines, and a nervous rash that swoops down like a whirlwind, covers me with red bands and white blisters that itch to the point of hysteria. In a couple of hours everything disappears just as instantaneously."

The end of 1933 brought yet more misfortunes. There was another family death that seemed to affect her more deeply than her brother's – that of her cousin, Yevgeny Davydov, who "was very dear," she wrote Bunin. "There are fewer and fewer people in the world for whom I am Nadya, Nadya Lokhvitskaya."[20] In addition she suffered a severe financial blow when *Vozrozhdenie* announced it was cutting its staff's pay in half. She wrote Amfiteatrov at the beginning of the new year: "This accumulation of horrors is so anti-artistic on Fate's part that it recalls a tasteless play in the Grand Guignol style."

Teffi did eke out a little extra money beginning in the spring of 1934 by renewing her association with *Segodnya*, but the added pittance did not help much, especially since she had moved the previous fall into a more spacious apartment in a large, elegant house on the Boulevard de Versailles. That might sound extravagant, given Teffi's straitened circumstances, but the extra space was necessary to accommodate Theakston, who moved in with her that winter, just at a time when his condition was steadily worsening. The added burden was so intolerable that she had to "take an exam to become an angel," she wrote the Amfiteatrovs – a calling for which she was ill-suited: "The thing is that angels are fleshless creatures, but I am made of flesh and everything hurts me, and I'm so tired I could howl like a wolf." Teffi's own health suffered, and in February, after a third bout of the flu, she complained: "I live like a dog. Beyond my strength […] I'm sliding down a slippery slope [*po naklonnoi ploskosti*]." She continued to adopt animal imagery to describe her deepening misery, comparing herself at Easter to the whipped horse in *Crime and Punishment*, and in October – to a dog expiring "from insane, inhuman exhaustion […] Cares and labor beyond measure, beyond one's strength."

Teffi's personal suffering, as well as the desperate struggle for survival she observed all around, darkened her already negative views of mankind. She wrote Lyatsky in early October: "Paris has changed a great deal. In general. But Russian [Paris] in particular. Malicious, spiteful, and evil-tempered [*Zol, zloben i zlitsia*]."[21] Her view of human nature sometimes became so negative that her writing crossed the line between witty satire and wrathful invective. In "Natural History," for example, she asserts that the saying "Man is a wolf to man" is an insult to wolves: "Why a wolf all of a sudden? Why not a pig, why not an ass, a snake? [...] Does a wolf really flatter, lie, play dirty tricks, spy, betray, sell out, slander? A wolf devours out of hunger, that's all."[22] This piece and others altered Amfiteatrov's view of Teffi's humor, which in 1931 he had described as "inoffensive, good-natured, and noble," expressing a "love of people" and imbued by the "Pushkinian spirit."[23] After reading "Natural History," however, he wrote, in a letter of 15 September 1934: "'Wolves,' eh? You've begun to remold yourself from a bright Pushkinian into a gloomy Gogolian."[24] He expanded upon this observation in a *Segodnya* article, commenting that her stories show

> that "papa Paris" [*batiushka Parizh*] is not living well, that Russian Parisians, stewing in their juice, have gone downhill, grown petty [*oposhleli*], spiteful, their lives are boring, rancorous – "man is a wolf to man." She tells her stories artistically, with inimitable wit, every word is apropos, every joke is right on the mark. You listen and laugh, you can't stop, but once she's finished – you're sad, sad to the point of tears. Oh, Russian people, poor, absurd, dear Russian people.[25]

Life became yet grimmer for Russians in France when another scandal involving an émigré erupted in 1934 – this one of such enormity that it threatened the stability of the French political system as a whole. The so-called *Affaire Stavisky* centered around the embezzler and confidence man Serge Alexandre Stavisky (1886–1934), a Jew born in Ukraine and a naturalized citizen of France since 1900.[26] While under investigation for fraud, Stavisky died suddenly on 8 January 1934, and, although the death was ruled a suicide, suspicion has lingered to this day that he was murdered by the police. The scandal brought down the Radical Socialist government, which had suspicious financial ties to Stavisky, and culminated in a right-wing demonstration on the Place de la Concorde on 6 February, in which 15 died and about 1,500 were wounded.[27] A prolonged period followed of almost daily violent demonstrations and massive workers' strikes.[28]

In a March feuilleton, Teffi conveys the unease that the *Affaire Stavisky* aroused among the émigrés. When two Russians, Mamashin and Sevryukov, meet on the *Métro*, the former warns the latter to shave off his beard to avoid falling under suspicion in the Stavisky case. When Sevryukov answers that he could prove he was not involved, Mamashin responds:

> Go ahead [...] and prove it. And in the meanwhile they'll put a rotten picture of you without a collar in the newspaper and will write that you speak French with a beastly accent and that you have the ears of a degenerate.[29]

Life occasionally offered diversions from this all-pervasive gloom. One involved Yevreinov, who in 1934 decided to put on a play by Teffi's sister, Varvara (written under her pseudonym, Myurgit). Teffi asked him on 24 May to "do a good deed" and "spare a few francs as an author's honorarium" for Varvara, "who is perishing from hunger in Leningrad."[30] Yevreinov's wife later recalled the numerous trips she and Teffi took "to register Myurgit's authorial rights at the French Society of Dramatists" – which also served a larger purpose: "I consciously diverted her [Teffi] in order to offer some distraction from her difficult domestic situation."[31]

That summer Theakston and Teffi again enjoyed a respite from Paris at Marly-le-Roi, and she was soothed by the tranquil setting.[32] Her undying coquettishness, moreover, was gratified by a piquant photograph of her by the river, clad in a bare-backed sundress, which she sent to friends, including Amfiteatrov and Lyatsky.[33] The former responded on 26 October with a mock-heroic poem that brought a moment of sorely needed levity to them both. It begins:

> Oh, Teffi! turned into a Naiad,
> You have filled my heart with poison!
> What words can express
> How ravishing you are naked?[34]

Lyatsky wrote playfully about the amorous feeling the picture reawakened: "Your photo is a living picture of you. You are beautiful in it, young, and... and... [...] Can it be that at this moment I'm compelled to sing: *nous arrivons toujours trop tard?*"[35]

Such light moments offered only brief reprieves from personal cares and the sense of impending doom that was hanging over Europe. In October 1934, the atmosphere grew yet more ominous when King Alexander I of Yugoslavia was assassinated in Marseilles. Teffi wrote a moving article on the king, an ardent anti-Bolshevik and one of the most steadfast friends of the Russian emigration. Summing up her gloomy view of émigré life, she observed that the Russians are no longer horrified by death, but are impatiently waiting their turn: "It's exactly as if we're sitting in the waiting room of a dentist. A door will now open and a calm voice will call: 'Who's next? Please come in.'"[36]

Theakston's turn was soon to come, but Teffi took the time to make an appearance at a major literary event that took place on 21–25 June 1935: the International Writers' Congress for the Defense of Culture. The idea of the chameleon-like writer and journalist Ilya Ehrenburg, and supported at the highest levels of the Soviet government, including Stalin, the congress was intended to promote the Soviet "experiment" as a positive alternative to fascism.[37] Famous French literary figures, most prominently André Gide and André Malraux, were among the organizers, who brought together writers from 35 countries. Although the event only emphasized the marginality of Russian émigrés, Teffi was bestirred to attend because her old chum Aleksei Tolstoy was head of the Soviet delegation. She reported to Bunin afterward that when he saw her, he exclaimed happily: "Nadyusha!" He seemed to be doing just fine, she added – "Not in the least bit frightened."[38] She justified her bold step, of which Zaitsev strongly disapproved: "I felt as if I were dreaming, when one dreams of Russia. You see something boorish but your very own. Both shameful and swe-e-et." Bunin responded that he heartily approved of her action and especially praised "*how* you wrote – I saw and felt Alyoshka as if in the flesh [*kak zhivogo*]."[39]

After this brief diversion, Theakston's illness totally consumed Teffi. In July she wrote the Zaitsevs: "I fear I won't be able to hold on to him for long. Poor thing, he has been so considerate [*delikatnyi*] all his life that he's not even leaving us rudely, but little by little." She was further saddened by the news she received that summer that her ex-husband had died. "I've been divorced for a long time," she wrote the Zaitsevs, "and he doesn't exist for [me]. But I somehow felt the news of his death – sent to me through […] the children we have in common. All of this is sad."

By September Theakston required round-the-clock care and Yevgenia Vasyutinskaya, who was to remain as Teffi's companion after his death, stayed overnight. His deteriorating state put yet more strain on Teffi. "Poor P.A. can no longer talk," she wrote Bunina, "so I carry on a monologue, of course very kind, cheerful, and entertaining. Because of that I have an unending migraine."[40] Pity, she added, made her suffering all the more intense: "What a terrible thing pity is. It knows absolutely no bounds or limits. It always seems one can give something more. 'Aha, bitch! You probably read a book at night, and he can't read!' There's no limit!" In the sketch "On Tenderness," published 6 October, Teffi reiterated: "Love-tenderness (pity) gives everything away, and there's no limit to it."[41] Theakston died soon after, on 17 October.

The funeral service was held a couple of days later at the Alexander Nevsky Cathedral. Among those in attendance were Prince Gavriil Konstantinovich (1887–1955), great-grandson of the last tsar, and numerous literary and theatrical friends.[42] The following month Teffi received unexpected condolences from Damascus, from the "sinful monk Gavriil," who identified himself as "in the world V. Fokht."[43] The monk, formerly the initiator of the Studio Franco-Russe, wrote: "The most gratifying memories bind me personally to the late Pavel Andreyevich [...] he was a peaceable, responsive man with a 'broad' soul (in the best sense), and I feel obliged to him for a number of bright memories."

After Theakston's death, friends advised Teffi to travel, and at the end of November she decided to visit her daughters in Warsaw. The effect was not salubrious, for Valya, as she wrote Zaitseva, was "sad and tired," her husband was down with the flu, and Gulya was suffering from a liver ailment. Her mood lifted somewhat at Christmas, when she visited Gulya's "enchanting villa" an hour's drive from Warsaw. It was located "right near the forest – fir trees and birches. The little house is warm, cozy, and very beautiful. The rooms are like the setting of northern plays at the Moscow Art Theater." The snow recalled lost Russia: "Through the window I can see snow on the roof. Winter. There has been no winter in my life for about fifteen years."[44] Once Teffi returned to Warsaw, though, she complained to Zaitseva that the thaw turned the fresh snow to black mud, and she again felt lonely, was suffering from migraines and unable to work. She was back in Paris by January 1936, with another difficult year ahead. One happy event, however, occurred in March: the publication of *The Witch*, Teffi's first collection since 1932.[45]

THE WITCH

During the summer of 1930, while taking the waters at Saint-Nectaire, Teffi wrote several feuilletons comparing the French countryside and its inhabitants to their Russian counterparts. Looking back at her native land after "ten years of separation," she saw with her "European gaze" what "a truly strange country" it was, inhabited by "amazing, incomprehensible people."[46] She wondered if Russia was so different from the West because of its climate – the "turbulent, short, mad spring, the difficult, black winter" – or its immensity – the "endless monotony of impressions (a forest that takes two days to cross, the steppe – four)."

Teffi probed more deeply into the peculiar nature of the Russian people – especially the simple country folk – in a series of stories published in *Vozrozhdenie* in 1931 but collected in *The Witch*, with a few additions, only five years later. It was one of Teffi's favorite books: "the only one," she wrote Bitsilli, "for which I feel absolutely no shame."[47] Her goal, she explained to Amfiteatrov, was a serious one: to portray "yesterday's gods" as they "live on in the lives of the people [*v narodnoi zhizni zhivut da pozhivaiut*]." In other words, what interests her is not so much Slavic paganism as such (although she does provide amusing and informative descriptions of some of the "gods"), but how the old beliefs continued to mold the Russian character. The emphasis is on *Russian*, as she declared in the title story:

> It goes without saying that it is completely impossible to tell a foreigner about this – he won't understand a thing and won't believe anything. Well, but a real Russian who has not completely forgotten the past will of course consider it all fully authentic and rightly so.[48]

Fantastic stories generally fall into two categories – those in which supernatural forces are actually in play and others where a rational explanation is provided in the end – but Teffi's tales belong to neither. Some strange events occur, which simple folk attribute to the intercession of unclean spirits, but nothing is unambiguously supernatural. On the other hand, no more plausible explanation is given, so that the reader is left in a state of disturbing uncertainty. The remarks of the narrator of "The Dog" bare Teffi's approach:

> People are often inclined to see the miraculous in trifles, and in general, where everything is ordinary and simple, they like to mix in some premonitions or dreams of theirs, which, depending on the circumstances, they interpret one way or another. Other sober natures, on the contrary, regard everything inexplicable very skeptically, analyzing and explaining stories that lie outside their understanding. I don't belong to one group or the other. I am not about to explain anything, but will simply tell honestly how everything was.[49]

The sober tone here is very characteristic of *The Witch*. Untypical of the genre, Teffi's stories are understated and restrained, and the narrators usually convince us of their level heads. In many of the pieces boring everyday life is disturbed by some strange occurrence, implying (as in a very different context in *An Adventure Novel*) that irrational forces are at work beneath the orderly surface of human life.

The title story illustrates how superstition disrupts the dull everyday life even of avowedly enlightened people. The narrator tells of an odd occurrence that took place when she was 19 years old and living with her husband and year-and-a-half-old daughter, Valya, in a dreary town in the steppes (some of the details reflecting the author's biography). When the maid, Ustyusha, disappears for four days without notice, the couple decides to fire her, but the cook enigmatically warns her mistress that they won't be able to do so: "Because every night she whispers against you and burns paper and blows in the chimney."[50] The narrator's husband attributes these words to the peasants' benightedness, but the couple is unable to dismiss Ustyusha. The main horror (in fact, not so very horrible) occurs one evening when the nanny shows her mistress that the 12 dining-room chairs, plus an unfamiliar thirteenth, have been placed with their backs to the table. She explains that they are being turned out: "Yes, a turn from the gates, here's God and here's the threshold. Turn and out with you!" (the incantatory repetitions of the original much more frightening: "*Da, ot vorot povorot, vot Bog, a vot porog. Povorachivaite i von otsiuda!*")[51] Nothing further occurs that night, but in the morning the husband decides that it would be best if they left.

As a supernatural phenomenon the chair turning is trivial. What is important is not the event itself, but the power the irrational exercises even over the "enlightened" couple. The narrator acknowledges Ustyusha's "turn" worked, after all, and "we were 'turned' from that house, turned and chased away. Laugh all you like, but it didn't turn out in our way, the rational, educated [*intelligentnomu*] way."[52] In the story both the outer world and the psyche exist on two levels. While the town is a model of dreary monotony, unexpected and disturbing events occur there, which echo in the minds of its ostensibly enlightened heroes.

Many of the stories in *The Witch* take place at Teffi's childhood summer retreat, Volynia (where, according to Kate Brown, belief in spirits lasted well into the Soviet period[53]). "Rusalka," one of the strongest, tells of how the alluring but treacherous Slavic water nymph inhabits an unlikely person: the unattractive and pious maid Kornela. Called *pannochka* (Polish for young lady) because of her gentry origins and affectations, she prays by the ice house on Sundays, her only *rusalka*-like feature her remarkably long hair, which she wears in an unbecoming crown on her head. Then one summer the family finds that Kornela has gotten married and, since she is living by the pond, now prays while sitting on a willow branch near the water. Otherwise she seems little changed until one day her hair comes cascading down after bringing sugar to the stable for the older sisters and their friends to feed the horses. A friend exclaims that Kornela is "a real *rusalka*," and when she asks the handsome young groom, Fedko, if he agrees, he responds, to please the young ladies: "Ekh, what beauty there is in the world!" The narrator comments that this is one of those instants when the line of fate is broken, and afterward Kornela no longer prays while sitting on the willow branch on Sundays, but combs her hair and sings in Polish: "*Złoty włosy, złoty włosy*" ("Golden hair, golden hair").[54]

Later the narrator, Nadya, and her little sister, Lena, witness a startling manifestation of Kornela's transformation. While she and the laundress are bathing in the pond, Fedko shouts out: "Ho – ho – ho! […] Ho! Ru – sal – alka!" and Kornela turns to him and, laughing hysterically, leaps waist-high out of the water, making a beckoning motion.[55] Then one evening Nadya hears a quiet groan from the pond, and the following day it looks as if Kornela has been crying. Nanny mutters (alluding to the *rusalka*'s habit of enticing men through weeping): "Crying! Such people are always crying. Try and pity her and she'll show you!"[56]

The final episode takes place at Fedko's wedding, which the two little girls, who have felt sick since morning, observe from the sofa. As they watch the peasant couples dance joylessly, Lena says, "Look, there's another wedding over there."[57] Nadya objects that she is pointing to a mirror, but Lena insists it is a door leading to another wedding, where Kornela is dancing. Nadya sees only the green, dim people, but when Lena says "Kornela is weeping," Nadya – confused by the similar-sounding verbs, "Dancing? Weeping?" ("*Pliashet? Plachet?*") – looks in the mirror again and sees that

the evil, green people are spinning, insistently stamping their feet, as if they were trampling someone into the ground. Isn't that Kornela, all black, turbid… She's looking with enormous fish eyes… And suddenly she leapt up, like that time in the pond, naked to the waist, her arms stretched out, and she lures, lures, and below her breasts are fish scales… Her mouth is open and she is singing or maybe crying: "O-o i o-o!"[58]

Echoing Kornela, the little girls scream hysterically. It turns out they have scarlet fever, and only later do they find out that Kornela drowned herself in the mill stream at about that time.

In conclusion, the narrator asks whether Kornela loved Fedko or simply went mad, but adds that there are times when neither rational alternative seems likely, when the truth is what little Nadya saw in the mirror. But what is that truth? The simplest answer is that Kornela turns into a *rusalka*, psychologically at least, that once again the boring surface – Kornela's initial proper demeanor – conceals powerful, irrational forces. But one may interpret the vision still further, for while the *rusalka* traditionally arouses people's pity through weeping, Kornela weeps, but nobody pities her. The image in the mirror, where evil, green people trample her, is emblematic of the triumph of hard-heartedness over pity. There is a striking reversal here, for if in the usual version the *rusalka* lures men to their death, in "Rusalka" the forces of everyday life – the grotesquely portrayed "green people" – destroy the mythical creature.

If "Rusalka" explores destructive passion associated with the old Slavic gods, "The Dog," centering upon "man's best friend," tells of a rare instance of love's positive power. The story, which takes place mostly in St. Petersburg during the 1910s, borrows from Teffi's contacts with the bohemia of the time, but by affixing the subtitle "The Story of a Stranger" she discourages an autobiographical reading. In any case, Teffi would have been in her forties by then, much older than her heroine, Lyalya.

The narrator starts her story when she was 15 years old, wildly merry, pretty, full of the joy of life. She is spending the summer at the family estate of her friend, Zina Katkova, and flirts with everyone – for which there is ample opportunity, what with the two Katkov sons (the older of whom, Volodya, she would later marry), their friend Vanya, and the steward's son, red-headed Tolya. It is Tolya, nice and not bad-looking, but painfully shy, who falls deeply and hopelessly in love with Lyalya.

The young people are in the habit of strolling in the evening to a hillock with a picturesque view of the river and an abandoned mill, and one time they decide that each should tell a story, the more terrifying the better. Tolya is first and recounts a true story about the mill, which long ago was rented to a reclusive old German whose enormous dog sat opposite him for days on end, not taking its eyes off him. Then one day, for no apparent reason, the dog jumped on the old man, bit through his throat, and disappeared, and ever since the mill has been empty. The others like Tolya's story, but Vanya complains that it wasn't scary enough, that he should have added that since that time the place is bewitched and whoever spends the night there will turn into a dog. Tolya, at Lyalya's prompting, decides to test Vanya's hypothesis and stay overnight at the mill and, although all of this is a joke, Lyalya can hardly sleep. When awakened in the morning by scratching on the shutters and she sees Tolya, she hugs him and screams: "How did you dare, you scoundrel [...] not to turn into a dog?" He objects: "I am a dog, Lyalechka, your hound forever true. I'll never leave you."[59]

During the next two years Tolya and Lyalya meet only once, and after their meeting he sends her an enormous bouquet of roses with a little heart-faced dog attached. The extravagant gift from the poor boy fills Lyalya with pity, and "the little dog was also so pitiful, with its glittering eyes, as if it were crying."[60] Then comes the "muddled period of [her] life," coinciding with the world war and revolution.[61] While Tolya and the Katkovs join the war effort, Lyalya remains in St. Petersburg to study voice at the conservatory and frequents the Stray Dog, where she meets a sickly but dandyish young man, Garri Edvers. At first repelled by him, Lyalya is soon drawn into his decadent circle and begins singing his nonsensical ditties, wearing a man's suit and with her hair cropped and dyed red. Garri advises her to "stick an abnormal rose in your lapel. Green. Enormous. Deformed," and the rose becomes emblematic of his circle:

> Also "abnormal, green, and deformed." A green girl cocaine addict, a certain Yurochka "whom everybody knows," a consumptive *lycée* student, and a hunchback who played the piano wonderfully. They were all bound by some kind of secrets, spoke in hints, were suffering over something, agitated by something, and, as I understand now, were sometimes simply striking poses in a void.[62]

Lyalya's relations with Garri were also "green and deformed": "when I was with him I felt an aversion, a sharp loathing toward him, as if I were kissing a corpse. But I couldn't live without him."

Things go from bad to worse for Lyalya. Garri is involved in some shady enterprises, which take him away for long periods, and during one trip he contrives to meet Lyalya's aunt and, pretending to be her husband, gets hold of Lyalya's money. At the time the mood of his circle is counter-revolutionary, but later, when they move to Moscow, Garri and his new friends call one another "comrades" – which Lyalya considers a joke until she finds out that they have joined the Cheka (the secret police).[63] Terribly frightened, she decides she must escape to her aunt's estate, and while scurrying around to get the proper papers, she runs into the younger Katkov brother, who promises to tell Tolya that "Lyalya is calling her dog for help."[64] After she collects the necessary documents, Lyalya needs to get her money from Garri, and on the day she plans to confront him a dog mysteriously appears in her room: "Big, reddish, lean, its fur ruffled, its breed something like a *chien-loup!*"[65] The landlady lets it out, but when Garri arrives, he screams, terrified, when he spies the dog lurking in the corner. It leaves a second time, but stands outside the window, its terrible eyes fixed on Garri.

Lyalya tells Garri of her intentions, and when he reacts violently, grabbing her by the throat, she calls for help, and something weird occurs: "The ringing of broken glass resounded, and something enormous, heavy, shaggy jumped in and fell on Garri from the side, throwing him down and covering him up."[66] Lyalya comes to and discovers that Garri's throat has been torn through and the dog has disappeared. She later discovers that Tolya, who was rushing to her aid, was shot by the Bolsheviks on the same day. The story concludes:

> I didn't make anything up [...] and didn't add anything. But I myself, when I turn to the past, clearly see all the rings of events and the pivot on which a certain power strung them. Strung them and joined the ends.[67]

In "The Dog," as in other stories in *The Witch*, nothing unambiguously supernatural occurs, and yet one would be hard put to give a rational explanation of the events. What is not typical for *The Witch*, or for Teffi more generally, is the depiction of Tolya the dog. Unlike other pathetic characters in her fiction, beginning with Aglaya in the 1905 story "Princess's Ruby," Tolya is not sickly and repugnant.[68] He is wholesome and nice-looking, the repulsive features transferred to the "green" freaks in Garri's sphere (as they were to the "green" wedding guests in "Rusalka"). Although Tolya perishes, like some of his predecessors, he does not share their weakness. On the contrary, his self-sacrificing love gives him the power to rescue Lyalya from Garri. To borrow from the story's canine imagery, his love has transformed Tolya from a weepy toy poodle to a fierce wolfhound. "The Dog" was written about a year after Teffi had completed most of the other stories in *The Witch* and almost two years after Theakston's stroke. Her experience of caring for the dying man may have influenced Teffi's depiction of selfless love in the story – the main theme of her next book, *On Tenderness*.

9

TENDERNESS AND ANGST

1936–8

After Theakston's death Teffi resumed her place in the émigré cultural world. In 1936 she delivered a talk at a benefit for Balmont, who was suffering from severe mental illness; held her own evening with proceeds going to *Sovremennye zapiski*; and participated in a variety of other good causes, ranging from the Cossack Museum in Courbevoie to the National Organization of Russian Scouts.[1] Teffi also hosted receptions at home, where, as Vasyutinskaya's daughter Valentina recalled many years later, "she liked to treat her guests to expensive hors d'oeuvres from the best stores. She could not endure abundant fare, saying it was petty bourgeois [*meshchanstvo*]."[2] (This was likely a case of Teffi concealing her material needs. Hors d'oeuvres – even from "the best stores" – were less expensive than a full dinner.)

Teffi was also developing new relationships, the most important with Ilya Fondaminsky (1880–1942), a revered figure in the emigration, whose wife had died in 1935.[3] An SR since his youth and a co-founder of *Sovremennye zapiski*, in exile Fondaminsky became more and more deeply involved in Orthodox Christianity (although he remained a Jew), and generously supported many needy individuals and cultural undertakings.[4] For Teffi he exemplified the selfless love she described in her 1929 Green Lamp talk – an "ideal Christian love that 'does not seek its own.'"[5]

Teffi's social activities notwithstanding, 1936 was a year of deep distress. She was again beset by grave illnesses – a serious kidney disease, nephritis, which began in January, and a worsening heart condition. She now looked back at her selfless devotion during Theakston's illness "as a special form of happiness," she wrote Zaitseva that summer: "Very painful, totally exhausting. The only [kind] for me. Blessed." She was painfully aware of how alone she was, and wrote the Zaitsevs in late June: "You are the only ones left in my life." But even they were growing more distant, as she acknowledged about a month later:

"Yes, our bond is lost, and it is not your distance on earth's surface that is to blame, but, most likely, your distance in some other dimension. Fate weaves its patterns, interlacing and pulling apart the threads." Her loneliness contributed, no doubt, to her "deep melancholy." She was at times "overcome by terror," she wrote Zaitsev, which only extreme measures might relieve:

> It's a shame that my dentist has gone away. I would have asked him to pull out a tooth. It seems to me this physical shock would be good [...]
> I'm now like a beetle turned over on its back. I'm seeking a straw with my legs. There is no straw.

The alarming economic and political situation in France in 1936 would only have intensified Teffi's anxiety. The disorders that had been plaguing the country since 1934 grew still worse, despite the electoral victory of the pro-labor Popular Front in May 1936. There was fear of revolution, and the Russians – "who," Teffi wrote wryly, "strongly recalled the old days in our native land, that is, 1917" – immediately sprang to action:

> Ladies with grocery bags speed through the streets. Russian speech rings out and is flung back and forth across the street.
> The conversations are exclusively businesslike and practical.
> "Did you get hold of any candles?"
> "Two of them [...] And have you stocked up on necessities?"
> "Why, of course we have, just like everyone else. A pound of rice, a pound of macaroni, and a stearin candle. In a word, I'm fully armed."[6]

Although revolution did not materialize, there was still much cause for concern, with almost 2 million workers participating in strikes and sit-ins in June alone. Among the disaffected were *Vozrozhdenie*'s printers, who staged a sit-in that closed the newspaper on 21 June and created "panic," as Teffi wrote the Zaitsevs, especially among writers like her, who were paid by the piece. The newspaper resumed publication as a weekly on 18 July, but the reopening brought Teffi only bad news, she wrote Amfiteatrov in late August, because "Gukasov, upon departing [for vacation], growled to the secretary to publish me every other issue [...] He's lowering everybody's wages, so that when he closes the paper he can give severance pay according to their final earnings." She decided to fight back, "to send protests over every omission by registered mail [*s obratnoi raspiskoi*]," with an eye to suing.

Teffi summed up to Amfiteatrov the calamities she had suffered during the past year: "In the fall I lost my friend. I myself was on my last legs [*izdykhaiush-chaia*]. Then the nephritis. Then the weakening of my heart. Now the unpleasant story with *Vozrozhdenie*." To top it all, she was alone in Paris. Teffi's doctor was urging her to get away, and fortunately, she wrote the Zaitsevs, a "kind soul forced me to take some money and go to Italy." Some acquaintances had invited her to Montecatini, in Tuscany, but when she arrived on 1 September, she discovered they had already left.[7] After a short stay there and in Florence, she went to visit the Amfiteatrovs in Levanto.

In a feuilleton published a couple of years later, Teffi described her first impression of her hosts: "An enormous man – such giants exist only in fairy tales – is standing at the threshold smiling. And next to him, like a spirit from Maeterlinck's plays – something almost incorporeal, with her silver eyes shining [...] These are the Amfiteatrovs."[8] She arrived on 12 September and was planning to spend three days, but stayed for nine, as Ilaria recalled in an unpublished memoir. She was ill at first and spent three days in bed, but during the entire time

> her stories and our laughter did not cease [...] She [...] lit up our quiet house with the bright flame of her talent and offered so much comforting [*uteshitel'noe*] merriment to my poor husband, downcast from his unhappy life, that I simply couldn't have been more delighted.[9]

Amfiteatrov himself wrote Gorny of Teffi's visit: "Clever and warm-hearted [*dushevna*] and simple and refined, and when it comes to wit, why even mention it: just say Teffi!"[10] Ilaria observed how Teffi wrote:

> Sick, she was lying down and wrote her regular feuilleton very, very fast in her bold hand. She finished, signed it, and began to fold the sheets and put them into an envelope.
> "Can I send it right away?"
> "Nadezhda Aleksandrovna! But won't you reread it?"
> "I never reread [...] Technique, my friend, technique is the only thing left. Pure technique, dear madam!" she exclaimed playfully.

Teffi left for Milan on 22 September, stayed overnight with the translator Rinaldo Küfferle (1903–55), and then headed to Lausanne, where she met her daughter Valya, there on business. While in Switzerland she wrote the

Zaitsevs that she had "come to love the Amfiteatrovs very much. Their life is very *hungry* [...] I'm frightened for them. They are totally good." Küfferle, who had previously made a positive impression, aroused more mixed feelings. He was "very nice" and "treated me wonderfully, showed me Milan," but "has become a fervent anti-Semite." In contrast "no sermon of hatred ever finds an echo in my soul."

Once back in Paris, Teffi expressed her gratitude to the Amfiteatrovs: "You don't know how much you've done for me. I can't reveal my *misères* to my friends [...] Now, thank God, I'm better." It was a good thing that she had recovered somewhat, because her fragile finances at once suffered further damage after a devaluation of the franc, although, as she wrote the Amfiteatrovs, "I hardly notice the process of my ruin, since I never know a single price." She could not, however, avoid noticing the situation at *Vozrozhdenie*, and she, Khodasevich, and two others decided to file a suit against the newspaper. When a court hearing on 24 September did not resolve their case, she wrote Amfiteatrov defiantly: "The rapiers are glittering, the steel is clanging." In December, however, Teffi had to admit to him that she was defeated, that it was "time to get to work, because I can no longer exist on half a ration." By then Amfiteatrov had already heard from Aldanov that Teffi was coming to *Poslednie novosti*, that Milyukov "has already announced that he would be glad [to have] her, Shmelyov, Zaitsev, and Korovin – those not associated politically with *Vozrozhdenie*."[11] On New Year's Day, 1937, Teffi's first feuilleton appeared in *Poslednie novosti*, but the change was not entirely advantageous.[12] "*Pos. nov.* has marked the New Year with a gift to Aldanov, Osorgin, me, and Polyakov-Litovtsev," she wrote Amfiteatrov. "They forbade us to print our articles simultaneously in *Segodnya*. In all they've reduced my budget by 5,200 francs." In response, he wrote indignantly: "Judging from your letter, by leaving for *Poslednie Novosti* you've exchanged a cuckoo for a hawk."[13]

At the beginning of 1937 Teffi looked back upon the turbulent previous year, which, "like every year consists of important or interesting events held together by a simple but essential connecting fabric."[14] This fabric is made up of everyday occurrences: "[T]he price of milk went up, the strike of the hotel *garçons*, the elimination of a tram line." The main events were the strikes of early 1936, followed by the onset of the Spanish Civil War, which stirred intense interest only to be eclipsed at the end of the year by the British drama of King Edward VIII's abdication in the name of love. Teffi concluded with a series of questions: "What awaits us? What is rushing toward us along the chain of eternity, link by link, ever faster and closer? War? Revolution? A new principle of immortality? A recipe to resurrect the dead?"

Hindsight, sadly, confirmed the first of Teffi's guesses, but early 1937 actually promised some respite from the crises of the recent past. The emigration was, for a change, given over to celebration, with the approach on 11 February of the hundredth anniversary of Pushkin's death. For once Russianness would be defined not by Soviet tyranny or the extremist ideology of some émigré factions, but by the glory of Russian culture. Two years earlier the Central Pushkin Committee, of which Teffi was one of many members, had been formed in Paris, and as the date approached, a plan was put into effect to mark the event "in all five parts of the world – in Europe, Asia, America, Africa, and Australia."[15] The celebration in Paris went on for several days, and included concerts, exhibits, theatrical performances, and various publications, ranging from a "one-day newspaper" to the poet's collected works.

Teffi's contribution was minimal, consisting only of a very brief and platitudinous piece, "The Miracle of Russia," for the one-day newspaper.[16] She was not more involved, perhaps, because at the time she was immersed in writing a play. She was in desperate need of money and hoped it would be a "way to get rich," she jokingly wrote the Amfiteatrovs in December 1936.[17] She had already tried to raise funds by holding two benefits in London, on 28 November and 1 December, but, although they brought her "much honor," there was "little crassly material tribute."[18] Since an evening in Brussels on 31 January 1937 brought no better results, she now had "to get down to work around the clock [vsploshnuiu] on the play for the Russian Theater."[19]

The Russian Dramatic Theater had been founded the previous year and, aside from Russian classical dramas, had already produced plays by Aldanov, Nabokov, Berberova, and other émigrés.[20] Teffi's contribution would be her first full-length play since *Satan's Hurdy-Gurdy*, and she warned the Amfiteatrovs of her likely failure:

It's my misfortune that all the editors of my youth trained me: compress, compress, and compress [...] That's excellent, of course [...] but on the other hand it's now terribly difficult [for me] to write an expansive, "large" thing. One act – if you please. Two – it's already worse. Three – simply disgusting.

She worked "like a madwoman" and finished by late February or early March: "And so I got up at 4:30 in the morning," she wrote the Amfiteatrovs, and, totally befuddled [*zabaldevshaia*], mixing up the names of the characters, dashed off the play. I handed it in still warm and damp, and now we're beginning to rehearse. Our brilliant actors will probably make such a mess of it that it will take a long time to wash away the shame.

The play, *A Moment of Fate*, based on Teffi's 1925 story "Marquita," tells of a sweet, maternal café singer, Sashenka, whose romance with a wealthy Tatar comes to an abrupt end when she adopts the guise of a demonic woman. The theatrical version is not simply a throwback, however, for Sashenka's position reflects the more desperate situation of the 1930s, when life, in her words, "seized [my soul], twisted, trampled it, and tossed it away."[21] It was Teffi's special gift to create a funny comedy out of such a sad tale and, contrary to her expectations, the play, which opened on 27 March, was a big hit. The writer and journalist Andrei Sedykh (pseudonym of Yakov Tsvibak, 1902–94) wrote of the "great [...] interest in a play into which N. A. Teffi put all of her subtle intellect, her best humor, and that intangible thing that distinguishes a play from a 'potboiler' and makes it a genuine work of art."[22] He predicted it would enjoy "a long, brilliant career," and it was indeed revived in Paris in December and played in many other émigré communities.[23]

Teffi's theatrical triumph must have brought a welcome infusion of cash, but the worth of the money was at once diminished when, in June 1937, the franc was again devalued. The Russians in France, moreover, soon were the center of yet another scandal. On 24 September General Yevgeny Miller, head of the ROVS (1867–1939), was kidnapped, and his aide, General Nikolai Skoblin (1893–1938?), who disappeared a few hours later, was suspected in the abduction. It was revealed that Skoblin and his wife, the famous singer Nadezhda Plevitskaya (1884–1940), had been Soviet agents for a number of years, and, in the absence of her husband, Plevitskaya was arrested as a co-conspirator, and in December 1938 condemned to 20 years of hard labor.[24]

Teffi, who attended the trial, attributed the shockingly long sentence to hostility toward foreigners, for which she blamed the hard times: "High prices, taxes, uncertainty about tomorrow, 'storm clouds on the horizon' [...] and here you have some incomprehensible people scurrying about, with an incomprehensible language and incomprehensible thoughts."[25] Plevitskaya, who, Teffi speculates, would have gone free had Skoblin not abandoned her, fits the pattern of Teffi's fictional victims of love (although with an admixture of Lady Macbeth):

What kind of person is the heroine of the trial? A vivid, talented Russian woman. She was simply a peasant and became a general's wife, a celebrated, beloved singer. She loved her Skoblin, was ambitious for him.
[…]
Lady Macbeth says with trembling, pale lips: "I only […] loved my husband."
"Twenty years of hard labor," answered the just but merciless judge.

Plevitskaya died in prison in 1941.

In 1938 the increasingly inimical atmosphere in France is encapsulated in Teffi's description of her 15 March benefit:

> The program of the evening is made up exclusively of merry things. We want to give the public only laughter and not "through tears"; if someone feels like crying – let him read the newspapers. Amidst the five-year plans, ten-year plans, twenty-year plans of tears, let there flash by a two-hour plan of simple, merry laughter.[26]

Contributing to Teffi's own gloom was news of the grave illness of one of her most loyal friends, Amfiteatrov. She wrote him on 13 January: "You can't imagine how pained I am that you're sick. This business is awfully unsuitable for you. You are so enormous, so silvery-pure, that a recumbent position doesn't become you." He died on 26 February, and the following day Teffi wrote to Ilaria to console her "that in this man's life, in his private life – deep, spiritual – you gave him everything that a wife and a true, devoted, self-sacrificing friend could give, love and faithfulness to the grave." Ilaria's devotion was precisely the form of love to which Teffi devoted her next book, *On Tenderness*.[27]

ON TENDERNESS

In the title story, "On Tenderness," written shortly before Theakston's death, Teffi writes: "Tenderness is the meekest, most timid, divine visage of love. The sister of tenderness is pity, and they are always together."[28] That such love runs counter to the self-interest that rules modern life is the theme of "The Monster." The heroine, Valentina, is exhausted from caring for her dying nanny, and her visitor, Shparagov, disapproves, since the sick and weak consume food and space better allotted to the healthy. He espouses a kind of eugenic cleansing: "First they'll eliminate only the hopelessly ill, then little by little they'll get to superfluous people in general."[29] Valentina brands Shparagov "a monster," and asserts: "It's terrifying without love. All these old and sick and poor and defenseless people don't need us, but we need them." The story ends with a reversal, since it turns out that Shparagov himself has been caring for a poor old person and now eagerly helps Valentina.

"The Easter Babe" tells of the relationship between a mother, Avdotya, and her baby, who is born on Easter night with a birth defect and dies the following Easter. Outsiders say he was a freak and it was good that he died, but his mother considers him as the sum of all virtues: "He's such a friend [...] that I don't understand how I lived in this world without him. My sweet Easter babe."[30] After his death Avdotya's life is "empty and difficult. Unilluminated and unsanctified [Ne osveshchennaia i ne osviashchennaia]."[31] All she has is the memory of her little one, "of the miracle of love, which gave strength and reason to the simplest and coarsest life."

The plight of another mother in "We, the Malicious Ones" – one of the most nuanced stories of the collection – points to the obstacles to maintaining such tenderness. Olga is beset by the many ills that have befallen the Russian emigration during the Depression: her husband is unemployed; her daughter, the nine-year-old Maruska, is seriously ill; she herself is in a constant state of exhaustion from performing physically arduous domestic tasks and caring for her irritable child, while her ineffectual husband is out unsuccessfully seeking work. One afternoon, while frantically trying to cope, she is visited by a "Slavic soul" (the endearing type of the 1920s now reduced to a mere pose) – a lady so focused on her absurd cause that she ignores the desperate situation confronting her. Once the visitor leaves, Olga contrasts herself to such "people with radiant souls," and asks: "Why is my soul all burned out? Only malice remains, like ash from a fire."[32] The malice soon flashes up when she grabs Maruska during one of her many temper tantrums and screams: "What are you torturing me for? What have I done to you?" At once, however, the concrete feel of Maruska's "fragile sick little body in her arms"– so different from the abstract love espoused by the "radiant souls" – overcomes her and, "overflowing with love and pity, she pressed it [the body] to herself, trembling and weeping."

That evening, instead of the usual bedtime story, Olga recounts to Maruska the dream in *Crime and Punishment* about the beaten nag, with whom she (like Teffi herself during Theakston's illness) identifies. She changes the ending, though, quoting mockingly the "radiant" souls: "Lift your head and look with your whipped eyes at the sky in which stars burn like diamonds [...] Look and, raising your hooves, rejoice."[33] But then her selfless tenderness wells up and she addresses her child: "Are you sleeping, my little kitten? Do you want some milk? I'll heat it, I'm not tired, it's nothing... Do you want some?"

Teffi devotes several stories in *On Tenderness* to what she considers the purest form of selfless love: between man and beast. Never before, she notes, have people kept so many dogs and cats, since whether you're a failure or a success they will always greet you with the same spontaneous joy.[34] She recounts various instances of animal love – of a cat, for example, who so adored her mistress that she placed on her lap her most precious belonging – a dead mouse.[35]

Teffi herself was sustained during these difficult times by the companionship of an animal – "a large, fluffy white cat," Miyuz – whom, according to a 1937 interview, "his mistress dotes upon. He strides importantly about the whole apartment, often sleeps right on the desk – sometimes on his mistress's manuscripts – but especially loves to sit on Nadezhda Aleksandrovna's knees, softly purring."[36] Feline love was becoming more of a necessity for Teffi because of cooling relations with her best human friends.

10

ZIGZAGS IN LIFE AND ART
1938–9

During the summer of 1938, after yet another illness, Teffi asked the Zaitsevs if she could join them in Monte Carlo (where Natasha and her husband were living), but Vera was "ominously silent," Teffi wrote Bunina.[1] She added bitterly: "That's friends for you! They've warmed and comforted [*oblaskali*] a sick and solitary friend. But I'm a pessimist, after all. It seems to me that this is how it should be." Teffi went instead to a "tiny resort not far from Vichy," and, by the time she returned to Paris, world events had taken a dangerous turn. In early September 1938, France called for a partial mobilization before French and British negotiations in Munich with the Germans, and troops headed for the Maginot line while panicky Parisians fled the city in droves.[2] Teffi wrote of the military measures, but concentrated on the "private mobilization," which confirmed her embittered view of friendship:

> You see, a man […] is respected in society, loved by those close to him, everything is in its proper place. To the left his friends, to the right his wife, behind his back acquaintances […] But then a tornado swoops down. And suddenly emptiness all around him. Especially behind his back and to the left […] No-bo-dy.[3]

Teffi looked to the future with foreboding. Previously we imagined a "peaceful" end, she wrote bleakly – "life under a bridge, death on a hospital cot, poverty, hunger, illness, solitude," but now we can't imagine what forms our future will take. "We know," however, "that they will be crueler, more ominous."[4] The Munich Pact actually provided an interlude of peace, although people remained uneasy, as Teffi noted in March 1939: "People's ears are cocked [*ushki na makushke*]. One ear listens to radio reports from the east, the other ear – reports from the south."[5] Despite the anxiety, however, there were more celebrations than ever in the Russian community (recalling the fevered gaiety preceding World War I): "Open a Russian Paris newspaper. 'A masquerade ball – merriment all through the night,' 'a concert,' 'a benefit evening and concert – dancing through the night.'" Teffi noted that the theater was also arousing greater interest, although there were "unfortunately few dramatists in emigration." She herself was, of course, among those few, and at the time was preparing a new play, to be directed by Yevreinov, with costumes by the popular political cartoonist MAD (Mikhail Drizo, 1887–1953) and music and lyrics by Teffi herself.[6]

The play, *Nothing of the Kind* (only the title borrowed from Teffi's 1915 collection), is very much in the tradition of Russian comedy, with echoes of Gogol's *Inspector General* especially strong. Here too the setting is a provincial town and the action is set in motion by a letter announcing the imminent arrival of an important outsider, in this case an American, Adam Kurzin. And once again the plot hinges on mistaken identity, but if Gogol's tsarist officials take the feckless hero for a government inspector, Teffi's townspeople – motivated, as Yevreinov observed, by the "dream of a million" so prevalent in the 1930s – assume the American is a millionaire and all claim to be his relatives.[7] When Kurzin tells them that he is in fact poor, there are all kinds of recriminations, but at the end, in a final twist, it turns out that he actually is a millionaire. He returns in his private plane and flies off to America with the shopgirl Marilka, who pitied him when she thought he was poor, and whose longing for escape (unlike that of earlier Teffi heroines) is fulfilled.

Nothing of the Kind opened at the Russian Theater 9 April 1939, and was very well received, one reviewer even judging it "the best of Teffi's large plays."[8] The author, however, was in no condition to enjoy her success, because the previous month she had fallen seriously ill with shingles. In late March she had written Bunina that she was *"terribly* sick," and later letters trace the unrelenting course of her ailment, which by mid-April had developed into polyneuritis (*polinevrit*) – "inflammation of the nerves, a prolonged and agonizing illness."[9] She gradually improved, but there were setbacks as late as July, when Gippius, Merezhkovsky, and Zaitseva went to visit and were told "that Teffi was worse and couldn't even see anyone."[10] Gippius remarked, with uncharacteristic sympathy, that Teffi "is totally spent, her heart isn't working, and she is spiritually broken."

The illness prevented Teffi from writing between mid-March and September 1939 – a hiatus that had a catastrophic effect on her already fragile finances. She wrote Bunina that "if you were in Paris, I know you would think something up for me," but even in her absence Bunina managed to help, enlisting as surrogates Zaitsev and Natalya Kulman (1877–1958), wife of the literary scholar Nikolai Kulman (1871–1940).[11] Teffi, however, proved an ungrateful beneficiary, complaining to Bunina on 1 May that Kulman "has no contact whatsoever with the 'rich.'"[12] Kulman in turn grumbled that, although things were not going badly, considering the hard times (they had raised about 8,700 francs), Teffi was expecting far more – about 20,000. And when in June Teffi suggested another appeal, Kulman refused.[13]

From her perspective Kulman was no doubt justified, but Teffi, with no income at present and with uncertain prospects for the future, was clearly desperate to amass a sufficient sum to see her through her illness and beyond. She feared, she wrote Bunina in early August, that she would have to leave her apartment because of a steep rise in the rent, and expressed dark forebodings: "I don't know what I'll be. A writer, an old almshouse invalid […] or a Warsaw *mamasha* come to live out her final days." She added: "Any decision will be a death sentence for me."[14] Bunina commented in her diary: "I received a heart-rending letter from Teffi – she cannot reconcile herself to either illness or old age […] For an artistic nature, greedy for earthly life, resignation is almost impossible, and without resignation there is neither peace nor joy."[15]

In the same letter to Bunina Teffi wrote that on 10 August (perhaps with money raised by the appeal) she was planning to go to the Fondation Foch, a "very luxurious and beautiful" rehabilitation sanatorium near Paris. It was in the "American taste," she wrote the Zaitsevs once she had moved in, "terribly comfortable, with immense terraces, more like a hotel or even an ocean liner." She would like to stay until the fall, she added, at which time "I'll see what kind of person I am and will arrange my life based on that inspection." Historical events, however, superseded any such personal decisions. On 3 September 1939, the French and British declared war on Germany and a new phase in Teffi's life began.

ZIGZAG, *ALL ABOUT LOVE*, HUES FROM *THE EARTHLY RAINBOW*: STORIES FROM THE 1930S

In the midst of all the turmoil Teffi published her last prewar book, *Zigzag*, in 1939. Two more story collections – *All about Love* (1946) and *The Earthly Rainbow* (1952) came out after the war, but the chronology is misleading, since all of the stories in the former and a substantial number in the latter first appeared in the 1930s – some as early as 1932. It therefore makes sense to look at the prewar stories in Teffi's three final books together, with an eye to the stories' original dates of publication.

In a letter to Amfiteatrov in early 1932, when Theakston's illness and other cares left Teffi with little creative energy to spare, she compared her writing to "knitting stockings. By technique alone." A significant number of stories in *Zigzag* and *All about Love* belong to the "stocking-knitting" category, Teffi often reverting to character types and plot patterns that hark back to her pre-revolutionary days.[16] One constant in her works, however, proved especially timely during the grim 1930s and serves as a major theme in *Zigzag* – the tendency of her characters to resort to artifice and deceit. She wrote in 1937: "How do people defend themselves? What are their weapons, their shield? [...] Youth, beauty, money, and success. Each person should have these four pistols. If they don't – they have to pretend they do."[17] Members of the younger generation, such as the friends in "The Dragonfly and the Ant" (1937), are especially adept at the beauty defense. Not only do their hair colors range from "red as a carrot" to lilac to striped; they utilize the modern weapons of cosmetic surgery to alter their noses, breasts, and chins "just like a thrifty housewife [who] turns old rags inside out."[18] Irochka, who is determined to become a star (although she is endowed with neither beauty nor talent), surpasses them all: she adopts a stage name of no identifiable nationality ("Ista Kruche"), appears before the public all in green against bright-green screens, so that only her face, hands, and feet are visible, and sings nonsensical songs in a non-existent language, accompanying herself with bronze rattles. The audience is befuddled, but, fearful of being accused of philistinism, they applaud wildly. Irochka's success is so great that she ends up on a tour of America.

Some of Teffi's stories on love (many of them, as the title indicates, included in *All about Love*) are of the "stocking knitting" variety, but several are among her best. These include "Time" (1938) and "Two Affairs with Foreigners" (1935), in which she succeeds in treating within the confines of a comic anecdote some of the large themes of her serious stories.[19]

"Time," like "Moonlight," centers upon an old woman and the corrosive effect of time, but the setting – in keeping with the lighter tone – has shifted from a dreary rented room to a "chic" Russian restaurant.[20] One of the guests, Gogosya Livensky – who, as a habitué of "the highest circles," has retained his juvenile nickname despite his 65 years – comments on three jolly old ladies eating and drinking with gusto at a neighboring table. While his dining companions contemptuously remark that if the dominant one – very elegantly dressed, a diamond brooch resting on her double chin – ever married, it was solely "for her money," Gogosya is kinder. He imagines that she might not have been bad looking once, but concedes that "now […] it's hard to tell. A lump of pink fat."[21]

The entertainment then begins, a performer intoning an old Russian romance that reminds Gogosya of the tragic love story of an enchanting beauty, Maria Nikolayevna Rutte: two men (one the composer of the song) fought a duel over her, after which her husband ran off to the Far East. The pair reunited only years later, when her husband was close to death. When the performance ends a friend of Gogosya's approaches and tells him that "Maria Nikolayevna remembers you very well […] and is very glad to see you." He points to the old ladies, and "the main old lady nodded her head and, merrily parting her strong fat cheeks with her painted mouth, gleamed affably with her even row of blue porcelain teeth."[22] For Maria Nikolayevna, as for Anna in "Moonlight," old age has erased all traces of even the most intense and tragic love, but – although the cheerful and prosperous patron of a chic restaurant does not arouse the same pity as the protagonist of the earlier story – her transformation from an "enchanting beauty" to a "lump of pink fat" presents in starker and more unsettling form the effect of time "taking its toll."

If time has blunted the torments of love for Maria Nikolayevna, laughter rescues one of the two women who tell of their unhappy love in "Two Affairs with Foreigners." While the first story evokes the usual melancholy, the second woman begins: "It was just a tragedy. Ha-ha-ha!"[23] It all began, she goes on, when a client at the *institut de beauté* where she was working – a decrepit old American – revealed her infatuation with a young man in her employ. The very same man – a Rumanian with the unlikely name of Kuritsu (*kuritsa* is chicken in Russian) – falls in love with the heroine; he even talks of marriage and brings her a most domestic present: an iron. Everything seems to be leading to a happy conclusion until the heroine tells Kuritsu of his employer's infatuation, after which he visits infrequently. She then learns that he has become the American's gigolo and writes him: "Come and I will silently bid you 'farewell'"[24] Kuritsu turns up a couple of days later, makes some lame excuse, and stalks from the room. The heroine opens the window, ready to fling herself at his feet, but then hears a cupboard door open and goes to see what he has taken. To her disbelief the iron is gone, and, struck by the absurdity of the situation, she sits on the floor and bursts out laughing:

I laughed so much […] and I felt so light and so good.

"Lord!" I said – "how enchanting it is to live in Your world!" […] An iro-o-on! I would have crashed on the street, my skull in smithereens, and he would have had an iro-on in his hands! What a picture!²⁵

Thus "Two Affairs with Foreigners" almost ends (like *An Adventure Novel*) with death, but – more typically for Teffi – the absurdity of the situation makes a tragic end seem inappropriate, laughter more suitable.

Some of Teffi's protagonists escape the absurdity of human existence by following the path of her early fantasizers (or liars). As she writes in "An Exciting Life" (1932), "a fact, in their opinion, can err just like a person," and therefore they "correct it with their fantasy […] In the vernacular, this is called lying [*vran'em*]."²⁶ "Nowhere" (1936) – included in Teffi's final book, *The Earthly Rainbow* – tells of three such fantasizers. The first episode begins at a Christmas party, the children wondering what their presents will be. A little girl whom people call "Katya the Fibber [*Katia-vratia*]" declares that they will get 12 crystal ships and pearl swans, all made of music.²⁷ When she receives instead a clown with a big nose, she insists: "Here's the swan […] Made completely of pearl. Do you see? Made of music." The second story is about a boy who spends all his time on the docks of a northern Russian city, enraptured by the exotic smells and the enticing names of the ships' destinations. He imagines there must be another unknown name, which one can hear only in the deepest sleep, and a drunken sailor tells of such a place. But when the boy asks adults about its location, they answer impatiently, "Nowhere," and now, a grown man, he often dreams that "a ship is carrying him to the land of Nowhere."²⁸

The hero of the third episode actually once caught of glimpse of Nowhere. When he was young he "was always searching for something" and for that reason took up mountain-climbing. One day he saw a sight of surpassing heavenly beauty:

The two cliffs before me […] were joined, forming an immense arch, the gates to heaven. And there, through the burning amber of the sunset, an unparalleled, ecstatic dawn blazed. And a quadriga, a chariot, was flying, speeding out from it, directing its path to the triumphal arch […] And in front of it, pointing the way, a crimson ray thundered like the Archangel's trumpet above the raging sea of the orchestra.²⁹

This celestial sight was the fulfillment of all his seeking for beauty, and he thought that if he closed his eyes the earth would push him away, and he would reach the land of Nowhere. Instead he fell. This final glimpse of the land of Nowhere recalls the exalted sphere of the sun reached through escape from the earth – an image from Teffi's early symbolist works that recurs later in different forms. "Nowhere," by creating a continuum from the comic "fibbing" of the first episode to the search for transcendent beauty of the third, confirms the common source of her comic and serious works.

In other stories in *The Earthly Rainbow*, mostly loosely autobiographical, Teffi continues her search for an alternative to the deadness of everyday life in the vanished Russian past.[30] This search for the essence of Russianness culminates in her essay "Freedom" (1936). Teffi begins by distinguishing the two Russian words for freedom, *svoboda* and *volia*:

> *Volia* is not at all the same as *svoboda*.
> *Svoboda* – *liberté* – is the lawful state of a citizen [...]
> *Svoboda* can be translated into all languages and be understood by all peoples.
> *Volia* is untranslatable.
> [...]
> *Svoboda* is lawful.
> *Volia* doesn't take anything into account.[31]

Volia, she goes on, manifests itself in the urge to free oneself from the bounds of civilization:

> We Russians are not as torn from nature as Europeans; culture lies on us in a thin layer, and it's simpler and easier for nature to break through this layer. In the spring, when the voices of the awakened earth sound more loudly and call more resoundingly to freedom – these voices lead us away.[32]

Teffi quotes one runaway on the unalloyed joy of such freedom:

> You'd wander through a dense, pathless forest. Only pines and the sky – alone in the whole world. And suddenly you'd begin shouting in a wild voice with all your might; this scream would overflow with such primeval joy that afterward you could only tremble and laugh for a long time.[33]

She ends with a recollection from her girlhood when she herself was swept away by such wild laughter. Late one white night, while standing on a balcony overlooking the Volga, she heard the singing of passing bargemen:

> "Free, boy, at freedom! / At freedom, boy, one's very own! [*Vol'no, mal'chik, na vole! / Na vole, mal'chik, na svoei!*]" And I lifted my arms [...] and waved to the dawn and to the wild song, and laughed, and cried: "Fre-e-e-e!"[34]

This freedom, Teffi implies, whose habitat is the dense forests and boundless rivers of Russia, has no place in the civilized, highly developed West. Nor, to her obvious regret, does the unbounded, joyful laughter that accompanies it and which she finds ever more impossible to summon up.

"Freedom" and "Nowhere," published a week apart in May 1936, both depict lost worlds: "Freedom" – defunct Russia, with its anarchic, joyous spirit; "Nowhere" – the non-existent but longed-for realm of transcendent beauty. They were written just a few years before Teffi was to experience a third loss: Russian émigré Paris as it had existed for the past 20 years.

11

WAR AND ITS AFTERMATH

1939–46

THE PHONY WAR: 1939–40

On 8 September 1939, in Teffi's first feuilleton since she fell ill, she gave her impressions of Paris preparing for war. In the daytime things seem close to normal, but "at night [due to the blackouts] the city changes its appearance […] It is quiet, dead, dark. Lights are extinguished and we see the moon. We see moonlight on the streets of Paris. A fantastic sight."[1] In her next piece, Teffi described frightening civil defense measures:

A siren is wailing.
You already hear it in your sleep.
Far off, persistent, challenging. Ever louder and louder. It wails maliciously, furiously, like a frightened and enraged beast. At once plaintively and menacingly.
[…]
And to the sounds of this wailing, shadows, undulating in the glimmer from flashlights, descend the stairs.
[…]
The air-raid shelter is long, like a corridor. The shadows try on their masks, and in the dancing light of flashlights it seems as if they have gathered for an eerie masquerade.[2]

Valentina Vasyutinskaya recalled that Teffi was still "bedridden" at the time, suffered from "acute neuritis of her left arm," and "fell asleep at night only after a morphine injection."[3] To add to her distress, she was wracked with anxiety about her daughters in Poland and was determined to stay in Paris, she wrote Bunina on 7 October, because "I don't want to lose contact with the Polish embassy so that I can have news of my children."[4] In fact (judging from a letter sent to Valya the same day) she had already moved from her unheated flat in Paris to Valentina Vasyutinskaya's apartment in the suburb of Vanves. What happens next, she wrote Valya, "will depend on you. If you come to Paris […] we'll arrange things differently."[5]

In an October feuilleton Teffi tried to make sense of the new conflict, comparing conditions with those preceding World War I:

> It is much more difficult than it was a quarter-century ago, when we believed in the strength of a treaty, the force of a promise. Now, when pacts are one thing and facts another, having nothing in common, how can we figure it out?[6]

The following week she echoed fears – widespread at the time – that technological advances would bring untold horrors:

> Technology! Technology! Technology!
>
> Airplanes flying at an altitude of ten kilometers, going by at twelve kilometers a minute; bombs incinerating whole cities with one strike, destroying the most powerful fortifications; the radio, which a quarter of a century ago was not yet so much in use in military affairs; moving fortresses – tanks. The wonders of technology are countless.[7]

So far, to be sure, there was strange quietude "between war and peace," for this was the time of the so-called "phony war" (*drôle de guerre*), when there was little military action, as the Allies tried to build up their strength.[8] Teffi remarked on a return to normal after the initial alarm: "Children will start going to school, trade is picking up, those who left are returning […] thieves have stopped stealing gas masks." Her anxiety about her daughters, moreover, was assuaged when Valya arrived in Paris in late October and bore the welcome news that Gulya was "alive and well" in Warsaw.[9]

Mother and daughter moved into the apartment of a friend in Paris,[10] but when Valya, who had been summoned to France by the minister of the Polish government-in-exile, left Paris to join her compatriots in Angers, Teffi returned to Vanves. Valentina writes warmly about that time, recalling that Teffi

> was able to create a sense of coziness and maintain emotional equilibrium. When returning home late at night, [she] brought with her

the enchanting aroma of Mitsouko by Guerlain and held a mysterious little package in her hands: pastry, fruit, or candy. To my objections, she invariably answered, "I like to look at a person who is pleased."[11]

While at Vanves Teffi wrote Bunina that she almost never saw their common acquaintances. Only on Thursdays did she run into Aldanov at the newspaper office, and she rarely saw Zaitseva – who, Teffi commented sourly, "is just as ardent [*plamennaia*] and categorical [as ever]."[12] The bitter cold was partly to blame for the lack of social interchange, but it also brought relative tranquility. "In general life is calm," Teffi wrote in March 1940; "nobody is expecting enemy raids – it's too cold."[13] By April, though, Teffi was feeling rather uneasy about the complacency. "One thing is required of us: not to worry. Sometimes we even go too far in not worrying."[14] She turned to the German attacks on "small nations," writing ironically of the aggressor's claim of moral rectitude:

Amazing as it might be, moral law is triumphant [...] People committing the most cutthroat [*banditskie*], bestial, wolfish acts try to explain them by their lofty and moral motives. No one until now has said: "Yes, we attacked a small, helpless nation because it's easier to skin a defenseless person alive." [...] On the contrary, those committing illegal acts, crimes, try their utmost to convince the world that precisely these acts are dictated by the most splendid, chivalric movements of the soul.

The following week Teffi published her last prewar fictional work, "Stages," in which she universalizes the human cruelty and violence that was unfolding around her. The narrator, Liza, recalls an Easter long ago in Russia, when she was a young girl. While in church her "heart aches" during the priest's account of Peter's betrayal of Christ, and she thinks how the terrible words Peter hears – "Crucify! Crucify Him" – have resounded through the centuries. She wonders: "How can we pay, how can we people atone so it would grow silent?"[15] The story then shifts to the civil war period, when Liza, aboard a ship, hears a droning sound, which a sailor tells her are church bells marking the Day of the Twelve Apostles. The words "Twelve Apostles" stir her memory of that time long ago in church, the question she asked herself then even more relevant during the fratricidal war that was destroying the old Russia: "What can we do, how can we people atone so the terrible cry might grow silent, so we wouldn't hear: 'Crucify! Crucify Him!'"[16] Far from falling silent, however, the cry was ringing out still more insistently at the time Teffi wrote the story, for in less than two weeks, on 10 May, the Germans attacked three small countries bordering on France – Luxembourg, Holland, and Belgium – and a few days later France's own borders were breached and the French army was in retreat.

On 19 May Teffi noted that sirens had again begun to sound.[17] They did not raise any particular alarm, since people "have gotten used to them," but by the following week airplanes, not so easily ignored, were flying overhead. A little over a week later Teffi was to witness the destructive power of the new armaments, when on 3 June Vanves was attacked from the air. Zaitseva, who was visiting Teffi, witnessed "a real bombardment," her husband wrote Bunin: "She saw blazing automobiles on the streets and collapsed houses."[18] In her feuilleton the following Sunday Teffi described their "battle baptism." It was

> as if we had landed at the very center of some demonic factory in full swing. Pipes were droning, wheels were clattering, screws were grinding, straps were smacking, chains were clanking, furnaces were blazing, steam was flying out with a whistle. There was no combat. No battle. We knew that somewhere high in the sky our defenders were pursuing the enemy – but we didn't see and didn't hear it. The demonic factory filled our entire world.[19]

In the midst of this mechanized hell, Teffi tells of one manifestation of traditional human values. A young woman always brought a large box with her during alerts and people guessed it contained valuables, but, as she had promised her son, she was carrying a turtle, sporting a ribbon with the French tricolor. Teffi concludes:

> They say the old world is collapsing. Brute force, violence, hypocrisy, lies, betrayal, and malice are smothering living life. But, you see, in God's unhappy world there is a box and in it is preserved the most precious human treasure: the inviolable traditions of our soul – belief in one's word, love, and loyalty.

This feuilleton, published on 9 June 1940, was to be Teffi's last for *Poslednie novosti* (which ceased publication two days later) and her last until the end of the war. The day after it appeared, on 10 June, she left Paris to join her daughter in Angers.[20]

ANGERS AND BIARRITZ: 1940–1

Teffi wrote of her departure in unpublished notes: "I had a pass and an invitation to Angers and Biarritz. I. Fondaminsky was concerned about me and called A. Kerensky and I was issued a pass." She commented: "I myself didn't want to go. I don't know why. Probably I was simply fed up. War and revolution had chased us so much all around the whole world. But before it was new and interesting and it stimulated the nerves. Now it was all so familiar and so boring."[21] She nevertheless set out, part of a huge and panic-stricken exodus that totaled an estimated three-quarters of the Paris population.[22] When her taxi arrived at the station, an enormous mass of humanity blocked its way: "Soldiers, children, peasant women, trunks, baby carriages, suitcases, bicycles, some kind of wheels, mattresses, an invalid on a stretcher, a group of children the same age – evidently [from] some orphanage [*priiut*]." Happily, Teffi wrote the Zaitsevs a day or two later, Yevgenia Vasyutinskaya came to her rescue, miraculously "forcing her way through the immense crowd, seeking out some fellows who agreed to drag my baggage."

Teffi's train arrived in Angers five hours late and, although suffering from leg cramps, she was forced to walk to Valya's place. The following day she wrote the Zaitsevs that, while sitting in a café, she had witnessed

> a file of refugees on carts, trucks; and even our Paris bus […] loaded with adolescents. There are mattresses on almost all the automobile roofs – [to protect] against splinters. They're transporting an enormous number of children, transporting dogs, cats, birds in cages.[23]

Judging from this and subsequent letters, Teffi's resentment toward the Zaitsevs had evaporated in the face of the danger they were facing in Paris. She expressed anguish that "I am not with you," but added that she was not sorry she had left, since "I see that Valya was so tormented at the thought that she would be cut off from me." Soon, however, Valya departed with the Poles – heading first for Portugal and then for their permanent refuge in London – and Teffi continued her own wanderings. She recalled in her notes how she was driven south by automobile: "Several times along the way sentries questioned us […] kept repeating – don't turn on the lights, airplanes are circling overhead."

By the end of June Teffi reached the Russian Children's Home in Salies-de-Béarn, close to Biarritz, which was founded by the Countess Nadezhda Leuchtenberg in 1929. After all she "had to suffer and endure," Teffi wrote the Zaitsevs, she felt "spiritually crushed," but her stay at the home appears to have had a salutary effect. "It seems I've never rested as well as now," she wrote Valya on 20 July, adding that the home was

> just like a Russian estate. The atmosphere is very pleasant, there are many children. The adults are all countesses, baronesses, and princesses. My "noble" origin helped me to be recognized as one of their own, and my literary position – to occupy a high rank.[24]

Teffi's anxiety about the Zaitsevs subsided once she found out that the city had not been bombed, although her renewed devotion to her friends was soon tested when she learned that Boris was writing on a biblical subject she herself had long been contemplating. She reacted on 24 July:

> Well, dear friend, you've pierced me to the very heart!
> Do you remember a couple of years ago, while sitting on my sofa, you and I conversed on a biblical theme and I spoke about David? I had begun writing about him at the time (more about Saul). Then I gave it up. And now, freed from my weekly trash, I thought of continuing, got hold of a Bible with difficulty, and settled down... And then – your letter.

The incident was not enough, however, to sever the bond. In any case, Teffi was most concerned about Valya, who was suffering not only the trauma of exile, but from the recent loss of her husband, and whom Teffi feared she would never see again.[25] On 10 July she sent Valya a "testament": "*Live*, create your life in the best possible way, think more about yourself."

Some time in early August, Teffi moved to Biarritz, where she came upon a number of old acquaintances, among them two famous literary couples: Gippius and Merezhkovsky; and Georgy Ivanov (1894–1958) and Irina Odoyevtseva (1895–1990). At first the Russians lived together at a hotel, the Maison Basque, which suited her: "I live cheaply here," she wrote the Zaitsevs on 27 August. "Nowhere can I settle in like this. And I'm not alone – there are many Russians, so there's no end of visitors." Nevertheless, conditions were difficult. Consumer goods were disappearing and the military situation was growing more alarming. Worst of all was Teffi's inner turmoil. "Everything is painful," she complained soon after her arrival. "Old age, loneliness, poverty, fear for loved ones, more than fear – horror." She was all right in the daytime, she wrote on 27 August, but "at dawn [I feel] such deadly fear and ineradicable melancholy that I could bash my head against the wall. And I'm alone in the entire world." One possibility would be to leave the country, which one of her acquaintances in Biarritz, the literary impresario Alexander Rognedov (d.1958), claimed he could arrange. She declined, she wrote the Zaitsevs, because "I'm weak, sick, old, and I'm afraid."

The Maison Basque closed in late September or early October, and Teffi moved, together with a Baroness Raut and a French mother and daughter, to a "marvelous apartment" on Avenue de la Reine Nathalie. The comfortable lodgings, however, only threw into relief her inability to write. "In general working conditions here are marvelous," she wrote the Zaitsevs in mid-October. "It's as though Fate has decided to show me that it's not a matter of circumstances, but that my head is finished." Once winter set in, moreover, the apartment proved anything but "marvelous." It was unbearably cold, and by New Year's Eve Teffi had to write in a café, since "at home my fingers freeze and I can't hold a pen." The food situation was also bad. "There's no tea," she wrote in December. "I make a brew of apple skin. I drink malt, but there's no milk." Then early in January 1941, disaster struck:

> We haven't had heat for two weeks. There's no coal. It's gone down to minus twelve. Two days ago I woke up at night because of some hissing. I turned on the light, looked – my shoes were floating near the door. I opened the door to the *cabinet de toilette* and at once a stream of icy water doused me. I called our Frenchwoman, who ran downstairs to have the concierge shut off the water. Then the two of us, standing in icy water up to our ankles, both wet from head to foot, since it was leaking on us from the walls, removed the water with towels, and I cried, my hands and feet hurt so much.

Teffi's misery while in Biarritz was compounded by her persistent writing block. "I've abandoned literature once and for all," she wrote the Zaitsevs in late March 1941. Even if she could write, there was nowhere to publish, and this added financial worries to Teffi's other cares. Some money did trickle in from external sources – unemployment compensation from *Poslednie novosti*; contributions from the philanthropic organization Zemgor; money transfers from Valya, mostly through Polish diplomats in Vichy.[26] And there was at least an expectation of help from compatriots in the New World.[27]

Teffi's spiritual malaise had a marked effect on her usually sociable nature. "I don't go anywhere, visit anyone," she wrote the Zaitsevs in April 1941. "I think it's not [other] people's fault, but my own. I'm bored and irritable, and stupidity does not amuse me as before, but drives me to distraction." Her misanthropy is apparent in her comments on the two famous couples who shared her exile in Biarritz – who in any case were not among her favorite people. In contrast to Odoyevtseva's warm memoir, which leaves the impression that they enjoyed very cordial relations, Teffi's few remarks on the Ivanovs were quite slighting (although she thought very highly of Ivanov's poetry).[28] The Merezhkovskys figure much more prominently in Teffi's letters, which, together with her later memoirs, provide a vivid glimpse of the pair's final years.[29]

At first Teffi expressed pity for the poverty-stricken old couple: "It's very sad," she wrote the Zaitsevs in mid-August. "They're both completely gaga. He is seething with malice [*zliushchii*], and she is senseless." After their departure from the Maison Basque, however, Teffi's pity turned to envy when the Merezhkovskys rented "a splendid villa – 1,000 francs a month" (for which they never paid, she later noted), but when their situation deteriorated, pity returned: "Things are bad for the Merezhkovskys," she wrote on 3 March 1941. "Their gas has been turned off. A disaster. Both are very old, pitiful, lopsided."

Teffi's attitude toward Merezhkovsky was especially negative. He could appear positively demonic: "He seethes with such malice," she wrote the Zaitsevs on 7 October 1940, "that, like a cuttlefish, he blackens the water around him. I don't offer him my hand – I'm terrified. He might tear off a finger." Given this personal revulsion, it is striking that Teffi was quite tolerant of his political views (his purported Nazi sympathies). Shortly after the celebration of his 75th birthday on 14 August 1940, in fact, she hinted about Merezhkovsky's anti-Nazi sentiments. He spoke "very well," but touched "tactlessly" (in the German-occupied city) on politics: "Of course, he spoke about the 'Antichrist.' You yourself know which one, and about the hope that when the Antichrists perish, holy Russia will unite with holy France." In her later memoir she could openly identify the Antichrists as the Bolsheviks, "tormenting Russia," and the Germans, "who are now strangling France."[30] There is a discrepancy between Teffi's letters and her memoir as to when Merezhkovsky's attitude toward the Nazis changed. In the former, she noted a shift by December 1940, but her memoir dates it to the German invasion of the Soviet Union in June 1941, and ascribes it to the principle that "even with the devil, but against the Bolsheviks."[31] She also states categorically that "nobody would dare say that the Merezhkovskys 'sold out' to the Germans. Just as they sat without a cent in Biarritz, so they returned without a cent to Paris." And she denies that Merezhkovsky was anti-Semitic.[32]

Teffi's feelings toward Gippius were more complex. While at the Maison Basque, she could be uncharacteristically "sweet," she wrote the Zaitsevs, but Teffi found her later visits to the apartment close to intolerable. On 7 October, she described how the half-blind and almost totally deaf Gippius would poke unceremoniously among her belongings,

> would grab a pencil from the table and scream: "What is this you have?" I answer: "A pencil." "And what for?" "To write things down." "What do you write down?" "Why, everything I need to." "Did you buy the pencil yourself?" "Yes, I did." "And what for?" And so it goes endlessly. Recently she stuck her head in my bidet and shouted: "And what is this? What do you keep here? Sugar? But we don't have any sugar." It's simply a disaster. She hears nothing, sees nothing, and rocks on her skinny legs.

As time passed, however, Teffi came to value Gippius's visits and conversation. "Zina drops in on me," she wrote in June 1941, "and we talk about timeless [*ne vremennye*] subjects and that's interesting."

Teffi's unhappiness in Biarritz was compounded by anxiety about family and friends. Her concern for Gulya eased when she received permission in February 1941 to write to her in Warsaw (also occupied territory) and, to her delight, soon received an answer. "She's alive and well," Teffi wrote Zaitseva. "She's working as a cashier – apparently theaters are stagnating. She's very proud that she's able to count." She also "received news via Vichy about Valya" soon afterward, but then had no word for about four months. Only in June did she learn that Valya was well, "but my anxiety does not leave me," she wrote. "The times, after all, are very frightening."

The friend whose situation most concerned Teffi was Fondaminsky, a Jew still living in Paris. Soon after her arrival in Biarritz in early August, she wrote Zaitseva that she was "very worried" about him, and on 27 August begged her to "stop in at Ilyusha's and write me how he looks to you […] He didn't answer my letter. I'm really afraid for him." Teffi's fear proved justified, for he was among the several hundred Russians in Paris who were placed in the internment camp in Compiègne on 22 June 1941 – the same day the Germans invaded the USSR.[33] A guarded comment to the Zaitsevs indicates that Teffi was aware that he and Zeyeler (1874–1954), head of the Union of Russian Writers and Journalists, had been arrested: "They say that Ilyusha and Vlad[imir] Feofilovich have left Paris." Most of the detainees were soon released, but Fondaminsky remained incarcerated, and in August 1942, as part of the mass roundup and deportation of Jews in France, was sent to Auschwitz.[34]

Teffi dreaded the prospect of returning to Paris, especially after the endless string of maladies – from neuralgia to the flu to heart problems – that struck her in Biarritz. "It's terrifying," she wrote Zaitseva in April 1941. "I fear the emptiness and loneliness and helplessness [...] I absolutely cannot live alone." Later in the spring she complained that her "heart has completely given out [...] Some kind of spasm in my chest and there's no way to get at it." It was the beginning, as she suspected, of a serious and prolonged illness. Happily, Teffi had made the acquaintance of a woman doctor – "an amazing friend" – she wrote effusively in May – who not only came to the rescue on medical matters, but in June found an apartment for the two women to share when Teffi had to vacate her room on Avenue de la Reine Nathalie. Later that summer they decided to live together in Paris as well, and by September Teffi and her new friend (who remains unnamed) were back in the French capital.

OCCUPIED PARIS: 1941–4

By the time Teffi returned to Paris, the Russian community was much diminished, what with the arrest of some and the departure of others abroad or to the unoccupied zone. Most prewar émigré institutions had also disappeared, since all foreign organizations, including "approximately 800 Russian cultural, educational, and charitable bodies," had been disbanded on 28 August 1940.[35] All the prewar Russian newspapers, magazines, and publishing houses had been shut down, and in October 1940, the Nazi-inspired Association of Russian Workers in Literature and Art replaced the old arts unions.[36]

It is generally accepted that attempts to enlist Parisian Russians to the Nazi cause produced few active collaborators.[37] A far larger number tried to go about their daily lives as best they could, making minor accommodations in order to survive – and in many cases, just barely. On 20 October 1941, Teffi sent Bunina a postcard written in French (the required form of communication with the unoccupied zone, where the Bunins lived) and conveyed in encoded form the desperate need of their compatriots in Paris:

If you have the chance, tell our Aunt Marie-Choura [Maria Tsetlina and her daughter, Alexandra, or Shura, Pregel, now in America] and our Aunt Fyodorovich de Keren [Alexander Fyodorovich Kerensky] that their nephews are very much disposed to die of hunger.[38]

Little concrete is known about Teffi's life at the time. We know that during the first half of 1942 she and her doctor friend moved from temporary quarters on Rue de Lübeck to an apartment on the elegant Rue Francisque-Sarcey in Passy. That summer she and the Zaitsevs were at the estate of the legal scholar Vasily Eliashevich (1875–1956) and his wife Faina (d.1941) in Bussy-en-Othe in the Yonne province. It was from there that she wrote Bunina about the loss of another link to her past: *"Mon pauvre Liatzky est mort."*[39]

There is no evidence that Teffi published anything during the occupation. She wrote the Tsetlins after the war: "I did not collaborate, in spite of requests and even threats on the part of the 'authorities.' I lived wretchedly, but didn't sell my soul."[40] Pressure rose in June 1942, with the appearance of a Russian-language newspaper sponsored by the occupying force, *Parizhskii vestnik* (Paris herald), but she did not contribute.[41] According to Berberova, Teffi also refused (as did Berberova herself and other prominent Russian writers) to have her works republished for distribution by the Nazis in the occupied regions of the Soviet Union.[42] Her only known attempt to publish was initiated by Yevreinov, who in 1942 arranged for her to submit a scenario, "Les héritiers de la jument grise" (The heirs of the gray mare) to a competition sponsored by the literary–political weekly *Comœdia* – "perhaps the only place in the occupied zone where non-collaborationist writers could appear unscathed," according to one source.[43] The scenario, clearly, did not win.

If Teffi published nothing, during the summer of 1943 she did receive unexpected recognition in another artistic field: music. She wrote Bunin the "amusing news" that on 6 August, on Radio Paris, the Verney Orchestra "will perform Brahms and... a *mélodie tsygane* [gypsy melody] by Teffi. That's the way it appears in the program. The things that go on in this world!" Bunin responded that, although they "all 'were hanging'" on the radio, "we didn't hear anything! Crackling, thunder, an earthquake! All the same I congratulate you on your new calling – as a composer!"[44]

This exchange was carried on in Russian, since after the Germans had occupied all of France on 11 November 1942, the earlier requirement that correspondence between the zones be carried on in French was abolished. With communication eased, Teffi wrote the Bunins more frequently and offered them a more detailed, yet still guarded, description of life in Paris. In the first surviving "Russian" letter, of 13 March 1943, she passed on the "melancholy" news that a friend of Bunina's, "Mme. [Olga] Apostol has died (not at home, but at Melita's)."[45] She used the name of Melitta Levina – another of Bunina's friends, who had perished in the camps – to signify those who had been arrested. Teffi added that Fondaminsky was dying of cancer, although he had by then perished at Auschwitz. One postcard from him – dated 8 August 1942, shortly before his deportation – is preserved in Teffi's archive. "I am holding up admirably," he wrote. "I am always tranquil, gay, and content, although I'm as skinny as Gandhi."[46] In her memoir of Fondaminsky, Teffi quotes his last card to her and Mother Maria, who sometimes wrote him jointly: "Don't let my friends worry about me. Tell them all that I feel very good. I am entirely happy. I never thought there was so much joy in God."[47] Fondaminsky, who became a Christian while in the camps, and Mother Maria, who perished there in 1945, were both canonized by the Patriarchate of Constantinople in 2004.[48]

In the letter to Bunina, Teffi was quite unsparing of herself. "I've become old and a kind of petty tyrant [*samodurka*]. At times I'm offended by everyone for some reason, at others every little dog I encounter fills me with tenderness and joy." Her material life was fine, she was unfazed by the constant alarms, and even her illness did not particularly bother her:

> I eat well, we have a grand apartment, there are interesting events, the sound of the D.C.A. [Défense Contre les Aéronefs – air defense] entertains me because I have the soul of a Valkyrie. My health, in the opinion of the doctors, is very bad – angina pectoris. It's more boring than painful, but then as the final accord of life it is much nobler than other illnesses.

During the summer of 1943 Teffi was again invited to the Eliasheviches', where she found herself in the company of Pyotr Struve and other distinguished Russian intellectuals. "It's very calm here, but insanely boring," she complained. "My companions [*sozhiteli*] are old, clever, talk about politics (that at least is interesting) but most of all about who received his professorship when and who published his paper when."[49] She had to leave earlier than expected, "since all was not well at our home," she wrote Bunina on 24 September; it turned out that she had been much mistaken about her doctor friend, whom she now considered "partly insane and partly raving mad."[50]

Teffi's precipitous return adversely affected her health, but her weak heart did not deter her from getting out when she could, since "from lying around a person becomes gloomy and even goes mad," she wrote Bunina in November.[51] She saw little of the Zaitsevs, her revived affection for her friends apparently not surviving closer contact, but she developed a rather unlikely bond with Gippius. "From among our mutual acquaintances," she wrote Bunin, "I see Zin. Nik. most often. She is almost incorporeal, but since she understands nothing about tickets and rations, one can have an interesting talk with her."[52] In her memoir on Gippius, Teffi goes into more detail:

> I always found it interesting to be with her. And it was best of all when there were just two or three of us. The third was the enchanting I. G. Loris-Melikov, an old diplomat, a man with a brilliant, well-rounded education [...]
>
> I valued our friendship. People gathered at Zinaida Nikolayevna's on Sundays, but a close circle [met] secretly on Wednesdays. You could come to her [and] without any polite [*svetskie*] introductions say what interested you at the moment and begin a long, interesting conversation.[53]

Such visits, however, were becoming ever more dangerous due to intensified air attacks by the allies. Berberova writes that when she was at Gippius's one evening in October 1943, she and Gippius's old friend Alexander Zlobin (1894–1967), saw through the kitchen window "American bombers flying in threesomes, like geese, dropping bombs." They decided they had to go down to the shelter, Berberova taking Gippius's arm and Zlobin helping Teffi: "In the terrible thunder all around we begin to descend the stairs (from the third floor), and suddenly I see that the marble staircase moves beneath my feet."[54]

Even in the midst of such havoc life went on – in fact it appears that Russian cultural life revived somewhat in 1943 and early 1944. Among other things, several theatrical enterprises opened or reopened: the Theater without a Curtain; the Russian Drama Theater (organized by the ballet master Serge Lifar [1904–86], Yekaterina Roshchina-Insarova, and Yevreinov); and the Bat. All three put on Teffi's miniatures and – although she wrote Bunin mockingly about these ventures – she sounded pleased that she was being performed at all: "I trade on my wit. Cheap, but lively [*boiko*] [...] 'It's shameful for an old writer to trade in trifles...' Not at all shameful. At least there's something [to trade]."⁵⁵ Meanwhile a more substantial theatrical event took place at the Russian Drama Theater: a revival in April 1944 of *A Moment of Fate*, this time with a new happy ending.⁵⁶ The change, "in the spirit of the time, made it somewhat anemic," Teffi wrote Bunina on 7 April; but, she added, "I'm indifferent to all that, because I have heart spasms and that subdues a person's aesthetic temperament to an amazing degree. It's all vanity of vanities."⁵⁷

Unlike Teffi, Bunin experienced a creative surge toward the end of the war. His wife later recalled that the stories, collected in *Dark Paths*, "came into being because we wanted to leave the world of war and enter one where blood did not flow and life was not being snuffed out."⁵⁸ At the end of 1943, Bunin sent many of them to Zaitsev, who had told him about an interested publisher.⁵⁹ Teffi asked Bunin in February 1944, to "order the Zaitsevs to let me read the stories," adding sourly that "they will not give them" to her on their own.⁶⁰ He agreed and wrote of his distress at the abashed comments by the strait-laced Zaitsev and others to these overtly erotic works. He insisted that the stories were "not at all frivolous, but tragic," and on 15 May, after reading some of them, Teffi echoed Bunin's judgment that the book was "very serious, somber, from the first word to the last. Tragic, hopeless [*bezyskhodnaia*]."⁶¹

Teffi's reaction brought about further rapprochement between her and Bunin. Her salutation in the May letter – "Adored friend and teacher!" – attests to her increasing devotion, and his response of 19 May – written on "an impenetrably dark, cursed night," the "deathly silence" interrupted by the "rapid clatter of machine guns" – was more emotional, perhaps, than it would have been at a calmer time. "What kind of 'teacher' am I," he began,

> to you, who all your life have sung like a nightingale [...] radiating brilliance! [...] I have always, always been amazed by you – in my entire life I have never met anyone like you! And what true happiness it is that God has allowed me to know you!

After her praise of his stories, he added, "like a vain, ambitious, vile adolescent I began snuffling, flushed with joy – and pulled another little notebook from my pocket – 'Here, I've got some more.'"⁶² After this exchange, Bunin decided to send his newly finished stories directly to Teffi and only then have her pass them on to Zaitsev.

Meanwhile, conditions in Paris further deteriorated. "We live badly," Teffi wrote Bunina in May. "I'm writing this letter to the howl of sirens. Many metro stations are closed, they're going to stop the elevators in the next few days, there's no coal and none is expected, electricity and gas are curtailed and it seems will be cut off entirely."[63] Her 2 July letter to Bunin indicates that things had gotten even worse: "I'm sick and tired of alerts and closed metro stations. You have to go on foot constantly. Because of that people with bad hearts die suddenly, and their friends envy them."[64] She asked forlornly: "Will we ever see one another again?" but then answered her own question reassuringly: "Everything, of course, will calm down, will somehow straighten out." Indeed, things did soon "calm down" – the liberation of Paris occurred less than two months later, on 25 August 1944.

LIBERATION AND WAR'S END

The renewed contact of Russians in France with the outside world brought Teffi some unnerving news: since 1943 word had spread that she had died. An obituary by Tsetlin had been published in the American *Novyi zhurnal* (The new review) and memorials held in other émigré communities.[65] In what was probably Teffi's first postwar feuilleton, "The Next World," she ruefully thanked those "who held funeral services for me," adding that the surmise that she had died was quite "rational":

> Can one possibly think that a weak, old, and sickly person could splendidly survive the winter in an unheated house, on a starvation ration, to the howling of sirens and roar of bombs, in a mental state of anguish and despair for those close, those distant, for people, for the world? O-oh, no. She has certainly died.[66]

Addressing the severe shortage of food and fuel, Teffi developed the conceit that she was writing from beyond the grave: "In our earthly life everybody knew that a person has a body," but in otherworldly Paris "nobody cares about the flesh."[67] There even entertainment focuses on death. In what is apparently Teffi's only comment in print on the holocaust, she describes a film she saw on the Majdanek concentration camp and expresses particular horror at its orderliness and ordinariness: the "rectangular little houses at a correct distance from one another," with a "big factory chimney" (the crematorium) protruding in the middle. The fact that this "regular, clean little picture" was "thought up by man" made it "even more horrifying than the heaps of skeletons" shown. The latter, after all, had been seen before, but only "on battle fields or in countries swept by the cyclone of revolution."[68]

Teffi's daughter Valya must have been overjoyed when word came that her mother was alive. In her first letter to Valya after the liberation, dated 25 September 1944, Teffi filled her in on her material deprivations and "quite wretched" health, greatly exacerbated by mundane cares: "Bombing doesn't affect my heart, it's brave, but it cannot tolerate worry, depression, everyday anxieties. It's noble and old. I'm still young, but it is over seventy."[69] She also wrote about the miseries she had endured living with the "crazy doctor," but these were soon to end. About a week later, in early October, Teffi moved to what was to be her final dwelling: a room rented from an old acquaintance, the actress Tamara Oksinskaya-Lavrova (1889–1963), and her sister, Maria Aitch (1893–1971), also an actress, at 49 Rue Boissière.

On the day before her move, Teffi wrote Valya of her new residence's shortcomings – it "will be more expensive there than here, the room is worse, and life will be more difficult in terms of conveniences." Her misgivings were justified, for the room was small, dark, and airless, and during the bitterly cold winter of 1944–5, was close to unbearable, due to lack of fuel. "Our main scourge now is the cold," Teffi wrote Valya on 24 January 1945.

> It went down to 0° in my room. If I heat it a little with branches (they're damp) then it reaches a maximum of 6°. I have terrible *engelures* [chilblains] on my hands, but nothing can be done – there's no coal.[70]

Adding to the misery, Teffi had to "clean the stove and also stoke it" herself, and "that means [...] coal soot, pieces of coal in my hair, *engelures*, and sores on my hands. Terrible!"

Aside from the coal crisis, there were also shortages of food and other basic necessities. Teffi wrote Valya on 4 June 1945 that "eggs, butter, meat, fish – in a word, everything – disappeared from the market," and when they reappeared, "everything became more expensive [...] Butter went up from 350 per kilo to 500." Clothing was also virtually unavailable, and Teffi had to apply her sewing skills to refurbish what she had on hand. On 24 January 1945, she wrote that she "sewed fur-lined velvet boots for herself" and later bragged that she had altered "two old-ladyish gray blouses" she had received through the Red Cross, which "turned out *très distinguées.*"

Valya frequently sent her mother parcels of food, clothing, and other consumer goods, for which she occasionally received reciprocal gifts. (The two also sent packages to Gulya when they could.) Confirming Yury Lotman's assertion that the material underpinning of everyday life "is discernible only when it is lacking or spoiled," Teffi attributed to the items she received after such long deprivation a heightened, even poetic significance.[71] She dubbed the long woolen underwear that Valya sent at the end of 1944 "divine pants [*shtantsy*] of the sort that angels probably wear on winter clouds in heaven." On 18 July 1945, she declared that when wearing the shoes from her daughter, "my toes can play a rhapsody of Liszt."

Valya's resources were also very limited, of course, and Teffi had to look for other sources of aid, particularly from colleagues overseas. On 9 January 1945, after having discovered that the Bunins were receiving packages from America, she wrote them: "I'm not expecting [anything], because in America they probably know I've died."[72] The Russian Americans must have soon realized their mistake, because by February some of her food was clearly of American origin: "I have semolina," she wrote Valya, "oatmeal [in] small American boxes, dry milk, coffee, margarine, cocoa, your most marvelous chocolate in the world, honey, a little rice." Such parcels were to sustain Teffi until as late as 1947.

Despite Teffi's straitened circumstances, she was soon hosting gatherings in her dark little room. Her circle of friends changed considerably after the war, many of her old acquaintances having died or moved to America. She and the Bunins remained close, but she wrote Valya in late 1944 that she hadn't seen the Zaitsevs "for a long time" because Vera "did something bad to me." (She didn't reveal what specifically the deed was.) Among Teffi's most steadfast new friends were the poet Vladimir Vereshchagin (Volodya) (1888–1981), and his wife Maria (Marochka), who were to be a constant source of support during her final years. There was also Um-El Banin Asadulayeva (1905–93), a woman writer born in Azerbaijan who wrote in French under the name Banine, who left a vivid description of Teffi's room

crammed with an enormous sofa strewn with cushions and a motley collection of furniture, pictures, and books. Incredible chaos reigned; everything was covered with dust [...] And the photographs! There were as many of them as books; they were standing, lying, hanging everywhere.[73]

It was in that room that Bunin first met Banine – the object of his last love affair – or "love duel," as she called it.

The closest of Teffi's new friends, however, was Boris Panteleimonov (1888–1950), whom she met in early 1946 in connection with a literary anthology he was putting together.[74] He was a chemist who in the late 1930s came to Paris from Palestine after an unsuccessful marriage and a feigned (or perhaps failed) suicide.[75] He befriended Remizov, through whom he met his new wife, the artist and sculptor Tamara Kristin. The couple disappeared during the war, apparently joining the resistance, and after returning to Paris Panteleimonov opened a large chemical laboratory and began to write. Teffi and Bunin, who also befriended him, became his literary mentors: he sent his manuscripts to them both (and sometimes to Remizov), and they carried on often heated discussions of his writing in their correspondence. This mutual friendship brought Teffi and Bunin still closer together. "The three of us liked to meet," she recalled. "They both called me sister [*sestritsei*]."[76]

If Teffi was gradually putting together her personal life, the task of resurrecting her career proved more intractable. "There are no newspapers, there's no work," she wrote Valya in September 1944. She therefore placed considerable hope on translations, and informed her daughter that the previous July she had reached an agreement with a French publisher for a collection of her stories.[77] Then, on 24 January 1945, she happily announced that another company "is taking my book *The Witch*," but added that there was a complication with the earlier book, which was "ready and *sous presse*, but the publisher has not yet been set free." (The detention was part of the *épuration* – a purge of suspected Nazi collaborators and participants in the Vichy government.[78]) Most of the publishers were soon released, but her books were further delayed by a paper shortage, and they appeared only in 1947.[79] Complications also arose with *All about Love*, whose publisher, O. Zeluck, was "stringing me along [*krutit*]," she complained to Bunin; "'hasn't gotten around' to signing the contract." Only after she followed Bunin's example (Zeluck also published *Dark Paths*) and sent an "abusive letter," did the book come out.[80]

Teffi had particular difficulty with "Saul," which had so long preoccupied her. Because of the dearth of Russian-language periodicals in France immediately after the war, she turned to the American *Novyi zhurnal*, co-founded by Aldanov and Tsetlin in 1942. In August 1945, she wrote the Tsetlins – her first contact with them since the war – and, after thanking him for the "obituary" he had so kindly written, continued the death imagery: "If, dear editor, my posthumous work suits you and you publish it, I would be very happy, because I'd feel that I'm still alive and perhaps would find the strength to continue working."[81]

Tsetlin died soon afterward, in November, and Teffi's subsequent correspondence with his widow (in charge of the journal's finances) proved highly frustrating. In a letter probably written in late 1946, she expressed dismay that her "unfortunate 'Saul'" had not appeared in the latest issue of the journal. Teffi feared it was competing with Zaitsev's "King David," as she wrote Bunin, and would come out "at the soonest in about ten years."[82] Although a joke, the prediction proved overly optimistic, since "Saul" appeared in *Novyi zhurnal* only in 1990.[83] Teffi also offered the New York journal her "recollections of [her] exodus in Biarritz," but had no response. She wrote Tsetlina in late 1946: "It is insulting that *Novyi zhurnal* regards me so sourly."[84] She never again submitted works to *Novyi zhurnal*.

"SAUL"

Although the similar subject matter of "Saul" and Zaitsev's "King David" was probably a factor in *Novyi zhurnal*'s decision not to publish the story, its artistic flaws likely also played a part. Uncharacteristically long and prolix, written in an orientalized style reminiscent of some of Teffi's early symbolist works (but lacking the exuberance), "Saul" betrays the author's fatigue, if not her outright despair. Despite such defects, the story is worth careful reading, since it re-examines, against the background of the world war, fundamental questions of divine justice and human will, which Teffi had addressed earlier and would turn to again in her last stories.

Teffi retells and comments upon the story of Saul (1 Kings; 1 Samuel in the Western Bible), in which the Israelites, heretofore ruled by judges, demand a king, and the prophet Samuel, the last of the judges "recognized Saul as one chosen of God." He anoints Saul and directs him to "do as seems right to you, for God is with you."[85] The implication here that Saul should be guided by his inner voice is not supported by future events, however, for – despite his having ruled justly and valiantly for two years – his well-founded decision to follow his judgment rather than Samuel's command leads to the reprimand: "You did not fulfill God's commandment and your reign will not continue."[86] The narrator asks:

Was Saul's crime so great? Did not circumstance force him to act independently? Was it not because, according to God's word, the Israelite
king should have been obedient first and foremost? And the prophet
felt in Saul a free reason and will, not pleasing to God.

Saul is given another chance when Samuel orders him before a battle to spare
no one. He obeys, and the graphic description (echoing the horrible slaughter
taking place in Teffi's own time) makes it difficult to maintain the notion of
a good God: "The terrible carnage, the sea of blood, howls, and groans, the
squeals of beasts, the death rattles and curses."[87] Saul's one act of mercy, toward
the enemy leader, Agaga, leads to his ruin, since he "pitied Agaga with human
pity […] He went against God's will with his limited human reason and so he
perished."[88] Samuel finds a new king, David, who, "all brightness, all joyous
[…] ringing with songs like a golden string," is the opposite of proud Saul.
Possessed by an "evil spirit" because David's single act of slaying Goliath with
his slingshot brings him greater glory "than the many exploits of the solicitous
and reasonable king," Saul attempts to kill David.[89] The latter, in contrast,
refuses to retaliate against "one anointed by God.[90] At the end Saul wills his
own death at the hands of one of his warriors.

In Teffi's version, as in the Bible, David emerges as the positive ideal, but
Saul's story is central, for it is his assertion of individual will and reason that
has prevailed in the modern world. He and David, however, are not simple
antipodes, for Saul was a good king, even his disobedience motivated by his
sense of "responsibility to the people entrusted to him."[91] He erred by not
recognizing that he "could in no way overstep God's will and even if what
was demanded of him through the prophet seemed excessively cruel […] he
dared not act contrary to the word of the prophet."[92] In her early poetry, Teffi
depicted the cruelty of pagan gods, who demand the sacrifice of the innocent,
and in her 1921 poem "The blessing of god's right hand," she questioned the
justice of the Christian God. In "Saul," written during a period of unspeaka-
ble violence, such doubts arise again with particular force, but Teffi does not
unambiguously side with Saul either, for he, like so many lesser figures in her
works, both comic and serious, relieves his sense of injury by lashing out at
others. The good, even heroic, man, in his excess of pride, turns evil, and his
refusal to recognize the limitations of human reason leads to his downfall.
Thus, the question of the interrelationship of human and divine will is left
unresolved – and is, perhaps, unresolvable.

12

STRUGGLE AND PERSEVERANCE

1945–51

Teffi's final years were filled with suffering and need. Living alone in the small, dark room she rented from an uncongenial landlady, wracked by tormenting spasms that only mind-numbing narcotics alleviated, she was able to work only sporadically and had to supplement her meager earnings with aid from others. Despite such impediments, Teffi succeeded in writing some of her most ambitious works during the postwar years. She also continued to participate in the affairs of Russia abroad – indeed, found herself at the center of the ideological conflicts that rent the fabric of the émigré literary world.

SOVIET BLANDISHMENTS

An underlying cause of the dissension was the political situation in France after the war. The French Communists won a plurality in the 1945 and 1946 elections, and as long as they wielded power, no "White Russian" newspaper was permitted.[1] Two Russian-language newspapers did appear in 1945, but both were pro-Soviet. The first, *Russkii patriot* (Russian patriot), was actually founded underground toward the end of the occupation by the pro-Communist Union of Russian Patriots. After joining forces with another pro-Soviet group in March 1945, they became the Union of Soviet Patriots and changed the name of its newspaper accordingly.[2] Teffi refused to write for *Russkii/Sovetskii patriot*, but she and other prominent writers – including Bunin, Remizov, Adamovich, Berdyaev – were willing to join forces with the second newspaper, *Russkie novosti* (Russian news), assured perhaps by the declaration of its founder, Arseny Stupnitsky (1893–1951), that it would be modeled on *Poslednie novosti*, where he had been a close associate of Milyukov. Any resemblance to its distinguished predecessor, however, was superficial, since Stupnitsky had become an ardent supporter of the Soviets, and *Russkie novosti* emerged as their second mouthpiece in France. Teffi wrote for the newspaper between 1945 and 1947, but avoided ideology – indeed, after her first feuilleton, "The Next World" (see Chapter 11), and a second, devoted to the momentous topic of the atomic bomb, she shunned the topical altogether, her favorite subjects the Russian language and the Russian past.[3]

Teffi's avoidance of politics in *Russkie novosti* did not mean, however, that she felt no sympathy for the Soviet Union, for she, like a significant number of Russians remaining in France after the war, shifted leftward, much to the dismay of those implacably opposed to the USSR. The journalist and historian Pyotr Berlin (1877–1962) tried to explain to his leftist, but anti-Soviet, colleagues in America that among those who

> had to endure and witness so many incredible horrors, a psychology involuntarily took hold – anyone who puts an end to this is holy and blessed. And [...] when the heroic exploits of the Red Army unfolded in all their splendor, we were ready to forgive [...] the Soviet government for everything and forget everything.[4]

The most significant attempt at rapprochement was made by Vasily Maklakov (1869–1957) – the last pre-Soviet ambassador to France and for over two decades the official liaison between the Russian emigration and the French government – whose visit to the Soviet embassy on 12 February 1945 and statement recognizing "the Soviet state as [Russia's] national state" created a furor in the emigration.[5] The Soviet ambassador, Alexander Bogomolov (1900–69), was intent on luring others he perceived as sympathetic to Maklakov's position – "from 20% to 30%" of the emigration, he estimated.[6] These included some writers, among whom he singled out "Bunin, Teffi."

Bogomolov, known for his lavish receptions, offered his hospitality to suitable émigrés, Teffi among them.[7] Two invitations are preserved in her archive – one to a celebration of the anniversary of the revolution in November 1946, the other to a dinner with the ambassador and his wife on 18 January (no year given).[8] She later denied attending either reception, but her contacts with the embassy may have been more extensive than she cared to admit. In November 1945, Yakov Polonsky wrote his brother-in-law, Mark Aldanov, that Teffi had told him that she had been at the consulate on business. The General Consul Yemelyanov […] came out to the reception room […] and addressed her loudly, for the whole room to hear: "Nadezhda Aleksandrovna, Russia's pride and glory," and led her to his office. Teffi is in ecstasy. She asked only not to have it printed in the newspaper […] Teffi (the sly fox has her practical considerations) is afraid it would harm her in a certain circle.[9]

Indeed, a visiting card from "Nicolaï Emelianov, Deuxième Secrétaire de l'Ambassade de l'U.R.S.S. en France," is preserved in Teffi's archive with a handwritten message on the other side: "Esteemed Nadezhda Aleksandrovna, Please accept my sincere greetings for the coming New Year. I wish you success in your work for the good of the Soviet Homeland."[10]

The Soviet attempt to woo émigrés intensified in June 1946, when an amnesty was declared for former subjects of the Russian Empire and Soviet citizens abroad, and an estimated 6,000 people received passports and returned to Soviet Russia.[11] Enticing such prominent figures as Bunin and Teffi was a priority, and the Soviets enlisted one of their most effective emissaries to carry out the assignment, the celebrated war poet and novelist Konstantin Simonov (1915–79). During the summer of 1946 he met with Teffi and Bunin a number of times, tempting them with his personal charm and culinary delicacies delivered directly from their long-lost homeland. In mid-August, Teffi wrote Valya:

Very talented and nice. He implored me [*strashno zval*] to go to Russia. He drove me about in his car and treated me to Moscow *kalachi* [a type of fancy loaf] and caviar, which he received by airplane the same day straight from Moscow. I ate the *kalachi*, but I'm not about to go anywhere.

Bunina described a "Moscow supper" for Simonov and his wife at their place, with Teffi and Banine in attendance. He provided "vodka, herring, sprats, caviar, [smoked] salmon, butter, white and black bread – all sent by airplane at [his] request."[12] On 26 August, after Simonov's departure from Paris, Teffi wrote Valya that they "became good friends […] He took my plays to Moscow and promised to stage them." In another letter she expanded on the privileges the Soviets promised her and explained why she resisted their blandishments:

Representatives of a certain northern country said that if I'd like to go there they would give me a house and dacha and servants and an automobile. But this would mean I would probably never see you again, and I don't want to go.

Banine's recollection of the dinner at the Bunins' suggests that it was not only personal considerations that accounted for Teffi's refusal. She describes how Teffi and Bunin, their tongues loosened by the freely flowing vodka, pounced upon Simonov's wife for her disparaging remarks about France:

> To my amazement [...] [they], usually so harsh regarding France, defended it with all their might on the principle "I can reproach [her], but I won't let others." In the depths of their souls, apparently, they loved their country of exile. Or did they feel like showing these Red missionaries that a Marxist paradise cannot live up to a capitalist hell? [...] They tried in every way to unnerve the citizens of a country in which Stalin ruled not only foreign policy, the army, the economy, the party, but also literature and, the main thing – conscience.[13]

An interview of November 1946 indicates that Teffi's awareness of the persecution of two of the Soviet Union's most gifted writers – which coincided with Simonov's Paris visit – also played a role. Asked if she was considering a return to Russia, she recalled

> the last time I was in Russia. It was in Pyatigorsk. I was driving into the city and saw an enormous placard across the road: "Welcome to the first Soviet Health Resort." The sign was held up by two posts, from which two hanged men were swinging. Now I'm afraid that when I enter the USSR I'll see a placard with the inscription: "Welcome, Comrade Teffi," and Zoshchenko and Akhmatova will be hanging from the supporting poles.[14]

OPPOSING CAMPS

Teffi did not publish in *Russkie novosti* after April 1947, and there is no indication of continued contact with Soviet officials, but by then the gulf between those regarded as too soft on Communism and their more staunchly anti-Soviet compatriots was unbridgeable. Old personal ties were severed, Teffi especially dismayed when she was accused of "turning red" (*pokrasnenie*) by the celebrated journalist, writer, and former leftist politician Ariadna Tyrkova-Williams (1869–1962), whom she had earlier praised as "the most intelligent, talented, and strongest woman spiritually I have had the occasion to meet."[15] The rift also had serious professional ramifications, for it served to limit further already severely restricted publishing options, with periodicals aligning themselves with one side or another. *Russkaia mysl'* (Russian thought), founded in the spring of 1947, and the first non-Communist Russian-language newspaper to appear in France since the war, would have been a natural outlet for Teffi, but its staff (which included Zaitsev, Berberova, and Shmelyov), was zealously anti-Soviet and antagonistic to those who had contacts with the Soviets. *Novyi zhurnal* also took an anti-Soviet stance and such prominent writers as Teffi, Bunin, and Remizov published instead in *Novosel'e* (Homecoming), a journal founded in New York in 1942, which, in Gleb Struve's words, gave off a "Sovietophile whiff" ("*sovetofil'skii dushok*").[16]

The decisive break between the two camps, however, grew out of a dispute that arose at the 24 May 1947 meeting of the Union of Russian Writers and Journalists in Paris, when a motion to exclude writers with Soviet passports was introduced but did not pass.[17] Both Bunin and Teffi were away, convalescing at the Russian House, a rest home in Juan-les-Pins, on the Côte d'Azur, but when Teffi (deputy chair of the union's board) heard of the motion, she protested to Zaitsev (the chair), and in a subsequent letter went so far as to assert its fascist nature: "Remember – Polonsky wrote to America that our board is fascist, and we quietly protested. Now this is underscored and exposed publicly."

At the union's annual meeting on 22 November the motion did pass, and a significant segment of the membership – including Bunina – resigned. The *coup de grâce*, however, occurred a couple of weeks later, when Bunin announced his decision to leave the union and give up the title of honorary member. Zaitseva wrote to Tsetlina, describing what she perceived as the extreme polarization of the two sides: "The emigration is divided *sharply* into two halves: Soviet and émigré. It is very painful when some close friends have turned up in the enemy camp."[18] Tsetlina in turn sent a furious letter to the Bunins, announcing that she was breaking off all relations, and Bunin reacted with equal outrage, seconding the decision to sever their warm, long-standing relationship.[19] He also ended his very close friendship with Zaitsev because of his role in the dispute.

If Teffi's name has thus far been absent it is because she was gravely ill at the time. During a benefit she held on 26 November she suffered a heart attack, followed a week later by life-threatening complications. Oksinskaya wrote Valya:

It was a miracle [...] that she survived! A heart vessel burst. It happened on 2 December, at 9 p.m. She had the will power to do exactly what [was needed] to save herself. Three injections of morphine. The doctor showed up only at 10:30 [...] For the first days after this hemorrhage the doctor stayed overnight with us, since she was catastrophically weak and, honestly, if I had your telephone number, I would have called for you [...] Now she's significantly better [...] But only God knows when she'll be back to her old self.[20]

Teffi did survive, but emerged bereft, both physically and emotionally. "I lie in bed in terrible anguish, totally alone," she wrote the Bunins at the beginning of January 1948. "Our ladies often go out in the evening and then I'm like the surviving sailor in a submarine."[21] Panteleimonov proved an attentive friend, but he wrote Bunin on the 19th that Teffi was "apathetic toward life," despite his "hundred-horsepower" attempt to lift her spirits."[22]

One thing that did arouse her was the still raging conflict over the Union of Writers. Even at the end of December, while still fighting for her life, she wanted to "submit a letter of resignation from the union's board," but Panteleimonov advised against it because "they'll be sure to skewer her and she must not get upset."[23] On 8 January, Teffi expressed to Bunin how "terribly upset" she was by Tsetlina's letter, and when Tsetlina contacted her in early February, she responded with a spirited defense of Bunin, denying that he, "who had rejected all [...] the promises of millions and immortal glory throughout all of boundless Rus," could have joined "those against whom we have struggled all our lives."[24] In a P.S. she added: "I consider it necessary to remind you that they also invited and lured me and I did not go." Tsetlina jotted her reaction: "Is it really a merit – *not* to go to the Soviet hell and not to unite with them spiritually for material advantage?!"

Teffi's fierce loyalty to Bunin did not abate even when, at his benefit of 23 October 1948, he sharply criticized many of his contemporaries, including Chekhov, shocking the audience and creating strong negative repercussions in the press. After an anonymous lampoon appeared in *Russkaia mysl'*, she came up with a plan "to compose a collective letter" in Bunin's defense.[25] Although she gathered only two signatures – her own and that of Leonid Zurov (a long-time member of the Bunin household) – and the letter was never published, there was word that *Russkaia mysl'* was bent upon "destroying" her.[26] Teffi wrote Bunin: "And so, brother, I will perish for you."[27] Happily, the attack did not materialize.

Teffi was no less protective of Panteleimonov when she sensed a threat from one who had long ago disappeared from her life: her former lover, Leonid Galich. At some point and for undetermined reasons, she and Galich – by then living in New York and writing for *Novoe russkoe slovo* (New Russian word) – had become irreconcilable enemies. Galich wrote Bunin in November 1948 that the two "cannot endure one another [...] and it is as inevitable as death," while the previous January Teffi described how Galich would heap praise on writers and then "drag them through the mud [*podgadit*]."[28] She was therefore appalled when he struck up an epistolary friendship with Panteleimonov and wrote a positive review of his book.[29] Her hysterical reaction led Panteleimonov to break off the relationship (if only temporarily), but it also somewhat marred his friendship with Teffi, who, he complained to Bunin, "went on and on, even frightened me."[30]

STRUGGLE FOR SURVIVAL, PHYSICAL AND MORAL

Teffi remained housebound through the winter and spring of 1948, but the time was not wasted. It allowed her to fix her attention on what was most important, she wrote Bunina in late January:

> You know, dear, I'm not at all bored. If my strength permits I read, if I don't read, I lie with my eyes closed and examine my life. And – it's strange – much that was very painful [now] pleases me. It's like the chaos of musical dissonances whose beauty is comprehended only when the last chord "brings resolution."[31]

A few days earlier she had confided to Bunin: "At the beginning of my illness I considered what I want from life. And I wrote: 'A sunrise. The overture to *Lohengrin*. A talk with Bunin.'"[32] That spring or early summer she included a version, but without Bunin's name, of those desires in her long, stream-of-consciousness narrative "And Time Was No More."[33]

Teffi wrote Bunin that she "couldn't help but write ['And Time Was No More'] – it sat inside me and gnawed at me."[34] She felt incapable, however, of carrying on her everyday journalistic pursuits, and therefore was in desperate financial straits. In late March she responded to Bunin's advice that she contact the New York newspaper *Novoe russkoe slovo*: "I can't even sit [...] Even reading exhausts me – well, how can I write, create?! It's difficult for me simply to *live*."³⁵ She tried to earn a little through translations of her works, but, although several of her stories had appeared in German in 1948, English versions were rejected by the *New Yorker* and the *Atlantic Monthly*.³⁶ After a film script, "Gnock the Benefactor," was turned down by a company that accepted "only American material," Teffi's translator suggested that she adopt an American pseudonym – "some Smith from Minnesota. All the more reason, since in *Gnock* you've truly captured [...] the primitivism of American psychology."³⁷ The ruse, not surprisingly, did not work.

Bunin, uncharacteristically, tried to help. He wrote Aldanov in June about a collection he and others had undertaken:

> You know what a terrible position Nadezhda Aleksandrovna is still in; she still has attacks of angina again and again, *and* very often, because all day and night she is entirely alone – the two ladies from whom she rents her forever dark, gloomy room are never home – and she herself has to make her bed and prepare something in the kitchen (the "something" so meager that, all else aside, she is exhausted from malnutrition) [...] Therefore we, several people close to her, have decided – in secret from her – to collect money [...] and give her a chance to live somewhere in a good pension outside Paris.³⁸

The effort was apparently quite successful, for Panteleimonov wrote Bunin in October that the money for Teffi "is topping a hundred [thousand]" – that is, about $350.³⁹ By then, however, her need was not quite as great, since she had resumed writing.

In June Teffi had begun a correspondence with Andrei Sedykh, city editor (later editor-in-chief) of *Novoe russkoe slovo* and a casual acquaintance since his Paris days. She warned him that she was not yet ready to write, but added in a July letter: "I have hope. 'Our sister poverty' [...] is very much prodding me to get down to business."⁴⁰ About a month later she wrote Bunin that she had thought up a project: "I am about to write memoirs about some of the departed. I have to work while my head hasn't yet become totally addled, but only partially."⁴¹ The result is a series of witty, penetrating essays on major literary and political acquaintances that came out in *Novoe russkoe slovo* over the next couple of years. In the preface to the first memoir, on Balmont, Teffi defined her approach:

Many interesting people have passed through my life [...] Their works have been and will be written about again and again, but not many will show them simply as living people. I want to tell about my encounters with them, about their characters, eccentricities, friendships and enmities.[42]

Teffi had begun to write again while convalescing at the Russian House at Noisy-le-Grand, a home for the poor and infirm founded by Mother Maria in the 1930s and reopened in September 1946. A few days after her arrival, on 4 August, she wrote Bunin that she liked the "prayerful" atmosphere, but after a couple of weeks she complained: "It's very cold and boring here. I'm afraid I'll adopt the bad habit of peering into church. Candles are glimmering, the priest is praying, it smacks of Shmelyov and Zaitsev. O-oh! A sin!"[43] Therefore it was a relief to get back to Paris at the end of August, where (an indication of her improved health) she and Panteleimonov "strolled, dined in a restaurant; the *côte de mouton* cheered her up after the pension."[44]

During late 1948 and early 1949 Teffi was well enough to attend cultural events, visit Bunin and other friends, go to the cinema, drop in on neighborhood bistros and cafés – but she continued to complain about her woeful state.[45] On 7 October 1948, for example, she wrote Bunin that she had an attack while buying shoes, couldn't utter a sound, and when the saleswoman told her to pay, she obeyed "like an automaton." She joked: "Probably the saleswoman thought I was mute and the only the word I knew was '*montrez*.'"[46] Teffi's precarious health continued to hamper her ability to write, and this severely limited her income, especially since *Novoe russkoe slovo* paid so little – five dollars for a small article and ten for two columns.[47] Producing "a large feuilleton takes me about ten days, sometimes more," she complained to Sedykh on 21 May 1949. "That's much less than my *femme de ménage* gets from me."

An opportunity to earn some more arose when a new journal with an old name – *Vozrozhdenie* – appeared in January 1949, published, like the prewar newspaper, by Abram Gukasov. Two of Teffi's poems appeared in the first issue, but she was unwilling to contribute anything else.[48] "Aside from the low level of literary material," she wrote Bunin on 19 April, "I would have to plunge into the same old pig swill [*svinaia luzha*] of relations with Gukasov."[49] Teffi's desperate financial state was exacerbated by the increasing difficulty of obtaining money from the usual charities. Aldanov warned her in March 1949 that she would be allotted no more than 25 dollars from the New York Literary Fund (Litfond) because of shrinking resources and burgeoning applications from postwar immigrants. He offered to send her his own money as a stop-gap, and when assured that he would be reimbursed, Teffi reluctantly agreed. Then on 24 June she resorted to another tried-and-true fundraising method – a benefit – but the yield, as she predicted, was not high, since "the benefactors have grown smarter and poorer."[50]

It was Sedykh who came up with a partial solution to the financial straits of Teffi and other old writers, whose woeful state she described on 21 May 1949 before his summer trip to Paris: "We're very frightening – our hair is thinning, our false teeth are falling out, heels twisted, words muddled, heads nodding, some affirmatively, some negatively, eyes malicious and puffy, cheeks caved in and stomachs blown out."[51] Sedykh found the description "close to the truth," and spoke to Solomon Atran – "a millionaire, a philanthropist, and quite an eccentric person, who denied himself little things, but gave large sums to charity" – who "agreed to pay a modest lifelong pension [of 10,000 francs a month] to four aged writers," including Teffi and Bunin.[52] When Sedykh sent Teffi the news, she reacted ecstatically: "Such a thing has never happened to me before! [...] One encounters such things only in Dickens, in stories for young people [...] This is truly a miracle."[53]

On 19 September Teffi wrote Sedykh that she had received a check from Atran and sent him an autographed copy of *All about Love*. She also sent Sedykh 11 books for sale to "tender hearts" – affluent Russian Americans to whom he sold autographed copies of Teffi's and Bunin's books.[54] The extra cash proved very timely, since in October Teffi again fell seriously ill – this time with a liver ailment, which, she wrote Valya on the 20th, "caused terrible intestinal upset – up to 15 times a day, and all water. Vomiting bile." In November she wrote that her physician, Dr. Verbov, ignored her conjecture that she was suffering from anemia and placed her on a dubious diet: 30 pieces of sugar a day. After two days of feeling "nauseous all the time," she "told Verbov that in Chekhov's time people were cured through inspiration, but now they do a blood test." It turned out that she was indeed anemic, but the injections prescribed only added to her misery, she wrote Sedykh, since they caused "an enormous abscess."

Teffi was not alone in her suffering, for by the fall of 1949 the health of her two "brothers" had greatly deteriorated – especially that of Panteleimonov, who had been battling neck cancer for the past year and a half. During Easter, 1950, Teffi went with him and his wife to Noisy, and Panteleimonov sent Bunin a comically bleak description of their departure:

From the sidelines this is how it looked: an old man, writhing in pain, is climbing into an automobile, his eyes bulging and filled with anguish like a wounded doe. There are ladies with him. One is pale, her face terribly tense, gripping Trinitrine in her hand. The old man's wife is hopping close by [...] For a passer-by – a sorry picture.[55]

Teffi had actually been feeling better for a while, but on 21 May she wrote Sedykh that she had suffered a relapse, and this brought on renewed money problems, since "all my income goes for doctors and medicine." Moreover, due to the recession in the United States, she complained, "no one will give a red cent [*grosha mednogo*] for my book." The Cold War exacerbated the situation: "In America they're not buying Russian books at all," she wrote Valya on 12 September, "and in one theater they weren't even allowed to perform old Russian plays."[56] Given the desperate situation, in June Teffi went so far as to submit an application to an old people's home, which Zemgor was opening outside Paris.[57] In the end, however, she decided to delay her move, because, as she wrote Roshchina (who had also applied) in September: "I want to spend one more winter at liberty. In general I think of a *bogadel'nia* [almshouse] with horror, and fear 'sweet old ladies' like fire."[58]

Meanwhile, both of Teffi's "brothers" were faring poorly, but Panteleimonov was "the worst of all in our trio," she wrote Sedykh on 24 July. "Of our entire group I pity only Pantel, because he is very *good*. Bunin and I are so-so." In August she went again with the Panteleimonovs to Noisy, Panteleimonov reporting to Bunin that their "sister" "embarrasses me with her solicitude and love."[59] He commented on Teffi's loneliness, which he had helped abate, but would not for much longer: he died soon after their return to Paris, on 17 September 1950. When Teffi informed Bunin of the death, he replied that the "terrible news tore my heart [...] Only now did I realize how much I loved him!"[60] Remizov used the occasion of Teffi's name day to express his distress in his characteristically half-playful, half-rueful tone: "I grieve for Boris Grigorievich. There is no one for me to play games with. Does he miss the earth or has all this passed into the earth?"[61]

While in life Panteleimonov had drawn Teffi and Bunin closer together, his death created a painful rift between them – the cause a eulogy she published in *Novoe russkoe slovo* on 8 October.[62] Everything was still fine on the 22nd, at the celebration of Bunin's eightieth birthday, when he and Teffi were filmed together and, as she wrote Valya, she "turned out to be an absolute *vedette*." The conflict erupted a week later, when Bunin published a letter in *Novoe russkoe slovo*, contesting certain details of Teffi's article – in particular her assertion that he had been an editor for the literary miscellany that Panteleimonov had published in 1946.[63] Teffi was "greatly disturbed," she wrote Aldanov on 17 November, that Bunin had sent the letter "totally unexpectedly, *not having said a single word to me*." She insisted that Bunin's version was "an out-and-out lie," motivated by his desire to avoid domestic discord, since Vera still harbored resentment over what she considered Zurov's unfair treatment by the collection's editors.

The fair-minded Aldanov acted as conciliator: "Not many of us so-called old writers are left," he wrote on 20 November.

> The Merezhkovskys, Shmelyov, Al. Tolstoy, Balmont, Muratov, have died. Zaitsev has quarreled with you and Bunin; Remizov always went his own way […] Essentially only the three of us are left: you, Bunin, and I. Let us, at least, not quarrel during the years of life left us.[64]

Teffi, apparently moved by his personal appeal, responded on the 26th that "the incident […] is liquidated, of course in accord with your wish. I wrote I.A. a letter worthy of Francis of Assisi himself."[65] The letter, to be sure – in which she characterized Bunin's behavior as "not at all befitting a friend" and "deeply insulting" – indicates that some rancor remained.[66] He in turn blamed Teffi for not warning him before publishing "untrue rumors," but concluded on a tender note: "I kiss your little hands and beg you to forget about this nonsense. Your true friend and slave, Iv. Bunin."[67]

Teffi no doubt found reconciliation easier because of Bunin's deplorable health. On 6 January 1951, she wrote Sedykh that he "mustn't be offended" by Bunin's insults, since first he came down with pleurisy, then was diagnosed with a "terrible disease," arteritis. She had to admit, moreover, that her own "character has become venomous," as she wrote Valya the previous December: "I curse everyone, everyone irritates me[…] Bunin has grown completely 'gaga' and malicious like me." All the same, resentment toward Bunin lingered, judging by a March 1951 letter to Sedykh, in which she calls Bunin "a traitor by nature. If he's frightened, he can disavow everything and even write a letter to the editor against you. I say this based on bitter experience."

Nevertheless, that same month Teffi paid Bunin a visit, afterward describing to Valya the supreme effort it entailed:

> I took all measures: [lists medicines she took] […] I went to the Place Victor-Hugo to look for a taxi. I stood in the pouring rain for half an

hour. Finally I found one. I stayed at Bunin's for a couple of hours. He doesn't go out, sometimes doesn't even get out of bed, gasps for breath. We chatted *très rigolet* about illness, death, and life beyond the grave. Verochka Bunina saw me off. Normally a walk to Place Muette, where there is hope of getting a taxi, takes six minutes. I stopped four times, took Trinitrine. A hurricane wind rose. We slowly made our way to the square. I sat down in a drugstore while Bunina ran around the square looking for a taxi.[68]

Bunina finally hailed a taxi and, after arriving home and climbing to the second floor, Teffi suffered from three spasms and was "out of commission" for two days.

Even in the best of times Teffi took a dim view of humanity, and during her final years her disappointment with close friends (the Zaitsevs, Bunin), not to mention the vituperative spirit prevalent within the émigré community as a whole, only confirmed her outlook. Therefore, Sedykh's unfailing kindness and generosity "amazed" her, she wrote him in March 1951; she thanked him "for [restoring] my faith in people, which has begun to waver a great deal." She had already expressed her appreciation the previous month by writing a glowing review of his new book, and in response, Sedykh "went completely berserk and sent me 60 dollars," Teffi wrote Valya in March.[69] She added that she had also received 25 dollars from the Kulayev Foundation, established by the small but active Russian colony in San Francisco.[70] Of greater moment was an invitation she had received the previous fall to contribute to a new San Francisco newspaper, *Delo* (The cause) – which promised to pay "no less than *Novoe Russkoe Slovo*."[71] *Delo* (by then a monthly journal) began publication in January 1951, with the first three (of four) issues dedicated to Bunin, Teffi, and Panteleimonov, respectively. The Teffi issue contains two of her poems and a story – apparently the last new literary works she published in her lifetime.[72]

On 13 April, Teffi wrote Valya how much she dreaded returning to Noisy because of "very painful memories (the dying Panteleimonov)." It turned out that she could not return in any case, since, as she wrote Sedykh in July, rooms were reserved for "legitimate old people." (Perhaps the problem was the false birth year – 1885 – given on her identity papers.) An alternative arose when the poet Perikl Stavrov (1899–1955), and his artist wife Masha (1895–1955), invited her to spend August at their summer cottage in Brunoy, outside Paris. She found the place "enchanting," she wrote Valya on the 6th, but painted a grimmer picture for Sedykh, complaining about how "wretched" she felt, "nauseous, physically, morally, and materially." She predicted that nothing good awaited her in Paris, where "life has become thoroughly savage. Visiting Americans are staggered by our prices. They ooh and aah and scurry back to their native Hudson."

A CHANGE OF FORTUNE

Two developments, however, promised to make Paris a little less "savage." Teffi had known about the first since 27 May, when Aldanov wrote her confidentially about a new publishing venture in New York.[73] Financed by the Ford Foundation, what was later to be called Chekhov Press was very much a product of the Cold War, its goal to aid Russian émigré writers as part of an ideological struggle with the Soviet Union. Teffi wrote Aldanov that she had two books ready – one of memoirs, the other of stories – and he replied in July that both were accepted "in principle," but the press would publish only one book a year by a given author.[74] The remuneration, he added, was generous:

> You will receive $1,500 for the first book (over a half-million francs) in three portions: 500 upon finalizing the terms, 500 at the moment of publication, and 500 three months after publication. These 1,500 cover the royalties for 2,000 copies. If more are sold, they will pay an additional $400 for every thousand copies. You can't wish for better terms.

Teffi had planned to submit the memoirs first, but found she would have to add more material to fill an entire book and therefore she sent a selection of her stories to the director of the press, Nicholas Wreden (1901–55).[75] Wreden, a former White naval officer turned author and translator, answered warmly in August that he had been Teffi's admirer since his St. Petersburg days and – more to the point – that the press would begin operation in September and would draw up an agreement at that time.[76] When matters were delayed, Teffi feared "opposing influences" (as Aldanov had warned), and also worried that her book did not conform to the press's "struggle with Communism […] I don't struggle at all, you see," she wrote Aldanov.[77] Her fears were allayed when on 8 October the literary editor, Vera Aleksandrova, wrote her that the book "was included in the publication plan for 1952" and the press was pleased that Teffi was working on her memoirs.[78]

Meanwhile, on 5 October, Sedykh – unaware of Teffi's dealings with Chekhov Press, because of her pledge of confidentiality – wrote that he was so upset by her "deplorable material situation" that he had decided to hold a benefit for her in New York. He had originally come up with the idea the previous spring, but soon gave up, since, as he wrote her on 10 April, even the "successful" benefit for Bunin had netted only 51 dollars. This time he was still somewhat dubious, but expectations rose after he found two sponsors (the Litfond and the Nadezhda [Hope] Society) and discovered that 1951 marked the fiftieth anniversary of Teffi's literary career, which he used as a fundraising tool. The event, which took place on 1 December, began with Sedykh relating amusing incidents from Teffi's life (which she had provided and which mostly attest to her absentmindedness and hopelessness with money).[79] There followed readings of her stories, performances of her miniatures, and musical performances by the highly regarded pianist Nadia Reisenberg and the violinist Misha Mishakov, Toscanini's concert master.

Sedykh anticipated that the take would be substantial, but on 2 December he wrote Teffi that the sum – $500 – exceeded all expectations. Even this proved too low an estimate, and on 11 December he dashed off a note written in giant letters: "Dear friend, Nadezhda Aleksandrovna! $694 (net!)." On the letter, Teffi calculated that the sum would convert to 297,600 francs. She responded exultantly to Sedykh and his wife:

Hurra-a-ah!
    So ecstatic that it hurts!
    Thank you!
    I hug you both!
    I kiss you both!
    […]
    My dears! How wonderful you are!!!
    Your rich friend,
    Teffi.

13

LAST WORKS, LAST DAYS
1952

DARK HUES OF *THE EARTHLY RAINBOW*:
STORIES OF THE 1940S

Teffi's first title for *The Earthly Rainbow* – "Good and Evil" – sounds rather ponderous for a book by a humorist (perhaps the reason the editor didn't like it[1]). Teffi explained her choice: "'Evil' is the suffering of our dark, crude life. 'Good' is the divine miracle (tenderness, love, pity), that one must find within this evil. Find, reveal, and then it will illuminate and sanctify [*osvetit i osviatit*] everything."[2] This vision of good and evil underlies all of Teffi's works, but during her final years, riven by both personal suffering and catastrophic world events, she concentrates more on evil, seeking an answer to a fundamental question that has recurred in her serious works from the very start: what is the source of human suffering and pain – humanity itself, the natural order, God?

In "Baba Yaga," one of three fairy tales published together in *Novosel'e* in 1947 under the heading "East and North," Teffi examines evil within the Russian context – the wild, anarchic Russian spirit portrayed in her essay "Freedom," embodied in the terrifying witch of Russian fairy tales.[3] Teffi had already told Baba Yaga's story in a 1932 picture book for children, a quite straightforward adaptation of the folk tale, in which a cruel stepmother sends a girl to visit "auntie" Baba Yaga in the forest, in the full expectation that the witch will eat her for dinner. Instead the girl outwits Baba Yaga, after which her father drives out his evil wife and he and his daughter live happily ever after.[4] In her later version, Teffi expands upon the nature of Baba Yaga, who, following a long tradition, is not simply a witch, but a deity – "a goddess of whirlwinds and snowstorms."[5] Her portrait, moreover, is more rounded than usual: not simply an embodiment of evil, Baba Yaga has ample reason to despise people, who always "came to her to wheedle out various wise secrets, and they always cheated her." She expects no better from the motherless girl, for "a human whelp, however little, however poor, is already crafty."[6] Thus the witch's vile deeds are a result of her own victimization – a more extreme version of the mutual hurt people so often inflict on one another in Teffi's works.

When winter arrives, Baba Yaga leaves her hut and is transformed into the embodiment of the anarchic Russian spirit: "Terrible, powerful, free."[7] She destroys everything and everyone in her path, but a traveler – like the sacrifices to the pagan gods in Teffi's early poetry – blissfully submits to his death. He forgets his sweet Mashenka, is enthralled by the hideous Baba Yaga: "Old, horrible! [...] Oh, how enchanting you are, song-filled, crystal-eyed! You are a GODDESS. Take me to your death – it is better than life."[8] While annihilating others, however, Baba Yaga herself (the curse of immortality!) must return to the tedious life in her hut once the blizzard subsides. The story ends: "Bo-o-ring [*sku-u-chno*]."

Striking are the correspondences between Baba Yaga and Teffi herself (who referred to herself as Baba Yaga[9]). The witch, like her creator, is old and alone, has a largely misanthropic view of humanity, and even finds the companionship of a cat essential: "Baba Yaga lived alone. Only she had a cat. Even Yaga couldn't bear total solitude."[10] Although Teffi did not possess the witch's goddess-like power of joyous destruction, she did succeed in wielding the literary equivalent in her fairy tale.

"Blind" is one of Teffi's most fully realized stories, in which she adopts the anecdotal form to probe fundamental questions. It was written soon after "Baba Yaga," but – in stark contrast to the wild nature of the fairy tale – here the usually turbulent sea is "completely stagnant, dead."[11] A lady in a hat, whose name we later learn is Vera Andreyevna, is sitting on a bench by the sea, evidently waiting for someone and looking peevish. Her gloom deepens at the sight of a group of blind girls walking along the shore and singing a "joyless blind song":

> Ah, open! Ah, open!
> To us the happy doors to our bright paradise.
> [. . . . . .]
>
> Ah, illuminate, illuminate
> My dark land with a welcoming ray.[12]

When the man Vera has been expecting finally arrives, she starts a senseless quarrel with him, the underlying cause the self-regard at the heart of Teffi's portrayal of romantic love. But if in "The Limit" and elsewhere such relations involve a struggle of wills, in "Blind" Vera's will is paralyzed: she "could not stop. It was as if she were rolling down some devilish rails, intoxicated by her despair, senseless and malicious."[13] In her rage she sees things (in contrast to the blind girls) all too clearly, penetrates the layer of artifice that makes life tolerable. She is incensed by the man's "porcelain tooth with a gold rim," which "was inserted for beauty into that faded, distended mouth," and another "beautiful" touch – an ox-eye daisy in the man's buttonhole – makes her lose control entirely and she orders him to leave. Once he is gone, however, she realizes the absurdity of her behavior toward that "sweet, wonderful man."[14] She is shaken "by strange, joyless laughter," but then finds she is crying – the melding of laughter and tears so typical of Teffi.

The story ends on an ironic note, for while Vera is forced to face ugly reality, the girls' blindness allows them to maintain their beautiful ideal. Two of them approach the bench where she is sitting, and one girl, coming upon the flower torn from the man's lapel, declares that

> millions of such flowers are strewn all over the earth. And butterflies hover over them, and everything is so beautiful [...] that an angel wouldn't be able to control himself and would flutter down from heaven on the sly and kiss such a flower or butterfly.[15]

The girl then takes Vera's quiet weeping for angelic laughter, and the pair hobbles off, "joyously smiling."

"Blind" seems to affirm, like so many of Teffi's works, the superiority of illusion to reality, yet it is doubtful that Vera's view is any more "real" than the blind girl's. (She called the girls "fools" and the man she so berated later seemed to her "sweet and wonderful."[16]) The narrator of Teffi's next major story, "And Time Was No More," remarks that "you won't find two people in the world who see a third [person] in the same way" – in other words, all of us are blind in our own way (thus expanding the significance of the story's title).[17] One might go still further and ask whether the blind girl's vision reflects some higher truth. Relevant is Teffi's poem "An old man resembling an old woman." Written about the same time as "Blind," it portrays a ridiculous old man sitting at a piano and intoning Fyodor Tyutchev's 1861 poem "The eyes I've known. Oh, those eyes" ("*Ia ochi znal. O, eti ochi*").[18] The poet at first asks mockingly: "What kind of eyes could he have known?" – but then shifts from the earth to the "blessedly clear" sky, where,

> above the sorrowful vision [of the sunset], a ray
> Reached out in the airy heights
> [. . . . . .]
> To beauty hidden from us.

The parallel between the dying sunset and the man approaching life's end intimates that such hidden beauty is concealed even in the ridiculous old man. It may be that the blind girl, cut off from the world of appearances, is able to penetrate to that beauty – that God, in the words of her song, has brightened her "dark land with a welcoming ray."

"And Time Was No More," inspired by Teffi's morphine-induced state during her illness of the winter of 1947–8, takes place entirely in the hidden world of dreams and visions. Sequential time and coherent plot are abandoned entirely, since, as the first-person narrator (henceforth N) explains: "That's how it is after morphine."[19] The body of the story recreates N's hallucinatory state as she wanders through the snow with a hunter who looks familiar, but whose face she cannot place. He later explains that he is a "collective person from [her] past life."[20] N talks to the hunter about many things, ranging from amusing recollections to observations about the natural world to large questions of good and evil.

Toward the end of the story, N turns to cosmic questions. She explains why she dislikes the starry nocturnal sky – here, as elsewhere in Teffi's works, emblematic of an inimical, or at best indifferent universe. Later, however – true to the eschewal of logic and consistency in the story – she offers a more comforting view of the world order, her "theory of a world soul" recalling Teffi's talk on love at the Green Lamp: "There is one soul, common to all people, animals, and in general to all creatures," and death is a "return to the one."[21] She then evokes an exalted vision of death and eternity associated with immortal art, telling of a woman who, after the death of a beloved man and under the influence of a Simone Martini painting, dreams that the air is "transparently gold, pierced, as if cut through by golden rays." This air, and the "blessed intensity" of the woman's love, arouse such ecstasy that "a person could not bear [it] for more than an instant. But time did not exist, and the instant felt like eternity." N quotes from Revelation: "And the angel lifted up his hand to heaven and swear by him that liveth forever and ever that there should be time no longer" (10:5–6).²² This timeless instant is death, "something tiny, indivisible, like a point, an instant when the heart stops and breathing ends and someone's voice says, 'And so he died' – that is what eternity is."²³

The drug-induced vision concludes with the disappearance of the hunter, N screaming after him: "'Return! I don't want to be alone!' What is his name [...] I don't know."²⁴ The ending suggests a connection between the hunter and the male figure in Teffi's poem "Again that dream!" about whom she writes:

> And in this dream someone is always leaving –
> I don't know who, but I love him.²⁵

Teffi wrote Bitsilli in October 1950 that "Thy Will" – her last major story – was "about free will within a religious context," a matter that "has always interested me, and I've never found an answer."²⁶ As in "The Limit" and elsewhere, she examines the interaction of human and divine will within the context of an unhappy love affair. At the beginning of the story, Anna Broun, a concert pianist, arrives at a dinner party and at once retreats to a corner to mull over her recent separation from her lover, the critic Gerbel. She herself, consumed by jealousy, initiated the separation, reasoning that (like the hero of "The Limit") she would thereby limit her suffering through her will. She acknowledges that she had no real evidence of Gerbel's unfaithfulness, but was guided by the irrational forces that (as in *An Adventure Novel*) lurk beneath life's surface:

> The thing is that we all live on two levels! One level is our artless real life. The other is made up entirely of premonitions, impressions, inexplicable but unconquerable sympathies and antipathies. Of dreams. This second life has its own laws, its own logic, for which we are not responsible. Brought to the light of reason, they astonish and frighten, but we cannot overcome them.²⁷

The breakup has only increased Anna's suffering, however, which she attributes to lingering hope. She thinks the hope would vanish only if Gerbel were to die, and imagines stealing into his apartment and slitting his throat. Later that evening, Gerbel actually does die, which Anna discovers when one of the guests, a doctor, receives a telephone call and announces: "Our poor Gerbel has perished under the knife [*Zarezali nashego bednogo Gerbelia*]."²⁸ He adds that the death occurred during an appendectomy, but Anna hears only the first words and collapses, sure that she is responsible.

The second part of the story takes place at a sanatorium in a southern town, where Anna has come to recover from a breakdown. She encounters two kindred spirits, neither human – a tree outside her room and a performing bear, with whom she identifies as "my sister, the artist Shura Ivanovna."[29] The sight of a human, however – a young man resembling an albino mouse who was present the night she learned Gerbel died – fills her with horror. Later during that oppressive night, all of nature seems to share Anna's suffering. She sees a single leaf trembling on the tree, "like the vein on [her] neck," then goes downstairs and finds the "albino mouse" crying while singing about a dying parrot who "bequeathed" to him "longing for a sun more beautiful than the suns of the universe." His torment is especially acute, he explains, because the parrot never existed, "but lived only inside me; not even that [...] but simply died inside me, and that is almost impossible to bear."[30] Thus, while Anna suffers the pains of earthly love, the albino (a final version of Teffi's pathetic failure) is haunted by a longing that recurs throughout the writer's work – for an illusory ideal.

Anna then goes out to the terrace and, seeing the bear tugging at her chain, chides her: "Is it really possible to hope? You must set a limit with your will, only then is it possible to live."[31] She returns to her room and, remembering the 40 ampoules of morphine she has to treat her neuralgia, thinks of how a scorpion, when surrounded by a circle of fire, stings itself in the chest, thereby limiting its suffering through its will.[32] It then occurs to her: "And what if it is not its will, not the scorpion's? What if it is the will of the one who surrounded it with the fiery circle?" Paraphrasing the Gospels, Anna identifies that "one": "And not a hair shall fall without His will."[33] She looks out the window at "the circle of thousands of stars in the sky, meaningless for us and merciless," and thinks: "So that is who surrounded me with a fiery ring!" Anna injects herself with the morphine, declaring: "Let the scorpion plunge the poison into its breast!" With Teffi's characteristic melding of laughter and tears, she then "smiled bitterly, as if weeping," and murmurs: "Thy will be done."

The notion of a cruel force ruling the universe attests to the constancy of Teffi's vision from her earliest poems, but "Thy Will" is especially dark, with all of nature plunged into hopelessness and despair. The vast universe arouses only horror, without the sense present in many of her earlier works that death brings a merging with transcendent grandeur. God himself appears as a cruel gamesman who has surrounded His prey with a circle of fire, then looks on indifferently.

AND YET...: TEFFI'S LAST WRITINGS

"Thy Will" presents Teffi's most embittered vision of the relations of the human and the divine, yet this was not her final word. Her very last writings reveal that to the end she preserved a glimmer of hope that some of the things she valued most on earth – art, the love of humble creatures – could bring salvation and eternal harmony.

In June 1949, at about the same time that Teffi was writing "Thy Will," she was invited to take part in a celebration of the 150th anniversary of Pushkin's birth.[34] The project filled her with dread, but afterward she told Valya that her speech was a "triumph" and had "all of (Russian) Paris buzzing."[35] The talk (delivered by Roshchina-Insarova) describes Pushkin as a unifying force – "the only sacred thing that has joined us all, of different minds, from the gray-haired monarchist to the Young Communist with his red necktie."[36] Alluding to Pushkin's "The Monument" (1836), she creates an image of all Russians striving upward toward the statue of the poet, "thousands and thousands of hands [...] stretching, awaiting from him some final word, unsaid and never before heard by anyone." One recalls Teffi's Green Lamp talk, "On the Unity of Love," in which people, united by love, are reaching toward the center where God dwells. Now, at the end of her long and painful life, which engendered much doubt about God's beneficence, she substitutes for a divine being the spiritual ideal of Russia's great poet.

If in "Thy Will" the star-filled firmament points to the existence of a cruel, implacable deity, in Teffi's two final published poems humble earthly creatures offer a path to salvation. In "Letter to America," she distinguishes between the actual "commercial" nation of the title and an otherworldly "azure [*golubaia*]" America. She expects that its inhabitants – "proud Angels" and "censuring saints" – will find her guilty of "all the sins that defile the world," but she will be saved by the bear fed by St. Serafim Sarovsky, who explains:

> Because you elevated a beast's soul
> To a saintly height,
> [...] gave away your last chicken leg
>
> To someone else's cat
> [. . . . . .]
> you, unworthy slave, will enter
> The door to paradise as a queen.[37]

"When I was a child" also centers upon an animal (although one who appears in a dream). The poet recalls that when she was about six she dreamed that she befriended a little tiger, a "fluffy, warm beast."[38] Then, when "close to fifty," "tired and gloomy," she saw a "real" tiger in the zoo – an "enormous beast" with a "stinking maw," but she still maintains that her childhood dream is true:

> We are the same now,
> I'm the same little girl Nadya,
> And you are my dream beast.

The two will be joined forever in the star-filled night – not cruel, as in "Thy Will," but imbued with Teffi's theory of a world soul:

> All that has and will happen to us,
> Dreams and life and death,
> All [will be] fused as golden stars
> Into God's eternity and immovable firmament.

Teffi's "Last [Poem]" ("Poslednee"), unpublished in her lifetime, offers a comforting view of death as surrender of self and a merging with surrounding nature.[39] The poet imagines herself dying; she is "pretty" (*khorosha*), with two roses on her breast, two in her hands, her dress strewn with violets and mimosa. She concludes with a vision that conjoins earth and heaven:

> My four roses
> I will give back to the earth […]
> In the evening heavens are the violets and mimosa,
> The sacred color of my shroud.[40]

A HUMORIST?

Until the end Teffi disliked the title of humorist. "I have almost never been a humorist in the full sense of the word," she wrote Zeyeler in June 1952. "That is, I have not sacrificed the literary worth of a work in the name of laughter."[41] At the same time she was unwilling to forgo the uniqueness of her position as a woman humorist. Repeating the commonplace that there are no women humorists, she asserted: "I do not deny my characteristic humor, because I am the only woman in WORLD literature possessing this gift."[42]

Teffi also refused to admit her frequent misanthropy. On 28 December 1951, she objected to Aldanov calling her a "*zloi* [malicious, unkind] writer." He tried to placate her, responding the next day: "Except for Pushkin, all our classic writers are '*zloi*.' But in life, my dear, you are kind." Teffi was not assuaged, for on 22 February 1952, she returned to the subject:

> You called me a *zloi* writer [...] How many ecstatic, heart-felt letters have I received from readers [...] I've received tender letters from dying old women thanking me precisely for my tenderness, and from those going off to war [...] No, I don't think I'm *zloi*. Alongside my freaks there is always a "victim" suffering because of them, there is a ray of light, a piece of blue sky.

The point is, of course, that Teffi was both. In her works, as Adamovich observed, "the deformities of ordinary life are [...] tightly intertwined with a belief in life's primordial beauty and purity."[43]

The subject of humor – and of *zloi* humor in particular – was no doubt on Teffi's mind because she was rereading Gogol in connection with the celebration of the hundredth anniversary of his death. She wrote Aldanov on 10 March that she was "up to my ears in Gogol," and pointed to her surprising conclusion – that his satirical characters are not grotesque and exaggerated at all, but ordinary Russians, "banal and flat, but nevertheless the most normal and natural people." In "After the Jubilee," she expanded on this perception in her description of the characters in *Dead Souls*: "They are all alive. The great master did not add and did not take anything away." The problem is that Gogol "didn't like them" and that prevented him from revealing their souls:

> He didn't want to know that they were people and not masks – that Sobakevich will bury his Feodulia and will at once shrivel up [...] Nozdryov will be struck by paralysis and, frightened and guilty, will look with terrified eyes [*perekoshennym glazom*] at some "fellow" poking a spoon of porridge into his mouth [...] They are all funny masks until the Lord stops them in their tracks [*okliknul*] through grief, through the illness of those near and dear, through anguish and death.[44]

Teffi, who showed such pity toward suffering humanity, is implicitly distinguishing herself from Gogol and refuting Aldanov's characterization of her as a *zloi* writer. "After the Jubilee" was apparently the last new work Teffi published in her lifetime. She wrote Aldanov on 10 March: "I'm not writing anything new. I've run dry."

A JUBILEE YEAR

1952 marked a double jubilee for Teffi – the fiftieth anniversary of her literary career and her eightieth birthday. The former actually fell in 1951, but – thanks to Sedykh's publicity for the December benefit – news spread widely only in early 1952 and called forth a gratifying outpouring of love and appreciation for the ailing writer. Greetings came from around the world, "from people and even organizations I don't know at all," Teffi wrote Sedykh on 21 April. Among the small gifts was a pair of stockings for which she had to pay so much to customs "that I could have bought two pairs here." Still, she was deeply moved, since "they write such tender letters that it simply tears my heart, which is sick without that."

There were also letters from acquaintances, including a gallant note from Remizov: "If I were not a blind man (an unfortunate blind man!), I would come to your place to eat ice cream." He went on magnanimously to compare his literary achievement to hers:

I've played the buffoon [*balaguril*] all my life and this laughter of mine will fade with the last person I drink tea with in the kitchen, while [...] your sparks will be preserved in the printed phrase [*v pechatnoi fraze*].

Merriment is so much more solid than all kinds of verbally worn-out (after Gogol and Dostoyevsky) tragedies, with gaping mouths and eyes staring into the void. That is how I judge myself; in sum: what have I lived for?[45]

The anniversary also received attention in the press. Teffi was especially gratified by Zeyeler's article in *Russkaia mysl'* on 13 June and wrote Valya: "A miracle! *Russkaia mysl'*, which has always regarded me very coolly, out of the blue printed a touching article about me with a portrait."[46] Teffi also attracted the attention of the postwar émigré Leonid Rzhevsky, editor of *Grani* (Facets), a new Russian literary journal published in Munich, who, after his visit on 2 July, commented that his gracious hostess looked far too young to be celebrating her fiftieth anniversary.[47] Rzhevsky brought along his review of *The Earthly Rainbow*, which Teffi liked, and she later sent him her early story, "Anyuta," which appeared in *Grani* shortly after her death.[48]

French-language newspapers also carried notices of Teffi's jubilee, and earlier in the year – probably in late February – she and other émigré writers were interviewed by *Nouvelles littéraires*.[49] The journalist wrote of her *"solitude la plus complète"* and remarked on the disadvantage she suffered by writing in Russian: "This great storyteller, so celebrated in imperial Russia that her name was given to dogs and racehorses, and whom her friends call 'our Collette,' would certainly have had greater fame had she written in French."[50]

Teffi celebrated the other milestone of 1952 – her eightieth birthday – on 9 May, and among the greetings was a very affectionate note from Bunin: "Dear Sister, dear friend, I congratulate you, kiss you, warmly wish you strength, health, and [that you] write at least one more wonderful book worthy of the glorious name Teffi!"[51] She responded with an uncharacteristically flowery letter, especially given her mixed feelings toward Bunin by then. "Dear Brother and Friend," she began, "I received your precious letter, kissed it and hid it. And in the evening I reread it and put it under my pillow. And so I slept with it. Thank you for this immense joy."[52] (Vera Bunina was understandably irritated by this "schoolgirl letter."[53])

Valya decided to come to Paris for her mother's birthday and "eat *soupe à l'oignon* to madly celebrate," she wrote on 26 April, but she feared Teffi would suffer a setback, as she had on previous visits. The fear was justified. "[My daughter] has only a two-week vacation," Teffi wrote Sedykh on 19 May. "We had a mass of plans, but it all came down to my lying in bed and her looking despondently at my green face." On 23 May, after Valya's departure, Teffi wrote her what sounds very much like a farewell letter. It ends: "Christ be with you, my sweet, dear one! I thank you for having been born, for having lived, and for still living without bitterness […] I kiss you, your worried little face, your sweet eyes, my beloved Valichka."

Another valedictory moment followed at Roshchina-Insarova's evening of 19 June, which featured a performance of Teffi's play *An Old-Fashioned Love Song*.[54] Teffi described the event to Aldanov on 22 June:

> The play really did go well. And what amazed me – it wasn't the funny spots that captured the audience, but precisely the touching ones.

They rapturously called for the author and demanded that she come out on the stage. But to do so she would have had to climb two little steps and the author decided against it and like a fool nodded from her seat. It was very strange that the audience was crying so. I walked past Zeyeler and said: "Look, they're crying." And Zeyeler said: "Yes, and I'm crying myself." And he very convincingly blew his nose. There's a humorist for you.

The two jubilees of 1952 lent a celebratory note to Teffi's final year, but anxiety about money persisted. At the beginning of the year her landlady, Tamara, upon learning of the windfall from the New York benefit and book royalties, informed Teffi (in writing, since "a conversation would inevitably bring on [...] an attack," she commented[55]) that she had decided – as she had done repeatedly before – to increase her rent substantially. Teffi protested vehemently, but finally relented, since Tamara's hysterical six-page response led to a "sharp deterioration in my health," she wrote Sedykh on 17 February.

It was encouraging, on the other hand, to learn that *The Earthly Rainbow*, which came out in March, was doing quite well. Sedykh wrote Teffi on 25 May that it occupied third place in sales (after books by two postwar émigrés, Sergei Maksimov and Vladimir Yurasov), and added "in secret" that "other famous writers are far behind you." But financial instability again loomed when Teffi's benefactor, Atran, died and, as she surmised, she would probably "no longer receive the usual ten thousand."[56] The news made her more anxious about the fate of her memoirs. "Atran was the foundation of my existence," she wrote Sedykh on 13 July, and "my memoirs are lying in the jungle [of Chekhov Press]. I'm afraid to ask – what if they reject it?" She did receive the good news that month that the press was planning to print 500 more copies of *The Earthly Rainbow*, and wrote Valya on 26 August: "I'm very glad the book is doing well. Maybe they'll take the second one also, then I can be sick in peace."

THE END

With the onset of summer Teffi once again was looking for a place to escape the Paris heat, but she did not want to return to the Stavrovs and the thought of Noisy filled her with "disgust," she wrote Valya. She finally found a rest home for taxi drivers (*dom shofferov*) in Morsang-sur-Orge, south of Paris. On

28 July, shortly before her departure, she saw Bunin for the last time.[57] The meeting was deeply satisfying, despite the adverse effect on Teffi's health, as she wrote Aldanov on 8 August:

> I found Ivan Alekseyevich in very good form. His mood was not bad, he cursed good-naturedly, as if amazed that such unfathomable swine live in this world. As always I found it very interesting to chat with him, but on my return taxi ride I began to feel bad. I arrived and took to my bed. All the same I'm very glad that I got to see I.A. Who knows if I'll ever again have the courage to go such a long way.

Vera Bunina later wrote of the visit:

> She arrived. Sat down. Couldn't utter a single word. An attack. She swallowed something and laughed at herself: "A fine guest." Yan also prepared himself for the meeting, took something for his asthma. I made tea and things she liked. She ate almost nothing. She was afraid. They both engaged in a lively conversation. They laughed. Joked. Remembered.[58]

Teffi had not fully recovered from the visit when she arrived at Morsang. She wrote Aldanov on 8 August: "I lay in bed for three days [...] Now I'm lying here at the dacha." In a couple of weeks she was feeling better, but on the 23rd her foot had begun to bother her, and on the 31st her "throat began to hurt somewhere deep down and it was difficult to speak and turn my neck. My *infirmière* said that the reason was the same as for my foot. Dampness, neuralgia."[59] She did find consolation in the kindness and respect shown her by the other pensioners, and was clearly moved by her send-off on 2 September, when, as she wrote Valya,

> the landlady's relatives, a boy of twelve and a girl of eight, approached me, and the boy said politely: "We ask you kindly to give us the pleasure of having our picture taken with you. When we're big, we'll show this portrait to our children."

On the 3rd, Teffi continued, Marochka Vereshchagina accompanied her home "and Volodya ran off to make purchases." She added: "In general I'd be lost without them!"

Once home, Teffi's leg was feeling better, but her spasms became unbearable, she wrote Valya on 18 September. (Valya marked this the *"poslednee pis'mo"* – "the last letter"):

Last Friday I called Dr. Makeyev and in his presence two spasms in a row took hold of me, my pulse over a hundred. He was horrified and finally understood what my spasms are like [...] That night I had a spasm that lasted an hour. Neither Trinitine nor valerian nor a suppository helped. I gathered my strength, boiled a syringe, and gave myself a *piqure* [injection], and in five minutes everything calmed down! A miracle.

Confronting Teffi on 30 September was a "menacing day – my name day!" she wrote Valya, and although her daughter urged her to cancel the celebration, she went ahead. Stavrov recalled her "smiling at everyone who had come to congratulate her" – perhaps aware that she would not see them again.[60] There were also written greetings, including one from Zaitsev, dated 29 September – one of several faint signs of reconciliation during Teffi's final year.[61] The most touching greeting, which best summed up the distinctive quality of Teffi's character, was sent by Alexander Rognedov on 30 September. Although "in the vulgar sense of the word" they had little in common, he wrote, he attributed their "inviolable friendship" to a

common trait that invariably enlivened our meetings and thoughts: skepticism tempered with tenderness. To see life as it is and forgive it is not easy. You were able to do so with your characteristic generosity of mind and heart, and that constantly attracted me to you.[62]

Teffi was long expecting her death, which, she claimed in a letter to Sedykh of 19 May 1952 (borrowing an image from a 1930s feuilleton), she was awaiting impatiently:

All my contemporaries are dying, but for some reason I go on living. As if I'm sitting in the waiting room at the dentist's, he calls the patients, clearly mixing up the order, and I feel awkward saying so and sit, tired and peevish [*zlaia*].[63]

Her time came in early October.

In her diary Bunina described Teffi's final days, evidently based on Oksinskaya's testimony:

> It began on Saturday evening [4 October]. The doctor from the municipality came at night. Morphine. He left with the words: the pain will subside and she'll fall asleep. But the pain continued, and Tamara Lavrova [Oksinskaya] sat with her until 6 a.m. Nadyusha sat and rocked from the most intense suffering [...] She didn't improve on Monday. They sent a telegram to her daughter.[64]

Valya indicated (apparently also based on Tamara's observation) how important appearance remained for Teffi to the very end: when Dr. Verbov arrived at about noon, "before admitting him N.A. asked for a mirror and powder."[65] She died approximately four hours later.

When Bunina learned of Teffi's death, she felt (despite some strain in their relations in recent years) that "it was like a blow to the heart." She went to the service held in Teffi's room that same evening, and seeing the face of the deceased – "darker than usual, her eyes shut tight, her mouth sunken" – felt "infinitely sorry for her and for ourselves; there will be nobody with whom to unburden our souls at times." Valya arrived later that night and recalled that her mother looked "peaceful, beautiful, with a garland on her head [...] And a small cypress cross, which she once brought from the Solovetsky Monastery and which she ordered to be placed with her in her coffin."[66]

Teffi's funeral took place on 9 October, a "bright, sunny day," according to a newspaper account.[67] Services were held at the Alexander Nevsky Cathedral, which was "filled with people who came to pay their respects [...] Many wept. One felt that with Teffi a particle of our soul, of our distant Russian past, had departed." She was buried at the Russian cemetery at Sainte-Geneviève-des-Bois, outside Paris. Ironically, but in its way suitably, Boris Zaitsev delivered the funeral oration "simply and touchingly."

Epilogue

LIFE AFTER TEFFI

At the conclusion of *Memories* Teffi commented on how unsatisfactory life's endings are, and her own story is no exception, for personal and professional difficulties survived her. During her last days one of Teffi's greatest concerns was the fate of her memoirs, and in mid-September 1952, she implored Sedykh to find out by any means possible whether Chekhov Press was planning to put them out. His response of 4 October was quite pessimistic, and therefore he was relieved that the letter arrived after Teffi's death.[1] Although the press had solicited the manuscript, he explained to Valya, "something changed in their politics," and only "an author, even a bad one, but a DP [displaced person, a war refugee] has a great many chances of getting published." In early 1953 Gukasov expressed some interest in putting out the book, but an agreement was never reached.[2] Only in 1955 did some of the memoirs come out in *Vozrozhdenie*.

Conflicts, both literary and personal, went on, adding to the burden of the grieving Valya. Teffi's archive, which she had earlier agreed to donate to the Russian (later the Bakhmeteff) Archive at Columbia University but had not sent, stirred up the still smoldering hostility between the two émigré camps.[3] Valya's decision to leave the papers with Vereshchagin created "real panic" among Teffi's friends, according to Tamara Panteleimonova, since he wrote for the detested *Russkaia mysl'* and there was fear that compromising correspondence would fall into the wrong hands.[4] The controversy subsided only when, following Aldanov's advice, a plan was devised to have Vereshchagin, "in the presence of Panteleimonova," pack the letters separately, after which both would affix signed seals.[5]

Teffi's domestic conflicts with her landlady, Tamara, were also inherited by Valya. Teffi had sent her daughter a couple of years earlier an "inventory of her things," with suggestions of who should receive what after she died.[6] Her daughters, naturally, were to get the bulk of her belongings, which included a diamond ring for Valya and turquoise earrings with diamonds for Gulya, but the ring mysteriously disappeared. Tamara, who had been willed nothing, wrote Valya a terribly vituperous letter, reproaching her "unbelievable ingratitude," denying that she (Tamara) had stolen the ring, and ending with a curse.[7] Valya, who wrote the Vereshchagins that she "felt I couldn't live after that letter," had not accused Tamara and her family of theft, but when the ring suddenly appeared in a heavy case in the stove in Teffi's room, there was no other explanation for its disappearance and reappearance.

Teffi's daughters did not outlive her by very long. Gulya, after visiting her sister in London in 1956, died aboard the ship back to Poland when she slipped on deck and a bone pierced an artery.[8] Valya, who as far back as 1953 had complained of heart pain – a sure sign, she believed, that she was "beginning [to suffer] from mama's illness" – died of heart failure on 26 October 1964.[9]

LITERARY DEMISE AND REBIRTH

During the couple of decades after her death, Teffi's works virtually disappeared from Russian-language publications in the West, focused as they were on the postwar emigration and dissident Soviet writers. It was in the Soviet Union, after Stalin's death in 1953, that her name was first cautiously reintroduced as part of a renewed interest in the *Satirikon* writers. It began when Kornei Chukovsky – the former provocative critic of the Silver Age, now a universally loved and admired children's writer – advised his young secretary, Lydia Yevstigneyeva, to study Sasha Chorny. After she and Chukovsky co-edited the first scholarly editions of Sasha Chorny's poetry, she went on (later under her married name, Spiridonova) to publish widely on the *Satirikon* writers, including Teffi.[10] During the 1960s and 1970s a few editions of Teffi's works appeared in the Soviet Union, but it was only toward the end of the twentieth century – during the glasnost period and afterward – that she began to be published widely in her native country, the high point so far the publication at the turn of the new century of her *Collected Works*.[11]

The English-speaking world has had to wait still longer. While Teffi began attracting attention earlier, due to the growing interest in women writers and in the Russian emigration, it is only in the second decade of the 21st century that very good English translations have appeared, allowing readers to savor Teffi's wit, virtuosic language, and deep humanity.[12]

That the response has been enthusiastic is not surprising, for Teffi's works have great contemporary resonance. During a time of mass displacement of whole populations, her portrayal of the trials (sometimes comical, sometimes tragic, often both simultaneously) of the Russians who after the revolution were forced to flee persecution and possible death in their homeland – only to find themselves in an alien and uncomprehending world – illuminates the plight and increases empathy for present-day refugees. More broadly Teffi's writings – even before her exile – capture the spiritual homelessness inherent in modern life. The preoccupation of her characters with outward appearance; their lack of true inner connection and understanding; their urge to dominate, eclipsing love and sympathy, have, if anything, become more prevalent with time. At the same time, Teffi's search for a refuge from such spiritual "homelessness" never ceased, although personal suffering and the epochal calamities to which she bore witness in the course of her long life made her ever more pessimistic. The ideal transcendent realm of her early poetry devolved to the land of Nowhere, and her belief in the benevolence of the Judeo-Christian God faltered, but, despite this crisis of faith – so typical of the modern age – she continued to seek until the very end. The most enduring value expressed in Teffi's work, however, is what she calls tenderness – the compassion and affection of one lone individual toward another, which result in acts of kindness and self-sacrifice that make the cruel and callous world a little more habitable.

Shortly after Teffi's death, her friend Maria Kallash (1886–1955) asserted that those who knew her through her newspaper pieces

have a poor idea of Teffi the writer as a whole. She made a great contribution to the treasure house of the Russian artistic word – in prose, in verse, in dramatic works. Such an appraisal is a matter for the future.[13]

The future is now at hand.

Notes

1. Works by Teffi

References to Teffi's works are, where possible, to the seven-volume *Sobranie sochinenii* (Collected works; abbreviated *Sob. soch.*), ed. D. D. Nikolayev and E. M. Trubilova (Moscow, 1997–2000), with details of original publication, when known, given in parentheses. For books or specific works not included in *Sob. soch.*, or when otherwise appropriate, citations are from the original periodical or from the editions listed below (with details of original publication given in parentheses, where necessary).

AR	*Avantiurnyi roman* [An adventure novel] (Paris, 1932)
Dym	*Dym bez ognia* [Smoke without fire] (St. Petersburg, 1914)
G	*Gorodok: Novye rasskazy* [The small town: new stories] (Paris, 1927)
I stalo	*I stalo tak…: Iumoristicheskie rasskazy* [And so it came to be…: humorous stories] (St. Petersburg, 1912)
Ium I	*Iumoristicheskie rasskazy* [Humorous stories] (St. Petersburg, 1910)
Ium II	*Iumoristicheskie rasskazy, kniga II: Chelovekoobraznye* [Humorous stories, book II: humanoids] (St. Petersburg, 1911)
K	*Karusel'* [Carousel] (St. Petersburg, 1913)
KI	*Kniga Iun': Rasskazy* [The June book: stories] (Belgrade, 1931)
NP	*Nichego podobnogo* [Nothing of the kind] (Petrograd, 1915)
NZ	*Nezhivoi zver'* [The lifeless beast] (Petrograd, 1916)
ON	*O nezhnosti: Rasskazy* [On tenderness: stories] (Paris, 1938)
P	*Passiflora* (Berlin, 1923)

P'esy	*P'esy* [Plays] (Paris, 1934)
Rys'	*Rys'* (The Lynx) (Berlin, 1923)
Sem'	*Sem' ognei* [Seven fires] (St. Petersburg, 1910)
Stambul	*Stambul i solntse* [Stamboul and the sun] (Berlin, 1921)
TZ	*Tikhaia zavod'* [A quiet backwater] (Paris, 1921)
V	*Ved'ma* [The witch] (Berlin, 1936)
Vchera	*Vchera* [Yesterday] (Petrograd, 1918)
VD	*Vechernii den': Rasskazy* [The twilit day: stories] (Prague, 1924)
Vos	*Vospominaniia* [Memories] (Paris, 1931)
Vse	*Vse o liubvi* [All about love] (Paris [1946])
Z	*Zigzag* [Zigzag] (Paris, 1939)
ZR	*Zemnaia raduga* [The earthly rainbow] (New York, 1952)

Other editions cited

Ium (1990)	*Iumoristicheskie rasskazy. Iz "Vseobshchei istorii," obrabotannoi "Satirikonom"* [Humorous stories. From "World History," adapted by the Satyricon], ed. D. D. Nikolayev (Moscow, 1990)
ML	*Moia letopis'* [My chronicle], ed. St. Nikonenko (Moscow, 2004)
Neatrour, Averin	*Sobranie sochinenii v 3 tomakh* [Collected works in 3 volumes], vol. 1, ed. Elizabeth Neatrour, Boris Averin, et al. (St. Petersburg, 1999)
V strane	*V strane vospominanii: Rasskazy i fel'etony 1917–1919* [In the land of memories: stories and feuilletons 1917–1919], ed. S. I. Knyazev and M. A. Rybakov (Kiev, 2011)

2. Correspondence and other archival material

Archival repositories

BAR	Bakhmeteff Archive of Russian and East European History and Culture, Rare Book and Manuscript Library, Columbia University (New York)
BRBML	Beinecke Rare Book and Manuscript Library, Yale University (New Haven, CT)

IRLI	Institut Russkoi Literatury (Pushkinskii Dom) / Institute of Russian Literature (Pushkin House) (St. Petersburg)
LA MCL	Literary Archive of the Museum of Czech Literature (Prague)
LL	Lilly Library, Manuscript Collections, Indiana University (Bloomington, IN)
LRA	Leeds Russian Archive, Brotherton Library, University of Leeds (Leeds, UK)
MD UIUC	Manuscript Division, University of Illinois Library (Urbana-Champaign, IL)
RGALI	Rossiiskii Gosudarstvennyi Arkhiv Literatury i Iskusstva / Russian State Archive of Literature and Art (Moscow)
TsGIA	Tsentral'nyi Gosudarstvennyi Istoricheskii Arkhiv Sankt-Peterburga / Central State History Archive of St. Petersburg
TsIAM	Tsentral'nyi Istoricheskii Arkhiv Moskvy / Central Historical Archive of Moscow

Published correspondence

TBits	"Perepiska N. A. Teffi i P. M. Bitsilli (1936–1950)" [Correspondence of N.A. Teffi and P.M. Bitsilli (1936–1950)], ed. Edythe Haber and Olga Fetisenko, in *Ezhegodnik Rukopisnogo otdela Pushkinskogo Doma na 2011 god* [Annual of the manuscript division of Pushkin House for 2011] (St. Petersburg, 2012), pp. 722–52.
TBun I	"Perepiska Teffi s I. A. i V. N. Buninymi, 1920–1939" [Correspondence of Teffi with I.A. and V.N. Bunin, 1920–1938], ed. Richard Davies and Edythe C. Haber, in *Diaspora: Novye materialy* [Diaspora: new material], vol. 1 (Paris and St. Petersburg, 2001), pp. 348–411
TBun II	"Perepiska Teffi s Buninymi, 1939–1948" [Correspondence of Teffi with the Bunins, 1939–1948], ed. Richard Davies and Edythe C. Haber, in *Diaspora: Novye materialy* [Diaspora: new material], vol. 2 (2001), pp. 477–584
TBun III	"Perepiska Teffi s Buninymi, 1948–1952" [Correspondence of Teffi with the Bunins, 1948–1952], ed. Richard Davies and Edythe C. Haber, in *Diaspora: Novye materialy* [Diaspora: new material], vol. 3 (2002), pp. 536–626

Unpublished correspondence

Teffi rarely dates her letters. Therefore I have provided minimal notes for some of the unpublished correspondence, usually giving the archival location only at first mention, then providing known dates in the text. The following are the major archives to which this practice applies:

Mark Aldanov: Mark Aleksandrovich Aldanov Papers, BAR
Alexander and Ilaria Amfiteatrov: Amfiteatrov MSS, LL
Waleria Grabowska: Nadezhda Aleksandrovna Teffi Papers, BAR
Andrei Sedykh: Andrei Sedykh Papers, General MSS 100, BRBML
Boris and Vera Zaitsev: Boris Konstantinovich Zaitsev Papers, BAR

3. Periodicals

Birzh	*Birzhevye vedomosti* [Stockmarket news] (St. Petersburg)
IR	*Illiustrirovannaia Rossiia* [Illustrated Russia] (Paris)
NRS	*Novoe russkoe slovo* [New Russian word] (New York)
NS	*Novyi Satirikon* [New Satyricon] (St. Petersburg)
NZh	*Novyi zhurnal* [The new review] (New York)
PN	*Poslednie novosti* [The latest news] (Paris)
RM	*Russkaia mysl'* [Russian thought] (Paris)
RN	*Russkie novosti* [Russian news] (Paris)
RS	*Russkoe slovo* [Russian word] (Moscow)
RZh	*Rampa i zhizn'* [Footlights and life] (Moscow)
Seg	*Segodnya* [Today] (Riga)
SZ	*Sovremennye zapiski* [Contemporary annals] (Paris)
TI	*Teatr i iskusstvo* [Theatre and art] (St. Petersburg)
Voz	*Vozrozhdenie* [Renaissance] (Paris)

4. Frequently cited secondary sources

DV	Boris Zaitsev, "Drugaia Vera: Povest' vremennykh let," in Boris Zaitsev, *Zolotoi uzor* (Moscow, 1991), pp. 333–433.
Johnston	Robert H. Johnston, *New Mecca, New Babylon: Paris and the Russian Exiles, 1920–1945* (Kingston and Montreal, 1988)

LERZ	A. N. Nikolyukin, ed., *Literaturnaia entsiklopediia russkogo zarubezh'ia (1918–1940)*, 4 vols. (Moscow, 1997–9)
Mnukhin I	L. A. Mnukhin, ed., *Russkoe zarubezh'e: Khronika nauchnoi, kul'turnoi i obshchestvennoi zhizni, 1920–1940*, 4 vols. (Paris and Moscow, 1995–7)
Mnukhin II	L. A. Mnukhin, ed., *Russkoe zarubezh'e: Khronika nauchnoi, kul'turnoi i obshchestvennoi zhizni, 1940–1975*, vol. 1(5) (Paris and Moscow, 2000)
TT	O. N. Mikhailov, D. D. Nikolayev, and E. M. Trubilova, eds., *Tvorchestvo N. A. Teffi i russkii literaturnyi protsess pervoi poloviny XX veka* (Moscow, 1999)
Ustami	*Ustami Buninykh. Dnevniki Ivana Alekseevicha Bunina i Very Nikolaevny i drugie arkhivnye materialy*, ed. Militsa Greene, 2 vols. (1977–82; 2nd edn., Moscow, 2004–5)
Weber	Eugen Weber, *The Hollow Years: France in the 1930s* (New York, 1994)

INTRODUCTION

1   "Nostal'giia," in *Sob. soch.*, vol. 3, p. 37 (originally in *PN* 17 [16 May 1920], p. 2).

2   Estimates of the number of refugees vary widely. See Johnston, pp. 22–6. For a more recent estimate, see Catherine Gousseff, *L'exil russe: la fabrique du réfugié apatride* (Paris, 2008). Here and elsewhere I use the word "Russian" loosely, to encompass all former subjects of the Russian Empire.

3   Greta N. Slobin, *Russians Abroad: Literary and Cultural Politics of Diaspora (1919–1939)*, ed. Katerina Clark, Nancy Condee, Dan Slobin, and Mark Slobin (Brighton, MA, 2013), p. 19.

4   See, for instance, *Subtly Worded and Other Stories*, trans. Anne Marie Jackson et al. (London, 2014); *Memories: From Moscow to the Black Sea*, trans. Robert and Elizabeth Chandler et al. (New York and London, 2016); *Tolstoy, Rasputin, Others, and Me: The Best of Teffi*, ed. Robert Chandler and Anne Marie Jackson, trans. Robert and Elizabeth Chandler et al. (New York, 2016). See also *Et le temps s'arrêta: nouvelles*, trans. Mahaut de Cordon-Prache (Paris, 2011); *Un roman d'aventures*, trans. Mahaut de Cordon-Prache (Paris, 2011).

1. "AN INTERESTING BUNCH"

1   "Nadezhda Teffi," in F. F. Fidler, ed. *Pervye literaturnye shagi: Avtobiografii sovremennykh russkikh pisatelei* (Moscow, 1911), p. 203. The first name is spelled variously "Kondrat" and "Kodrat."

2   TBits, 25 June 1947, p. 740.

3   Nadezhda Kokhanovskaya, "Starina. Semeinaia pamiat'," *Otechestvennye zapiski* 3 (1861), pp. 209–46; 4 (1861), pp. 355–90. My thanks to Mary Zirin for tracking down this work.

4   Ibid., 3, p. 214.

5   Ibid., p. 215.

6   Ibid., pp. 217.

7   "Materialy dlia istorii mistitsizma v Rossii (Zapiski K. A. Lokhvitskogo)," ed. F. Ternovsky, *Trudy Kievskoi dukhovnoi akademii* 10 [otd. 2] (1863), pp. 161–203.

8   Ibid., p. 168 n. 1.

9   For Chebotaryov, see G. V. Vernadsky, *Russkoe masonstvo v tsarstvovanie Ekateriny II*, ed. M. V. Reizen and A. I. Serkov (1917; 3rd ed., St. Petersburg, 2001), pp. 112, 368 n. 326.

10   "Materialy dlia istorii mistitsizma," p. 177. For such principles, see Douglas Smith, *Working the Rough Stone: Freemasonry and Society in Eighteenth-Century Russia* (DeKalb, IL, 1999), p. 91.

11   "Materialy dlia istorii mistitsizma," pp. 201–2.

12   Ibid., p. 170.

13   For Alexander I, see ibid., p. 165; Smith, *Working the Rough Stone*, pp. 182–3. For Nicholas I, see David L. Ransel, "Pre-Reform Russia: 1801–1855," in Gregory L. Freeze, ed., *Russia: A History* (Oxford, 1997), p. 159.

14   A. I. Serkov, "Lokhvitskii Kondrat Andreevich," *Russkoe masonstvo 1731–2000: Entsiklopedicheskii slovar'* (Moscow, 2001), p. 492.

15   Nikolai Zakrevsky, *Opisanie Kieva*, vol. 1 (Moscow, 1868), pp. 417–18; 324–5.

16   Serkov, *Russkoe masonstvo 1731–2000*, p. 492.

17   The Moscow researcher Tamara Aleksandrova discovered in the document "Delo o prieme v chislo studentov Aleksandra Lokhvitskogo 1847 goda" (TsIAM [f. 418, op. 16, d. 193]) that Teffi's grandfather, Vladimir Lokhvitsky, was not a member of the hereditary nobility (as K.A.'s son would have been), but of the merchant estate. Aleksandrova kindly provided me with this and other findings in a series of emails from early 2015, which I will acknowledge in the appropriate place. She also called my attention to the exhibit at TsGIA: "Sem'ia Teffi (Lokhvitskoi N. A.) v Sankt-Peterburge" (chief archivist A. G. Rumyantsev, Dec. 2015). I accessed this exhibit in spring 2017 at https://spbarchives.ru/cgia_exhibitions/-/asset_publisher/. The exhibit is the source of some of the information on the Lokhvitsky family. Henceforth TsGIA exhibit.

18   Tamara Aleksandrova, in her researches in Tikhvin, found Iosif's first name and describes him as a "distinguished Tikhvinian [...] chosen as mayor (*gorodskim golovoi*)" (email to the author, 2 Dec. 15). See also Tatyana Aleksandrova, *Istaiat' obrechennaia v polete: Zhizn' i tvorchestvo Mirry Lokhvitskoi* (St. Petersburg, 2007), pp. 72–3.

19   A. Matte-Gené, "A. V. Lokhvitskii. Nekrolog," *Moskovskie vedomosti* 137 (1884), p. 3; N. Nevyadomsky, "A. V. Lokhvitskii," *Zhurnal grazhdanskogo i ugolovnogo prava* xiv/6 (June 1884), p. 48.

20   Robert S. Wortman, *The Development of Russian Legal Consciousness* (Chicago, 1976), pp. 45–6. Much of the following account is based on this source.

21   Ibid., pp. 223–4.

22   B. A. Chicherin, *Vospominaniia Borisa Nikolaevicha Chicherina: Moskva sorokovykh godov* (Moscow, 1929). Quoted in Wortman, *The Development of Russian Legal Consciousness*, p. 223.

23   Alexander Lokhvitsky, "Zamechaniia na stat'iu g-na Filippova," *Russkoe slovo* 10 [otd. 2] (1859), p. 22. See also N. S. Vertinsky, *Gazeta v Rossii i SSSR. XVII-XX v.v.* (Moscow and Leningrad, 1931), p. 44.

24 Alexander Lokhvitsky, "Po povodu sudebnoi reformy Stat'ia tret'ia i posledniaia (politicheskie i nravstvennye nachala sudebnoi reformy," *Golos* 28 (28 Jan. 1865), p. 1. For "great foundations," see Lokhvitsky, "Zamechaniia na stat'iu," p. 21.

25 TsGIA exhibit. The books by A.V. in question are: *Obzor sovremennykh konstitutsii* (St. Petersburg, 1862–3); *Guberniia, ee zemskie i pravitel'stvennye uchrezhdeniia* (St. Petersburg, 1864); *Kurs russkogo ugolovnogo prava* (St. Petersburg, 1868).

26 Lokhvitsky, "Po povodu sudebnoi reformy," p. 1.

27 Nevyadomsky, "A. V. Lokhvitskii," p. 48. I adopt the term used by Samuel Kucherov, *Courts, Lawyers and Trials under the Last Three Tsars* (New York, 1953), pp. 155–60.

28 Nevyadomsky, "A. V. Lokhvitskii," p. 48. Among A.V.'s publications is a series on crime novels, of which he judged *Crime and Punishment* the best of the lot.

29 Lokhvitsky, "Po povodu sudebnoi reformy," p. 1.

30 Louise McReynolds, *The News under Russia's Old Regime: The Development of the Mass-Circulation Press* (Princeton, NJ, 1991), p. 41.

31 See F. M. Dostoevsky, *Polnoe sobranie sochinenii v 30 tomakh*, vol. 29 (Leningrad, 1986), bk. 2, pp. 330–1. A.V.'s *Guberniia* was positively reviewed in the Sept. 1864 issue of Dostoevsky's journal *Epokha* (ibid., p. 347).

32 Alexander Amfiteatrov, "Iumor posle Chekhova," *Seg* 31 (31 Dec. 1931), p. 2.

33 Nevyadomsky, "A. V. Lokhvitskii," p. 50. For a detailed account of the trial in English, see Kucherov, *Courts, Lawyers and Trials*, pp. 163–8.

34 Kucherov, *Courts, Lawyers and Trials*, pp. 163–4; N. Nevyadomsky, *Vechnye voprosy advokatury: Po povodu "Etiuda po advokatskoi etike" Gr. Dzhanshieva* (Moscow, 1886), p. 30. The following account is based on these sources.

35 Quoted in Nevyadomsky, *Vechnye voprosy advokatury*, p. 47.

36 Nevyadomsky, "A. V. Lokhvitskii," p. 52.

37 V. O. Mikhnevich, *Nashi znakomye: Fel'etonnyi slovar' sovremennikov* (St. Petersburg, 1884), p. 181.

38 Nevyadomsky, "A. V. Lokhvitskii," p. 53.

39 "Zolotoi naperstok," in *Sob. soch.*, vol. 4, p. 131 (originally published in *Voz* 1804 (11 May 1930), p. 2; then in *KI*).

40 Ibid., p. 132.

41 Ibid., p. 133.

42 See "Davydova (Goyer) Sof'ia Aleksandrovna," in I. I. Yukina and Yu. E. Guseva, *Zhenskii Peterburg: Opyt istoriko-kraevedcheskogo putevoditelia* (St. Petersburg, 2004), pp. 181–2. I am grateful to Rochelle Ruthchild for calling my attention to this book. Teffi had relatives with the surname Davydov. See Teffi to Bunin, TBun I, no. 53, p. 393; Leonid Galich to Bunin, LRA (1066/2575).

43 "Davydova, Sof'ia Aleksandrova," in *Novyi entsiklopedicheskii slovar'*, vol. 15 (St. Petersburg, 1913), p. 412; Yukina and Guseva, *Zhenskii Peterburg*, pp. 181–2. On 19 Nov. 2015, Davydova's activities were the subject of a paper at the annual convention of the Association for Slavic, East European, and Eurasian Studies in Philadelphia: K. Andrea Rusnock, "Ladies and Lace: Sofia Davydova and the Collecting and Exhibiting of Russian Lace during the Late Imperial Period."

44 From http://nadezhdmorozova.livejournal.com/183222.html (link no longer working). My thanks to Tamara Aleksandrova for finding this website.

45 The dates of birth are taken from the "Metricheskaia kniga na 1872" in the TsGIA exhibit. (A *metricheskaya kniga* was a register of births.) According to the New Style calendar, adopted after the Bolshevik revolution, Teffi's birth date was 9 May. Until the

TsGIA exhibit, there was no documentary evidence of Vadim's existence, although Teffi mentions a second brother, a *lycée* student, twice at least in her autobiographical fiction. (See "Liubov'," in *Sob. soch.*, vol. 3, pp. 242–3; "Chuchelo," *Voz* [11 Jan. 1931], p. 2.)

46 "Nadezhda Teffi," in Fidler, ed. *Pervye literaturnye shagi*, p. 204.

47 Ibid.

48 "Moi pervyi Tolstoi," *PN* 179 (21 Nov. 1920), p. 3.

49 "Nadezhda Teffi," in Fidler, ed. *Pervye literaturnye shagi*, p. 204.

50 Teffi, "Moi pervyi Pushkin," *RS* 24 (29 Jan. 1912), p. 4. It turns out that the poem was not Pushkin's but one with the same title by his contemporary Fyodor Tumansky. A few days after the feuilleton was published, Teffi explained (not very convincingly) that the mistake was intentional – that she believed "it was quite a funny picture, that a little girl […] was persuading Pushkin that he wrote Tumansky's 'Little Bird'" ("Kommentarii k anekdotu," *RS* 28 [4 Feb. 1912], p. 2).

51 "Domovoi," in *Sob. soch.*, vol. 2, p. 223 (originally published in *Voz* 2147 [19 Apr. 1931], p. 2; 2154 [26 Apr. 1931], p. 2; then in *V*).

52 "Rusalka," in *Sob. soch.*, vol. 2, pp. 272–3 (originally published in *Voz* [29 Mar. 1931], p. 2; [5 Apr. 1931], p. 2; then in *V*).

53 See "Volynskaia guberniia," in *Entsiklopedicheskii slovar' Brokgauza i Efrona*, vol. 7 (St. Petersburg, 1892), pp. 119–25.

54 "Leshachikha," in *Sob. soch.*, vol. 2, p. 236 (originally published in *Voz* 2091 [22 Feb. 1931], p. 2; 2098 [1 Mar. 1931], p. 2; 2105 [8 Mar. 1931], p. 2; then in *V*).

55 "Liza," in *Sob. soch.*, vol. 3, pp. 235–9 (published in *G*).

56 "Moi pervyi Tolstoi," *PN* 179 (21 Nov. 1920), p. 3.

57 Tamara Aleksandrova discovered Teffi's record while at the school, in the gymnasium's "Imennaia kniga uchenits […] postupivshikh s 1882 goda." The document, as well as Teffi's diploma ("Attestat o zrelosti") is included in the TsGIA exhibit.

58 Unsigned letter, Paris, 4 Feb. 1929, Teffi Papers, BAR.

59 See Robin Bisha, Jehanne M. Gheith, Christine Holden, and William G. Wagner, eds., *Russian Women, 1698–1917: Experience and Expression, an Anthology of Sources* (Bloomington, IN, 2002), pp. 180–1, 183, 162–4. Maria (Mirra) Lokhvitskaya graduated from the Aleksandrovsky Institute in Moscow in 1888. See Christine D. Tomei, "Mirra Lokhvitskaia," in Christine D. Tomei, ed., *Russian Women Writers*, vol. 1 (New York, 1999), p. 419. In her stories Teffi mentions that her other older sisters also studied at institutes.

60 Teffi, "O chestoliubii," *Seg* 305 (5 Nov. 1935), p. 2.

61 Tatyana Shchepkina-Kupernik, *Dni moei zhizni: Teatr, literatura, obshchestvennaia zhizn'* (Moscow, 1928), pp. 151, 152. Quoted in Charlotte Rosenthal, "Carving Out a Career: Women Prose Writers, 1885–1917, the Biographical Background," in Rosalind Marsh, ed., *Gender and Russian Literature: New Perspectives* (Cambridge, 1996), p. 130. I am much indebted to Rosenthal's essay.

62 See D. S. Mirsky, *A History of Russian Literature*, ed. Francis J. Whitfield (New York, 1964), pp. 333–4.

63 Ibid., p. 346; Victor Terras, *A History of Russian Literature* (New Haven, CT, 1991), p. 383.

64 Alexander Benois, *Moi vospominaniia v piati knigakh*, vol. 2 (Moscow, 1990), p. 47. Benois writes that this occurred in 1890, but Nadezhda was 16 in 1888 – the same year that Merezhkovsky's first poetry collection came out. See also Judith E. Kalb, "Dmitrii Sergeevich Merezhkovsky," in Judith E. Kalb, J. Alexander Ogden, and I. G. Vishnevetsky, eds., *Dictionary of Literary Biography*, vol. 295: *Russian Writers of the Silver Age, 1890–1925* (Farmington Hills, MI, 2004), pp. 307–18.

65 See Camilla Gray, *The Russian Experiment in Art 1863–1922* (1962; rev. edn., London, 1986), pp. 37–64; G. G. Bunatyan and M. G. Charnaya, *Peterburg serebrianogo veka: Doma, sobytiia, liudi* (St. Petersburg, 2002), pp. 8–28.

66 "Chuchelo," *Voz* (11 Jan. 1931), p. 2. A somewhat shorter version, entitled "Pervoe poseshchenie redaktsii," appeared in *Seg* 270 (29 Sept. 1929). See also "Kak ia stala pisatel'nitsei," *IR* 50 (8 Dec. 1934), p. 8.

67 Varvara, who wrote under the pseudonym Myurgit (taken from the title of one of Mirra's poems), contributed sketches to the newspaper *Novoe vremia* and wrote one-act plays. Yelena, under the pseudonym Elio, also wrote theatrical miniatures. She and Teffi were co-translators of two prose works and a play from the French: Guy de Maupassant, *Sur l'eau* (*Na vode, Polnoe sobranie sochinenii*, vol. 22 [St. Petersburg, 1911]); G. Lenotre, *Paris révolutionnaire* (*Parizh v dni revoliutsii* [Moscow, 1912]); André Rivoire, *Le bon roi Dagobert* (*Korol' Dagober* [Moscow, 1915]). For the production of the play, see Chapter 5.

68 Tamara Aleksandrova discovered that at some point Vadim served as an official under the governor general of Turkmenistan. The information about Nikolai is from V. G. Chicheryukin-Meingardt, "Lokhvitskii Nikolai Aleksandrovich (1867–1935)," *Novyi istoricheskii vestnik* 9 (2003). Available at http://nivestnik.ru/2003_1/13.shtml.

69 See "Nadezhda Teffi," in Fidler, ed. *Pervye literaturnye shagi*, p. 204.

70 "Chuchelo," *Voz* (11 Jan. 1931), p. 2.

71 "Vasilisk," *Voz* 2056 (18 Jan. 1931), p. 2.

72 I. I. Yasinsky, *Roman moei zhizni* (Moscow and Leningrad, 1926), pp. 258–9.

73 "Chuchelo," *Voz* (11 Jan. 1931), p. 2.

74 Ibid. "Kak ia stala pisatel'nitsei" presents a different version, in which Nadya wrote the poem with Lena and they went together to the editorial office. For what is apparently one publication of the poem, see "Pesn' o ful'skom korole (Na sovremennyi lad)," *Birzh* 319 (30 June 1903; evening edn.), p. 4.

75 Tamara Aleksandrova found this information in the *Alfavitnyi spisok dvorianskikh rodov, vnesennykh v rodoslovnye knigi Mogilevskoi gubernii* (Alphabetic list of noble families entered into the family registers of the Mogilyov province). The following details about Teffi's life in Tikhvin also come from Aleksandrova, who had access to the registry book (*metricheskaia kniga*) of the Spaso-Preobrazhensky Cathedral.

76 Information from Tamara Aleksandrova. The specific date of Valeria's birth is based on an interview by Elizabeth Neatrour of Jan Fryling, with additional information from Guana Sokolnica. See Elizabeth Baylor Neatrour, "Miniatures of Russian Life at Home and in Emigration: The Life and Works of N. A. Teffi," Ph.D. dissertation, Indiana University, 1972, p. 9.

77 "Ved'ma," in *Sob. soch.*, vol. 2, p. 198 (originally published in *Voz* 2070 [1 Feb. 1931], p. 2; 2077 [8 Feb. 1931], p. 2; then in *V*).

78 See "Helena Buczyńska," in Stanisław Dabrowski, ed., *Słownik biograficzny teatru polskiego: 1765–1965* (Warsaw, 1973), p. 73.

79 "Volch'ia noch'," in *Sob. soch.*, vol. 2, p. 363 (originally published in *Voz* 3141 [7 Jan. 1934]; then in *V*). The other two stories are "Chudesa!" in *Sob. soch.*, vol. 4, pp. 218–22 (originally published in *Voz* 3756 [15 Sept. 1935], p. 2; then in *ON*); "Feia Karabos," in *Sob. soch.*, vol. 7, pp. 32–7 (originally published in *PN* 6238 [24 Apr. 1938], p. 2; then in *Vse*).

80 "Chudesa!" in *Sob. soch.*, vol. 4, pp. 218–19.

81 "Volch'ia noch'," in *Sob. soch.*, vol. 2, p. 366.

82 Marcelline J. Hutton, *Russian and West European Women, 1860–1939: Dreams, Struggles, and Nightmares* (Lanham, MD, 2001), p. 30.

83 Neatrour, "Miniatures of Russian Life," pp. 9, 11.

84 Clippings of the stories are preserved in the Teffi Papers, BAR: Helena Buczyńska, "Sentymentalna historja," "Jahor," "Jedno zdarzenie," "Kołym," "Wielka noc." Only on the last story is the place and date of publication recorded: *Gazeta polska* (4 Apr. 1931), p. 5. Written in pencil on the top is the abbreviated word "Autobiogr."

85 According to Tamara Aleksandrova, Jan or Janek was born on 5 Sept. 1896.

86 In Teffi's story "Valya" this line is given to her little daughter.

87 "Staryi dom," in *Sob. soch.*, vol. 6, pp. 85–90 (originally published in *PN* 6131 [7 Jan. 1938], p. 3).

88 Teffi to Waleria Grabowska, 6 Nov. 1947, Teffi Papers, BAR.

2. LITERARY BEGINNINGS

1 I am grateful to Charlotte Rosenthal for this information.

2 Anastasya Verbitskaya, *Kliuchi schast'ia*, vol. 4 (Moscow, 1915), pp. 206–9.

3 See "Zabytyi put'," in *Ium* (1990), pp. 117–26 (originally published in *Zvezda* 39 [7 May 1903]; then in *Ium* I) and *Sharmanka Satany. P'esa v 4-kh deistviiakh* (Petrograd, 1916).

4 Marcelline J. Hutton, *Russian and West European Women, 1860–1939: Dreams, Struggles, and Nightmares* (Lanham, MD, 2001), p. 30.

5 Verbitskaya, *Kliuchi schast'ia*, vol. 4, p. 210.

6 T. L. Shchepkina-Kupernik, *Iz vospominanii* (Moscow, 1959), p. 280.

7 See Charlotte Rosenthal, "Carving Out a Career: Women Prose Writers, 1885–1917, the Biographical Background," in Rosalind Marsh, ed., *Gender and Russian Literature: New Perspectives* (Cambridge, 1996), pp. 129–40; Maria Mikhailova, "The Fate of Women Writers in Literature at the Beginning of the Twentieth Century," in ibid., pp. 129–30, 142.

8 For more detail, see Judith E. Kalb and J. Alexander Ogden, "Introduction," in Judith E. Kalb, J. Alexander Ogden, and I. G. Vishnevetsky, eds., *Dictionary of Literary Biography*, vol. 295: *Russian Writers of the Silver Age, 1890–1925* (Farmington Hills, MI, 2004), pp. xv–xxv; Ewa M. Thompson, "Symbolism," Evelyn Bristol, "Decadence," in Victor Terras, ed., *Handbook of Russian Literature* (New Haven, CT, 1985), pp. 460–4, 94.

9 M. A. Lokhvitskaya (Zhiber), "Safo," in *Stikhotvoreniia* (Moscow, 1896), p. 177.

10 Tatyana Aleksandrova, *Istaiat' obrechennaia v polete: Zhizn' i tvorchestvo Mirry Lokhvitskoi* (St. Petersburg, 2007), p. 113. The quotation "ecstatic outpourings" is from G. Byaly, "Poety 1880–1890-kh godov," in L. K. Dolgopolov and L. A. Nikolayeva, eds., *Poety 1880–1890-kh godov* (Moscow and Leningrad, 1964), p. 89.

11 I. I. Yasinsky, *Roman moei zhizni* (Moscow and Leningrad, 1926), p. 260.

12 See Robert Bird, "Konstantin Dmitrievich Bal'mont," in Kalb, Ogden, and Vishnevetsky, eds., *Dictionary of Literary Biography*, vol. 295, p. 57.

13 "Bal'mont," in *ML*, p. 233 (originally published in *NRS* 13821 [5 Sept. 1948], p. 2). The meeting apparently took place in 1900. See Tatyana Aleksandrova, *Istaiat' obrechennaia v polete*, p. 195.

14 "Bal'mont," in *ML*, p. 237 (originally published in *NRS* 13821 [5 Sept. 1948], p. 2).

15 Yasinsky, *Roman moei zhizni*, p. 259.

16 Leonid Galich, "Strastotsvet," *Rul'* 745 (15 May 1923), pp. 2–3.

17 IRLI (f. 486, no. 69). Quoted in Tatyana Aleksandrova, *Istaiat' obrechennaia v polete*, p. 50.

18 N. Buchinskaya, "Chetyre inzhenera," *Pochtal'on* 10 (1902), pp. 637–8; "Volshebnyi son,"

Pochtal'on 1 (Jan. 1903), p. 3; "Shansonetka," *Beseda* 7 (July 1903), p. 340. (In 1903 *Pochtal'on* was renamed *Beseda* and remained under Yasinsky's editorship.)

19 "Aleksei Tolstoi," in *ML*, p. 203 (originally published in *NRS* 13344 [7 Nov. 1948], p. 2).

20 Ibid., p. 204.

21 See "Iakovleva, Zoia Iulianovna," in *Entsiklopedicheskii slovar' Brokgauza i Efrona*, vol. 41a (St. Petersburg, 1904), p. 607.

22 "Nadezhda Teffi," in F. F. Fidler, ed. *Pervye literaturnye shagi: Avtobiografii sovremennykh russkikh pisatelei* (Moscow, 1911), pp. 204–5.

23 Quoted by Vladimir Vereshchagin, "Teffi," *RM* (21 Nov. 1968), p. 8.

24 "Novyi god u pisatelei," *Zvezda* 52 (29 Dec. 1901), pp. 14–16, 18. The pseudonym was also used a couple of weeks earlier for the poem "Pokaiannyi den'," *TI* 51 (16 Dec. 1901), p. 955.

25 "Psevdonim," *Voz* (20 Dec. 1931), p. 2. On pseudonyms, see Rosenthal, "Carving Out a Career," p. 131.

26 "How the First Letter Was Written," "How the Alphabet Was Made," *Just So Stories* (New York, 1970), pp. 116–51.

27 The above edition gives the date of the two stories in question as 1901, but apparently they appeared in book form only in 1902. In any case, it is unlikely that Teffi could have become familiar with the stories so quickly, especially since she did not know English well.

28 As early as 1902 the song "Dogadaites' sami. Tsyganskii romans," with lyrics by "Lokhvitskaya-Buchinskaya" and music by N. Zubov, was published in *Tsyganskaia zhizn': Izliublennye romansy i pesni repertuara A. D. Vial'tsevoi, N. I. Tamara, V. Paninoi, N. G. Severskogo i dr.* (St. Petersburg, 1902).

29 "Mne snilsia son," *Sever* 35 (1901), p. 1101.

30 "Vampir," *Zvezda* 41 (13 Oct. 1901), p. 18.

31 "Osen' zhizni," *Zvezda* 73 (10 Sept. 1903), p. 1190.

32 "Ne podkhodi ko mne!..." *Zvezda* 15 (19 Feb. 1903), p. 242.

33 "Osennee priznanie," *Zvezda* 83 (16 Oct. 1903), p. 1352.

34 Galich's letters to Ivan Bunin from the late 1940s and early 1950s indicate that he and Teffi were close in the early 1900s. See Galich to Bunin, 8 July 1947, LRA (1066/2556); 12 May 1951, LRA (1066/2659).

35 See D. M. Magomedova, "Galich Leonid Evgen'evich," in *Russkie pisateli 1800–1917: Biograficheskii slovar'*, vol. 1 (Moscow, 1989), pp. 517–8.

36 Leonid Galich, "Moi gazetnyi debiut (Peterburg na poroge 20 veka)," *NRS* 12467 (16 June 1946), pp. 3, 8.

37 "Skonchalsia Leonid Galich," *NRS* (13 Sept. 1953), p. 1.

38 Quoted in Vladimir Vereshchagin, "Teffi," *RM* (21 Nov. 1968), p. 8.

39 See June Sochen, "Introduction," in June Sochen, ed., *Women's Comic Visions* (Detroit, 1991), p. 9. For a fuller exploration of the subject, see Edythe C. Haber, "Fashioning Life: Teffi and Women's Humor," in Lesley Milne, ed., *Reflective Laughter: Aspects of Humour in Russian Culture* (London, 2004), pp. 63–71, 200–3.

40 Teffi, "Novyi god u pisatelei," *Zvezda* 52 (29 Dec. 1901), p. 14.

41 "Vesennii otlet. Dramaticheskaia stsena v odnom akte," *Zvezda* 22 (1 June 1902), p. 17.

42 Ibid., p. 12.

43 "Letiat! Pereleteli!" *Zvezda* 42 (19 Oct. 1902), p. 10.

44 "Plach doktorov," *Zvezda* 16 (20 Apr. 1902), p. 24.

45 "45 let," in *ML*, p. 244 (originally published in *NRS* 13939 [15 June 1950]).

46 I have not seen the entire run of the newspaper. My observations are based on my findings from May 1903 to early 1905.

47 "Malen'kii dialog," *Birzh* 657 (19 Dec. 1904; morning edn.), p. 2.

48 "Smekh," *Birzh* 31 (18 Jan. 1904), p. 2.

49 Kornei Chukovsky, "Dve 'korolevy': Stranitsy vospominanii," in Kornei Chukovsky, *Sobranie sochinenii v 15 tomakh* (Moscow, 2001), vol. 4, p. 511 (originally published in *Literaturnaia Rossiia* [1 Sept. 1967]). I am grateful to Richard Davies for calling my attention to this article.

50 *Birzh* 135 (16 Mar. 1903). Quoted ibid., p. 513.

51 Ibid., p. 517.

52 "Slovo o polku plagiatorov," *Zvezda* 28–9 (5 Apr. 1903), p. 486.

53 "Beskrylye dushi," *Birzh* 384 (29 July 1904), p. 2.

54 *Thus Spoke Zarathustra*, part 1. In Walter Kaufmann's translation: "I love those who do not first seek behind the stars for a reason to go under and be a sacrifice, but who sacrifice themselves for the earth, that the earth may some day become the overman's" (*The Portable Nietzsche*, ed. and trans. Walter Kaufmann [New York, 1959], p. 127).

55 "Mgla," *Birzh* 495 (28 Sept. 1904; morning edn.), p. 3.

56 Mikhail M. Zoshchenko, "N. Teffi," *Ezhegodnik Rukopisnogo otdela Pushkinskogo Doma na 1972 god* (Leningrad, 1972), p. 142. See also Edythe C. Haber, "The Roots of NEP Satire: The Case of Teffi and Zoshchenko," *The NEP Era: Soviet Russia, 1921–1928* i/1 (2007), pp. 89–99.

57 "Veselaia vecherinka," in *Ium* (1990), pp. 50–7 (originally published in *Birzh* 183 [11 Apr. 1904], pp. 2–3; then in *Ium* I).

58 "Zabytyi put'," in *Ium* (1990), p. 126 (originally published in *Zvezda* 39 [7 May 1903]; then in *Ium* I).

59 Ibid.

60 Ibid., pp. 118, 126.

61 Ibid., pp. 118, 123.

62 Ibid., p. 122.

63 "Den' proshel," *Prilozhenie Nivy* 2 (Aug. 1905), pp. 603–16. See also Rosenthal, "Carving Out a Career," p. 129.

64 "Rubin Printsessy," in *Sob. soch.*, vol. 2, p. 26 (originally published in *Prilozhenie Nivy* 1 [Feb. 1905], pp. 333–50).

65 Ibid., p. 30.

66 Ibid., p. 34.

67 Ibid., p. 37.

68 "Utkonos," *Niva* (17 Dec. 1905), p. 966.

69 The account of the historical events of 1905 is based on Reginald D. Zelnik, "Revolutionary Russia, 1890–1914," in Gregory L. Freeze, ed., *Russia: A History* (Oxford, 1997), pp. 214–18; Hugh Seton-Watson, *The Decline of Imperial Russia: 1855–1914* (New York, 1952), pp. 219–25.

70 "45 let," in *ML*, p. 243.

71 Ibid., p. 244.

72 "Znamia svobody," *Vpered* (2 Mar. 1905).

73 "Pchelki," in *Sem'*, pp. 57–8.

74 "Poluson," *Birzh* 8987 (20 Aug. 1905), p. 2.

75 See Tatyana Aleksandrova, *Istaiat' obrechennaia v polete*, p. 241.

76 Teffi to A. V. Amfiteatrov, Amfiteatrov MSS, LL.

77 "Novaia zhizn'," in *ML*, p. 251 (originally published in *NRS* 13953 [9 July, 1950]). Essentially the same account is given in the multiple-authored introduction to *Novaia zhizn': Pervaia legal'naia S.-D. bol'shevistskaia gazeta, 27 oktiabria–3 dekabria 1905 goda*, vyp. 1 (Leningrad, 1925): L. Krasin, "Kak voznikla 'Novaia zhizn'," pp. vi–vii; M. Litvinov, "Stranichka vospominanii," pp. vii–ix; Is. Gukovsky, "Iz vospominanii I. E. Gukovskogo," p. x.

78 Gukovsky, "Iz vospominanii," p. x. Litvinov lists Galich, Teffi, and Platonov as department heads (p. ix). Teffi does not mention her prominent role in *ML*.

79 "Novaia zhizn'," in *ML*, p. 252.

80 "18 oktiabria," *Novaia zhizn'* 1 (27 Oct. 1905), p. 7.

81 Ibid., p. 8.

82 Ibid., p. 9.

83 "Pchelki" was republished at least three times between 1905 and 1907: in *V grozu* (St. Petersburg, 1905), *Pod krasnym znamenem* (Moscow, 1905), and *Pesni truda i nevoli* (St. Petersburg, 1907).

84 "Patrony i patron," *Novaia zhizn'* 5 (1 Nov. 1905), p. 16.

85 "Novaia zhizn'," in *ML*, p. 253.

86 Ibid., p. 245.

87 Ibid., p. 247.

88 Ibid., pp. 260–1.

89 Zelnik, "Revolutionary Russia," p. 218.

90 "Oni pridut," *Krasnyi smekh* 2 (1906), p. 2.

91 Among the periodicals I have seen, her works appeared with particular frequency in *Rus'* and *Rech'*.

92 "Evrei i russkaia literatura," *Zritel'* iv/2 (10 Feb. 1908).

93 Kornei Chukovsky, "Evrei i russkaia literatura," in Chukovsky, *Sobranie sochinenii*, vol. 7, pp. 315–22 (originally published in *Svobodnye mysli* [14 Jan. 1908]).

94 Leonid Galich, "Fedor Sologub," *NRS* 13009 (7 Dec. 1947), p. 2.

95 "45 let," in *ML*, p. 248.

96 A. M. Remizov to Teffi, 28 Mar. 1950, Teffi Papers, BAR.

97 "45 let," in *ML*, p. 248.

98 E. Anichkov, *Novaia russkaia poeziia* (Berlin, 1923; repr. The Hague, 1969), p. 48.

99 *Aleksandr Blok v vospominaniiakh sovremennikov v 2-kh tomakh*, vol. 2 (Moscow, 1980), pp. 331–2. Quoted in G. G. Bunatyan and M. G. Charnaya, *Peterburg serebrianogo veka: Doma, sobytiia, liudi* (St. Petersburg, 2002), p. 73.

100 N. A. Berdyaev, *Samopoznanie* (Leningrad, 1991), p. 155. Quoted in Bunatyan and Charnaya, *Peterburg serebrianogo veka*, p. 73.

101 Vyacheslav Ivanov, *Borozdy i mezhi* (Moscow, 1916), pp. 276, 280–1. Quoted in Konstantin Rudnitsky, *Russian and Soviet Theater: 1905–1932*, trans. Roxane Permar, ed. Lesley Milne (New York, 1988), p. 9.

102 Ibid., pp. 9–10.

103 Leonid Galich, "Dionisovo sbornoe deistvo i misticheskii teatr 'Fakely'," *TI* 8 (1906), p. 139.

104 Galich, "Dionisovo sbornoe deistvo," *TI* 9 (1906), p. 127.

105 N. Volkov, *Meierkhol'd*, vol. 1 (Moscow and Leningrad, 1929), pp. 218–19.

106 "Avtor i postanovka," in *NP*, pp. 85–9 (originally published in *RS* 64 [17 Mar. 1913], p. 4).

107 "Georgii Chulkov i Meierkhol'd," in *ML*, pp. 187, 188 (originally published in *Voz* 42 [1955]).

108 For more details, see Edythe C. Haber, "The Queen of Laughter and the Knight of Death: Nadezhda Teffi and Fedor Sologub," in Catherine Ciepiela and Lazar Fleishman, eds., *New Studies in Modern Russian Literature and Culture: Essays in Honor of Stanley J. Rabinowitz*, part 1, Stanford Slavic Studies 45 (Stanford, CA, 2014), pp. 173–87.

109 "Fedor Sologub," in *ML*, p. 190 (originally published in *NRS* 13407 [9 Jan. 1949], p. 2).

110 Ibid., p. 191. Sologub's poem "Shveia" appeared in *Voprosy zhizni* 9 (1905), p. 1, accompanied by a note from the editor: "Mr. Sologub has asked us to warn his readers that the theme of his poem 'The Seamstress' coincides with that of the poem 'Bees,' which was written independently by one of our contemporary poets" (Fyodor Sologub, *Stikhotvoreniia*, ed. M. I. Dikman [2nd edn., Leningrad, 1975], p. 613).

111 Teffi writes that the meetings took place on Saturdays, but O. L. Fetisenko points out that they were held on Sundays: "Teffi i Fedor Sologub (K tvorcheskoi istorii knigi 'Sem' ognei')," *Trudy Gosudarstvennogo muzeia istorii Sankt-Peterburga* 4 (1999), pp. 290, 298 n. 11.

112 Some biographical details are taken from M. I. Dikman's introduction to Fyodor Sologub, *Stikhotvoreniia*, pp. 5–20.

113 See Victor Terras, *A History of Russian Literature* (New Haven, CT, 1991), pp. 422–4.

114 Stanley Rabinowitz, *Sologub's Literary Children: Keys to a Symbolist's Prose* (Columbus, OH, 1980), p. 6.

115 "Fedor Sologub," in *ML*, p. 190.

116 Ibid., p. 192.

117 "Russkii den'," *PN* (7 Jan. 1940), p. 2.

118 Teffi to Olga Kuzminichna Teternikova, Arkhiv Sologuba, F. K., IRLI (f. 289, op. 8, ed. khr. 21).

119 "Fedor Sologub," in *ML*, p. 193; Teffi to Fyodor Sologub, 30 June (n.y.), Arkhiv Sologuba, F. K., IRLI (op. 3, ed. khr. 692). All further citations from Teffi's letters to Sologub are to this source, and will not receive separate annotation. Dates, when known will appear in the text.

120 "Fedor Sologub," in *ML*, p. 194.

121 "Vzamen politiki," *Ium* (1990), pp. 38–41 (originally published in *Birzh* 10497 [11 May 1908; morning edn.], p. 3; then in *Ium* I).

122 Teffi to A. A. Izmailov, Arkhiv Izmailova, A. A., IRLI (f. 115, op. 3, ed. khr. 331, n. 14).

123 "Fedor Sologub," in *ML*, p. 196.

124 Teffi to Fyodor Sologub, postmarked 10 Nov. 1908, Arkhiv Sologuba, F. K., IRLI (op. 3, ed. khr. 692).

125 Teffi to Fyodor Sologub, postmarked 23 May 1908, Arkhiv Sologuba, F. K., IRLI (op. 3, ed. khr. 692). For the other literary gatherings, see O. L. Fetisenko, "Teffi i Fedor Sologub," p. 290.

126 "'Al'manakh Shipovnika', Kniga 7-ia," *Rech'* (15 Dec. 1908), p. 3; "Fedor Sologub," in *ML*, p. 198.

127 "Fedor Sologub," in *ML*, p. 198.

128 *Rech'* 315 (22 Dec. 1908), p. 3. Republished as "Retsenziia N.A. Teffi na knigu stikhov Andreia Belogo", together with the ensuing articles, in "Polemika v gazete 'Rech','" ed. M. D. Klyagina, in *TT*, pp. 267–79. See also Klyagina's interesting article "Teffi i Andrei Belyi," in *TT*, pp. 260–6.

129 "Retsenziia N.A. Teffi," in "Polemika v gazete 'Rech','" p. 267.

130 "Zinaida Gippius," in *ML*, p. 224 (originally published in *NRS* 13834 [12 Mar. 1950]).

131 Anton Krainy, "Belaia strela," in "Polemika v gazete Rech'," p. 273.

132 Ibid., p. 275.

133 "Zinaida Gippius," in *ML*, p. 224.
134 Teffi, "Chaiushchie ot iurodivogo," in "Polemika v gazete Rech'," p. 276.
135 Ibid., p. 277.
136 Ibid., p. 278.
137 Andrei Bely, *Mezhdu dvukh revoliutsii* (Leningrad, 1934), p. 199.

3. ASCENT

1 "Arkadii Averchenko," in *ML*, p. 286 (originally published in *NRS* 13407 [9 Jan. 1949]).
2 "Smekh," *RS* (18 Nov. 1910), p. 2.
3 "O 'Monodrame' N. N. Evreinova," Neatrour, Averin, pp. 422–4 (originally published in *Rech'* 127 [11 May 1909], p. 3).
4 A. Shn., "Literaturno-khudozhestvennogo obshchestva teatr," in P. A. Markov, ed., *Teatral'naia entsiklopediia*, vol. 3 (Moscow, 1964), p. 547.
5 *Zhenskii vopros*, in *P'esy*, p. 84.
6 Ibid., pp. 90–1.
7 Yulia Zagulyayeva, "Peterburgskie pis'ma," *Moskovskie vedomosti* 86 (13 Apr. 1907), p. 3.
8 See Lyudmila Tikhvinskaya, *Povsednevnaia zhizn' teatral'noi bogemy serebrianogo veka. Kabare i teatry miniatiur v Rossii 1908–1917* (Moscow, 2005), p. 12 ff.
9 A. Rostislavov, "O postanovkakh kabare," *TI* 51 (1908), p. 914.
10 "Kulisy 'Doma intermedii'," *Birzh* (16 Apr. 1910). Quoted in Tikhvinskaya, *Povsednevnaia zhizn' teatral'noi bogemy*, p. 20.
11 Tikhvinskaya, *Povsednevnaia zhizn' teatral'noi bogemy*, pp. 44–5. The following account is taken largely from this source.
12 Ibid., p. 46. For more details, see Nikolai Yevreinov, *V shkole ostroumiia: Vospominaniia o teatre "Krivoe zerkalo"* (Moscow, 1998), pp. 56–7.
13 Quoted in Nikolai Yevreinov, *V shkole ostroumiia*, p. 58.
14 Tikhvinskaya, *Povsednevnaia zhizn' teatral'noi bogemy*, p. 72.
15 This form was to become typical of the Crooked Mirror, according to Yelena Bryzgalova, *"Liricheskaia satira" v dramaturgii serebrianogo veka* (Tver, 2004), p. 207.
16 The music was written by I. Chekrygin. Sketches and photographs of the production appear in *Zhizn' iskusstva* 50 (1908), p. 892; 52, pp. 940, 942.
17 The play is unpublished, but a typed manuscript, entitled "'Krug liubvi' ili 'Istoriia odnogo iabloka'" (The circle of love, or, the history of one apple; censor's mark dated 25 Nov. 1908), has been preserved in Sankt-Peterburgskaia Gosudarstvennaia Teatral'naia Biblioteka, w. 40011. Despite the different title, the manuscript text appears to be the same as the staged version.
18 Boris Brazol, "Khronika: Teatral'nyi klub," *TI* 50 (1908).
19 "Muzhskoi s"ezd" (censor's mark dated 21 Apr. 1909), Sankt-Peterburgskaia Gosudarstvennaia Teatral'naia Biblioteka. The Women's Congress opened 10 Dec. 1908. See Rochelle Goldberg Ruthchild, *Equality and Revolution: Women's Rights in the Russian Empire, 1905–1917* (Pittsburgh, PA, 2010), p. 102.
20 See Harold B. Segel, *Pinocchio's Progeny: Puppets, Marionettes, Automatons, and Robots in Modernist and Avant-Garde Drama* (Baltimore, MD, 1995), p. 36.
21 Tikhvinskaya, *Povsednevnaia zhizn' teatral'noi bogemy*, p. 173 ff.
22 Dukh-Banko, "Literatura 'Miniatiur'. (Drugaia storona medali)," *TI* 28 (8 July 1912), p. 554.

23   "Ominiatiurennye," in *Sob. soch.*, vol. 5, pp. 351–2 (originally published in *RS* 113 [17 May 1913], p. 3; then in *Dym*).
24   Ibid., pp. 352, 353.
25   "Intimomaniia," *RS* (17 Nov. 1911), p. 2.
26   At least four collections of Teffi's plays were published in Russia before her emigration: *Vosem' miniatiur* (St. Petersburg, 1913); *Novye miniatiury* (Petrograd, 1914); *Miniatiury i monologi* (Petrograd, 1915); *Novye miniatiury* (Petrograd, 1917).
27   Quoted in Yelena Bryzgalova, *Tvorchestvo satirikontsev v literaturnoi paradigme Serebrianogo veka: Monografiia* (Tver, 2006), p. 233.
28   "Quelque lignes de Nadejda Teffi sur elle-même," *France et monde, septième fascicule de l'encyclopédie des humanités contemporaines* (1929), p. 11.
29   Waleria Grabowska, "U groba N. A. Teffi," *RN* (9 Oct. 1952).
30   See Dimitry Aleksandrovich Levitsky, *Zhizn' i tvorcheskii put' Arkadiia Averchenko* (Moscow, 1999), pp. 29–30.
31   "Arkadii Averchenko," in *ML*, p. 287.
32   Levitsky, *Zhizn' i tvorcheskii put' Arkadiia Averchenko*, p. 31.
33   L. Yevstigneyeva, *Zhurnal "Satirikon" i poety-satirikontsy* (Moscow, 1968), p. 6.
34   "Arkadii Averchenko," in *ML*, p. 287.
35   Ibid., p. 288.
36   L. Yevstigneyeva, *Zhurnal "Satirikon"*, p. 106 ff.
37   P. Ryss, "O smekhe," *Den'* 51 (22 Feb. 1914). Quoted in L. Yevstigneyeva, *Zhurnal "Satirikon"*, p. 105.
38   "Arkadii Averchenko," in *ML*, p. 290.
39   Kornei Chukovsky, "Sovremennye Iuvenaly," in Kornei Chukovsky, *Sobranie sochinenii v 15 tomakh* (Moscow, 2001), vol. 7, p. 442 (originally published in *Rech'* [16 Aug. 1909]).
40   See Bryzgalova, *Tvorchestvo satirikontsev*; L. A. Spiridonova (Yevstigneyeva), *Russkaia satiricheskaia literatura nachala XX veka* (Moscow, 1977), p. 142.
41   See Dimitry Dmitrievich Nikolayev, "Tvorchestvo N. A. Teffi i A. T. Averchenko. Dve tendentsii razvitiia russkoi iumoristiki," candidate's dissertation, Moscow State University, 1993, p. 54.
42   Mikhail Kuzmin, "O prekrasnoi iasnosti," *Apollon* 4 (Jan. 1910), p. 10.
43   See A. G. Mendeleyev, *Zhizn' gazety "Russkoe slovo": Izdatel'. Sotrudniki* (Moscow, 2001), pp. 4, 10, 32. Most of the information on *Russkoe slovo* is from this source.
44   Quoted ibid., p. 17.
45   *Vos*, p. 108.
46   "Vystavka noveishikh izobretenii (Pis'mo iz Peterburga)," *RS* 102 (6 May 1909), p. 2.
47   Teffi to F. I. Blagov, Gosudarstvennaia biblioteka Lenina (now Rossiiskaia Gosudarstvennaia Biblioteka), Moscow (f. 259, k. 22, ed. khr. 66, l. 27). Quoted in Boris Averin and Elizabeth Neatrour, "Taina smeiushchikhsia slov," in Teffi, *Smeshnoe v pechal'nom*, ed. Boris Averin (Moscow, 1992), p. 9.
48   See Marietta Chudakova, "Zametki o iazyke sovremennoi prozy," *Novyi mir* 1 (1972), p. 215.
49   *Vos*, p. 108.
50   M. Tsetlin, "N. A. Teffi," *NZh* 6 (1943), p. 384.
51   M. A[ldanov], "Teffi, 'Passiflora,'" *SZ* 18 (1923), p. 485.
52   "Igra i rabota: Otvet na anketu N. A. Teffi," *Zhurnal zhurnalov* 1 (1915), p. 14.
53   A. Izmailov, "Novye knigi," *RS* 88 (17 Apr. 1910), p. 2.
54   N. Gumilyov, "Pis'ma o russkoi poezii," *Apollon* (Apr. 1910), pp. 35–6; Valery Bryusov,

"Belletristika," *RM* 8 (1910), p. 248. The latter republished as "Zhenshchiny-poety," in Valery Bryusov, *Dalekie i blizkie* (Moscow, 1912), p. 151.

55 For the influence of Sologub and Balmont, see O. L. Fetisenko, "Kommentarii," in Neatrour, Averin, p. 436; O. L. Fetisenko, "Teffi i Fedor Sologub (K tvorcheskoi istorii knigi 'Sem' ognei')," *Trudy Gosudarstvennogo muzeia istorii Sankt-Peterburga* 4 (1999), pp. 288–99. On the influence of Lokhvitskaya, see "Poeticheskie otgoloski," Mirra Lokhvitskaya [website]. Available at http://mirrelia.ru/echo/?1=teffi.

56 D. S. Mirsky, *A History of Russian Literature*, ed. Francis J. Whitfield (New York, 1964), p. 472.

57 On symbolism, see N. A. Bogomolov, "Postsimvolizm (obshchie zamechaniia)," in *Russkaia literatura rubezha vekov (1890-ye–nachalo 1920-kh godov)*, vol. 2 (Moscow, 2001), p. 381.

58 N. Gumilyov, "Pis'ma o russkoi poezii," p. 35.

59 Catriona Kelly, *A History of Russian Women's Writing, 1820–1992* (Oxford, 1994), p. 204.

60 For the structure, see D. D. Nikolayev, "Kontseptsiia 'knigi' v tvorchestve N. A. Teffi," in *TT*, pp. 22–3.

61 Konstantin Balmont, *Budem kak solntse* (Moscow, 1903).

62 *Polden' Dzokhary*, in *Sem'*, p. 109.

63 Ibid., p. 110.

64 "Zhertva," ibid., p. 81.

65 "Gulda," ibid., p. 66.

66 "Mar'ionetki," ibid., p. 14.

67 "Moia liubov' – kak strannyi son…" ibid., p. 20. Teffi's memoir, "Fedor Sologub," indicates that the poem was completed by mid-1905 (in *ML*, p. 190).

68 "Lunnoe," ibid., p. 45.

69 M. Kuzmin, "Zametki o russkoi belletristiki," *Apollon* 9 (Jul.–Aug. 1910), p. 34.

70 N. Lerner, "N. Teffi. Dym bez ognia," *Prilozhenie Nivy* 2 (Feb. 1914), p. 459.

71 Anastasya Chebotarevskaya, "Teffi. I stalo tak…" *Novaia zhizn'* 7 (July 1912), p. 255.

72 "N. A. Teffi," *Argus* 2 (1913), p. 88.

73 Arkady Bukhov, "Teffi," *Zhurnal zhurnalov* 14 (1915), p. 17.

74 *Ium* (1990), p. 19.

75 See D. D. Nikolayev, "Kommentarii," ibid., p. 391.

76 "Chelovekoobraznye," in *Sob. soch.*, vol. 1, p. 95 (published in *Ium* II). Chukovsky observed that Nietzsche's influence was running rampant among the *Satyricon* humorists: "Perhaps they only write 'Arkady Averchenko,' but one should read 'Friedrich Nietzsche?' Indeed, just think, such proud hatred of the average, worn-down, gray man, of the crowd, of the Philistine […] in this splendid magazine" ("Ustritsy i okean," *Rech'* [20 Mar. 1911]).

77 "Duraki," in *Sob. soch.*, vol. 1, p. 307 (published in *Ium* II).

78 Ibid., p. 306.

79 "Ostraia bolezn'," in *Sob. soch.*, vol. 5, p. 127 (published in *K*).

80 Ibid., p. 131.

81 "Rozovyi student," in *NP*, p. 103.

82 Ibid., p. 105.

83 Ibid., p. 107.

84 Ibid., p. 108.

85 "Svetlyi prazdnik," in *Ium* (1990), p. 209 (published in *Ium* II).

86 "Mar'onetki," in *Sem'*, p. 14.

87 Henri Bergson, "Laughter," in Wylie Sypher, ed., *Comedy* (Garden City, NY, 1956), p. 97.

88   "Providets," in *Sob. soch.*, vol. 4, p. 343 (published in *Dym*).
89   "Vzamen politiki," in *Ium* (1990), p. 38 (published in *Ium* I).
90   "Pis'mo," in *Sob. soch.*, vol. 5, p. 224 (published in *Dym*).
91   "Schastlivaia liubov'," in *Sob. soch.*, vol. 5, pp. 59–63 (published in *K*).
92   "Broshechka," in *Sob. soch.*, vol. 1, p. 117 (published in *Ium* II).
93   "O dnevnikakh," in *Sob. soch.*, vol. 5, pp. 258–60 (published in *Dym*).
94   "Kurortnye tipy," in *Sob. soch.*, vol. 5, p. 192 (published in *K*).
95   "Demonicheskaia zhenshchina," in *Sob. soch.*, vol. 5, p. 218 (published in *Dym*).
96   Ibid., p. 220.
97   "Zhizn' i tvorchestvo," in *Sob. soch.*, vol. 5, p. 279 (published in *Dym*).
98   Ibid., pp. 279–80.
99   "Pis'ma," in *Sob. soch.*, vol. 5, p. 52 (published in *K*).
100   "Solov'inye grezy," in *NP*, p. 74.
101   Ibid., p. 75.
102   "Igrushki i deti," in *NP*, p. 117.
103   "Sokrovishche zemli," in *Sob. soch.*, vol. 1, p. 300 (published in *I stalo*).
104   "Dobroe delo startsa Vendimiana," in *Sob. soch.*, vol. 5, p. 73 (published in *K*).
105   "Za stenoi," in *Ium* (1990), pp. 89–90 (published in *Ium* I).
106   Ibid., p. 90.

4. FEASTS AND PLAGUES

1   Lyudmila Tikhvinskaya, *Povsednevnaia zhizn' teatral'noi bogemy serebrianogo veka. Kabare i teatry miniatiur v Rossii 1908–1917* (Moscow, 2005), p. 18.
2   A.G., "Dva mira," *Satirikon* 26 (12 Dec. 1909), p. 5.
3   Richard Pipes, *The Russian Revolution* (New York, 1991), pp. 191–4.
4   "Geroistvo sil'nykh," *RS* (15 Apr. 1912), p. 4. See also "Teper'," *RS* (5 Dec. 1910), p. 2.
5   Quoted in Sergei Glezerov, *"Petersburgie tainy" nachala XX veka* (Moscow, 2005), p. 284. Some details are taken from Glezerov.
6   "Ubiistvo peterburgskoe i ubiistvo moskovskoe," *RS* 34 (10 Feb. 1913), p. 4.
7   "Geroistvo sil'nykh," p. 4.
8   "Stydno," *RS* 252 (1 Nov. 1913), p. 3. See also "O dele ne Beilisa," *RS* 241 (18 Oct. 1913), p. 2; "Svidetel'nitsa, kotoroi nekhvataet," *RS* 242 (20 Oct. 1913), p. 4; "Chto mozhet sluchit'sia zavtra," *RS* 248 (27 Oct. 1913), p. 3.
9   Tikhvinskaya, *Povsednevnaia zhizn' teatral'noi bogemy*, pp. 16, 19.
10   S. Auslender, "Bal 'Satirikon'," *Russkaia khudozhestvennaia letopis'* 5 (1911), p. 75; Ave[rchenko], "Bal 'Satirikona'," *Satirikon* 10 (6 Mar. 1911), p. 7; "Khronika," *Zhizn' iskusstva* 51 (20 Dec. 1909), p. 926.
11   "Igor' Severianin," in *ML*, pp. 311–16. First published by Ye. M. Trubilova, in "Materialy iz arkhiva N. A. Teffi (SShA)," in *TT*, pp. 343–5.
12   See Yury Tsivian, "The Tango in Russia," *Experiment* 2 (1996), pp. 307–35.
13   "Predprazdnichnoe 1914 g.," *RS* 79 (5 Apr. 1914), p. 3. The feuilleton hardly exaggerated: in *RS* one finds advertisements for such items as "Tango Liqueur" and "Tango Perfume." See, for example, 26 Jan. 1914.
14   "Malen'kaia khronika," *TI* 16 (20 Apr. 1914), p. 371.
15   Tikhvinskaya, *Povsednevnaia zhizn' teatral'noi bogemy*, p. 16.
16   "Sinie vtorniki," in *ML*, pp. 299–302 (originally published in *NZh* 180 [1990], pp. 116–20).

17 Ibid., p. 300.

18 "A. I. Kuprin," in *ML*, pp. 177–86 (originally published in *Voz* 42 [1955]).

19 *Desiatiletie restorana "Vena". Literaturno-khudozhestvennyi sbornik* (St. Petersburg, 1913), p. 93.

20 My main sources for the Stray Dog (*Brodiachaia sobaka*) are: A. E. Parnis and R. D. Timenchik, "Programmy 'Brodiachei sobaki'," *Pamiatniki kul'tury: Novye otkrytiia: Pis'mennost', iskusstvo, arkheologiia. Ezhegodnik 1983* (Leningrad, 1985), pp. 160–257; Tikhvinskaya, *Povsednevnaia zhizn' teatral'noi bogemy*; S. S. Shults ml. and V. A. Sklyarsky, *Brodiachaia sobaka: Vek nyneshnii – Vek minuvshii* (St. Petersburg, 2003).

21 Parnis and Timenchik, "Programmy 'Brodiachei sobaki'," p. 161.

22 Quoted by Parnis and Timenchik, "Programmy 'Brodiachei sobaki'," p. 166.

23 N. N. Yevreinov, "Tvorcheskii put' S. Sudeikina kak zhivopistsa v teatre. 1926," RGALI (f. 982, op. 1, ed. khr. 33, ll. 34–6). Quoted in Parnis and Timenchik, "Programmy 'Brodiachei sobaki'," p. 173.

24 D. Burlyuk, Alexander Kruchonykh, V. Mayakovsky, and Viktor Khlebnikov, "Poshchechina obshchestvonnumu vkusu" (1912), in N. L. Brodskii and N. P. Sidorov, eds., *Literaturnye manifesty* (Moscow, 2000), p. 142. For "Noah's Ark," see Tikhvinskaya, *Povsednevnaia zhizn' teatral'noi bogemy*, p. 115.

25 See R. D. Timenchik's introduction to E. M. Prilezhayeva-Barskaya, "Brodiachaia sobaka," ed. R. D. Timenchik, *Minuvshee* 23 (1998), pp. 381–2.

26 "Kuzmin," in *ML*, pp. 307, 309. Teffi's view contrasts starkly with Anna Akhmatova's in her "Poem without a Hero" (1965) and elsewhere, where Kuzmin emerges as a satanic figure, whom she blames for the suicide of the young poet Vsevolod Knyazev. See John E. Malmstad and Nikolay Bogomolov, *Mikhail Kuzmin: A Life in Art* (Cambridge, MA, 1999), p. 221.

27 B. K. Pronin, "V 'Brodiachei sobake'" (1939), Arkhiv E. B. Pronina. Quoted in Shults ml. and Sklyarsky, *Brodiachaia sobaka*, p. 105.

28 Quoted in Prilezhayeva-Barskaya, "Brodiachaia sobaka," p. 392.

29 Ash [A. E. Shaikevich], "Peterburgskie katakomby," *Teatr* (Berlin) 14 (1922), p. 4. Quoted in Prilezhayeva-Barskaya, "Brodiachaia sobaka," p. 411 n. 34. Some "sly songs" (none of which contains the line remembered by Shaikevich) were published in *Argus* 1 (Jan. 1913), pp. 51–3.

30 On 26 Jan. 1914, Teffi was included in an "Evening of Lyric Poetry" (*Vecher liriki*); on 23 Feb. in an "Evening of Lenten Magic"; on 26 Apr. she sang some of her ditties at a banquet honoring the Moscow Art Theater. See Parnis and Timenchik, "Programmy 'Brodiachei sobaki'," pp. 224, 235.

31 "Tainopis'," *RS* 93 (23 Apr. 1913), p. 3.

32 "Kuzmin," in *ML*, p. 308; "Nichegoki," *RS* 296 (24 Dec. 1913), p. 4.

33 "V eti dni," *PN* 6738 (8 Sept. 1939), p. 3.

34 "Noch'," *PN* 6999 (26 May 1940), p. 2; "Na severe," *PN* 6887 (4 Feb. 1940), p. 2.

35 *Russkie vedomosti* (19–21 July 1914). Quoted in A. V. Lavrov and M. G. Petrov, eds., *Letopis' literaturnykh sobytii v Rossii kontsa XIX–nachala XX v. (1891–okriabr' 1917)*, vyp. 3: *(1911–oktiabr' 1917)* (Moscow, 2005), p. 335.

36 One event of a military bent in which Teffi participated was an "Evening of Poets" (27 Jan. 1915), at which Gumilyov (who had volunteered for the military) appeared. See Parnis and Timenchik, "Programmy 'Brodiachei sobaki'," p. 239.

37 Ibid., p. 166.

38 V. V. Mayakovsky, "Vam!" in V. V. Mayakovsky, *Izbrannye proizvedeniia*, vol. 1 (Moscow and Leningrad, 1963), p. 90.

39 Parnis and Timenchik, "Programmy 'Brodiachei sobaki',"' p. 166.

40 Shults ml. and Sklyarsky, *Brodiachaia sobaka*, p. 127.

41 Based on a contemporary newspaper article, reprinted in V. Shumikhin, "Iz kommentariia k 'Zapisnym knizhkam' A. A. Bloka," *Novoe literaturnoe obozrenie* 2 (1993), p. 235. I thank Olga Kushlina for calling my attention to this publication.

42 L. E. Gabrilovich to I. A. Bunin, 8 Apr. 1949, LRA (1066/2604).

43 "Doktor Niurenberg," *Russkaia volia* 52 (8 Apr. 1917), p. 3. I thank Richard Davies for providing me with the obituary and other information about the doctor.

44 Admiral Pogoulaieff to Chef État-Major Armée, Ekaterinodar, 30 Apr. [1919], Petr Vrangel' Collection, Correspondence of Gen. D. Shcherbachev, Hoover Institution Archives (Stanford, CA) (Box 76, Folder 3).

45 Telegram from Lt. Col. Shubert to Shcherbachev, 25 June 1919; Shcherbachev to Viazmitinov, 3 Feb. 1920, Petr Vrangel' Collection, Hoover Institution Archives (Stanford, CA).

46 The photograph is preserved in the museum of IRLI (f. 3, inv. 29366).

47 "Avtor," in *Sob. soch.*, vol. 5, pp. 154–6 (originally published, without the dedication, in *RS* 273 [27 Nov., 1912], then in *K*).

48 "Kuzmin," in *ML*, p. 310.

49 M. Kuzmin, *Dnevnik, 1908–1915*, ed. N. A. Bogomolov and S. V. Shumikhin (St. Petersburg, 2005). In the index, the editors identify him as Nikolai Aleksandrovich Shcherbakov, an actor at Meyerhold's studio (p. 858). Kuzmin, however, never uses the first name and does not indicate that Shcherbakov is an actor. For the reviews, see Dmitry Shcherbakov, "Petrogradskie pis'ma," *RZh* 48 (27 Nov. 1916), pp. 13–14; "Pis'mo iz Petrograda," *RZh* 8 (19 Feb. 1917), p. 14.

50 "Il'ia Repin," in *ML*, p. 336.

51 "Belaia odezhda," *Niva* 44 (1914), p. 835; Vladimir Berenshtam, "Voina i poety," *Russkie vedomosti* (1 Jan. 1915). Quoted in Lavrov and Petrov, eds., *Letopis' literaturnykh sobytii v Rossii*, vyp. 3, p. 358.

52 See N. Rogozhin, ed., *Literaturno-khudozhestvennye al'manakhi i sborniki: Bibliograficheskii ukazatel'*, vol. 2: *1912–1917 gody* (Moscow, 1958), p. 144.

53 "Dva estestva," in L. Andreyev, M. Gorky, and F. Sologub, eds., *Shchit: Literaturnyi sbornik* (3rd edn., Moscow, 1916), p. 223.

54 Ibid., p. 224.

55 For the photograph, see *TI* 18 (3 May 1915), p. 307.

56 "Okolo voiny. Voennye miniatiury. Na punkte G.," *RS* 61 (15 Mar. 1915), p. 5.

57 *Zarevo bitvy* (Petrograd, 1915).

58 "Predislovie," in *Sob. soch.*, vol. 2, p. 374.

59 "Shamash" was originally published in *Rech'* 86 (29 Mar. 1909), p. 5.

60 "Zaiats," in *Sob. soch.*, vol. 2, p. 97 (originally published in *RS* 67 [21 Mar. 1912], p. 3).

61 "Par," in *Sob. soch.*, vol. 2, p. 145.

62 "Chortik v banochke," in *Sob. soch.*, vol. 2, p. 164 (originally published in *RS* 67 [22 Mar. 1915], p. 6).

63 Ibid., p. 165.

64 Ibid., p. 166.

65 Ibid., p. 167.

66 "Nezhivoi zver'," in *Sob. soch.*, vol. 2, p. 64 (originally published in *RS* 297 [25 Dec. 1912], p. 7).

67 Ibid., p. 67.

68 Ibid., pp. 67, 66.

69 Ibid., p. 67.

70 Ibid., p. 69.

71 Ibid., p. 70.

72 "Yavdokha," in *Sob. soch.*, vol. 2, p. 150 (originally published in *Birzh* 14793 [26 Oct. 1914; morning edn.], p. 2.

73 Ibid., p. 151.

74 "Dezi," in *Sob. soch.*, vol. 2, p. 188 (originally published in *RS* 31 [1 Feb. 1915], p. 4). See also "Geroi," originally published as "Lazaretnye vpechatleniia: Geroi," *RS* 9 (13 [26] Jan. 1915), p. 3, and "Vanya Shchegolek," originally in *Otechestvo* 13 (1915). Neither is included in *Sob. soch.*

75 Ibid., pp. 189–90.

76 Ibid., p. 190.

77 "Serdtse," in *Sob. soch.*, vol. 2, p. 176.

78 Ibid., p. 178.

79 Ibid., p. 181.

80 "Tikhaia zavod'," in *Sob. soch.*, vol. 2, p. 159 (originally published in *RS* 151 [2 July 1915], pp. 2–3).

81 Ibid., p. 158.

82 Ibid., p. 163.

5. A FAREWELL TO RUSSIA, PAST AND FUTURE

1   Edvard Radzinsky, *The Rasputin File*, trans. Judson Rosengrant (New York, 2000), pp. 299–301, 306.

2   "Rasputin," in *ML*, p. 267. Originally as "Koldun: Iz vospominanii o Rasputine," *Seg* 179, 181, 182 (10, 13, 14 Aug. 1924).

3   Ibid., p. 268.

4   Ibid., p. 267.

5   Ibid., p. 272.

6   Ibid., p. 274.

7   Ibid., p. 273.

8   Ibid., p. 276.

9   Ibid., p. 280.

10 Edvard Radzinsky, *The Rasputin File*, pp. 40–1. For more on the Khlysty, see James H. Billington, *The Icon and the Axe* (New York, 1968), pp. 174–7.

11 "Rasputin," in *ML*, p. 280.

12 Ibid., p. 281.

13 Ibid., p. 282.

14 Ibid., p. 285.

15 Edvard Radzinsky, *The Rasputin File*, pp. 309–10.

16 "Rasputin," in *ML*, p. 286.

17 Michael T. Florinsky, *The End of the Russian Empire* (New York, 1969), p. 139.

18 "V kafe," in *Vchera*, pp. 102–6 (originally published in *RS* 215 [20 Sept. 1915], p. 2).

19 "Byt glubokogo tyla," *RS* 26 (2 Feb. 1916), p. 2.

20 A. Rivoire, *Korol' Dagober. Komediia v 3-kh aktakh v stikhakh*, trans. Elio i Teffi (Moscow, 1915). See N. Efros, "Moskovskie pis'ma," *TI* 8 (1915), pp. 132–4.

21 Teffi to Sumbatov-Yuzhin, postmarked 13 Dec. 1915, RGALI (f. 875, op. 1, ed. khr. 2053, l. 1).

22 The information about the contract is from Teffi to Sumbatov-Yuzhin, n.d., ibid. The play was reviewed on 6 Mar. 1916, by Yak. Lvov: "Malyi teatr," *RZh* 10, pp. 10–11.

23 See ibid., p. 10; Averchenko, *NS* 49 (1 Dec. 1916), p. 6; Shcherbakov, "Petrogradskie pis'ma," *RZh* 48 (27 Nov. 1916), pp. 13–14.

24 *Sharmanka Satany. P'esa v 4-kh deistviiakh* (Petrograd, 1916), p. 26.

25 Ibid., p. 14.

26 Ibid., p. 27.

27 "Ohkraniaemyi idiot," *RS* (6 Dec. 1916), p. 2; "Nash Klondaik," *RS* 131 (8 June 1916), p. 1; "Na kavkazskikh vodakh," in *Vchera*, pp. 126–36 (originally published in *RS* 170 [23 July 1916], p. 3); "Eshche o kavkazskikh vodakh," *RS* 190 (18 Aug. 1916), p. 3; "Gospodin Purvits," *RS* 221 (29 Sept. 1916), p. 2; "Essentuki. U vody. V. N. Il'narskaia, Lolo, Teffi," *RZh* 30 (24 July 1916), p. 12; "Kislovodsk. Rampiitsy i ikh druz'ia," *RZh* 32 (7 Aug. 1916), p. 15. She was also photographed at a charity event, "An Evening of Arias, Romances, and Songs," *RZh* 31 (31 July 1916), p. 12.

28 "V khvostakh," *RS* 233 (9 Oct. 1916), p. 2.

29 "V teatre," in *Vchera*, pp. 98–101 (originally published in *RS* 239 [16 (29) Oct. 1916], p. 3). The name here and in other Teffi wartime satires indicates the protagonist is Jewish. The implication that Jews were prominent in war speculation indicates a shift from the unswerving Judeophilia of her earlier works. For another fictional depiction of Jewish war speculators from a Jewish perspective, see Irène Némirovsky, *The Wine of Solitude: A Novel*, trans. Sandra Smith (New York, 2011), p. 82 ff.

30 "Ohkraniaemyi idiot," *RS* (6 Dec. 1916), p. 2.

31 "Zliushchie," in *Vchera*, pp. 110–14 (originally published in *RS* [6 Dec. 1916]).

32 "Po povodu bukvy 'iat'," *RS* (22 Jan. 1917), p. 2.

33 Dmitry Shcherbakov, "Pis'mo iz Petrograda," *RZh* 8 (19 Feb. 1917), p. 14.

34 "V Gosudarstvennoi Dume," *RS* 42 (21 Feb. 1917), p. 4.

35 "Srednii," *NS* 13 (2 Apr. 1917), p. 6.

36 Ibid., p. 7.

37 "Napoleon," *NS* 24 (July 1917), p. 3.

38 "Revoliutsionnaia dama," *NS* 25 (July 1917), pp. 2–3.

39 "Oratory," *RS* 131 (11 June 1917), p. 1.

40 "Dezertiry!" *RS* 134 (15 June 1917), p. 2. Many of the feuilletons of this period are collected in *V strane*.

41 "Nemnozhko o Lenine," *RS* 141 (23 June 1917), p. 1.

42 *Vinegret*: literally a mixed vegetable salad.

43 "Dozhdalis'," *RS* 155 (9 July 1917), p. 1; "My verim," *RS* 161 (16 July 1917), p. 2.

44 "Razgovor s bestolkovym," *RS* 242 (22 Oct. 1917), p. 3.

45 My account is based largely on Richard Pipes, *The Russian Revolution* (New York, 1991), pp. 489–96.

46 A May 1917 article in *Rech'* states that the society organized a "permanent commission for the protection of monuments of antiquity and art" (A. R-v, "Khudozhestvennye vesti. Revoliutsiia i khudozhestvennaia zhizn'," *Rech'* 102 [3 May 1917], p. 6). For Sologub's role in the society, see Jason Merrill, "Fedor Sologub," in Judith E. Kalb, J. Alexander Ogden, and I. G. Vishnevetsky, eds., *Dictionary of Literary Biography*, vol. 295: *Russian Writers of the Silver Age, 1890–1925* (Farmington Hills, MI, 2004), p. 367.

47 "Fedor Sologub," in *ML*, p. 200.

48 A. G. Mendeleyev, *Zhizn' gazety "Russkoe slovo": Izdatel'. Sotrudniki* (Moscow, 2001), p. 34.

49 "Petrogradskoe zhitie," *RS* 252 (17 Nov. 1917), p. 1.

50 Mendeleyev, *Zhizn' gazety "Russkoe slovo"*, pp. 35, 36.

51 "Budushchii den'," *NS* 1 (Jan. 1918), p. 6.

52 "Retrospektivnyi vzgliad i udivlenie," *NS* 6 (Mar. 1918), pp. 10–11, 13.

53 "Vse eshche zhivem," in *V strane*, p. 158. The editor was unable to find the original publication, but context indicates that it was the winter of 1917–18.

54 Richard Pipes, *The Russian Revolution*, p. 558.

55 "Novyi psikhoz," in *V strane*, p. 156 (originally published in *Nashe slovo* 58 [30 June 1918]).

56 W. Bruce Lincoln, *Sunlight at Midnight: St. Petersburg and the Rise of Modern Russia* (New York, 2000), p. 243.

57 "Letuchaia mysh'," *RZh* 20 (19 May 1918), p. 11.

58 "Khronika," *TI* 1 (7 Jan. 1918), p. 5. In *Vos* (p. 13), Teffi places the incident at a later date.

59 "Iz mertvogo goroda," in *V strane*, p. 149 (originally published in *Novoe slovo* 34 [8 (21) Mar. 1918]).

60 Ibid., p. 151.

61 "Peterburg," in *V strane*, p. 171 (originally published in *Kievskaia mysl'* [17 Oct. 1918]).

62 "Letuchaia mysh'," *RZh* 20 (19 May 1918), p. 11.

63 "Helena Buczyńska," in Stanisław Dabrowski, ed., *Słownik biograficzny teatru polskiego: 1765–1965* (Warsaw, 1973), p. 73.

64 See Nina Serpinskaya, *Flirt s zhizn'iu*, ed. Sergei Shumikhin (Moscow, 2003), p. 313 n. 22. For eurhythmy, or eurhythmia, see Rudolf Steiner, lecture of 26 Aug. 1923, quoted in "Rudolf Steiner and Eurythmy," Rudolf Steiner Web [website]. Available at http://www.rudolfsteinerweb.com/Rudolf_Steiner_and_Eurythmy.php. Steiner conceived of the form in 1911.

65 Serpinskaya, *Flirt s zhizn'iu*, pp. 218, 220–1.

66 Alexander Avdeyevich Otsup to Teffi, 27 Mar. 1948, Teffi Papers, BAR.

67 The cover of *RZh* 31–3 (5 [18] Aug. 1918), features a photograph of A. I. Zakom, who played the title role. In *Vos*, Teffi gives the title of the work as *Catherine the Great* (p. 11).

68 "Lolo," in *ML*, p. 317. An undated clipping (Teffi Papers, BAR) reports the attempt to revise the play for a Soviet audience: "O postanovke 'Ekateriny II' (Beseda s S. E. Radlovym)."

69 *Vos*, p. 18.

70 Ibid., p. 12.

71 Ibid., p. 15.

72 Ibid., p. 7.

73 Ibid., p. 28.

74 Ibid., p. 47.

75 Ibid., p. 40.

76 Ibid., p. 92.

77 Ibid., p. 93.

78 Ibid., p. 95.

79 Yury Kaplan, "Boevoi vosemnatsatyi god," *Kievskie vedomosti* 210 (23 Sept. 2003).

80 *Vos*, pp. 100–1. See Teffi's contemporary account: "Ispanskaia bolezn'," in *V strane*, pp. 194–6 (originally published in *Kievskaia mysl'* 227 [29 Nov. 1918]). The name of the hotel is given in Natalya Goncharenko, "Neznakomaia Teffi i ee znakomye personazhi: Vospominaniia o 'krasnom terrore'," *Moskovskie novosti* 24 (16–23 June 1996), p. 25.

81 *Vos*, p. 112.

82 "Raz"ezd," in *V strane*, p. 216 (originally published in *Nash put'* 49 [24 Jan. 1919]).

83   *Vos*, p. 122.

84   Ibid., pp. 126–7.

85   Ibid., p. 125.

86   Ibid., p. 141.

87   Bunina, diary, 27 Feb. 1919, LRA (1067/362). See also *Ustami*, vol. 1, p. 179.

88   Yury Olesha, "Vstrechi s Alekseem Tolstym," in Yury Olesha, *Povesti i rasskazy* (Moscow, 1965), p. 382. It is possible that Olesha's memory was blurred, since Amari was the pseudonym of Mikhail Tsetlin, also in Odessa at the time.

89   *Vos*, p. 130.

90   Ibid., p. 131.

91   Ibid., p. 132.

92   Ibid., p. 133.

93   Ibid., p. 135.

94   Ibid., p. 138.

95   Ibid., p. 142.

96   "Na skale Gergesinskoi," in *V strane*, p. 226 (originally published in *Griadushchii den'* 1 [Mar. 1919], pp. 32–4).

97   Ibid., pp. 224, 225.

98   "Poslednii zavtrak," in *V strane*, p. 230 (originally published in *Nashe slovo* [20 Mar. 1919]).

99   *Vos*, p. 150. The date is based on Bunina's diary (*Ustami*, vol. 1, pp. 184–6).

100   *Vos*, p. 165. For Teffi and Gorny, see K. I. Finkelshteyn, "O Sergee Gornom." Available at http://kfinkelshteyn.narod.ru/Literat/O_Sergee_Gornom.htm.

101   *Vos*, p. 178.

102   Ibid., pp. 205, 206.

103   Ibid., p. 208.

104   Ibid., pp. 208–9.

105   Ibid., p. 250.

106   Ibid., p. 252.

107   Ibid., p. 259.

108   Ibid., p. 261.

109   Ibid., pp. 262–3.

110   Ibid., p. 263. In his notes to the translation of *Memories*, Robert Chandler writes that the hanged anarchist went by the name of Ksenya Mikhailovna G. – the initial the pseudonym of her husband, whose surname was Goldberg. See Teffi, *Memories: From Moscow to the Black Sea*, trans. Robert and Elizabeth Chandler (New York and London, 2016), p. 267 n. 137.

111   *Vos*, p. 264.

6. MIGRATION

1   "Mirnaia zhizn'," *PN* 6427 (30 Oct. 1938), p. 3.

2   *Stambul*, p. 7. In the nineteenth and early twentieth centuries, Westerners used "Constantinople" to refer to the city as a whole, "Stamboul" for the central, historic part.

3   Ibid., pp. 8–9.

4   Ibid., pp. 28, 29.

5   Ibid., 18.

6   See Marc Raeff, *Russia Abroad: A Cultural History of the Russian Emigration, 1919–1939* (Oxford, 1990), pp. 18–19.

7   Weber, p. 11; Raeff, *Russia Abroad*, pp. 29, 33.

8   Raeff, *Russia Abroad*, pp. 25–7.

9   "Prokliat'e," "Korabl'," *Griadushchaia Rossiia* 2 (Feb. 1920), p. 71.

10 "Que faire?" in *Subtly Worded and Other Stories*, trans. Anne Marie Jackson et al. (London, 2014), p. 139.

11 Don-Aminado, *Poezd na tret'em puti* (Moscow, 2000), pp. 246–7.

12 Ibid., p. 247.

13 "Aleksei Tolstoi," in *ML*, p. 207.

14 Ibid.

15 Bunina, diary, 24 Apr. 1921, LRA (1067/372), p. 63.

16 TBun I, no. 9, p. 359.

17 Mnukhin I, vol. 1, p. 10.

18 "Fedosya," *Russkii sbornik* (Paris, 1920) (originally published in *Ogonek* 39 [27 Sept. 1915], p. 1).

19 See L. G. Golubeva, "Soiuz russkikh pisatelei i zhurnalistov v Parizhe," in *LERZ*, vol. 3, p. 47; A. F. Golovenchenko, "Komitet pomoshchi russkim pisateliam i uchenym vo Frantsii," ibid., vol. 2, p. 35.

20 Mnukhin I, vol. 1, p. 9. In 1921 and early 1922 Teffi also participated in benefits for the Russian Turgenev Public Library (1 Jan. 1921 [Mnukhin I, vol. 1, p. 20]) and for needy Russian students (28 Jan. 1922 [Mnukhin I, vol. 1. p. 61]).

21 Mnukhin I, vol. 1, pp. 35–6, 56.

22 Teffi to Lyatsky, n.d., E. A. Liatskii Papers, LA MCL (LA52/69/2439). Lyatsky responded on 20 Dec. 1920 (Arkhiv Liatskogo, E. A., IRLI [f. 163, op. 2, n. 611, l. 39].)

23 *Chernyi iris*; *Tak zhili* (Stockholm, 1921).

24 *Tikhaia zavod'* (Paris, 1921); *Sokrovishche zemli* (Berlin, 1921); *Vostok i drugie rasskazy* (Shanghai, 1921). *Stambul i solntse* (Berlin, 1921).

25 "Nostal'giia," in *Sob. soch.*, vol. 3, p. 37 (originally published in *PN* 17 [16 May 1920], p. 2; then in *Rys'*).

26 "Vspominaem," in *Sob. soch.*, vol. 3, p. 41 (originally published in *PN* 86 [5 Aug. 1920], p. 2).

27 "Syr'e," in *Sob. soch.*, vol. 3, p. 56 (originally published in *PN* 65 [11 July 1920], p. 2; then in *Rys'*).

28 "Ke fer," in *Sob. soch.*, vol. 3, p. 126 (originally in *PN* 1 [27 Apr., 1920], p. 2, then in *Rys'*).

29 Ibid., p. 127–8.

30 "Dve vstrechi," in *Sob. soch.*, vol. 3, p. 23 (originally published in *Svobodnye mysli* 1 [20 Sept. 1920], p. 2; then in *Rys'*).

31 Ibid., pp. 25–6.

32 Ibid., p. 26.

33 Ibid., p. 27.

34 "Faifokloki," in *Sob. soch.*, vol. 3, p. 93 (originally published in *PN* 74 [22 July 1920], p. 2; then in *Rys'*).

35 Ibid, p. 94.

36 "Nostal'giia," in *Sob. soch.*, vol. 3, p. 38.

37 "Toska," in *Sob. soch.*, vol. 3, pp. 99, 100 (originally published as "Nostal'giia," *Svobodnye mysli* 4 [11 Oct. 1920], p. 2; then as "Toska" in *Rys'*).

38 G. Aleksinsky, "Ee dobroi i svetloi pamiati (Vospominaniia o N. A. Teffi)," *Grani* 16 (1952), p. 135.

39 D. D. Nikolayev writes that Teffi published three poems in *Ogni* in 1921: "Angel," *Ogni* 1 (8 Aug.); "Stambul"; "Ia ne zdeshniaia, ia izdaleka…" *Ogni* 3 (22 Aug.). See "N. A. Teffi i

russkie periodicheskie izdaniia v Chekhoslovakii," in *TT*, pp. 120–1. A handful of Teffi's poems and feuilletons also appeared in 1921 and 1922 in Latvian newspapers. See Yury Abyzov, *Russkoe pechatnoe slovo v Latvii, 1917–1944 gg.: Bio-bibliograficheskii spravochnik*, part 4, Stanford Slavic Studies 3 (Stanford, CA, 1991), pp. 194–5.

40 Bunina, diary, 28 July 10 Aug. 1921, LRA (1067/372). For Teffi's "truly terrible condition," see TBun I, no. 11, p. 360. Teffi had already undergone treatment at Contrexéville the previous summer (see Teffi to Bunina, ibid., nos. 4, 5, pp. 356–7 [postmarked 27 Aug. 1920]). Since Teffi almost never dated her letters, the chronology and dating in the text is approximate, based on context.

41 TBun I, no. 11, p. 360; no. 13, p. 362.

42 Bunina, diary, 22 Jan./4 Feb. 1922, in *Ustami*, vol. 2, p. 65.

43 See Robert C. Williams, *Culture in Exile: Russian Émigrés in Germany, 1881–1941* (Ithaca, NY, 1972), p. 115.

44 In Teffi's passport, issued by the Russian General Consulate in Paris on 7 Feb. 1922, a stamp *"pour pays Rheinans et retour"* is dated 8 Feb. 1922. Stamps for several later dates suggest that she traveled to and fro a few times (Teffi Papers, BAR).

45 Don-Aminado to Bunin, 29 Jul., 1922, LRA (1066/2263).

46 Ilnarskaya to Bunina, n.d., LRA (1067/2932).

47 Ilnarskaya to Bunina, n.d., LRA (1067/2935).

48 See Jamie H. Cockfield, *With Snow on Their Boots: The Tragic Odyssey of the Russian Expeditionary Force in France during World War I* (New York, 1998). I am grateful to Richard Davies for calling my attention to this source.

49 Teffi to A. L. Volynsky, RGALI (f. 95, op. 1, ed. khr. 851).

50 TBun I, no. 18, p. 365.

51 *Vos*, p. 213.

52 On 2 Oct. 1922, Lyatsky wrote to a Lieutenant Lindgren that Teffi was in Berlin (Arkhiv Liatskogo, E. A., IRLI [f. 163, op. 2, n. 64]). Information about Berlin from Williams, *Culture in Exile*, p. 114.

53 Iu. A. Azarov, *Dialog poverkh bar'erov. Russkoe literaturnoe zarubezh'e: tsentry, periodika, vzaimosviazi (1918–1940)* (Moscow, 2005), p. 121.

54 Williams, *Culture in Exile*, pp. 133, 137; Azarov, *Dialog poverkh bar'erov*, p. 126.

55 E. A. Liatskii Papers, LA MCL (LA52/69/2438).

56 "Podsolnechnik," in *P*, p. 45 (originally published in *Energiia* 3 [1914]).

57 "Strastotsvet," in *P*, p. 7.

58 "Krai moi," in *P*, p. 9 (originally published in *Zhar-ptitsa* 9 [1922], p. 8).

59 "Ia ne zdeshniaia, ia izdaleka," in *P*, p. 10; "Pela-pela belaia ptitsa," in *P*, p. 12.

60 For a thorough linguistic analysis, see Catherine V. Chvany, "Analysis of a Poem by Teffi," in C. E. Gribble, ed., *Studies Presented to Professor Roman Jakobson by His Students* (Cambridge, MA, 1968), pp. 61–9.

61 "Serebrianyi korabl'," in *P*, p. 8 (published as "Korabl'" in *Griadushchaia Rossiia* 2 [1920]).

62 "Ia serdtsem krotkaia byla," in *P*, p. 11 (originally published in *Lit. – khudozh. al'manakhi izd. "Shipovnik,"* vol. 17 [St. Petersburg, 1912], p. 212).

63 "Angelika," in *P*, p. 39 (originally published as "Khodila Fedos'ia," *Ogonek* 39 [27 Sept. 1915], p. 1; then as "Fedos'ia" in *Russkii sbornik* [Paris, 1920], p. 176).

64 Ibid., p. 40.

65 "Blagosloven'e Bozh'ei desnitsy," in *P*, pp. 15–16 (originally published in *SZ* 10 [1922], p. 125).

66 Author's interview with Natalya Borisovna Sollogub (née Zaitseva), Paris, 14 Mar. 2000.

67 Teffi to Roshchina-Insarova, Ekaterina Nikolaevna Roshchina-Insarova Papers, BAR.

68 Zaitseva to Bunina, 21 Feb. 1923, in DV, p. 345; Bunina, diary, 7 Mar. 1923, in *Ustami*, vol. 2, p. 90.

69 *Novaia russkaia kniga* 3–4 (1923), p. 45; 5–6 (1923), p. 53.

70 The letter has not survived. Its contents are surmised from Teffi's response.

71 Teffi to P. N. Milyukov, RGALI fond Redaktsii zhurnala "Zveno" (f. 2475, op. 1, d. 58).

72 Teffi to M. M. Vinaver, ibid. (f. 2475, op. 1, d. 44).

73 "Dollar," *Zveno* 31 (3 Sept. 1923), p. 2. The second feuilleton: "Kommunisty v El'stere," *Zveno* 32 (10 Sept. 1923), p. 3.

74 A transit visa in Teffi's passport was issued in Cologne on 16 Aug. 1923 (Teffi Papers, BAR).

75 "Malen'kii fel'eton: Moe quartier," *Zveno* 65 (28 Apr. 1924), p. 2.

76 "Vozvrashchenie," *Russkii golos* (Harbin) (4 Dec. 1923). I am grateful to Richard Davies for calling my attention to this feuilleton.

77 "Parizh," *Rul'* 1007 (27 Mar. 1924), p. 2.

78 Her works also turned up occasionally in *PN* and *Rul'* (Rudder), as well as the Latvian *Russkii kur'er* (Russian courier). This is not an exhaustive list.

79 "Kryl'ia," *IR* 1 (1924), pp. 12–13.

80 See Mnukhin I, vol. 1, pp. 112, 117, 125, 126, 133, 135.

81 This *Ogni* should not be confused with earlier Prague newspaper of the same name, edited by Aleksinsky, to which Teffi also contributed. See D. D. Nikolayev, "N. A. Teffi i russkie periodicheskie izdaniia v Chekhoslovakii," in *TT*, pp. 120–1. For the Czechoslovak state and Russian emigration, see Azarov, *Dialog poverkh bar'erov*, pp. 144–63; Raeff, *Russia Abroad*, pp. 61–4.

82 Excerpts from Teffi's letters have been published in *Evgenii Liatskii: Materialy k biografii*, ed. S. I. Mikhalchenko (Bryansk, 2000), pp. 141–58.

83 There is material about Lyatsky's wife, Vera Aleksandrovna Pypina-Lyatskaya (1864–1930), dating from 1912 through the 1920s, in his archive at IRLI (f. 163, op. 4).

84 E. A. Liatskii Papers, LA MCL (LA52/69/2445).

85 Ibid. (LA52/69/2418).

86 Ibid. (LA 52/69/ 2441, 2445; LA 52/69/2454).

87 Ibid. (LA 52/69/2473).

88 Ibid. (LA 52/69/2465).

89 Ibid. (LA 52/69/2455).

90 Zaitseva to Bunina, 5 June 1924, in DV, pp. 354–5.

91 E. A. Liatskii Papers, LA MCL (LA52/69/2451).

92 "Volch'ia dolina," *Zveno* 69 (28 May 1924), p. 2; "Lastochka," *Rul'* 1198 (9 Nov. 1924), pp. 2–3; 1199 (11 Nov. 1924), pp. 2–3; 1201 (13 Nov. 1924), pp. 2–3; 1202 (14 Nov. 1924), p. 13; "Virtuoz slavy (Iz vstrech Shatobriana)," *Seg* (25 Nov. 1924).

93 Teffi to Bunina, TBun I, no. 23, p. 372.

94 E. A. Liatskii Papers, LA MCL (LA52/69/2463).

95 Teffi informed Zaitseva on 19 Sept. that Lyatsky would be in Paris "in two weeks." Teffi to Zaitseva, Zaitsev Collection, BAR. The letter is undated, but Teffi refers to an article by Merezhkovsky published that day in *PN* 1350, pp. 2–3.

96 Teffi to Lyatsky, 11 Oct. (n.y.), E. A. Liatskii Papers, LA MCL (LA52/69/2467). The contents suggest the year was 1924.

97 In Jan. 1926, Zaitsev recalled the Lyatskys' recent "wonderful trip" to Paris (Zaitsev, *Sobranie sochinenii*, vol. 11 [Moscow, 2001], p. 26). Lyatsky's wife is identified as a writer

and translator at http://ruslo.cz/index.php/dummy-category/163-cpisok-zakhoronenij-na-pravoslavnom-uchastke-kladbishcha-l.

98 I judge the date by a review that came out in late Oct.: B.K., "Vechernii den'," *Rul'* 1182 (22 Oct. 1924), p. 5.

99 Teffi wrote Lyatsky that "Solovki" was one of her best stories (E. A. Liatskii Papers, LA MCL [LA52/69/2446]).

100 "Solovki," in *VD*, p. 19 (originally published in *Zhar-ptitsa* [1921], pp. 7–15).

101 Ibid., p. 20.

102 Ibid., pp. 21–2.

103 Ibid., p. 23.

104 F. I. Tyutchev, "Posledniaia liubov'," in F. I. Tyutchev, *Lirika*, ed. K. V. Pigarev, vol. 1 (Moscow, 1965), p. 156.

105 "Martselina," in *VD*, pp. 128.

106 Ibid., p. 129.

107 "Lapushka," in *VD*, p. 133 (originally published in *Zveno* [5 Nov. 1923], pp. 2–3).

108 Ibid., p. 137.

109 Ibid., p. 138.

110 Ibid., p. 140.

111 For a similar observation, see M[ark] Sl[onim], "Teffi, N. A., *Vechernii den'*," *Volia Rossii* 18–19 (Nov. 1924), p. 262.

112 "Predel," in *VD*, p. 31 (originally published in *Okno* 3 [1924]).

113 Ibid., p. 48.

114 Ibid., p. 54.

115 Ibid., p. 63. In her last feuilleton for *NS*, Teffi made an almost identical remark: "Look at the butterfly's head under a microscope. You will never encounter a more sinister mug" ("Mysli o zhivotnykh," *NS* 18 [Aug. 1918], p. 6).

116 Ibid., p. 53.

117 Ibid., p. 72.

118 Ibid., p. 62.

7. RUSSIA ABROAD

1 O. A. Rostova, *"Napishite mne v al'bom…"*: *Besedy s N. B. Sollogub v Biussi-an-Ot* (Moscow, 2004), p. 102.

2 "Tsvetik belyi," in *Sob. soch.*, vol. 3, pp. 209–12 (originally published in *Zveno* 60 [3 Mar. 1924], p. 2; then in *G*).

3 Teffi to Zaitsev, n.d., Boris Konstantinovich Zaitsev Papers, BAR. The date given is approximate, based on context. Unless otherwise noted all further letters to the Zaitsevs are located in the Zaitsev Papers, BAR. Precise dates, when established, will be given in the text.

4 E. A. Liatskii Papers, LA MCL (LA52/69/2428).

5 Bunina, diary, 16/29 Jan. 1925, in *Ustami*, vol. 2, p. 110.

6 Rostova, *"Napishite mne v al'bom…"*, p. 141.

7 TBun I, no. 26, p. 374.

8 Bunina, diary, 22 Jan. 1925, in *Ustami*, vol. 2, p. 109.

9 DV, p. 359.

10 E. A. Liatskii Papers, LA MCL (52/69/2449, 52/69/2418).

11   Author's interview with Natalya Borisovna Sollogub (née Zaitseva), Paris, 14 Mar. 2000.

12   "Pervyi dzhentl'men. Pamiati P. A. Tikstona," *Voz* 298 (27 Oct. 1935), p. 2.

13   "Pavel Andreyevich Tikston," *Voz* 3791 (20 Oct. 1935), p. 4.

14   TBun I, no. 28, p. 375.

15   "Kak ia zhivu i rabotaiu," *IR* 9 (27 Feb. 1926), p. 7.

16   Teffi's miniatures were performed on 19 Oct., 11 Nov., and 14 Nov. (Mnukhin I, vol. 1, pp. 206, 207, 212, 213).

17   See Zaitsev to Bunin, 19 Oct. 1925, in "Pis'ma B. K. Zaitseva k I. A. i V. N. Buninym," ed. Militsa Greene, *NZh* 139 (1980), p. 165.

18   Four of Teffi's stories were published there: "Markita," *Perezvony* 3 (22 Nov. 1925), pp. 61–4; "Sirano de Berzherak," *Perezvony* 16 (Mar. 1926), pp. 463–7; "Ignat," *Perezvony* 27 (Dec. 1926), pp. 852–6; "Neproshchenoe derevo," *Perezvony* 20 (8 June 1926), p. 632.

19   Anna Kashina-Yevreinova, "N. A. Teffi: Zapozdalyi venok na mogilu," *RM* 817 (5 Nov. 1955), p. 4.

20   Ibid., p. 5.

21   See Remizova-Dovgello correspondence, A. Remizov and S. Dovgello-Remizova Archive, Amherst Center for Russian Culture, Amherst College, Amherst, MA (box 21, folder 3, scrapbook 2, 1926, nos. 29, 39). Other items in the scrapbook (nos. 45, 46, 47, 49) indicate that the Remizovs were in Belgium 27–29 March (Teffi presumably arriving on the 28th) and that he was paid 200 francs. Neatrour, in her Ph.D. dissertation, "Miniatures of Russian Life at Home and in Emigration: The Life and Works of N. A. Teffi" (Indiana University, 1972), points to a notice in *PN*: "N. A. Teffi i A. M. Remizov v Briussele," *PN* 1843 (9 Apr. 1926), p. 3.

22   Mnukhin I, vol. 1, pp. 278–9. Mnukhin's list of events for 1925 takes up 60 large pages (vol. 1, pp. 165–225); 1926, 73 pages (pp. 226–99); 1927, 100 pages (pp. 300–400). The numbers continued to increase until the end of the decade.

23   "Chestvovanie B. K. Zaitseva," *PN* 2092 (14 Dec. 1926), p. 2.

24   "Vecher N. A. Teffi," *Voz* 628 (20 Feb. 1927), p. 4.

25   Mnukhin I, vol. 1, pp. 211, 232, 233, 238, 240, 249.

26   Vysheslavtsev to Teffi, 7 May 1930, Teffi Papers, BAR.

27   B. P. Vysheslavtsev, *Khristianstvo i sotsial'nyi vopros* (Paris, 1929).

28   See Teffi to K. I. Zaitsev, n.d.; P. B. Struve to Teffi, 5 Nov. 1926; Teffi to P. B. Struve, received 9 Nov. [1926], Petr Struve Collection, Hoover Institution Archives (Stanford, CA) (Box 14, Folder 21).

29   A. V. Lomonosov, "Vozrozhdenie," in *LERZ*, vol. 2, pp. 64–5. See also G. P. Struve, "Stranitsa iz istorii zarubezhnoi pechati: Nachalo gazety 'Vozrozhdenie'," *Mosty* 3 (1959), pp. 374–9.

30   See Marc Raeff, *Russia Abroad: A Cultural History of the Russian Emigration, 1919–1939* (Oxford, 1990), pp. 83–4; Johnston, p. 48; Iu. A. Azarov, *Dialog poverkh bar'erov. Russkoe literaturnoe zarubezh'e: tsentry, periodika, vzaimosviazi (1918–1940)* (Moscow, 2005), pp. 50–4.

31   Zaitseva to Bunina, 13 July 1927, in *DV*, p. 367.

32   Zaitseva to Bunina, 24 May 1927, ibid., p. 365. Teffi wrote two feuilletons on Aix-les-Bains: "Eks," *Voz* 733 (5 June 1927), p. 4; "Eshche Eks," *Voz* 740 (12 June 1927), p. 3.

33   Neatrour, "Miniatures of Russian Life," p. 10.

34   A.D., "Teffi v Varshave," *Seg* 255 (11 Nov. 1927), p. 8.

35   "K Vostoku," *Voz* 887 (6 Nov. 1927), p. 3.

36   "Pis'mo iz za-granitsy," *Voz* 901 (20 Nov. 1927), p. 3. Teffi presented a more sympathetic picture of native Polish culture and especially singled out Julian Tuwim (1894–1953): "An

excellent lyric poet, a witty satirist, a poet of Heine-like moods." The admiration must have been mutual, because Tuwim translated into Polish a selection of Teffi's stories: *Kobieta demoniczna*, trans. Juljan Tuwim (Warsaw, n.d.). The copy in the Harvard library has 4 Apr. 1928 stamped inside. For Teffi on the impoverishment of the Russian language, see "Narodnyi iazyk," *Voz* 873 (23 Oct. 1927), p. 3; 880 (30 Oct. 1927), p. 3.

37   Zaitseva to Bunina, 14 Dec. 1927, in DV, p. 200.

38   See, for example, "Zlaia kniga: Teffi. Gorodok," *Rossiia* 18 (24 Dec. 1927), p. 4.

39   B. K. Zaitsev, "Teffi N. Gorodok: Novye rasskazy," *SZ* 34 (1928), pp. 498–9.

40   Ivelich [pseudonym of Berberova], "'Gorodok' Teffi," *Voz* 1017 (18 Mar. 1928), p. 3.

41   "Gorodok," in *Sob. soch.*, vol. 3, p. 146 (originally published as "Khronika," *Zveno* 45 [10 Dec. 1923], p. 3; then in G).

42   Ibid., p. 147. Elsewhere Teffi satirized this splintering in more detail: "Whoever wants to live amicably with everyone should not offer a hand to: anarchists, monarchists, legitimists, nationalists, interventionists, socialists, defeatists, degenerates, regenerates [*vyrozhdentsam*, *vozrozhdentsam* – the latter meaning also contributors to *Voz*], bolshevizers, appeasers, temporizers" (*IR* 30 [1 Nov. 1925], p. 1). Even the sympathetic W. Chapin Huntington observed: "Never was a small nation so torn with political schisms as Russia-out-of-Russia." See W. Chapin Huntington, *The Homesick Million: Russia-out-of-Russia* (Boston, 1933), p. 169.

43   "Maiskii zhuk," in *Sob. soch.*, vol. 3, p. 198 (originally published in *Rul'* 1101 [19 July 1924], pp. 5–6; then in G).

44   "Razgovor," in *Sob. soch.*, vol. 3, p. 173 (originally published in *Zveno* [19 Nov. 1923], p. 3; then in G).

45   "Gedda Gabler," in *Sob. soch.*, vol. 3, pp. 177, 178 (published in G).

46   "L'ame slave," *Ogni* 13 (13 Mar. 1924), p. 2. Quoted in D. D. Nikolayev, "N. A. Teffi i russkie periodicheskie izdaniia v Chekhoslovakii," in *TT*, p. 130. This is actually the introduction to the second part of the story.

47   "L'âme slave," in *Sob. soch.*, vol. 3, p. 158 (originally published in *Zveno* 60 [24 Mar. 1924], pp. 2–3; then in G).

48   "Markita," in *Sob. soch.*, vol. 3, p. 149 (originally published in *Perezvony* 3 [Nov. 1925], pp. 61–4; then in G).

49   Ibid., p. 151.

50   Ibid., pp. 152–3.

51   Ibid., p. 155.

52   Ibid., pp. 155, 156.

53   "Kryl'ia," in *Sob. soch.*, vol. 3, p. 225 (originally published in *IR* 1 [1924], pp. 12–13; then in G).

54   Ibid., p. 226.

55   "Chudovishchnaia mamka i neozhidannyi kon'. Shutka N. A. Teffi," *IR* 5 (28 Jan. 1928), pp. 1–2, 4, 6–7.

56   Alexander Yablonovsky, "Bal pisatelei. Pis'mo v redaktsiiu," *Voz* 953 (11 Jan. 1928), p. 2; "Trinadtsatogo noch'iu," ibid.

57   Mnukhin I, vol. 1, p. 412 ff.; Papers of the Union of Russian Writers, Amherst Center for Russian Culture, Amherst College, Amherst, MA (box 2, folder 56).

58   "O detiakh," *Voz* 1039 (6 Apr. 1928), p. 2.

59   "Vyzov gruppy russkikh pisatelei," *Voz* 1447 (19 May 1929), p. 2 (Teffi was among many signers); "V piatnitsu 13-go," *Voz* 1655 (13 Dec. 1929), p. 3.

60   "Vybory krasavits," *Seg* 151 (2 June 1929), p. 4. See also Mnukhin I, vol. 1, p. 525; "Miss Rossiia," *IR* 6 (2 Feb. 1929), pp. 9, 10.

61 See TBun I, no. 33, p. 379.

62 Teffi to Lyatsky, 22 Jan. 1929, E. A. Liatskii Papers, LA MCL (LA52/69/2497).

63 Bunina, diary, 9, 17 Jan. 1929, in *Ustami*, vol. 2, p. 159.

64 Teffi to Don-Aminado, n.d., Aminad Petrovich Shpolianskii Papers, BAR.

65 See Temira Pachmuss, "Zelenaia lampa," in *LERZ*, vol. 2, p. 168; Yury Terapiano, *Vstrechi* (New York, 1953), p. 43 ff.

66 "Zelenaia lampa. Beseda II," *Novyi korabl'* 1 (1927), pp. 39, 42. I thank Oleg Korostelev for leading me to this publication.

67 "Oskolki," in *Sob. soch.*, vol. 3, p. 200 (originally published in *Zveno* 148 [30 Nov. 1925], p. 2; then in G).

68 "Ne zabud'te," *Voz* 992 (19 Feb. 1928), p. 2.

69 "Ot avtora," in *Vos*, p. 5.

70 M. Tsetlin, "N. A. Teffi. Vospominaniia," *SZ* 48 (1932), p. 482.

71 See "Zhiul'etta," *Seg* 165 (16 June 1929), p. 4; "Zhanin," *Voz* 628 (20 Feb. 1927), p. 3; "Serdtse Val'kirii," *Voz* 971 (29 Jan. 1928), p. 2.

72 "Chuzhie liudi," *Voz* 1727 (23 Feb. 1930), p. 2.

73 See Leonid Livak, *How It Was Done in Paris: Russian Émigré Literature and French Modernism* (Madison, WI, 2003), pp. 21–2. For a full transcript of the meetings, see Leonid Livak and Gervaise Tasis, eds., *Le Studio franco-russe, 1929–1931*, Toronto Slavic Library 1 (Toronto, 2005).

74 Leonid Livak, "Introduction," in Leonid Livak and Tasis, eds., *Le Studio franco-russe*, p. 13.

75 See Wsevolod de Vogt, "Introduction," in Robert Sébastien and Wsevolod de Vogt, *Rencontres: Soirées franco-russes des 29 octobre 1929–26 novembre 1929–18 décembre 1929–28 janvier 1930* (Paris, 1930), p. 10. Republished in Livak and Tasis, eds., *Le Studio franco-russe*, pp. 46–7.

76 At the end of the fourth meeting, Fokht asked her to speak on Proust, since she "likes this writer very much," but she "protested energetically." She delivered Vysheslavtsev instead, who at the following meeting delivered the talk "Proust et la tragédie objective" (*Cahiers de la quinzaine* xx/5 [5 Mar. 1929], pp. 23–31).

77 "Au couvent de Solovki," "Marquita," *France et monde, septième fascicule de l'encyclopédie des humanités contemporaines* (1929), pp. 11–20, 20–4. The stories are prefaced by a brief autobiographical note: "Quelques lignes de Nadejda Teffi sur elle-même," p. 11. Preserved in Teffi Papers, BAR.

78 *France et monde*, p. 1.

79 See Leonid Livak, "Introduction," in Livak and Tasis, eds., *Le Studio franco-russe*, pp. 40–1.

80 "Po povodu chudesnoi knigi. I. A. Bunin – 'Izbrannye stikhi'," *IR* 27 (29 June 1929), p. 8.

81 "Ikh teatr," *Voz* 1853 (29 June 1930), p. 2.

82 See Johnston, pp. 101–4; O. G. Goncharenko, *Beloemigranty mezhdu zvezdoi i svastikoi: Sud'by belogvardeitsev* (Moscow, 2005), pp. 120–2. My account borrows from these sources.

83 Bunina, diary, 29 Jan., 2 Feb. 1930, in *Ustami*, vol. 2, pp. 175, 176.

84 Weber writes that "France began to suffer" only in 1932 (Weber, p. 33).

85 Mnukhin I, vol. 2, p. 47.

86 "Dozhdlivyi sezon," *Voz* 1860 (6 July 1930), p. 2.

87 Amfiteatrov's letter has not survived. I am judging its contents from Teffi's response (Amfiteatrov MSS, LL). All of Teffi's letters to Amfiteatrov are located at LL, his letters in the Teffi Papers, BAR. Known dates will be noted in the text.

88 Bunina, diary, 7 Mar. 1931, in *Ustami*, vol. 2, p. 193.

89 Zaitseva to Bunina, 23 Dec. 1930, in DV, pp. 345, 388.

90   Zaitseva to Bunina, 25 Dec. 1930, in DV, p. 389.

91   TBun I, no. 42, p. 384.

92   A receipt for 1,000 francs from the Casa Editrice Bietti, dated 24 Feb. 1931, is preserved in the Teffi Papers, BAR.

93   *Un romanzo di avventure*, trans. Ilaria Amfiteatrov (Milan, 1932).

94   Teffi to M. S. Milrud, in Yury Abyzov, Boris Ravdin, and Lazar Fleishman, *Russkaia pechat' v Rige: Iz istorii gazety Segodnya 1930-kh godov*, vol. 2, Stanford Slavic Studies 14 (Stanford, CA, 1997), pp. 288, 287.

95   A death notice of *Voz* employee Sofya Andreyanova appeared in the newspaper: *Voz* 2380 (8 Dec. 1931), p. 1.

96   *Satirikon* was published from 4 Apr. to 15 Oct. 1931. See L. Spiridonova, *Bessmertie smekha: Komicheskoe v literature russkogo zarubezh'ia* (Moscow, 1999), pp. 51–75.

97   "O edinstve liubvi. (Iz besedy v 'Zelenoi Lampe')," Teffi Papers, BAR.

98   Irina Odoyevtseva, "Na beregakh Seny," *Mosty* 15 (1970), p. 112.

99   Mikh[ail] Os[orgin], "Teffi. – Kniga Iiun'," *SZ* 46 (1931), pp. 498–9.

100 "Kniga-Iiun'," in *Sob. soch.*, vol. 4, p. 19 (originally in *Voz* 1680 [7 Jan. 1930], p. 4; then in *KI*).

101 Ibid., p. 21.

102 "Ty ne ego v nem vidish' sovershenstva" (emphasis mine). From the poem "Ty klonish' lik, o nem upominaia" (1858), ibid., p. 15.

103 "Zhena," in *Sob. soch.*, vol. 4, p. 65 (originally published in *Voz* 1664 [22 Dec. 1929], p. 2; then in *KI*).

104 Ibid., p. 66.

105 "Tikhii sputnik," in *Sob. soch.*, vol. 4, p. 88 (originally published in *Voz* 859 (9 Oct. 1927), p. 1; then in *KI*).

106 Ibid., p. 91.

107 "Lunnyi svet," in *Sob. soch.*, vol. 4, p. 42 (originally published in *Voz* 949 [7 Jan. 1928], p. 4; then in *KI*)).

108 Ibid., p. 43.

109 Ibid., p. 44.

110 See Victor Erlich, *Russian Formalism: History, Doctrine* (3rd edn., New Haven, CT, 1965), p. 149.

111 P. Dneprov, "Avantiurnyi roman," *Voz* (24 Mar. 1932), p. 2.

112 *Avantiurnyi roman*, in *Sob. soch.*, vol. 6, p. 69 (originally published in *Voz* from 17 Apr. 1930 to 4 Jan. 1931; then in *AR*).

113 The Russian *avantiura* is defined as an "unprincipled, risky business of dubious honesty" (S. N. Ozhegov, *Slovar' russkogo iazyka* [10th edn., Moscow, 1975], p. 20).

114 Boris Zaitsev, "N. A. Teffi, 'Avantiurnyi roman,'" *SZ* 44 (1932), pp. 452–3.

115 *Sob. soch.*, vol. 6, p. 96.

116 Ibid., p. 43.

117 The quotation "flowed on evenly and as usual" is ibid., p. 42.

118 Ibid., p. 102.

119 Ibid., pp. 96, 112.

120 Ibid., pp. 75, 76. For a similar view of maternal love and its potentially ghastly consequences, see "Mat'," in *Sob. soch.*, vol. 4, pp. 52–9 (published in *KI*).

121 Ibid., p. 85.

122 Their names, as O. L. Fetisenko has observed, hint at this: Lyubasha is a diminutive for love (*liubov'*), whereas Natasha's real name, Marusya, is a diminutive of Maria (Mary),

the perfect embodiment of motherly love ("'Avantiurnyi roman' Teffi kak roman-mif," in *TT*, pp. 69–82).

123 *Sob. soch.*, vol. 6, p. 71.
124 Ibid., p. 40.
125 Ibid., p. 73.
126 Ibid., p. 102.
127 Ibid., p. 106.
128 Ibid., p. 113.
129 Ibid., p. 116.
130 Ibid., p. 117.
131 Ibid., p. 105.
132 Ibid., p. 118.

8. A SLIPPERY SLOPE

1 Mnukhin does not mention Teffi a single time in 1931. Teffi wrote Amfiteatrov that they were planning to leave on 28 Feb. On La Colline, see "Na kholmakh sv. Antoniia," *Voz* 2182 (24 May 1931), p. 2.

2 Between 12 July and 13 Sept. 1931, Teffi wrote a series of feuilletons from Uriage for *Voz* under the general heading "Liudi malen'kogo otelia."

3 Theakston to Zaitseva, 19 July 1931, Boris Konstantinovich Zaitsev Papers, BAR.

4 Teffi to Bunina, TBun I, no. 45, p. 386; Zaitseva to Bunina, 27 Nov. 1931, in DV, p. 395.

5 See Johnston, pp. 104–9.

6 Weber writes that at the end of 1931 "'a wave of xenophobia' was sweeping over France" (Weber, p. 89). See also Johnston, pp. 105, 107.

7 See "Vecher v Marli," *Voz* 2602 (17 July 1932), p. 2.

8 N.P.V., "Iubilei 'Sovremennykh Zapisok': Torzhestvennyi banket v zalakh Sen-Did'e," *PN* 4272 (2 Dec. 1932), p. 2. On the same page Teffi is listed as a member of the Society of Friends of SZ. See "Obshchestvo druzei 'Sovremennykh Zapisok.'"

9 R.R., "Beseda s N. A. Teffi," *Voz* 2784 (15 Jan. 1933), p. 4; "Na vechere N. A. Teffi," *Voz* 2793 (24 Jan. 1933), p. 4.

10 Bor. Zaitsev, "Bunin uvenchan," *Voz* 3083 (10 Nov. 1933), p. 1. Boldface in the original.

11 TBun I, no. 50, pp. 390–1. The telegram, dated 10 Nov. 1933, reads: "*À la gloire de la literature russe. Salut*" (RGALI [f. 44, op. 2, ed. khr. 137, l. 28]).

12 N. Gorodetskaya, "I. A. Bunin v 'Vozrozhdenii,'" *Voz* 3090 (17 Nov. 1933), p. 1.

13 Ch., "Chestvovanie I. A. Bunina: Sobranie v teatre Shan z-elize," *Voz* (28 Nov. 1933), p. 2.

14 "Torzhestvo," *Voz* 3092 (19 Nov. 1933), p. 2. For "friendly 'defense,'" see TBun I, no. 50, p. 391.

15 See Amfiteatrov to Teffi, 14–16 Mar. 1934, Nadezhda Aleksandrovna Teffi Papers, BAR; Aldanov to Amfiteatrov, 4 Mar. 1934, in "'Parizhskii filosof iz russkikh evreev': Pis'ma M. Aldanova k A. Amfiteatrovu," ed. E. Garetto and A. Dobkin, *Minuvshee* 2 (1997), p. 576. For Bunin's setting aside 10 percent, see DV, p. 412.

16 TBun I, no. 55, p. 396; "Dnevnik Ia. B. Polonskogo: Ivan Bunin vo Frantsii," ed. Yefim Etkind, *Vremia i my* 55 (1980), p. 273.

17 TBun I, no. 54, p. 394.

18 See "Pamiati N. A. Lokhvitskogo," *Voz* 3080 (7 Nov. 1933), p. 2; "Skonchalsia gen. N. A. Lokhvitskii," *PN* 4621 (7 Nov. 1933), p. 4.

19   "Pokhorony gen. N. A. Lokhvitskogo," *Voz* 3082 (9 Nov. 1933), p. 3.

20   TBun I, no. 53, p. 393.

21   Teffi to Lyatsky, received 7 Oct. 1934, E. A. Liatskii Papers, LA MCL (LA52/69/2502).

22   "Estestvennaia istoriia," *Seg* 201 (24 July 1934), p. 3.

23   "Iumor posle Chekhova," *Seg* 31 (31 Dec. 1931), p. 2.

24   Amfiteatrov to Teffi, 15 Sept. 1934, Teffi Papers, BAR.

25   "Gorodok 'Segodnia,'" *Seg* 284 (14 Oct. 1934), p. 17.

26   See Paul F. Jankowski, *Stavisky: A Confidence Man in the Republic of Virtue* (Ithaca, NY, 2002), p. 12. The scandal inspired a 1974 film, *Stavisky...*, directed by Alain Resnais.

27   Weber, pp. 131–6. See also Dudley Andrew and Steven Ungar, *Popular Front Paris and the Poetics of Culture* (Cambridge, MA, 2005), p. 16.

28   Weber, p. 140.

29   "O vershkakh I koreshkakh," *Voz* 3203 (11 Mar. 1934), p. 2.

30   Nikolai Nikolaevich Evreinov Papers, BAR (dated according to the postmark). According to Marina Litavrina, the play, entitled *Chego eshche ne bylo*, depicted "the absurdity of Soviet law and order" (Marina Litavrina, *Russkii teatral'nyi Parizh* [St. Petersburg, 2003], pp. 126–7).

31   Anna Kashina-Yevreinova, "N. A. Teffi," *RM* 817 (5 Nov. 1955), p. 5.

32   See "Mir na Marne," *Voz* 3350 (5 Aug. 1934), p. 2.

33   She also sent it to newspapers. See "Posledniaia fotografiia pisatel'nitsy N. A. Teffi na beregu Marny vo Frantsii," *Seg* 270 (1 Oct. 1934), p. 10. Preserved in the Teffi Papers, BAR.

34   "*O, Teffi! Prevratias' v naiadu / Vy v serdtse mne nalili iadu! / Kakie vyraziat glagoly, / Skol' upoitel'no vy goly?*"

35   Box 1, Arranged Correspondence A–N, Teffi Papers BAR. Only fragments of the letter survive.

36   "Nashi dni," *Voz* 3420 (14 Oct. 1934), p. 3.

37   For the role of the Soviets, see Boris Frezinsky, "Velikaia illiuziia – Parizh, 1935 (Materialy k istorii Mezhdunarodnogo kongressa pisatelei v zashchitu kul'tury)," *Minuvshee* 24 (1998), pp. 166–239.

38   TBun I, no. 59, pp. 398–9.

39   Ibid., no. 60, 26 June 1935, p. 400.

40   Ibid., no. 58, p. 398.

41   "O nezhnosti," *Voz* 3777 (6 Oct. 1935), p. 2.

42   "Pavel Andreyevich Tikston," *Voz* 3791 (20 Oct. 1935), p. 4.

43   Box 1, Arranged Correspondence A–N, Teffi Papers, BAR.

44   Teffi to Zaitseva. Reproduced in O. A. Rostova, *"Napishite mne v al'bom..."*: *Besedy s N. B. Sollogub v Biussi-an-Ot* (Moscow, 2004), p. 138. The commentary misdates the letter on the basis of Teffi's sarcastic assertion that she was 82 years old.

45   Teffi wrote Amfiteatrov in Feb. that the book was about to come out and the first reviews appeared in March: Georgy Adamovich, "Literaturnye zametki," *PN* 5474 (19 Mar. 1936), p. 2; Yury Mandelshtam, "Ved'ma," *Voz* 3949 (26 Mar. 1936), p. 2.

46   "Udivitel'nye liudi," *Voz* 188 (27 July 1930), p. 3. See also "Nasha zemlia i ee liudi," *Voz* 1888 (3 Aug. 1930), p. 2; "Medvezh'i dela," *Voz* 1895 (10 Aug. 1930), p. 2.

47   TBits, 25 June 1947, p. 739.

48   "Ved'ma," in *Sob. soch.*, vol. 2, p. 198 (originally published in *Voz* 2070 [1 Feb. 1931], p. 2; 2077 [8 Feb. 1931], p. 2; then in *V*).

49   "Sobaka," in *Sob. soch.*, vol. 2, p. 296 (originally published in *Voz* 2651 [4 Sept. 1932]; 2658 [11 Sept. 1932]; 2665 [18 Sept. 1932]; then in *V*). The translation is from "The Dog," trans.

Edythe C. Haber, *Russian Literature Triquarterly* 9 (spring 1974), p. 117. Page references to *Sob. soch.*

50 "Ved'ma," in *Sob. soch.*, vol. 2, p. 202 (originally published in *Voz* 2070 [1 Feb. 1931], p. 2; 2077 [8 Feb. 1931], p. 2; then in *V*).

51 Ibid., p. 206.

52 Ibid., p. 211.

53 Kate Brown, *A Biography of No Place: From Ethnic Borderland to Soviet Heartland* (Cambridge, MA, 2004), p. 67.

54 "Rusalka," in *Sob. soch.*, vol. 2, pp. 275, 276 (originally published in *Voz* 2126 [29 Mar. 1931], p. 2; 2133 [5 Apr. 1931], p. 2; then in *V*).

55 Ibid., p. 276.

56 Ibid., p. 278.

57 Ibid., p. 279.

58 Ibid., pp. 279–80.

59 "Sobaka (Rasskaz neznakomki)," in *Sob. soch.*, vol. 2, p. 302 (originally published in *Voz* 2651 [4 Sept. 1932]; 2658 [11 Sept. 1932]; 2665 [18 Sept. 1932]; 2672 [25 Sept. 1932]; then in *V*). The translation is from "The Dog," trans. Edythe C. Haber, *Russian Literature Triquarterly* 9 (spring 1974), pp. 117–35. Page references to *Sob. soch.*

60 "Sobaka," p. 303.

61 Ibid., p. 304.

62 Ibid., pp. 306–7.

63 Ibid., p. 314.

64 Ibid., p. 316.

65 Ibid., p. 317.

66 Ibid., p. 319.

67 Ibid., p. 320.

68 A particularly close parallel to "The Dog" is "The Sticker" ("Nakleika," in *KI*), in which an adolescent also falls hopelessly in love with a frivolous young woman and gives her a "pitiful" toy dog that "looks as if it were crying" (*Sob. soch.*, vol. 4, p. 152), but he, unlike Tolya, is sickly and unattractive.

9. TENDERNESS AND ANGST

1 Mnukhin I, vol. 3, pp. 192, 196, 181, 209. On Teffi's evening, see *Voz* 3991 (7 May 1936), p. 4. The program is preserved in the Teffi Papers, BAR. Since May 1935, Balmont had been suffering from delirium and hallucinations. See P. V. Kupriyanovsky and N. A. Molchanova, *Poet Konstantin Bal'mont. Biografiia. Tvorchestvo. Sud'ba* (Ivanovo, 2001), p. 416.

2 Valentina Dmitrievna Vasyutinskaya-Marcadé, in "Tsvetaeva v pis'makh: Iz Bakhmetevskogo arkhiva Kolumbiiskogo universiteta," ed. John Malmstad, *Literaturnoe obozrenie* 7 (1990), p. 104 n. 8.

3 See "Il'ia Fondaminskii," in *ML*, p. 321 (originally published in *NRS* 14248 [29 Apr. 1951], pp. 2, 3).

4 See O. Korostelev, "Fondaminskii (Fundaminskii) Il'ia Isidorovich," in Oleg Korostelev and Manfred Shruba, eds., *"Sovremennye zapiski" (Parizh, 1920–1940) Iz arkhiva redaktsii*, vol. 1 (Moscow, 2011), pp. 291–3.

5 "Il'ia Fondaminskii," in *ML*, p. 321. For the talk, see "O edinstve liubvi. (Iz besedy v 'Zelenoi Lampe')," Teffi Papers, BAR.

6   "V tekushchii moment," *Voz* 4028 (14 June 1936), p. 2.

7   Postcard to Amfiteatrov, postmarked 1 Sept. 1936, Amfiteatrov MSS, LL.

8   "V poslednii raz," *PN* 6356 (21 Aug. 1938), p. 2.

9   "Teffi i Bal'mont," Amfiteatrov MSS, Box 4, Ilaria V. Amfiteatrov writings, LL.

10   Amfiteatrov to A. Otsup (fragment), Teffi Papers, BAR. Otsup apparently sent the fragment on to Teffi.

11   Aldanov to Amfiteatrov, 14 Nov. 1936, in "'Parizhskii filosof iz russkikh evreev': Pis'ma M. Aldanova k A. Amfiteatrovu," ed. E. Garetto and A. Dobkin, *Minuvshee* 2 (1997), p. 605.

12   "Zimnii sport," *PN* 4059 (1 Jan. 1937), p. 3.

13   Amfiteatrov to Teffi, 7 Jan. 1937, Teffi Papers, BAR.

14   "Retrospektivnyi vzgliad," *PN* 5703 (3 Jan. 1937), p. 2.

15   "Pushkinskii komitet," *PN* 5779 (19 Jan. 1937), p. 4.

16   "Chudo Rossii," *Pushkin. Odnodnevnaia gazeta* (1937).

17   It was around this time that Teffi applied to the Union of Russian Journalists and Writers for 400 francs to pay the tax collector. The number "400," penciled in on the letter, suggests that the request was granted (Vladimir Feofilovich Zeeler Papers, BAR). A loan from the Société Franco-Russe de Prêts et Avances also apparently dates from 1937 (Teffi Papers, BAR).

18   See "Vecher Teffi v Londone," *Voz* 4053 (21 Nov. 1936), p. 5. The program for 28 Nov., at which Gleb Struve gave the opening remarks, is preserved in the Teffi Papers, BAR. See also O. A. Kaznina, *Russkie v Anglii. Russkaia emigratsiia v kontekste russko-angliiskikh literaturnykh sviazei v pervoi polovine XX veka* (Moscow, 1997), p. 384.

19   The evening repeated the program of the Paris *SZ* benefit of the previous May, with Tsetlin giving the introductory remarks. See Zinaida Shakhovskaya, *Otrazheniia* (Paris, 1975), pp. 267–73.

20   Marina Litavrina, *Russkii teatral'nyi Parizh* (St. Petersburg, 2003), p. 135. Teffi's miniatures were included in evenings of one-act plays performed in May and Dec. 1936; Jan., Feb., and June 1937. See Mnukhin I, vol. 3, pp. 268, 276, 290, 344.

21   "Moment sud'by. P'esa v chetyrekh deistviiakh," RGALI (f. 1174, op. 2, ed. khr. 8).

22   Andrei Sedykh, "Uspekh novoi p'esy N. A. Teffi v Parizhe," *Seg* (2 Apr. 1937), p. 3. See also K. P., "Russkii teatr. 'Moment sud'by' Teffi," *PN* 5849 (30 Mar. 1937), p. 3.

23   Teffi told V. Unkovsky that fall that it had been produced "in Berlin, Riga, Revel [Tallinn], London, and Prague, and – in France – in Nice, Marseilles, and Grenoble" ("Nadezhda Aleksandrovna Teffi o sebe," *Rubezh* [20 Nov. 1937], p. 7).

24   For an absorbing and meticulous account, see Pamela A. Jordan, *Stalin's Singing Spy: The Life and Exile of Nadezhda Plevitskaya* (Lanham, MD, 2016). Nabokov's 1943 story "The Assistant Producer" (*Nabokov's Dozen* [New York, 1958], pp. 59–75), is closely based on this incident.

25   Teffi, "Na protsesse Plevitskoi (Vpechatleniia)," Teffi Papers BAR. I have not ascertained the newspaper in which this appeared.

26   "N. A. Teffi o svoem vechere," *PN* 6196 (13 Mar. 1938).

27   *O nezhnosti* was put out by the book-publishing arm of the journal *Russkie zapiski* (Russian annals), founded in Shanghai in 1937. Somewhat in the style of *SZ* (with whom it at first shared an editorial board), but of broader geographic reach and greater popular appeal, *Russkie zapiski* also published Teffi's one-act play, *An Old-Fashioned Love Song*, in 1938 and her last prewar book, *Zigzag*, in 1939.

28   "O nezhnosti," in *Sob. soch.*, vol. 4, p. 192 (originally published in *Voz* 3777 [6 Oct., 1935]; then in *ON*).

29 "Chudovishche," in *Sob. soch.*, vol. 4, p. 211 (originally published in *Voz* 3959 [5 Apr. 1936], p. 2; then in *ON*).

30 "Paskhal'noe ditia," in *Sob. soch.*, vol. 4, p. 204 (originally published in *Voz* 3616 [28 Apr. 1935], p. 2; then in *ON*).

31 Ibid., p. 206.

32 "My, zlye," in *Sob. soch.*, vol. 4, p. 284 (originally published in *Voz* [31 Mar. 1935], p. 2; then in *ON*).

33 Ibid., p. 285.

34 "Znamenie vremeni," in *Sob. soch.*, vol. 4, p. 214 (originally published in *PN* 5902 [23 May 1937], p. 3; then in *ON*).

35 "Bez slov," in *Sob. soch.*, vol. 4, p. 264 (originally published in *Voz* 3896 [2 Feb. 1936], p. 2; then in *ON*).

36 Unkovsky, "Nadezhda Aleksandrovna Teffi o sebe," p. 6. Teffi wrote a two-part "biography" of Miyuz: "Biografiia nevazhnoi persony," *PN* 5993 (22 Aug. 1937), p. 2; *PN* 6000 (29 Aug. 1937), p. 2.

10. ZIGZAGS IN LIFE AND ART

1 TBun I, no. 66, p. 405.

2 Weber, p. 176.

3 "Repetitsiia i ekzamen," *PN* 6405 (9 Oct. 1938), p. 2.

4 "Mirnaia zhizn'," *PN* 6426 (30 Oct. 1938), p. 3.

5 "Nastroenie v Parizhe (Pis'mo iz Frantsii)," *Seg* 64 (6 Mar. 1939), p. 2.

6 *Nichego podobnogo* (1939), Drizo Collection, BAR. This copy is accompanied by Drizo's vivid sketches and a letter from Teffi describing the characters in detail.

7 Quoted by A.N.T., "Na repetitsii 'Nichego podobnogo,'" *PN* 6583 (6 Apr. 1939), p. 4.

8 K. P—v, "Russkii teatr. 'Nichego podobnogo,'" *PN* 6588 (11 Apr. 1939), p. 3.

9 TBun I, no. 72, p. 413; no. 75, p. 415.

10 Gippius, diary, 10 July 1939, in Zinaida Gippius, *Dnevniki*, ed. A. N. Nikolyukin, vol. 1 (Moscow, 1999), p. 419.

11 Teffi's letter to Bunina is in TBun I, no. 72, p. 414.

12 Ibid., no. 76, p. 416.

13 N. I. Kulman to V. N. Bunina, 12 May 1939, LRA (1067/3572); 16 June 1939, LRA (1067/3573).

14 TBun I, no. 80, p. 421.

15 Bunina, diary, 10 Aug. 1939, in *Ustami*, vol. 2, p. 263.

16 See, for example, "Virtuoz chuvstva," in *Sob. soch.*, vol. 7, pp. 177–81 (originally published in *Voz* [3 Dec. 1933], p. 2; then in *Vse*), whose hero, like that of "'Tonkaia psikhologiia" (1911), imagines he is a Don Juan; "Na svoikh gvozdiakh," in *Z*, pp. 66–74 (originally published in *Voz* [1 Feb. 1935], p. 2), whose hero's senselessly rigidity recalls that of the protagonist of "Maliar" (1914).

17 "Zhil'tsy belogo sveta," in *Z*, p. 21 (originally published in *PN* 5833 [14 Mar. 1937], p. 3).

18 "Strekoza i muravei," in *Z*, pp. 134, 135 (originally published in *PN* 5965 [25 July 1937], p. 2). The title refers to Ivan Krylov's adaptation of the La Fontaine fable "La cigale et la fourmi."

19 See also "Flirt," in *Sob. soch.*, vol. 7, pp. 16–25 (originally published in *Voz* 2410 [7 Jan. 1932], p. 2; then in *Vse*); "Feia Karabos," in *Sob. soch.*, vol. 7, pp. 32–7 (originally published in *PN* 6238 [24 Apr. 1938], p. 2; then in *Vse*).

20 "Vremia," in *Sob. soch.*, vol. 7, p. 26 (originally published in *PN* 6161 [6 Feb. 1938], p. 2; then in *Vse*). The translation is from "Time," trans. Edythe C. Haber, in Clarence Brown, ed., *The Portable Twentieth Century Reader* (New York, 1985), pp. 67–73. Page reference to *Sob. soch.*

21 Ibid., pp. 27, 29.

22 Ibid., p. 31.

23 "Dva romana s inostrantsami," in *Sob. soch.*, vol. 7, p. 81 (originally published in *Voz* 3574 [17 Mar. 1935], p. 2; 3581 [24 Mar. 1935], p. 2 [the latter as "Eshche odin roman"]; then in *Vse*).

24 Ibid., p. 84.

25 Ibid., p. 85.

26 "Iarkaia zhizn'," in *Sob. soch.*, vol. 7, p. 164 (originally published in *Voz* [11 Dec. 1932], p. 2; then in *Vse*).

27 "Nigde," in *Sob. soch.*, vol. 7, p. 228 (originally published as "O strane 'Nigde,'" *Voz* 4015 [31 May 1936], p. 2; republished as "Nigde" in *NRS* 14121 [24 Dec. 1950], p. 2; then in *ZR*).

28 Ibid., p. 230.

29 Ibid., p. 231.

30 Some relate further adventures and misadventures of little Nadya and Lena: "V Ameriku" (To America; originally published in *PN* 6286 [12 June 1938], p. 2); "Kishmish" (originally published in *PN* 6957 [14 Apr., 1940], p. 2). Others, grouped under the title "Tipy proshlogo" (Types from the past) and originally published in *Voz* under the general title "Letnii repertuar" (A summer repertoire) shortly after most of the *Witch* stories, continue Teffi's exploration of the odd Russian types she encountered as a child: "Diadia Polkasha" (Uncle Polkasha; originally published in *Voz* 2980 [30 July 1933], p. 2); "Verzila" (A lanky fellow; originally published in *Voz* 2994 [13 Aug. 1933], p. 2); "Ernest s iazykami" (Ernest with the languages; originally published in *Voz* 3001 [20 Aug. 1933], p. 2; later republished in *NRS* in 1951).

31 "Volia," in *Sob. soch.*, vol. 7, p. 367 (originally published in *Voz* 4008 [24 May 1936], p. 2; then in *ZR*).

32 Ibid., p. 369.

33 Ibid., p. 370.

34 Ibid., p. 371.

11. WAR AND ITS AFTERMATH

1 "V eti dni," *PN* 6738 (8 Sept. 1939), p. 3.

2 "Dni i minuty," *PN* 6747 (17 Sept. 1939), p. 3.

3 Valentina Vasyutinskaya, "Nadezhda Aleksandrovna Teffi (Iz lichnykh vospominanii)," *Voz* 131 (Nov. 1962), p. 88.

4 TBun II, no. 82, p. 478 (in French; dated according to the postmark).

5 Teffi to Grabowska, 7 Oct. 1939, Teffi Papers, BAR (in French). All subsequent letters from Grabowska are preserved in the Teffi Papers, BAR. All known dates will be given in the text.

6 "Letopis'," *PN* 6768 (8 Oct. 1939), p. 3.

7 "Chetvert' veka," *PN* 6775 (15 Oct. 15), p. 3. Weber notes that beginning in the 1920s there was a flood of books and articles warning of the "danger of air attack, bombs, chemical and bacterial warfare" in the next war (Weber, p. 238).

8   See Julian Jackson, *France: The Dark Years, 1940–1944* (Oxford, 2002), p. 113.

9   Teffi to Bunina, TBun II, no. 83, p. 479.

10   Zaitsev to Bunin, 2 Nov. 1939, in "Pis'ma B. Zaitseva I. i V. Buninym," ed. Militsa Greene, *NZh* 150 (1983), p. 207.

11   Valentina Vasyutinskaya, "Nadezhda Aleksandrovna Teffi," p. 89.

12   TBun II, no. 83, p. 479.

13   "Sinie dni nashei zhizni. Iz byta zatemnennogo Parizha," *Seg* 62 (4 Mar. 1940), p. 5.

14   "Razmyshleniia," *PN* 6964 (21 Apr. 1940), p. 2.

15   "Etapy," in *Sob. Soch.*, vol. 7, p. 213 (originally published in *PN* 6071 (28 Apr. 1940), p. 2; then in *ZR*).

16   Ibid., p. 215.

17   "Shestaia colonna," *PN* 6992 (19 May 1940), p. 2.

18   Zaitsev to Bunin, 4 June 1940, in "Pis'ma B. Zaitseva I. i V. Buninym," pp. 217–18.

19   "I vse-taki…" *PN* 7013 (9 June 1940), p. 2.

20   Teffi wrote the Zaitsevs from Angers on Tuesday, 11 June, that she had decided to leave Paris on Sunday, but received a reserved seat only for Monday.

21   Unpublished MS, Teffi Papers, BAR.

22   Weber, p. 276.

23   Unless otherwise noted, the following account is based on Teffi's correspondence with the Zaitsevs, Boris Konstantinovich Zaitsev Papers, BAR. For a vivid description of the exodus, see Irène Némirovsky, *Suite Française*, trans. Sandra Smith (New York, 2006), p. 28 ff.

24   Teffi gave similar positive descriptions – both on 24 July – to the Zaitsevs and Bunina (TBun II, no. 84, pp. 481–2).

25   See Teffi to Zaitsevs, 30 June, 24 July [1940], Zaitsev Papers, BAR.

26   In Aug. 1940, Teffi wrote the Zaitsevs that Boris "can receive *chômage* [unemployment, here unemployment compensation]" and the following spring she informed them that she had received 4,000 francs. Then in the summer she "received [something] from Dolgopolov [of Zemgor]." A couple of postcards from Teffi to Dolgopolov, written in 1942, are preserved in LRA, MS 1500 (Zemgor), Box 15 (Provisional). Letters and receipts documenting transfers from Valya are preserved in the Teffi Papers, BAR.

27   Teffi wrote Zaitsev rather sourly on 15 June 1941: "I think our overseas benefactors estimate our needs at about 200 francs a month. Don't expect anything better."

28   For more detail, see Edythe Haber, "Skvernaia pora. Teffi v Biarritse: 1940–41," *Vyshgorod* (Tallinn) 1–2 (2007), pp. 81–2. See also Irina Odoyevtseva, *Na beregakh Seny* (Paris, 1983), pp. 87–117

29   Later memoirs: "O Merezhkovskikh," *NRS* 13792 (29 Jan. 1950); "Zinaida Gippius," *NRS* 13834 (12 Mar. 1950), p. 2. The memoir of Gippius was reprinted in *Voz* 43 (July 1955), pp. 87–96.

30   "O Merezhkovskikh," in *ML*, p. 216.

31   Ibid., p. 220.

32   "Zinaida Gippius," in *ML*, pp. 227–8.

33   Mnukhin II, p. 22.

34   R. A. Uritskaya, *Oni liubili svoiu stranu: Sud'ba russkoi emigratsii vo Frantsii s 1933 po 1948 g.* (St. Petersburg, 2010), p. 90.

35   Mnukhin II, p. 6; Johnston, p. 162.

36   Mnukhin II, p. 9.

37 See especially Robert H. Johnston, "The Great Patriotic War and the Russian Exiles in France," *Russian Review* xxxv/3 (July 1976), p. 306 ff.

38 *"Si vous avez l'occasion – dites à notre tante Marie-Choura et à notre tante Fyodorovich de Keren que leurs neveux sont très disposés à crever de faim"* (TBun II, no. 85, p. 483 [postmarked 20 Oct. 1941]).

39 Teffi to Bunina, TBun II, no. 86, p. 484 (postmarked 29 Sept. 1942).

40 Teffi to Tsetlins, 27 Aug. [1945], S. Iu. Pregel and V. V. Rudnev Collection, MD UIUC.

41 Mnukhin II, p. 28.

42 "'Tsirkuliarnoe' pis'mo N. N. Berberovoi M. A. Aldanovu," ed. Maksim Shrayer, Yakov Klots, Richard Davies, in O. Korostelev and R. Davies, eds., *I. A. Bunin: Novye materialy*, vol. 2 (Moscow, 2010), p. 106.

43 Alan Riding, *And the Show Went On: Cultural Life in Nazi-Occupied Paris* (New York, 2011), p. 69. Yevreinov's official letter to Teffi, dated 24 Nov., 1942, stipulates that if her scenario should win, he would receive 33 percent of the money, if not, and he would have to make the rounds of producers, he would get 50 percent. The agreement, signed by Teffi and returned to Yevreinov on 9 Dec. 1942, is preserved in the Yevreinov Papers, RGALI (f. 982, op. 1, ed. khr. 127).

44 TBun II, no. 90, p. 491; no. 92, p. 495 (9 Aug. 1941). The newspaper clipping announcing the concert is preserved in Box 11, Teffi Papers, BAR.

45 TBun II, no. 87, p. 486 (13 Mar. 1941).

46 Teffi Papers, BAR. In the original French: *"Moi, je tiens admirablement. Je suis toujours tranquille, gai et content, quoique maigre comme Gand[h]i."*

47 "Il'ya Fondaminskii," in *ML*, p. 327.

48 R. A. Uritskaya, *Oni liubili svoiu stranu*, p. 124 n. 20.

49 Teffi to M. N. Vereshchagina, n.d., in "Pis'ma Teffi N. A. Vereshchaginoi Marii Nikolaevne. Nekotorye s odnovremennym obrashcheniem k Vereshchaginu Vladimiru Aleksandrovichu," RGALI (f. 1174, op. 2, ed. khr. 15).

50 Teffi to Bunina, TBun II, no. 93, p. 496; no. 94, p. 497.

51 Teffi to Bunina, TBun II, no. 95, p. 500.

52 Teffi to Bunin, TBun II, no. 90, p. 492.

53 "Zinaida Gippius," in *ML*, p. 228.

54 Nina Berberova, *The Italics Are Mine*, trans. Philippe Radley (New York, 1969), p. 428.

55 TBun II, no. 105, p. 515 (2 July [1944]). For the staging of the miniatures, see Mnukhin II, pp. 47, 51, 52, 53, 54, 55, 56, 59, 60.

56 The play was performed 9, 16, 23 Apr. 1944 (Mnukhin II, p. 57).

57 TBun II, no 101, p. 509.

58 Bunina to a Soviet critic, 8 June 1959. Quoted in *Ivan Bunin: The Twilight of Émigré Russia, 1934–1953: A Portrait from Letters, Diaries, and Memoirs*, ed. Thomas Gaiton Marullo (Chicago, 2002), p. 382.

59 TBun II, no. 96, p. 503 n. 7.

60 TBun II, no. 98, p. 505.

61 TBun II, no. 99, p. 505 (24 Feb. 1944); no. 103, p. 512 (dated according to the postmark).

62 TBun II, no. 104, pp. 513–14.

63 TBun II, no. 103, p. 512 (a short note to Bunina added to Teffi's 15 May letter to Bunin).

64 TBun II, no. 105, p. 515.

65 M. Tsetlin, "N. A. Teffi," *NZh* 6 (1943), pp. 384–6.

66 "Tot svet," *RN* 12 (3 Aug. 1945), p. 4. Republished in "N. A. Teffi v gazete 'Russkie novosti' (1945–1947)," ed. E. G. Domogatskaya, in *TT*, p. 211. Page references are to the latter pub.

67 Ibid., p. 213.

68 Ibid., p. 214.

69 Published with two other letters to Grabowska, with introduction and notes by Edythe Haber, in "Povsednevnaia zhizn' Teffi mezhdu voinoi i mirom," in *Povsednevnost' kak tekst kul'tury: Materialy mezhdunarodnoi nauchnoi konferentsii "Povsednevnost kak tekst kultury"*, ed. G. Yu. Sternin, N. O. Osipova, N. I. Pospelova (Kirov, 2005), pp. 259–76.

70 The *New Yorker* journalist Janet Flanner wrote in Dec. 1945: "Smart, chilblained Parisiennes beg transatlantic travelers for American vaseline the way smart New Yorkers used to beg for Paris perfume" (Janet Flanner [Genêt], *Paris Journal: 1944–1965* [New York, 1965], p. 47).

71 Yu. M. Lotman, *Besedy o russkoi kul'ture: Byt i traditsii russkogo dvorianstva (XVIII–nachalo XIX veka)* (St. Petersburg, 1994), p. 10.

72 TBun II, no. 108, p. 518.

73 Um-El Banin, "Poslednii poedinok Ivana Bunina" [part 1], trans. E. Zvorykina, *Vremia i my* 40 (Apr. 1979), pp. 6–7.

74 *Russkii sbornik* (Paris, 1946). Teffi's contribution, "Tsep'" (pp. 49–69), is composed of feuilletons originally published in *PN* between Sept. 1939 and June 1940.

75 The account of Panteleimonov's life is based primarily on Mikhail Agursky, "Sibiriak na Mertvom more. O Borise Panteleimonove," in Mikhail Parkhomovsky, ed., *Evrei v kul'ture russkogo zarubezh'ia: Sbornik statei, publikatsii, memuarov i esse*, vol. 1 (Jerusalem, 1992), pp. 82–96. See also Aleksei Remizov, "Stekol'shchik," in Aleksei Remizov, *Myshkina dudochka* (Paris, 1953), pp. 129–50.

76 "Moi drug Boris Panteleimonov," *ML*, p. 331 (originally published in *NRS* 14044 [8 Oct. 1950]).

77 A contract dated 5 July 1944 with Les Éditions Fernand Sorlot for the publication of a collection of stories, *La lumière des humbles*, is preserved in the Teffi Papers, BAR.

78 See Antony Beevor and Artemis Cooper, *Paris after the Liberation: 1944–1949* (London, 1994), p. 164.

79 *La lumière des humbles* (Paris, 1947); *Vourdalak*, trans. G. Barbizan and B. Escassut (Paris, 1947).

80 TBun II, no. 118, p. 529; no. 123, p. 533.

81 Teffi to the Tsetlins, 27 Aug. [1945], S. Iu. Pregel and V. V. Rudnev Collection, MD UIUC.

82 TBun II, no. 116, p. 527. Zaitsev's "Tsar' David" was published in *NZh* 11 (1945).

83 "Saul," *NZh* 178 (1990), pp. 108–49.

84 Tsetlina to Teffi, n.d., Pregel and Rudnev Collection.

85 Ibid., pp. 112, 113.

86 Ibid., p. 117.

87 Ibid., p. 119.

88 Ibid., p. 120.

89 Ibid., pp. 122, 128.

90 Ibid., p. 139.

91 Ibid., p. 117.

92 Ibid., p. 120.

12. STRUGGLE AND PERSEVERANCE

1 See Nina Berberova, *The Italics Are Mine*, trans. Philippe Radley (New York, 1969), p. 453.

2 S. I. Drobyazko et al., *Mezhdu Rossiei i Stalinym: Rossiiskaia emigratsiia i Vtoraia mirovaia voina* (Moscow, 2004), pp. 177–9.

3 The feuilleton about the atomic bomb was "Rytsar' i mel'nitsa," *RN* (21 Sept. 1945). Republished in "N. A. Teffi v gazete 'Russkie novosti' (1945–1947)," ed. E. G. Domogatskaya, in *TT*, pp. 215–21.

4 P. A. Berlin to B. I. Nikolayevsky, 20 May 1945. Quoted in O. V. Budnitsky, "Popytka primireniia," in Vladimir Alloy, ed., *Diaspora*, vol. 1 (Paris and St. Petersburg, 2001), p. 225.

5 For details, see Budnitsky, "Popytka primireniia," pp. 179–240; Johnston, pp. 171–9.

6 Bogomolov to Deputy of the People's Commissar of Foreign Affairs of the USSR V. G. Dakanozov, 4 Apr. 1945. Quoted in Budnitsky, "Popytka primireniia," pp. 213–14.

7 For the lavish receptions, see Antony Beevor and Artemis Cooper, *Paris after the Liberation: 1944–1949* (London, 1994), pp. 127–8, 297.

8 Box 1, Arranged Correspondence A–N, Teffi Papers, BAR.

9 Polonsky to Aldanov, 21 Nov. 1945, Fond Aldanova, Dom-Muzei Mariny Tsvetaevoi, Moscow.

10 Teffi Papers, BAR.

11 Johnston, pp. 179–80.

12 Bunina, diary, 15 Aug. 1946, in *Ustami*, vol. 2, p. 386.

13 Um-El Banin, "Poslednii poedinok Ivana Bunina" [part 2], trans. E. Zvorykina, *Vremia i my* 41 (May 1979), p. 13.

14 A. Dii, "'Dobro pozhalovat', tovarishch Teffi!' *Russkaia zhizn'* (San Francisco) (14 Nov. 1946). Clipping preserved in Teffi Papers, BAR. The Communist Party resolution attacking Akhmatova and Zoshchenko – "Postanovlenie Orgbiuro TsK VKP (b) O zhurnalakh 'Zvezda' i 'Leningrad'" – was issued on 14 Aug. 1946.

15 Tyrkova-Williams to Teffi, 22 Jan. 1947, Teffi Papers, BAR; Teffi to Tyrkova-Williams, 18 Nov. 1939, Ariadna Vladimirovna Tyrkova-Williams Papers, BAR.

16 Gleb Struve, *Russkaia literatura v izgnanii* (New York, 1956), p. 382.

17 Mnukhin II, p. 202; A. M. Dubovnikov, "Vykhod Bunina iz parizhskogo Soiuza pisatelei," in V. G. Bazanov et al., eds., *Literaturnoe nasledstvo*, vol. 84: *Ivan Bunin* (Moscow, 1973), bk. 2, pp. 401–2.

18 V. A. Zaitseva to M. S. Tsetlina, 15 Dec. 1947, in "Konflikt M. S. Tsetlinoi s I. A. Buninym i M. A. Aldanovym. Po materialam arkhiva M. S. Tsetlinoi," ed. Mikhail Parkhomovsky, in Mikhail Parkhomovsky, ed., *Evrei v kul'ture russkogo zarubezh'ia: Sbornik statei, publikatsii, memuarov i esse*, vol. 4 (Jerusalem, 1995), p. 314.

19 Tsetlina to the Bunins, 20 Dec. 1947, ibid., p. 315; Bunin to Tsetlina, 1 Jan. 1948, in Dubovnikov, "Vykhod Bunina," pp. 402–4.

20 Oksinskaya to Grabowska, 23 Dec. [1947], Teffi Papers, BAR.

21 TBun II, no. 135, p. 547 (postmarked 7 Jan. 1948, but Teffi writes that she began it a week before).

22 Panteleimonov to Bunin, 19 Jan. 1948, LRA (1066/4380).

23 Panteleimonov to Bunin, 29 Dec. 1947, LRA (1066/4372).

24 TBun II, no. 136, p. 548; Teffi to Tsetlina, Pregel and Rudnev Collection, MD UIUC.

25 The anonymous lampoon was "Emu, velikomu," *RM* 83 (10 Nov. 1948), p. 3. The author, it was later revealed, was S. V. Yablonovsky. For the text, see TBun III, no. 166, pp. 564–5 n. 2.

26 Panteleimonov to Bunin, 23 Nov. 1948, LRA (1066/4447).

27 TBun III, no. 167, p. 566.

28 Galich to Bunin, 2 Nov. 1948, LRA (1066/2583), quoted in TBun III, no. 165, p. 563 n. 5; TBun II, no. 136, p. 549 (8 Jan. 1948).

29 Galich, "Plemiannik diadi Volodi," *NRS* 13253 (8 Aug. 1948), pp. 2, 8.

30   Panteleimonov to Bunin, 19 Nov. 1948, LRA (1066/4445), quoted in TBun II, no. 165, p. 563 n. 6.
31   TBun II, no. 141, p. 559.
32   TBun II, no. 139, p. 556 (20 Jan. 1948). A notebook preserved in Box 4, Teffi Papers, BAR contains a somewhat different list: "*I want*: The overture to Lohengrin. The Louvre. A summer morning on the terrace of the Café Régence. A talk with Bunin."
33   "I vremeni ne stalo," in *Sob. soch.*, vol. 7, pp. 237–49 (originally published in *Novosel'e* 39–41 [1949], pp. 19–32; then in *ZR*).
34   TBun III, no. 163, p. 558.
35   TBun II, no. 152, pp. 579–80. Bunin had actually suggested that she contact *NZh*: TBun II, no. 148, p. 573 (16 Feb. 1948).
36   R. D. Pollett to Teffi, 6 Mar. 1948, Box 2, Arranged Correspondence O–Z, Teffi Papers, BAR. Several of Teffi's stories, translated into German by Fred Ottow, are preserved in Teffi Papers, BAR: "Rjuljas Mama springt ein," *Die Neue Zeitung* (30 May 1948); "Marusja erzieht sich selbst," *Die Neue Zeitung* (21 Sept. 1948).
37   Pollett to Teffi, 5 Apr. 1948, ibid.
38   Bunin to Aldanov, 14 June 1948, in "Perepiska I. A. Bunina s M. A. Aldanovym," ed. A. Zveyers, *NZh* 153 (1983), p. 144.
39   Panteleimonov to Bunin, 14 Oct. 1948, LRA (1066/4440).
40   Teffi to Sedykh, 18 July 1948, Andrei Sedykh Papers, Gen MSS 100, BRBML. Teffi's letters to Sedykh are preserved in this repository, Sedykh's letters to Teffi at Teffi Papers, BAR. Known dates of Teffi's letters will be included in the text.
41   TBun III, no. 163, p. 558.
42   "Vstrechi," in *ML*, p. 169 (originally published in *NRS* [5 Sept. 1948], p. 2).
43   TBun III, no. 160, p. 554 (4 Aug. 1948); no. 163, p. 558.
44   Panteleimonov To Bunin, 28 Aug. 1948, LRA (1066/4428).
45   Panteleimonov to Bunin, 29 Nov.; 3, 15, 23 Dec. 1948; 10, 12 Jan., 8, 14, 21 Feb., 5, 27 Mar., 9 May 1949, LRA (1066/4446, 4449, 4451, 4452, 4454, 4455, 4458, 4459, 4462, 4468).
46   TBun III, no. 164, pp. 559–60 (7 Oct. 1948).
47   Sedykh to Teffi, 7 Nov. 1948, Teffi Papers, BAR.
48   "Opiat' tot son! Opiat' poludremota!…"; "Starik, pokhozhii na starukhu…" *Voz* 1 (Jan. 1949), pp. 50–1.
49   TBun III, no. 177, p. 585.
50   Aldanov to Teffi, 30 Mar. 1949, Teffi Papers, BAR; Teffi to Aldanov, 14 Apr., 9 June 1949, Mark Aleksandrovich Aldanov Papers, BAR. On the date of the benefit, see Mnukhin II, p. 318.
51   Quoted in Andrei Sedykh, "N. A. Teffi v pis'makh," *Vozdushnye puti* 3 (1963), p. 194.
52   Ibid., pp. 194–5.
53   Sedykh wrote "48?" on the top of the letter, but the contents indicate it was written in 1949.
54   Andrei Sedykh, "N. A. Teffi v pis'makh," p. 195. No date given, but "48?" written on the original MS.
55   Panteleimonov to Bunin, 13 Apr. 1950, LRA (1066/4519).
56   Teffi is repeating news she received from Aldanov.
57   "Oprosnyi list dlia zhelaiushchikh byt' priniatymi v Dom Zemsko-Gorodskogo Komiteta dlia prestarelykh v Kormei-An- Parizi (Cormeilles-en-Parisis)" (Zemgor Archive, LRA). The archive contains an unsigned carbon copy of a letter from the administrator, Nedoshivina, to Teffi and the original of Teffi's response.

58 Teffi to Roshchina-Insarova, 7 Sept. 1950, Roshchina-Insarova Papers, BAR.
59 Panteleimonov to Bunin, 18 Aug. 1950, LRA (1066/4526).
60 TBun III, no. 196, p. 608 (24 Sept. 1950).
61 Remizov to Teffi, 30 Sept. 1950, Teffi Papers, BAR.
62 "Moi drug Boris Panteleimonov," NRS 14044 (8 Oct. 1950), p. 2.
63 "Pis'mo I. A. Bunina," NRS 14065 (29 Oct. 1950), p. 3, quoted in TBun III, no. 198, p. 611
    n. 1.
64 Aldanov to Teffi, Nov. 20, 1950, Teffi Papers, BAR.
65 Quoted in TBun III, no. 198, p. 612 n. 1.
66 Teffi quoted the letter in full in her 17 Nov. letter to Aldanov. The original has not survived.
67 TBun III, no. 198, p. 610.
68 The letter is dated 1 Apr. 1951, but Teffi writes that she visited Bunin the previous Tuesday.
69 Written on the top of the letter: "marzec" (March in Polish). For Teffi's review, see
    "Sumasshedshii sharmanshchik Andreia Sedykh," NRS 14178 (18 Feb. 1951), p. 8.
70 The Teffi Papers, BAR, contains several letters from N[ikolai] V[iktorovich] Borzov,
    chairman of the board of the Kulayev Foundation, which – as of 2006 – still exists. See
    I. V. Kulayev, Pod schastlivoi zvezdoi (Moscow, 2006).
71 A. N. Mazurova to Teffi, 28 Oct. 1950, 21 Nov. [1950], Teffi Papers, BAR. Inserted in the
    second letter is a copy of a letter from the editor, Rodion Berezov, the original of which
    has not been preserved.
72 "Pis'mo v Ameriku" (n.p.), "Kogda ia byla rebenkom" (p. 7), "Assotsiatsii" (pp. 1–6), Delo 2
    (Feb. 1951). The issue also includes Georgy Adamovich, "Perechityvaia Teffi" (pp. 68–75). In
    the first issue, Teffi's "Sviataia" (pp. 6–12) was published (originally published as "Kishmish"
    in PN 6957 [14 Apr. 1940], p. 2), and in the third her NRS memoir of Panteleimonov
    (pp. 44–51) and Ye. Malozemova's "Chitateli o Teffi" (pp. 85–90).
73 Aldanov to Teffi, 27 May 1951, Teffi Papers, BAR.
74 Aldanov to Teffi, 16 July 1951, Teffi Papers, BAR.
75 On Teffi's finding that she would have to add more material, see Teffi to Aldanov, 5 Aug.
    1951, Aldanov Papers, BAR.
76 Wreden to Teffi, 12 Aug. 1951, Teffi Papers, BAR.
77 Aldanov to Teffi, 16 July 1951, Teffi Papers, BAR; Teffi to Aldanov, 10 Oct. 1951, Aldanov
    Papers, BAR.
78 Aleksandrova to Teffi, 8 Oct. 1951, Teffi Papers, BAR.
79 Sedykh published the anecdotes as "Teffi pisatel' i chelovek," NRS (7 Dec. 1951), pp. 3, 4.
    A variation appears in "Tri iumorista," in Andrei Sedykh, Dalekie, blizkie (2nd edn., New
    York, 1962), pp. 85–90.

13. LAST WORKS, LAST DAYS

1 Teffi to Vera Aleksandrova, 8 Sept. [1951], Chekhov Publishing House Papers, BAR.
2 Teffi, Nadezhda, "Dobro i zlo," Pervoistochniki russkoi kul'tury za rubezhom, Sobranie
   unikal'nykh arkhivnykh i pechatnykh materialov, Arkhiv russkogo zarubezh'ia, Dom-
   Muzei Mariny Tsvetaevoi, Moscow.
3 "Vostok i sever," Novosel'e 33–4 (Apr.–May 1947), pp. 29–37.
4 Baba-Yaga: Narodnaia skazka (Paris, 1932). For the source, see "Baba-Yaga," in Narodnye
   russkie skazki A. N. Afanas'ieva, ed. L. G. Barag and N. V. Novikov, vol. 1 (Moscow, 1984),
   pp. 125–7.

5   "Baba Yaga," in *Sob. soch.*, vol. 2, p. 368 (originally published in *Novosel'e* 33–4 [Apr.–May 1947], pp. 29–37; then in *ZR*). For Baba Yaga as a goddess, see Andreas Johns, *Baba Yaga: The Ambiguous Mother and Witch of the Russian Folktale* (New York, 2004), pp. 16–20.

6   "Baba Yaga," pp. 369, 370.

7   Ibid., p. 371.

8   Ibid., p. 372.

9   Teffi to Aldanov, n.d., Mark Aleksandrovich Aldanov Papers, BAR.

10   "Baba Yaga," p. 369.

11   "Slepaia," in *Sob. soch.*, vol. 7, p. 264 (originally published in *Novosel'e* 37–8 [1948], pp. 35–41; then in *ZR*). Although published in 1948, the story was scheduled to appear in Sept. 1947. See Panteleimonov to Bitsilli, 12 Aug. 1947, Arkhiv Bitsilli, P. M., IRLI (f. 804, op. 1, l. 10).

12   Ibid., p. 265.

13   Ibid., p. 266.

14   Ibid., pp. 266–7.

15   Ibid., p. 269.

16   Ibid., p. 265.

17   "I vremeni ne stalo," in *Sob. soch.*, vol. 7, pp. 237–49 (originally published in *Novosel'e* 39–41 [1949], pp. 19–32; then in *ZR*).

18   "Starik, pokhozhii na starukhu" was published in 1949 (*Voz* 1 [Jan., 1949], pp. 50–1), but a draft, dated March 1947, is preserved in Nadezhda Aleksandrovna Teffi Papers, BAR.

19   "I vremeni ne stalo," p. 245.

20   Ibid., p. 244.

21   Ibid., p. 247.

22   Quoted from the King James version.

23   "I vremeni ne stalo," pp. 247–8.

24   Ibid., p. 248.

25   "Opiat' tot son!" *Voz* 1 (1949), p. 50. A draft, dated 28 Feb. 1947, is preserved in the Teffi Papers, BAR.

26   TBits, 16 Oct. 1950, p. 749.

27   "Volia Tvoia," in *Sob. soch.*, vol. 7, pp. 253–4 (originally published in *Novosel'e* 42–44 [1950], pp. 34–7; then in *ZR*).

28   Ibid., p. 256.

29   Ibid., p. 259.

30   Ibid., pp. 261, 262.

31   Ibid., p. 262.

32   Ibid., p. 263.

33   A paraphrase of Matthew 10:29–30: "Are not two sparrows sold for a farthing? and one of them shall not fall on the ground without your Father. But the very hairs of your head are all numbered."

34   The evening took place on 21 June 1949 (Mnukhin II, p. 317).

35   For Teffi's dread, see Teffi to Aldanov, 7 June 1949, Aldanov Papers, BAR.

36   "Pushkinskie dni," *NRS* 13582 (3 July 1949), p. 2.

37   "Pis'mo v Ameriku," *Delo* 2 (Feb. 1951), n.p.

38   "Kogda ia byla rebenkom," *Delo* 2 (Feb., 1951), p. 7.

39   Whether this is actually Teffi's last poem is unclear. A typed version is preserved in the Teffi Papers, BAR, together with other poems she wrote over the years.

40 "Poslednee," Teffi Papers, BAR. Published in Nadezhda Teffi, *Chernyi iris. Belaia siren'*, ed. Yelena Trubilova (Moscow, 2006), p. 334.

41 Teffi to V. F. Zeyeler, 3 June 1952, Soiuz Russkikh Pisatelei Papers, BAR. In her 1925 obituary of Averchenko, Teffi implicitly denies, in her description of his humor, that she is a humorist pure and simple: "He is a pure-blooded Russian humorist, without heartbreak and without laughter through tears. His place in Russian literature is his very own; I would say – that of the only Russian humorist" ("Arkadii Averchenko," *Segodnia* 56 [22 Mar. 1925]).

42 A few weeks later (22 June 1952) Teffi wrote something similar to Aldanov.

43 Georgy Adamovich, "Perechityvaia Teffi," *Delo* 2 (Feb. 1951), p. 70.

44 Teffi, "Posle iubileia (Otryvki vpechatlenii i razgovorov)," *NRS* 14,569 (16 Mar. 1952), p. 2.

45 Remizov to Teffi, 17 June 1952, Teffi Papers, BAR.

46 Zeyeler's article was "Nadezhda Aleksandrovna Teffi: K piatidesiatiletiiu literaturnoi raboty," *RM* (13 June 1952), p. 2.

47 L. Rzhevsky, "U N. A. Teffi," *Grani* 16 (1952), p. 7.

48 "Aniuta," *Grani* 16 (1952), pp. 3–5. Rzhevsky's review was "Zhizneutverzhdaiushchee masterstvo," *Grani* 14 (1952).

49 Teffi wrote Sedykh on 17 Feb. of an interview that week. On 19 July Aleksinsky sent Teffi a notice he wrote for *Nouvelles littéraires* and mentioned another to appear in *Figaro littéraires*. On 21 July he wrote her that a notice had appeared in *La nation belge* (Teffi Papers, BAR).

50 François-Régis Bastide, "Rendez-vous à Paris. V. avec les Russes," *Nouvelles littéraires* (n.d.), p. 4. The clipping has been preserved in the Teffi Papers, BAR.

51 TBun III, no. 207, p. 622 (9 May 1952).

52 TBun III, no. 208, p. 622 (the date 16 May 1952 written in by Bunin).

53 Bunina, diary, 25 May 1952, LRA (1067/427).

54 Mnukhin II, p. 514.

55 Oksinskaya to Teffi, n.d., Teffi Papers, BAR.

56 Teffi to Aldanov, 3 June 1952, Aldanov Papers, BAR.

57 On that date in her calendar Teffi entered: "Byla u Bunina" (Teffi Papers, BAR).

58 Bunina, diary, 12 Oct. 1952, in *Ustami*, vol. 2, p. 404.

59 Teffi to Vereshchagina, RGALI (f. 1174, op. 2, ed. khr. 15). Date on second letter written in another hand.

60 P. Stavrov, "O N. A. Teffi (Vmesto kriticheskogo ocherka)," *NRS* (26 Oct. 1952).

61 Teffi had received a New Year's greeting from the Zaitsevs, and her name was included among those congratulating Zaitsev on his January jubilee.

62 Rognedov to Teffi, 30 September 1952, Teffi Papers, BAR.

63 Quoted in Andrei Sedykh, "N. A. Teffi v pis'makh," *Vozdushnye puti* 3 (1963), p. 212. See "Nashi dni," *Voz* 3420 (14 Oct. 1934), p. 3.

64 Bunina, diary, 12 Oct. 1952, LRA (1067/427).

65 "U groba N. A. Teffi," *RN* (9 Oct. 1952).

66 V. V. Grabovskaya, "To, chto ia pomniu," Vospominaniia. Ruskopis' M. N. Vereshchaginoi [1953], RGALI (f. 1174, op. 2, ed. khr. 21). It is noted on the MS that this was for a Russian-language BBC broadcast.

67 "K konchine N. A. Teffi. Na pokhoronakh," Teffi Papers, BAR. The following account is based on this source.

EPILOGUE: LIFE AFTER TEFFI

1   Sedykh to Grabowska, 12 Dec. 1952, Teffi Papers, BAR.
2   Grabowska to Vereshchagins, 20 Feb. 1953; 12 Mar. 1953, Teffi Papers, BAR.
3   See Aldanov to Teffi, 21 Mar. 1952, Teffi Papers, BAR; Teffi to Aldanov, 29 Mar. 1952, Aldanov Papers, BAR.
4   Panteleimonova to Grabowska, received 21 Oct. 1952, Teffi Papers, BAR.
5   Grabowska to Vereshchagin, 3 Nov. 1952; Panteleimonova to Grabowska, 8 Nov. 1952; Vereshchagin to Grabowska, 17 Nov. 1952, Teffi Papers, BAR.
6   The list is preserved in the Teffi Papers, BAR. Most of Teffi's friends were bequeathed small items, such as books and pictures.
7   Oksinskaya to Grabowska, 29 Oct. 1952, Teffi Papers, BAR.
8   Elizabeth Baylor Neatrour, "Miniatures of Russian Life at Home and in Emigration: The Life and Works of N. A. Teffi," Ph.D. dissertation, Indiana University, 1972, pp. 10–11. See also "Helena Buczyńska," in Stanisław Dabrowski, ed., Słownik biograficzny teatru polskiego: 1765–1965 (Warsaw, 1973), p. 73.
9   The causes listed on her death certificate are: "(a) Coronary Thrombosis (b) Angina Pectoris (c) Arteriosclerosis." My thanks to Richard Davies for finding this document. For Valya's heart pain, see Grabowska to Vereshchagina, 12 Feb. 1953, Teffi Papers, BAR.
10 The scholarly editions of Chorny's poetry are S. Chorny, Stikhotvoreniia, ed. K. Chukovsky and L. A. Yevstigneyeva, Biblioteka poeta, Bol'shaia seriia (Leningrad, 1960); Sasha Chorny, Stikhotvoreniia, Biblioteka poeta, Malaia seriia (Moscow and Leningrad, 1962). I am grateful to Yevstigneyeva-Spiridonova for providing me with this information during a personal meeting in 2000 and an email exchange in Oct. 2015. Among her publications are Poety "Satirikona," ed. L. A. Yevstigneyeva, Biblioteka Poeta, Bol'shaia seriia (Moscow and Leningrad, 1966); L. Yevstigneyeva, Zhurnal "Satirikon" i poety-satirikontsy (Moscow, 1968); L. A. Spiridonova (Yevstigneyeva), Russkaia satiricheskaia literatura nachala XX veka (Moscow, 1977).
11 N. A. Teffi, Sobranie sochinenii, ed. D. D. Nikolayev and E. M. Trubilova (Moscow, 1997–2000).
12 As evidence of the growing interest in women writers and in the Russian emigration, see, for example, Edythe C. Haber, "Nadezhda Teffi," Russian Literature Triquarterly 9 (spring 1974), pp. 454–72; Elizabeth Baylor Neatrour, "Teffi," in Marina Ledkovskaia-Astman, Charlotte Rosenthal, and Mary Fleming Zirin, eds., Dictionary of Russian Women Writers (Westport, CT, 1994), pp. 640–3; Catriona Kelly, A History of Russian Women's Writing, 1820–1992 (Oxford, 1994), pp. 195–205; Greta N. Slobin, "Nadezhda Teffi," in Christine D. Tomei, ed., Russian Women Writers, vol. 2 (New York, 1999), pp. 811–33.
13 M. Kallash, "Svetlaia dusha: Pamiati N. A. Teffi," RN (17 Oct. 1952). A copy is preserved in Teffi Papers, BAR.

Select Bibliography and Further Reading in English

WORKS BY TEFFI

Books

Subtly Worded and Other Stories, translated by Anne Marie Jackson with Robert and Elizabeth Chandler, Clare Kitson, Irina Steinberg, and Natalia Wase (London, 2014).
Memories: From Moscow to the Black Sea, translated by Robert and Elizabeth Chandler, Anne Marie Jackson, and Irina Steinberg (New York and London, 2016).
Tolstoy, Rasputin, Others, and Me: The Best of Teffi, edited by Robert Chandler and Anne Marie Jackson, translated by Robert and Elizabeth Chandler, Rose France, and Anne Marie Jackson (New York, 2016).

Other translated works

"Time," translated by Edythe C. Haber, in Clarence Brown, ed., *The Portable Twentieth-Century Russian Reader* (New York, 1985), pp. 67–73.
"The Woman Question," translated by Elizabeth Neatrour; "Walled Up," translated by Catriona Kelly, in Catriona Kelly, ed., *An Anthology of Russian Women's Writing, 1777–1992* (Oxford, 1994), pp. 174–201.
"When the Crayfish Whistled: A Christmas Horror," "A Little Fairy Tale," "Baba Yaga" [1932 picture book], "The Dog," "Baba Yaga" [1947 article], translated by Robert and Elizabeth Chandler, in Robert Chandler, ed., *Russian Magic Tales from Pushkin to Platonov* (London, 2012), pp. 168–217.
"A Few Words about Lenin," "The Guillotine," translated by Rose France, in Boris Dralyuk, ed., *1917: Stories and Poems from the Russian Revolution* (London, 2016), pp. 124–35.

WORKS ON TEFFI

Haber, Edythe C., "Nadezhda Teffi," *Russian Literature Triquarterly* 9 (spring 1974), pp. 454–72.
——— "Fashioning Life: Teffi and Women's Humor," in Lesley Milne, ed., *Reflective Laughter: Aspects of Humour in Russian Culture* (London, 2004), pp. 63–71, 200–3.

———— "N. A. Teffi," in Maria Rubins, ed., *Dictionary of Literary Biography*, vol. 317: *Twentieth-Century Russian Émigré Writers* (Farmington Hills, MI, 2005), pp. 307–19.
———— "The Roots of NEP Satire: The Case of Teffi and Zoshchenko," *The NEP Era: Soviet Russia, 1921–1928* i/1 (2007), pp. 89–99.
———— "The Queen of Laughter and the Knight of Death: Nadezhda Teffi and Fedor Sologub," in Catherine Ciepiela and Lazar Fleishman, eds., *New Studies in Modern Russian Literature and Culture: Essays in Honor of Stanley J. Rabinowitz*, part 1, Stanford Slavic Studies 45 (Stanford, CA, 2014), pp. 173–87.
Kelly, Catriona, *A History of Russian Women's Writing, 1820–1992* (Oxford, 1994), pp. 195–205.
Neatrour, Elizabeth Baylor, "Miniatures of Russian Life at Home and in Emigration: The Life and Works of N. A. Teffi," Ph.D. dissertation, Indiana University, 1972.
———— "Teffi," in Marina Ledkovskaia-Astman, Charlotte Rosenthal, and Mary Fleming Zirin, eds., *Dictionary of Russian Women Writers* (Westport, CT, 1994), pp. 640–3.
Slobin, Greta N., "Nadezhda Teffi," in Christine D. Tomei, ed., *Russian Women Writers*, vol. 2 (New York, 1999), pp. 811–33.
Starostina, Natalia, "The Construction of a New Émigré Self in 20th-Century Russian Paris in Short Stories by Nadezhda Teffi," *Canadian Review of Comparative Literature* xlii/1 (2015), pp. 81–93.

SECONDARY WORKS

Beevor, Antony, and Artemis Cooper, *Paris after the Liberation: 1944–1949* (London, 1994).
Berberova, Nina, *The Italics Are Mine*, translated by Philippe Radley (New York, 1969).
Bisha, Robin, Jehanne M. Gheith, Christine Holden, and William G. Wagner, eds., *Russian Women, 1698–1917: Experience and Expression, an Anthology of Sources* (Bloomington, IN, 2002).
Bunin, Ivan, *Accursed Days: A Diary of Revolution*, translated by Thomas Gaiton Marullo (London, 2000).
———— *Dark Avenues*, translated by Hugh Aplin (London, 2008).
Ciepiela, Catherine, and Honor Moore, eds., *The Stray Dog Cabaret: A Book of Russian Poems*, translated by Paul Schmidt (New York, 2007).
Engelstein, Laura, *The Keys to Happiness: Sex and the Search for Modernity in Fin-de-siècle Russia* (Ithaca, NY, 1992).
Freeze, Gregory, *Russia: A History* (Oxford, 1997).
Goscilo, Helena, and Beth Holmgren, eds., *Russia – Women – Culture* (Bloomington, IN, 1996).
Huntington, W. Chapin, *The Homesick Million: Russia-out-of-Russia* (Boston, 1933).
Hutton, Marcelline J., *Russian and West European Women, 1860–1939: Dreams, Struggles, and Nightmares* (Lanham, MD, 2001).
Jackson, Julian, *France: The Dark Years, 1940–1944* (Oxford, 2002).
Johnston, Robert H., *New Mecca, New Babylon: Paris and the Russian Exiles, 1920–1945* (Kingston and Montreal, 1988).
Jordan, Pamela A., *Stalin's Singing Spy: The Life and Exile of Nadezhda Plevitskaya* (Lanham, MD, 2016).
Karlinsky, Simon, and Alfred Appel, Jr., eds., *The Bitter Air of Exile: Russian Writers in the West, 1922–1972* (Berkeley, CA, 1977).
Lincoln, W. Bruce, *Between Heaven and Hell: The Story of a Thousand Years of Artistic Life in Russia* (New York, 1998).
———— *Sunlight at Midnight: St. Petersburg and the Rise of Modern Russia* (New York, 2000).

Livak, Leonid, *How It Was Done in Paris: Russian Émigré Literature and French Modernism* (Madison, WI, 2003).

McReynolds, Louise, *The News under Russia's Old Regime: The Development of the Mass-Circulation Press* (Princeton, NJ, 1991).

Matich, Olga, *Erotic Utopia: The Decadent Imagination in Russia's Fin de Siècle* (Madison, WI, 2005).

Mirsky, D. S., *A History of Russian Literature*, ed. Francis J. Whitfield (New York, 1964).

Némirovsky, Irène, *Suite Française*, trans. Sandra Smith (New York, 2006).

———— *The Wine of Solitude: A Novel*, trans. Sandra Smith (New York, 2011).

Pipes, Richard, *The Russian Revolution* (New York, 1991).

Raeff, Marc, *Russia Abroad: A Cultural History of the Russian Emigration, 1919–1939* (Oxford, 1990).

Riding, Alan, *And the Show Went On: Cultural Life in Nazi-Occupied Paris* (New York, 2011).

Robinson, Marc, ed., *Altogether Elsewhere: Writers on Exile* (San Diego, 1994).

Rosenthal, Charlotte, "Carving Out a Career: Women Prose Writers, 1885–1917, the Biographical Background," in Rosalind Marsh, ed., *Gender and Russian Literature: New Perspectives* (Cambridge, 1996), pp. 129–40.

Ruthchild, Rochelle Goldberg, *Equality and Revolution: Women's Rights in the Russian Empire, 1905–1917* (Pittsburgh, PA, 2010).

Slobin, Greta N., *Russians Abroad: Literary and Cultural Politics of Diaspora (1919–1939)*, ed. Katerina Clark, Nancy Condee, Dan Slobin, and Mark Slobin (Brighton, MA, 2013).

Verbitskaya, Anastasya, *Keys to Happiness*, ed. and trans. Beth Holmgren and Helena Goscilo (Bloomington, IN, 1999).

Weber, Eugen, *The Hollow Years: France in the 1930s* (New York, 1994).

Williams, Robert C., *Culture in Exile: Russian Émigrés in Germany, 1881–1941* (Ithaca, NY, 1972).

Index